WASHINGTON WINES AND WINERIES

WASHINGTON WINES AND WINERIES

The Essential Guide

Paul Gregutt

UNIVERSITY OF CALIFORNIA PRESS

Berkeley   Los Angeles   London

THE PUBLISHER GRATEFULLY ACKNOWLEDGES THE GENEROUS
CONTRIBUTION TO THIS BOOK PROVIDED BY THE GENERAL
ENDOWMENT FUND OF THE UNIVERSITY OF CALIFORNIA PRESS
FOUNDATION.

University of California Press, one of the most distinguished university
presses in the United States, enriches lives around the world by advancing
scholarship in the humanities, social sciences, and natural sciences. Its
activities are supported by the UC Press Foundation and by philanthropic
contributions from individuals and institutions. For more information,
visit www.ucpress.edu.

University of California Press
Berkeley and Los Angeles, California
University of California Press, Ltd.
London, England

Library of Congress Cataloging-in-Publication Data

Gregutt, Paul.
    Washington wines and wineries : the essential guide / Paul Gregutt.
        p. cm.
    Includes index.
    ISBN 978-0-520-24869-4 (cloth : alk. paper)
    1. Wine and wine making—Washington (State)   2. Wineries—Washing-
ton (State)—Guidebooks.   3. Vineyards—Washington (State)   I. Title.

TP557.G745   2007
641.2'209797—dc22

                                                        2007015645

Manufactured in the United States

10   09   08
10 9 8 7 6 5 4 3

The paper used in this publication meets the minimum requirements of
ANSI/NISO Z39.48-1992 (R 1997) (Permanence of Paper).∞

Cover illustrations: Above, Seven Hills Vineyard, Walla Walla; below, Cabernet Sauvignon grapes, Grand Ciel Vineyard, Red Mountain. Photographs by
Sara Matthews.

For all those whose dedicated, purposeful work in vineyard, laboratory, and wine cellar has, in a remarkably short time, built a world-class wine industry in Washington state

It sloweth age, it strengtheneth youth, it helpeth digestion, it abandoneth melancholie, it relisheth the heart, it lighteneth the mind, it quickeneth the spirits, it keepeth and preserveth the head from whirling, the eyes from dazzling, the tongue from lisping, the mouth from snaffling, the teeth from chattering, and the throat from rattling; it keepeth the stomach from wambling, the heart from swelling, the hands from shivering, the sinews from shrinking, the veins from crumbling, the bones from aching, and the marrow from soaking.

From a thirteenth-century manuscript

CONTENTS

LIST OF WINERIES

PREFACE

In *McCall's Guide to Wines of America*, published in 1970, author William E. Massee allows one short page for "Washington, Oregon, and Elsewhere." (Elsewhere, we soon discover, is Arkansas, Georgia, and Illinois.) Washington gets a single paragraph, in which we are told that "there have always been plenty of fruit and berry wines from the Willamette Valley in Washington [sic], along with lots of Concords." The author goes on to recommend the state's sylvaner, pinot blanc, zinfandel, pinot noir, and carignane.

Writing at the same time, Philip M. Wagner (in *American Wines and Wine-Making*) suggests that the Yakima Valley has "immense potential [for] some of the hardiest north and central European vinifera, plus some of the better French hybrids." Outside of Leon Adams' celebrated work, that was the most informed coverage of Washington state wine country less than 40 years ago!

Most of the books written since have lumped Washington and Oregon together as the Pacific Northwest and often included their wineries as a northern adjunct to California. They offer thumbnail sketches of recent releases and information on wine touring. Virtually no wine writer who does not live and work in Washington state has any real chance of knowing what remarkable growth has occurred here in recent years. They jet in, taste a few new releases, get the quick tour of Woodinville and Walla Walla, and jet out.

I believe it's time for a more thorough and comprehensive look at Washington. It should be examined apart from Oregon, as its own place, except of course where the Washington appellations spill across the border. And it is long past time for a critical appraisal of the state as a world-class winemaking region, taking into account its geography and its unique viticulture and winemaking history and pointing out its current challenges and its proven successes. That is the purpose of this book.

As serious as that may sound, I wrote this book for consumers, knowing that consumers want to be entertained as well as guided. Through my weekly wine columns, which are carried in newspapers throughout Washington state, I hear regularly from a wide range of consumers of all ages. Their interest in wine—in Washington wine—is undeniable. Their knowledge and curiosity about the minutiae of wine varies dramatically. At the risk of trying to be all things to all people, I've worked here to cut a swath through the jungle of wine dweebisms without sacrificing the technical detail that is legitimately meaningful and important.

It's not easy making informed choices about wine, even for those inside the business. Anyone who has ever stood, utterly befuddled, in front of retail shelves overflowing with unknown labels understands the despair that such displays can induce. Vintages, grape varieties, entire regions of the earth whirl out of control as the would-be wine drinker struggles desperately to recall some lost factoid, some lifeline to a bottle that just might go well with the evening meal.

This is not another book claiming that it will take the stuffiness out of wine. Wine is not stuffy. There's no need to remove stuffing that doesn't exist. Much of wine's appeal is its mystery, its old-fashioned insistence that one must take time to understand it. It's a little like learning to speak Mandarin Chinese—very rewarding after the first few years. The problem is that not a lot of people want to make that commitment. Most people just want to eat Mandarin Chinese.

The bottom line is this: It's not often that a brand-new wine region with world-class capabilities comes along. I've been privileged to see this one grow from a tiny cutting into a major vine. Washington has moved out of the shadow of California. My sincere hope is that this book will help you to understand what makes this state and its wines unique and memorable so that you can make your own delicious discoveries.

To Washington wine!

ACKNOWLEDGMENTS

I owe my wine education not to any particular course of study, but to the thousands of individuals who have taken the time to sit with me over the years and taste and discuss wine. They come from all sides of the business—growers and winemakers, importers and distributors, retail shop owners and sommeliers. Some are academics, some are journalists, some are marketers, but all share a wonderful passion for this inexhaustible subject. They come from all countries, and many may not ever know the profound impact they have had on my thinking about wine.

I would like to single out a few close friends and mentors for special thanks. Richard Hinds and Henry Stoll introduced me to the pleasures of wine drinking in college, and they have kept plying me with fine old wines ever since. The members of my two long-running tasting groups, many of them winemakers and wine sellers themselves, have sparked numerous memorable debates and kept my palate on its toes. My many tastings with retailer and fellow author Dan McCarthy have had a profound impact on my ability to evaluate wines systematically.

My ability to write about wine both enthusiastically and critically has been honed by the many talented and supportive editors with whom I have been privileged to work. My deep appreciation goes to Harvey Steiman, who first published my work for a national readership; to David Brewster, who supported my wine column in the *Seattle Weekly* for more than a decade; to Adam Strum and the editors at the *Wine Enthusiast*, who have recognized the importance of Washington state viticulture and given me many opportunities to write about it; to Tom Stevenson, whose books have provided a model for wine criticism to which I can only aspire; and to the publisher and editors at the *Seattle Times* and its family of newspapers, who for the past five years have allowed me the privilege of covering this most fascinating of all possible subjects for the hometown crowd.

The staff, past and present, at both the Washington Wine Commission and the Walla Walla Wine Alliance have been enormously helpful in arranging numerous tastings and compiling current statistics on the industry. And most of all, I wish to thank my best friend, partner, and muse, my wife, Karen, for her seemingly inexhaustible enthusiasm and unwavering support of this work.

INTRODUCTION

A DELICIOUS MOMENT IN TIME

Most wine books promise to take the snobbery out of wine, to cut through the "meaning-less" ritual associated with wine, and to give you the inside scoop on what to drink with your hamburger. Some drown you in technical detail; others pretend to reinvent the art of food and wine pairing (imagine—fish with red wine!) or point you to the best value wines (usually corporate plonk). We're not going there.

This is a book about a special time and a unique place in the history of wine. It's about a state whose meaningful exploration of vinifera grapes is barely 40 years old, a state that has only recently discarded the deeply held conviction that it was too cold to grow serious wine grapes, a state where many of the best winemakers live hundreds of miles from the vineyards and truck their dusty bins of grapes over mountains and (sometimes) the Puget Sound to crush and ferment and barrel the wines.

They work in tiny rented spaces in faceless office parks, with battered forklifts, used barrels, and borrowed de-stemmers and rented bottling lines. And they make better wines, in many instances, than the biggest, best-funded mega-wineries in the world.

I believe—and I hope you will come to agree with me—that Washington state is going to become one of the greatest wine regions in the world in the twenty-first century. This despite (or perhaps because of) its fringe location, its reliance on irrigation, its extreme desert growing conditions, its separation of growers and winemakers, its preponderance of tiny, underfunded start-ups, and the persistent myth that it is too cold, too wet, and too far north—in other words, despite the fact that Washington is not, and never will be, California.

When it comes to exploring unknown viticultural territory and crafting stylistically original, world-class wines, Washington has come as far as or farther than California, in less time. Without California's vast advantages, little Washington has plugged along, driven by dreamers and doers who believed there was something magical in the land. People such as John Williams and Jim Holmes, who bought some barren acreage on a desolate hill called Red Mountain back in 1975 and decided to grow cabernet there. People such as Dr. William McAndrew, who planted gewürztraminer and a variety of other grapes in an old apple orchard high above the Columbia Gorge in 1972, dubbed it Celilo, and waited to see what, if anything, would survive. People such as Christophe Baron, a native Champenois who made wine in half a dozen places around the world before circling for a landing in Walla Walla and then doggedly searched for land to plant until he found the rockiest, least likely, most difficult, and most labor-intensive soil in the region and hand-planted his Cailloux vineyard to syrah.

Today Red Mountain cabernet and merlot and cabernet franc can stake a legitimate claim to greatness, as can Celilo gewürztraminer and Cailloux syrah. They have all passed the test of time and also the test of timelessness. These vineyards express that elusive, often-abused (and misspelled) term *terroir*, which is not *terrior* (some sort of small dog/grape hybrid?) but the Holy Grail of winemaking. It is the pot of enological gold at the end of a long, dusty rainbow. Washington's vignerons are beginning to find it, and therein lies the point and purpose of this book.

There *is* something magical in this land. These pioneers were right about that, as are those who continue to explore and expand viticulture in Washington today. It's true that the nine AVAs now officially recognized include millions of acres of land that are not, and will never be, dedicated to wine grape growing. But tucked away here and there are the sites that work, that have the potential, if properly managed, to create exceptional wines. Finding those places is what has obsessed those who have pioneered winemaking during the first few decades of Washington's modern wine era.

There is nothing easy about this work, and the rewards, if they come at all, are often more artistic than financial. But for a wine lover, Washington has reached a delicious moment in time. How many people in the history of the world could say that they were or are witnessing the emergence of a brand-new, world-class wine region? Who among us has tasted, in each new vintage, wines that push the envelope a bit farther than it has previously been pushed, that reveal unknown or unsuspected layers of flavor and bouquet, nuances previously locked away in a piece of scrub desert or a rocky riverbed or a mountainside blanketed in volcanic dust?

WHY NOW, WHY ME?

Any wine book about a specific place is essentially a snapshot in time. When it first appears, it promises to deliver an update, breaking news on the region's wines and wineries. But once that time window passes, a good book becomes a valuable historical document. One of the oldest in my Pacific Northwest library, *Winery Trails of the Pacific Northwest*, was written by the late Tom Stockley, who covered this region for readers of the *Seattle Times* for almost 30 years. It was published in 1977—not so long ago—and promised to be "a complete guide to the wineries of Washington, Oregon, and British Columbia." It is astonishing to see that there were just a dozen in Oregon, eight in Washington, and five in British Columbia—25 wineries in the entire Pacific Northwest.

It certainly made good sense at that time to bind them all together in a single, slim volume. Stockley, a Washington native, was the first important locally based writer to cover the region's emerging wine scene. As he noted in his introduction, up until the late 1960s the Pacific Northwest was "a vast wasteland when it came to wine. [Its] wines were," he continued, "to put it rather unkindly, laughable."

Stockley wrote with great excitement of the renaissance he saw blooming all around him. Now, 30 years later, I can chronicle the astonishing fruits of those pioneering efforts. The region covered in *Winery Trails* now includes roughly 1000 wineries. Washington alone has over 500, more than enough to justify a book of its own.

But it is not merely numbers that suggest that the time is right for a comprehensive look at Washington wines. There is history here now. There are vineyards moving into their fourth or even fifth decade and wineries that can put together vertical tastings going back 25 years or more. There are winemakers who have been working in Washington since Stockley wrote his book and are working still, and there is a second generation of their sons and daughters stepping in to move the industry forward.

Steve Burns, who was executive director of the Washington Wine Commission from 1996 to 2004, was famously quoted a few years ago as noting that a new winery opened in Washington every 10 days. That remarkable statistic captured the frenetic growth of the industry during his tenure. The almost-daily changes made it difficult for any writer to take the snapshot accurately. Though my own guides to northwest wines were long out of date, I wanted to wait a bit longer and let the dust settle before tackling this book.

The dust has not entirely settled, to be sure, but it has been mapped, studied, ripped, planted, trellised, irrigated, fertilized, chronicled, and delineated into more and more meaningful appellations. The wineries and vineyards that survived the mistakes and trials of Washington's early years have learned some hard-won lessons, making it easier for young, artisanal winemakers to craft superb wines. The growth of the state continues, but it is now possible to look closely at the past and present of Washington viticulture and make meaningful predictions about the future.

I have lived in Washington state for 35 years, and I have observed its wine industry from its modern beginnings. I have been writing about the wines of Washington since 1984, always with a strong conviction that the long-term wine-producing potential of the region was virtually limitless. That said, I have always been a critic, not a cheerleader. Any region whose aspirations are to become world-class must have its wines evaluated in the context of the global competition. Yes, Washington is making some exciting syrah. So are Australia, California, Spain, and France. How do Washington syrahs compare? Do they have a style all their own? Are they priced competitively?

Questions such as these are what the consumer asks every time he or she walks down the wine aisle looking for a bottle to go with dinner. That global perspective, coupled with my insider's knowledge of Washington wines and wineries, is important to readers. I live in Washington and spend half my time in the heart of wine country. I do not work and have never worked in the wine business; I make my living solely as an independent journalist. In my newspaper columns and magazine profiles I strive to provide both consumers and wine professionals with a unique point of view on the industry, its successes, its experiments, and its failures.

It's a fascinating occupation. A wine writer is a bit of a wandering comet, riding in from the outer limits, streaming past the steady orbits of the grape growers, the vintners, the négociants, the importers, the distributors, the wholesalers, the retailers, and the marketers, extracting from the fruits of all of their labors the best information, the most interesting anecdotes, the most thrilling wines, and above all the very best wine values, always with the reader's interest foremost in mind.

And it's a rare position—part critic, part advocate, part educator, and part coach—that I value immensely. Please join me as we explore the history and the vineyards of Washington state, visit its wineries, and get inside the heads of its leading winemakers as they pour their wines. We'll taste the best and critique the rest.

THE ESSENTIAL GUIDE'S 100-POINT SCORING SYSTEM

Each winery profiled in these pages has been awarded an overall ranking based on a 100-point scale. Let's be clear: This is *not* the standard 100-point scale. The scale I propose has been designed to correct the many deficiencies of that simplistic rating of specific wines.

This practice of promoting wine, a multifaceted, subjective sensory experience, simply by broadcasting numbers has gradually devalued the numbers while shrinking the original 100-point scale. At first blush, such a rating system sounds generous, allowing room for a lot of subtlety in the grading curve. But in actual practice it's not a 100-point scale at all, not even close. It has become a 10-point scale. Wines rated under 85 are ignored completely. Wines rated 85–89 must be marketed as value wines (those numbers only work for wines priced at the low end of the scale). If your wine is going to sell for $15 or more, it must hit 90 points at least. One prominent retailer even makes a point of selling (at discount) wines that have scored the "dreaded" 89. Once a wine moves up the ladder from there, it becomes increasingly rare and expensive. As a result, wines scoring 95 or above are virtually unobtainable for the average consumer.

In this book, the perfect score of 100 points is made up of four components. The first three components award points for style, consistency, and value. Each has a potential (e.g., perfect) score of 30. The final points (up to 10) are awarded for the contribution being made by the individual winery to the development and improvement of the Washington wine industry. This can include such things as vineyard development, experimentation with new varietals, marketing and promotional excellence, number of medals and high-scoring wines, even unusually attractive packaging. So this 100-point system is spread out over much broader and more meaningful territory. The most important point I want to make is that every winery included in this book has made the cut. These are all well above average. Every score is a good score.

This is not specifically designed as a comprehensive touring guide. You will find only a quarter of the state's wineries even mentioned here. The focus is on who delivers quality. Everyone included here has made the quality cut. If your favorite winery is not among them, please do not take offense. Perhaps it is simply too new to evaluate. Perhaps it is one of those that stubbornly refuse to acknowledge the world outside their own tasting room. More than a few wineries in Washington prefer to take a combative "my way or the highway" stance when their wines are critiqued. They are content to muddle along on tasting room sales, making wines to suit their own tunnel palates, and defending their right to do things their way. I support that right, but I cannot endorse the wines.

Many sources, both in print and online, offer opinions and ratings about wines. Experience has proven time and again that even the most educated palates can disagree about many subjective aspects of taste. I belong to two long-established tasting groups that count among their members winemakers, distributors, retailers, and salespeople, many of them with impressive credentials and decades of experience. The roundtable discussions that our blind tastings ignite are never dull, usually hilarious, and frequently combative. They certainly sharpen my thinking and my palate, and I thank my fellow tasters (you know who you are) for sharing your time and talents so generously.

I think there is value in such group discussions. But at the end of the day, any group or panel judgments about wine are watered-down compromises. When you read of medals awarded or points given to individual wines by tasting or judging panels, no matter how well credentialed, you may be certain there was compromise involved. Although much lip service is paid to the value of blind tastings, I find that they are simply one tool in the reviewer's tasting toolkit. Blind tastings can layer a veneer of impartiality over any group of ratings, but they can also lead to some bizarre conclusions. As often as not, the results at which such competitive blind judgings arrive seem to fly in the face of experience.

When wines are reviewed and scored by a single individual, it is easier for consumers to gauge. You are dealing with one person's palate, not the decision of a committee. You can agree or disagree, but at least you have a compass and an orientation. Over time, as you come to know a particular writer, and come to your own conclusions about his or her palate, you may find a kindred spirit, whose recommendations you can trust. Or you may find someone whose palate is not exactly your own, but whose descriptions and summaries are informative enough for you to find the wines that best suit your tastes.

The final score awarded to each winery included here is the numerical summation of all the points awarded for style, for consistency, and for value. The perfect total is 100 points, a nice, round number that is familiar and comforting to many wine enthusiasts and that has become a bit of a Holy Grail for many wineries. One winery in this book earns that score.

I have chosen to grade wineries rather than individual wines. A single wine may get a high grade, but what does that tell you, other than that the critic or panel who awarded the score liked that bottle on that day? Often these high-scoring wines are made in miniscule quantities. They can change dramatically over time, for better or for worse. All wines are prone to bottle variation, and any wine, no matter how good, may suffer from a failed cork or irreversible damage during shipping and storage. And inevitably, once a big number has been awarded to a particular bottle, the price climbs and the wine quickly disappears from the market.

Grading the winery resolves these issues. A high score indicates that the winery does a good job with all of its wines and has done so consistently, vintage after vintage. The breakdown of each score also tells you where a given winery's strengths may lie. This scoring system places a high premium on consistency, value, and longevity. Since it reflects a winery's entire output and track record, it utilizes a much broader range of numbers than the 85-and-up scores in the major wine publications.

In this guide, only the greatest wineries score above 90. A score in the 80s is superb and indicates that the winery has some real experience under its belt. The best of the newer wineries might reach scores in the 60s and 70s because they have not yet been here long enough to rack up big scores for longevity. In rough numbers, something like three-quarters of the wineries in the state have released five or fewer vintages. The jury is still out, in my view. So I am asking you to adjust your parameters when considering their scores. The bottom line is this: Any winery scored here is among the top 15 percent of all the wineries in Washington and well worth your time and attention.

Here is how this 100-point system awards its points.

Style

26–30   a winery with a unique, clearly defined, technically flawless style

21–25   a winery with a majority of its wines better than its peers, with rarely a technical flaw

16–20   a winery whose wines generally meet industry standards for varietal character and technical competence

11–15   a winery whose wines lack varietal character and occasionally have more serious flaws, such as excessive volatility, or brettanomyces

0–10   a winery whose wines are frequently marred by technical flaws

Consistency

26–30   a winery with at least a 20-year track record of good to excellent wines

21–25   a winery with at least a 10-year track record of good to excellent wines

16–20   a winery with at least a five-year track record of good to excellent wines

11–15   a winery with fewer than five vintages and/or mixed success in different vintages

0–10   a winery with little or no consistency in style or quality, wine to wine and vintage to vintage

Value

26–30   a winery whose wines offer exceptional value in relation to the global wine market

21–25 a winery whose wines offer good value in relation to the global wine market

16–20   a winery whose wines offer good value in relation to their Washington peers

11–15   a winery whose wines offer fair value in relation to their Washington peers

0–10   a winery whose wines are overpriced in relation to the rest of the wine market

Contribution

0–10   a sliding scale, with points awarded according to the winery's contribution to the development and improvement of the Washington wine industry

METHODOLOGY

I taste roughly 6000–8000 wines annually, mostly at home, in peer group flights. I supplement these tastings with numerous trips to wineries throughout Washington, along the West Coast, and abroad. I live half the time in Seattle and the other half in Walla Walla County. This places me in the heart of some of Washington's most exciting wine country. I sometimes attend trade tastings but do not use those notes in my final database. As often as time permits, I taste new releases with winemakers, believing that the information gleaned from our conversations outweighs any chance that my impressions will be overly influenced by their presence.

I am not of the currently fashionable critical school that practices and preaches hit-and-run wine judging. There are snapshots and movies; I think wines are movies that should be observed in motion. With that in mind, I taste wines slowly, over many hours, with and without food, and sometimes over several days. I believe there are times when we must extend ourselves to a wine and give it a decent chance to show its stuff.

One reason that massive, jammy, oaky, fruit-bomb wines tend to win high scores and gold medals is that they stand out quickly during rapid-fire "shotgun" wine tastings. If a wine is one in a group of 50 or more bottles that are each being given a minute or two to demonstrate their worth, is it any wonder that only the biggest, brawniest, most forward, and ripest will be noticed?

I have lost count of the times that a wine, just opened, failed to perform. Wines submitted for review are new releases; many have just recently been blended and bottled. They have had little time to settle down, and they are often a bit "shocked." It is not uncommon for such wines to seem dumb, devoid of any scent or flavor.

To quote Bob Dylan, "you know something is happening, but you don't know what it is." The scents and flavors are often buried under a blanket of SO_2 or still showing aggressive barrel tannins that obliterate the fruit. But give these wines a few hours or even days and they will (sometimes) open up beautifully so that you can see their true selves. Which is the more accurate impression: the instant snapshot or the film clip?

Of course, there are many, many wines whose simplistic structure or generic character are instantly apparent. Retasting after some hours have passed merely serves to confirm the original opinion. Flawed wines with TCA, excess brett, oxidation, volatile acidity, and so on are also easily and quickly chronicled. But in my experience the very wines that best demonstrate terroir, whose innate structure, balance, clarity, precision, and depth portend age-worthiness, are frequently wrapped up tight as mummies when first opened. These are the gems that most benefit from extra hours of breathing or decanting. These are the wines that are easiest to miss in a hit-and-run evaluation.

I especially value wines that do not obliterate nuance in favor of the crowd-pleasing flavors of new oak, wines built on grapes ripened to appropriate levels for their particular vineyard site, wines with complex and detailed aromas, with well-defined fruit, and balancing acids and tannins that are harmoniously integrated into the whole. The wines I most enjoy and constantly search for are wines that have a focus. They taste like something specific—a particular grape variety or varietal blend, grown and made into wine in a particular place.

The best wines reflect the soil, climate, and vintage conditions of the vineyard. The French word *terroir*, which has no English equivalent, when used correctly suggests a wine that expresses the grape, the soil, the site, and the climate through its complex scents and flavors. Excessive ripeness, superextraction, alcohol topping 15, 16, or even 17 percent (in unfortified dry wines), and the ham-handed application of expensive new oak—the formula for many so-called cult wines—will obliterate terroir (if it is there to begin with).

Washington vintners are not all immune to the siren song of such wines, which seem to get the medals, the scores, the high prices, and the cover stories in the glossy magazines. Who doesn't want to be the captain of the cheerleading squad? But such jammy, flashy, high-octane, hedonistic wines are rarely fit companions at mealtime. Their very bigness—portlike levels of fruit and alcohol married to a small forest (air-dried of course)—makes it difficult to down a second glass.

The best vintners in Washington state recognize that bigger is not necessarily better. Washington's unique geography gives them the opportunity, the potential, to ripen grapes to physiological maturity while retaining good acid levels and keeping sugars and pH in check. If the vineyard is sited well, the vines are managed well, the picking is done at the right time, and the winemaker gets out of the way and leaves well enough alone, there is a real chance to find that elusive terroir.

For the first few years of the twenty-first century, the total vineyard plantings in Washington stayed unchanged, at just under 30,000 acres. But behind and beyond that statistic, enormous changes were taking place. Old vineyards were being replanted with new vines; new vineyards were going in to places such as Red Mountain, the Wahluke Slope, the Horse Heaven Hills, the Walla Walla Valley, and the Columbia Gorge, places where someone who took a big leap of faith had demonstrated that it was possible to grow extremely good grapes.

Experiments in vine density, row orientation, pruning, trellising, water management, and sustainable viticulture are well under way, many with the express purpose of finding better methods to achieve maximum flavor complexity at lower alcohol levels.

Back in the 1970s a typical bottle of Washington cabernet would have between 12 and 12.5 percent alcohol. Today the average is at least two percentage points higher. The interesting thing is that some of those older wines have aged beautifully. They may have been underripe by today's standards, but with the passing of time they have evolved flavors that are closer to European wines than any others made in America. These occasional early successes clearly point the way to a Washington winemaking style that straddles the border between the massive, fruit-powered wines of California and the more acidic, austere, mineral-laced, terroir-driven wines of Europe.

A number of wineries in Washington are actively exploring this borderline, crafting superb wines that suit the twenty-first-century palate, that beautifully accompany the foods we most enjoy, wines that will not only persist but will evolve over time. These wines are the beacons that show us where to find true terroir in these brand-new, New World vineyards. They are the wineries that draw my highest praise in these pages.

PART I

HISTORY AND BACKGROUND

1

WHICH SIDE OF THE POTOMAC?

A Brief History of Washington Wines

For many years Bob Betz, a Master of Wine (MW) who now has his own Betz Family winery, traveled the globe speaking to audiences on behalf of Stimson Lane (the corporate parent of Columbia Crest and Chateau Ste. Michelle, among others). His standard spiel neatly encapsulated the story of the wineries, their vineyards, and the growth of winemaking in Washington. Nonetheless, he found that a certain amount of confusion persisted among a significant percentage of his audiences. At one particular East Coast appearance, he recalls, his audience seemed to be paying close attention, following his every word, carefully studying the charts and photographs, and showing keen interest in his subject. Wrapping up his presentation, Betz asked if there were any questions. A hand shot up. "Just one question, Bob. Which side of the Potomac did you say the grapes were grown on?"

The story illustrates what has been an especially difficult problem for Washington wineries. For most consumers who do not live on the West Coast of the United States, Washington is the capital of the country, not some obscure state in its most distant, upper left-hand corner. For foreigners it's even worse. Of course they know where California is, and that state's reputation for being the land of entertainment, beauty, the arts, and the Good Life has attached itself quite naturally to its wine industry. But ask even a well-traveled foreigner to conjure up an image of Washington state, and, once you work your way past the coastal confusion, the best you can hope for is a vague sense that it is somewhere north of the redwood forests and south of Alaska's glaciers—and most certainly not wine country!

Compounding the confusion caused by this state's name is its schizophrenic geography. In terms of climate, precipitation, and the overall look and feel of the landscape, it splits neatly into two completely different halves, which may conveniently be labeled the *wet side* and the *dry side*. If you hold out your left hand, palm facing you, fingers folded, thumb spread, you have a perfect map of Washington state. Your thumb is the Olympic Peninsula, with the Pacific Ocean on the left and Puget Sound on the right. Follow the line between your ring and middle fingers on down to your wrist; there you have the Cascade Mountains, a relatively young and still active range of volcanoes best known for Mount Baker, Mount Rainier, and of course Mount St. Helens. Pretty much everything from the bottom of the other three fingers to the wrist is desert or, as the locals like to think of it, wine country.

On the wet side, the Olympic Mountains, which would run down the center of your thumb, parallel to the Cascades, are the first shield against the massive storms that blow in from the Pacific. They turn the Puget Sound into a perpetual convergence zone, with weather systems coming up from the south or down from the north and colliding, usually somewhere right around Seattle. Though not nearly as wet or cold as its reputation would have it, the weather in the western part of the state is substantially less hospitable to growing wine grapes than that east of the Cascades.

The Cascades act as the second barrier to the moisture-laden Pacific fronts and pretty much soak up the lion's share of the rain and snow that those storms bring. Once across the mountain passes, you descend through alpine forests into dryer and dryer meadows and valleys that ultimately open out into the great deserts of eastern Washington.

Leon Adams, in his seminal history of American viticulture (*The Wines of America*, 3rd ed., McGraw-Hill), stated that the first wine grapes were grown in Washington during the 1860s in the Walla Walla Valley. In *The Wine Project* (Sketch Publications, 1997), a more thorough investigation of the state's viticultural history, Ronald Irvine and Dr. Walter Clore date the first grapevine plantings to 1825, at Fort Vancouver.

The century of winemaking that led into Prohibition left few traces in Washington. There are no commercially viable old vines here that date back to those times, as there are in California. Prohibition in Washington began in 1917, ahead of the rest of the nation, and brought winemaking progress to a standstill. Grape growers were able to survive, and even prosper, selling rustic, thick-skinned, winter-hardy grapes to home winemakers. But the handful of commercial wineries had to close their doors.

It would be misleading to say that the modern era of winemaking in Washington began with Repeal, as it did in California. Although it is true that many new wineries were bonded at that time, they made no varietal wines and only occasionally and haphazardly used vinifera grapes. In western Washington, most wines were produced from Island Belle grapes, grown on Stretch Island in south Puget Sound. In the vineyards of eastern Washington, field blends might have included anything and everything, from Concord and Campbell Early (another name for Island Belle) to zinfandel, muscat, and alicante bouschet.

These grapes were harvested all together, tossed into fermenters together, and made into unfortified sweet wines. Many of the best-selling wines were produced by a so-called "high fermentation" technique that added plenty of sugar to the fermenting grapes and used special yeasts to boost alcohol levels to 17 percent, the maximum allowed by the state.

Labeled Burgundy, Rhine Riesling, Sauternes, and so on, these wines accounted for the lion's share of wine sales right through the 1960s. A thirsty public, freed from the restrictions of Prohibition and beginning to recover from the Great Depression, wanted a good buzz, not terroir.

In retrospect, post-Prohibition liquor laws in Washington seem to have been designed, purposely or not, to block meaningful attempts to make European-style dry table wines and to create a protected market for sweet, high-fermentation wines. In 1934, the Washington State Liquor Act was passed, which created the Liquor Control Board. The Washington State Liquor Control Board regulates and controls the sales of all hard liquor to this day. Initially, it allowed only beer and wine to be sold by the glass, in licensed restaurants and taverns. Wine, according to the WSLCB, was anything fermented that contained no more than 17 percent alcohol.

Ironically, this created the incentive to manufacture wines with unnaturally high levels of both sugar and alcohol, to satisfy the desires of consumers who couldn't get served a cocktail or glass of whiskey. Part and parcel of these laws were trade restrictions that taxed out-of-state wineries heavily but allowed Washington wineries to sell directly to retail accounts. The price advantages, designed to foster the local industry, also meant that few quality wines from California or anywhere else could find much of a market in Washington.

By 1937, 42 wineries were licensed in the state, mostly small and making fruit wines rather than grape wines. The local products were the mainstay alcoholic beverages of the taverns, while the California brands were offered (at substantially higher prices) in the state liquor stores and some restaurants. The Washington wineries banded together to push their advantage, and taxes on California wines were repeatedly raised. By the end of 1942, *The Wine Project* reports, there were just 24 Washington wineries, but they controlled almost two-thirds of the total wine sales in the state.

Permissible alcohol levels continued to rise, and fortified wines replaced the sugar-enhanced, 17-percenters of the prewar years. By 1948, Irvine notes, 85 percent of all Washington wines were fortified. But the Washington wine industry was again in decline, and the number of wineries in the state began dropping steadily.

The legislative tug-of-war between competing interests and the conflicted attempts by the state legislature to support the Washington wine industry with tax breaks and other measures while its own Liquor Board promoted the sales of California wines, has been well chronicled elsewhere. It delayed for two decades the birth of the modern-day Washington wine industry.

Despite ongoing pioneering efforts by a handful of growers, producers, and university scientists, who continued to experiment with vinifera vines and wines, the "smart thinking" about Washington was that it was too cold ever to compete with California for quality, European-style wines.

But in the late 1960s, two startling events brought revolutionary change virtually overnight. The first was a chance encounter between author Leon Adams, making a visit to the Yakima Valley in 1966, and Victor Allison, the manager for American Wine Growers, who had begun to take notice of California varietal wines and experiment with a few of their own. As Adams explains, he happened across just a single memorable Washington wine on that trip, a rosé of grenache, made by Associated Vintners (A/V), a group of amateur winemakers from the University of Washington.

The members of A/V had originally come together in the 1950s in order to purchase grapes and winemaking equipment so that they could make dry, varietal wines for their own consumption. They incorporated in 1962 and a year later purchased and planted a small vineyard, Harrison Hill, in the heart of the Yakima Valley.

Dr. Cornelius Peck, one of the 10 who started the enterprise, recalls that very little was known about growing vinifera grapes in Washington. So the group's members planted nine different varieties on their five acres, in order to see which grapes, if any, might survive. The mix included gewürztraminer, riesling, semillon, chardonnay, and cabernet sauvignon. (Happily, some of the original cabernet vines are still bearing and are now being used by DeLille Cellars to make a vineyard-designated wine.)

At the time, vintage-dated, domestic varietal wines made from the great European wine grapes were a curiosity at best. Published in 1965, Angelo Pellegrini's classic *Wine and the Good Life* passionately promoted the pleasures of good wine and food made with local ingredients. The book's finale, an account of two monumental dinner parties, is entitled "Is There an American Wine Fit to Drink?"

At the conclusion of a lengthy discourse on the subject, professor Pellegrini notes that "in our own [Washington] state, a group of dedicated wine men have planted several acres of choice hybrids." Was he speaking about the Associated Vintners? Maybe so, though they were planting French vinifera grapes rather than hybrids.

In any event, and despite his unbridled enthusiasm for Cascade mountain mushrooms, Dungeness crab, Cougar Gold cheese, and all things Northwest, Pellegrini rather summarily concludes the chapter by saying "as wine drinkers we wish them luck, . . . meanwhile we must look to California for most of the dinner wines in our cellars."

Fortunately, the Associated Vintners were looking to Washington, and author Leon Adams, impressed with the rosé he had tasted, suggested to Victor Allison that a good California winemaker might be able to make something even better with Washington grapes. Adams mentioned the name of André Tchelistcheff, the man behind the great wines of Beaulieu Vineyards. Allison brought Tchelistcheff to the state the following year, and, after plowing through a selection of dismal offerings, he tasted another Associated Vintners wine, this one a gewürztraminer, and was immediately convinced that the potential existed to make great wine from Washington grapes. He signed on as a consultant with American Wine Growers and began making their wines that same year. Ron Irvine has found an unpublished memo dating from the early 1970s that quotes Tchelistcheff as saying that someday he expects eastern Washington to produce wines from grenache and petite sirah.

Encouraged by the praise of Adams and Tchelistcheff, the Associated Vintners decided to sell their wines commercially. "We were winemakers," Dr. Peck recalled in a 2006 interview, "and we knew we were onto something pretty darn good. In 1966 we all made wine in our basements; afterwards we said holy Christopher—if it's this good we should make wine commercially!"

Tchelistcheff's first releases for American Wine Growers were a cabernet, a pinot noir, a sémillon, and a grenache, also from the 1967 vintage. The reds were still in barrel when the second paradigm-shifting event occurred. In March of 1969, the California Wine Bill was passed, ending the trade barriers that had propped up the Washington wine industry since Repeal and allowing specialty wine shops to open their doors for the first time.

As the turbulent decade of the 1960s drew to a close, the Washington wine industry finally entered the twentieth century.

THE 1970s

In 1970, no more than a half dozen commercial wineries were operating in Washington state. The two of lasting importance, Associated Vintners and AWG's Ste. Michelle brand, were making varietal wines from a growing number of different grapes, and they quickly began attracting the attention of wine lovers from out of state.

A group called the San Francisco Wine Sampling Club tasted a number of Ste. Michelle wines in 1970 and pronounced them "a serious challenge" to California varietal wines. The influential California wine writer Robert Balzer conducted a riesling competition a few years later and announced that a 1972 Johannisberg riesling from Ste. Michelle had bested entries from California, Germany, and Australia.

Spurred by the growing interest in varietal wines, Ste. Michelle, which was acquired by conglomerate U.S. Tobacco in 1974, began planting extensive vineyards in eastern Washington. Others were conducting their own experiments in far-flung corners of the state. The Associated Vintners continued to cultivate their vines in the Yakima Valley, near Sunnyside. Jim Holmes and John Williams began their exploration of Red Mountain. Gary Figgins tended an acre or two in Walla Walla. Charles Henderson planted riesling, gewürztraminer, pinot noir, and other grapes in the Bingen–White Salmon area of the Columbia Gorge, and in 1972 Dr. William McAndrew followed suit at his Celilo vineyard. A few miles farther west, Lincoln and Joan Wolverton planted pinot noir, chardonnay, and riesling at La Center, somewhat whimsically calling their vineyard the northernmost extension of the Willamette Valley.

This was the first great wave of Washington viticulture, boosted along by more and more visionaries, such as Mike Wallace, Bill Preston, Maury Balcom, Don Mercer, Mike Sauer,

In January 2006, through the generosity of private collectors and the winemakers themselves, I assembled an extraordinary tasting of Washington cabernets from the 1960s and 1970s. From Chateau Ste. Michelle and its predecessor, Ste. Michelle Vineyards, were cabernets from 1978, 1977, 1976, 1975, 1974, 1973, 1970, and 1969. From A/V (Associated Vintners), the very first winery in Washington to produce vintage-dated varietal wines, were cabernets from 1980, 1979, 1976, 1970, 1969, and 1967.

The guests at the tasting table included Dr. Cornelius Peck and his wife, Gloria. Dr. Peck is a founding member of the group of 10 men, most of them University of Washington professors, who bonded Associated Vintners back in 1962. Seated next to him was David Lake, the winemaker at A/V (now Columbia) from 1979 until his retirement in 2006. Also in attendance were Bob and Cathy Betz. Betz worked at Ste. Michelle for almost 30 years before leaving to devote attention full time to the Betz Family winery.

What did these old wines have to tell us as we tasted through them? First, that despite the primitive vineyard and winemaking techniques of the day, they had matured amazingly well. Lower in alcohol and far more acidic than today's cabernets, they were in many instances perfectly structured for long-term aging.

As Betz explained, "We were harvesting under much different criteria then. People were not willing to take chances on longer hang time; the Bordeaux model was bring the grapes in at 23 1/2 to 24 1/2 brix."

There was also plenty of SO_2 added, both during fermentation and at bottling, and far less exposure to new oak. The wines, most of them 100 percent cabernet sauvignon (merlot was not used as a blending grape prior to 1976), were all still drinkable.

Standouts among the Ste. Michelle wines were the following: the 1978, fragrant and beautiful, the color of sunset, with round, supple, fully mature flavors of plum, pie cherry, and hints of tobacco; the 1976, best of the decade, dark and extracted, smooth and supple, mixing black cherries with hints of berries and plums, set off against spices and caramel; the 1975, dark, heavy, tannic, and beginning to tire; the 1974, Bordeaux-like, herbaceous, and very light, tart, and frail; the 1973, assertive, herbal, very deeply colored, and searingly tart; the 1970, the most like Bordeaux, elegant and delicate, with hints of rose petals, pale cherry, and chocolate shavings; and finally, the 1969, hard, tannic, and angular but quite drinkable, tasting of tobacco and caraway seed spice.

The first commercial A/V wines to be released were a 1967 riesling and a gewürztraminer, both very well received according to press accounts of the day. Their first red wine was a 1967 cabernet sauvignon, the centerpiece of this tasting. Beginning with the youngest wine, the standouts from Associated Vintners were: the 1979—extraordinary, dense, hard, and rich, with traces of mineral, spice, herb, and other subtle elements; the 1970—100 percent cabernet from Harrison Hill grapes, deep, full, rich and evocative, with flavors of mixed dried fruits, molasses, caramel, and light spice; the 1969—also pure cab from Harrison Hill (though beginning to oxidize, it remained interesting), with powerful flavors of cooked cherry, sweet brown sugar, and a whiff of iodine; and finally, the cherished 1967—a lovely amber color, its plush bouquet reminiscent of a dry tawny Port, dusty and raisined, with an extremely long finish of butter and caramel.

and Jerry Bookwalter, among many others. Ste. Michelle Vintners became Ste. Michelle Vineyards and planted the first cabernet and riesling at their Cold Creek site. But the most far-reaching event was the purchase of the brand, vineyards, and winemaking facilities by U.S. Tobacco in 1974. From then on, the company controlled the vast majority of Washington state's varietal wine vineyards and production.

By the end of the decade, Washington had roughly a dozen wineries and 2600 acres of vinifera vineyard. Despite a severe freeze in the winter of 1979, the future, as a very young Bill Gates might have said, was so bright you needed sunglasses.

THE 1980s

Washington had shown that it could make competitive varietal wines. But the state's reputation for periodic arctic blasts seemed intact. If its vines were constantly being frozen back to the roots, it seemed a gamble to look beyond winter-hardy Germanic grapes and even hardier hybrids.

Somehow, a critical number of growers were not deterred. Many were farmers, whose view of wine grapes was that they were just another crop to be added to the mix of hops, potatoes, mint, asparagus, apples, cherries, Concords, and so on that was already in the ground. They were used to the weather problems. Grapes were planted, as a general rule, in the most fertile soils, watered heavily, and harvested early. Getting the crop in, rather than maximizing wine quality, was paramount.

The Yakima Valley, a fertile crescent extending from the city of Yakima in the west almost to the Tri-Cities in the east, attracted the most attention. It had plenty of water, well-established agricultural enterprises, and was already planted to some of Washington's oldest, most proven vineyards. Other significant vineyard plantings were concentrated in the Columbia Basin, north of the Tri-Cities, and south of Prosser, in the Horse Heaven Hills, above the Columbia River.

As the decade began, Ste. Michelle (now owned by UST) and Associated Vintners (now renamed Columbia Winery) werse the state's big players, recently joined by a few smaller, family-owned vineyard and winery operations (Kiona, Hinzerling, Mont Elise, Preston, Yakima River) and a handful of boutiques (Leonetti Cellar, Neuharth, Quilceda Creek, Worden's).

But as the '80s swung into full stride, several large-scale, family-run, and cooperative enterprises appeared: Hogue Cellars, Hyatt Vineyards, Gordon Brothers, Mercer Ranch Vineyards, Quail Run, Quarry Lake Vintners, and Tagaris among them. A wave of smaller mom-and-pop wineries, many without vineyards of their own, followed quickly: Arbor Crest, Barnard Griffin, Bonair, Bookwalter, Chinook, Latah Creek, L'Ecole Nº 41, Pontin del Roza, Portteus, Salishan, Tucker Cellars, Woodward Canyon, and dozens more.

When it opened in 1982, Chateau Ste. Michelle's Paterson Winery, as Columbia Crest was first known, represented an extraordinary $25 million commitment to the future of Washington wine. Along with the state-of-the-art winery (capacity 2 million gallons) came almost 2000 acres of new vineyard (a net 50 percent increase overall for the state).

Perhaps the most important development of the decade, even more than the wine industry's steady growth, was the state's burgeoning reputation for making superb red wines. Though Ste. Michelle and Columbia were certainly doing a very good job, especially with their single-vineyard cabernets, the real excitement centered on the wines of a handful of boutique bottlers whose products are still considered among the very best in the state: L'Ecole Nº 41, Leonetti Cellar, Quilceda Creek, and Woodward Canyon.

A big splash was also made by newcomer Hogue Cellars, whose first vintage was 1982. Hogue astonished the judges at the Atlanta Wine Festival with their 1983 Reserve cabernet sauvignon, which was named Best of Show. Made by Rob Griffin (whose Barnard Griffin winery was begun that same year), it revealed a combination of silky elegance and pure fruit-driven power that few outside the state had ever witnessed in a Washington red.

Other big, gutsy wines from small, gutsy producers were also making their mark. Leonetti's 1978 cabernet sauvignon (the winery's first commercial release) made the cover of a long-gone wine publication (*Wine and Spirits Buying Guide*), touted as the best cab in the country. Quilceda Creek's first vintage, the 1979 cabernet sauvignon, brought home the Grand Prize from the prestigious Enological Society competition in 1983. L'Ecole's 1983 merlot (their first commercial vintage) won a gold medal from the Enological Society a few years later. Latah Creek's 1983 merlot was given a gold medal at the Sixteenth International Wine and Spirits Competition in Bristol, England. And the fledgling Washington Wine Writers' Association voted the 1984 Woodward Canyon Dedication Series cabernet sauvignon the wine of the year in 1986.

Throughout the decade, vineyard-designated wines began to appear, first as a trickle and then with increasing regularity. The state's first AVAs were named in quick succession: Yakima Valley, Walla Walla Valley, and the all-encompassing Columbia Valley. The first significant European investment in Washington's wine industry was made when Germany's F. W. Langguth family, along with a group of Washington investors, planted the

265-acre Weinbau vineyard and built an ultramodern, 35,000-square-foot winery in the desolate sagebrush desert outside Mattawa.

Langguth's commitment to producing Germanic rieslings was decades ahead of its time, as was its foresight in developing the region that would later become known as the Wahluke Slope, recently named Washington's eighth AVA and home to some of its most important vineyards.

The number of wineries tripled, from fewer than 20 at the beginning of the decade to 60 by 1989. Vineyard acreage grew more slowly, from 7742 acres in 1981 (more than half of them newly planted and nonbearing) to 9000 bearing acres in 1989. But although Washington's total wine production lacked the sheer quantity to command much of a presence outside the state, trends were appearing that would set the stage for vast changes in the decade ahead.

In the mid-1980s, the Washington Wine Commission and its companion Washington Wine Institute were funded and began their efforts to promote and legislate for Washington vintners. The Commission's first World Vinifera Conference, held in Seattle in the summer of 1989, brought winemakers from around the world to Washington state and matched Washington's rieslings with the best from elsewhere. *Wine Country* magazine named Chateau Ste. Michelle "Best American Winery" in 1988. *Wine Spectator* magazine included five Washington wines in its Top 100 list for 1989.

Meanwhile, Columbia winemaker David Lake and grower Mike Sauer were quietly laying the foundation for some of the most exciting Washington red wines of the next decade. At Sauer's Red Willow vineyard, just east of the Cascades, syrah cuttings from Joseph Phelps went into the ground in 1986, and the first varietal Washington syrah was produced by Columbia in 1988. As the decade drew to a close, syrah remained a virtually unknown experiment, but merlot was about to become the ticket to Washington's first real stardom.

THE 1990s

When television's *60 Minutes* broadcast the legendary "French Paradox" segment in November 1991, little did the producers realize that it would ignite a revolution in wine drinking and that tiny Washington state would benefit hugely as a result. At the time most wine drinkers in America were sticking to white wines and sweet pink versions of red grapes. The very notion of wine as a beverage of moderation was under attack from a neo-Prohibitionist movement that seemed to be gaining strength from month to month. In the eyes of that powerful lobby, wine was just another addictive drug, no different than heroin. The "French Paradox" story suggested otherwise. Wine, it said, was not only an essential part of a meal; red wine was a beverage that actually had proven health benefits. Voila! Suddenly, drinking red wine was a certifiably Good Thing. Given permission to enjoy their red wines guilt-free, consumers embraced them. And merlot, which until then had been a rather listless player on the world stage, became the red wine of choice.

As luck would have it, the Washington Wine Commission's second World Vinifera Conference, held in July of 1991, had chosen merlot as its focus. In a *Wine Spectator* interview some years later, Simon Siegl, who was executive director of the Washington Wine Commission from 1988 to 1996, recalled that the topic was selected for marketing reasons more than anything else. California already "owned" cabernet, but merlot remained unclaimed; there was far less competition in the category. Furthermore, Stimson Lane (the umbrella company for all of the UST wineries) had planted a lot of merlot, particularly at their Columbia Crest winery and vineyard. The company was eager to back any event that would promote Washington merlot to the rest of the world. And finally, merlot enjoyed the same general advantages as chardonnay: It was French, and it was a lot easier to pronounce than, say, gewürztraminer.

The merlot conference clicked, and along with the *60 Minutes* story it resulted in a perfect marketing storm, propelling the image of merlot. Washington, many were coming to believe, was making better merlots than any place outside of France, and not just the limited, expensive boutique bottlings; Columbia Crest was the state's (and later the country's) leading producer of value merlot, priced for supermarket shelves. Early in the decade, Washington's merlot vineyard acreage had overtaken plantings of cabernet to become the state's most widely planted red wine grape. During the next eight years that acreage increased by a factor of 5, to 5600 acres in 1999.

By the mid-1990s it seemed that Washington merlot was everywhere. Merlot specialists such as Leonetti Cellar began to command Bordeaux-like prices for wines that sold out months before being released. Merlot was both trendy *and* spendy. National publications that had scorned Washington as the land of cheap riesling were falling all over themselves to honor the state's reds, especially its merlots, as the most Bordeaux-like in the land.

Columbia introduced the "Milestone" merlot from the Red Willow vineyard. DeLille Cellars' "D2" blend featured merlot in the starring role. Andrew Will made as many as six different merlots annually, including four vineyard-designated bottlings, a blended Washington version, and a few cases of an "R" reserve. And Chateau Ste. Michelle expanded its own program of single-vineyard merlots to include bottlings from Cold Creek, Canoe Ridge, and Indian Wells, plus its Columbia valley and reserve merlots.

With the 1994 introduction of Northstar, then a merlot-only brand, parent company Stimson Lane made it clear that in its deep-pocket, corporate view, merlot was Washington's star grape variety. California's Jed Steele was hired as consulting winemaker and charged with making a Pomerol-style Washington merlot. A dedicated winery and vineyard were established in Walla Walla in 2002, and Northstar began producing both a Columbia Valley and a Walla Walla Valley merlot bottling. (But how times do change: In 2006, the winery released, for the first time, a very limited amount of Northstar syrah.)

Meanwhile, a second red wine revolution was quietly gaining strength. The syrahs that the Columbia winery had been turning out since 1988 were beginning to attract attention. McCrea Cellars made its first varietal syrah in 1994, with fruit from vines planted in 1990 at a site above the Columbia Gorge. Ripe, rich, and seductive, McCrea's wine proved that Red Willow was not the only site where the grape could thrive.

Another of Washington's periodic arctic blasts struck in 1996, severely reducing vineyard yields and wiping out much of the state's prime merlot for that vintage. But Red Willow's syrah vines survived the freeze just fine, as did other, younger syrah vineyards in the Columbia Valley and on Red Mountain. Once its winter-hardiness had been tested, more growers began to get interested in trying syrah, spurred on by winemakers' eagerness to work with the grape. Even Columbia Crest jumped on the syrah bandwagon, making a few cases beginning in 1994 and then ramping it up with a spectacular 1996 bottling, lushly scented with smoke, black fruit, and pepper.

The rush was on as new wineries, dedicated specifically to making syrah, began springing up like chanterelles after an autumn rain. "I spent two years in Australia immersed in shiraz," recalled Glen Fiona's Rusty Figgins. "I came back home and I fell in love with the variety. I knew the conditions were right, especially in Walla Walla." Though Figgins departed Glen Fiona some years ago, it was originally conceived by him as a syrah specialist, making three different, limited-production syrahs. Among them was the first to bear a Walla Walla Valley designation and the first to be cofermented (Rhône style) with viognier.

Vigneron Christophe Baron also saw the syrah potential of Walla Walla and settled in the area in the mid-1990s to plant his vineyards on the stony soil of an ancient, dry river bed. When his first crop appeared, in the autumn of 1999, there were only 290 bearing acres of syrah in the entire state, though four times that amount was already in the ground. Despite its limited availability, syrah was already on the way to claiming its place as the signature wine for Walla Walla.

As the century drew to a close, Washington could claim 144 commercial wineries and almost 25,000 acres of vinifera vineyard. In addition to the Yakima Valley, Columbia Valley, and Walla Walla Valley AVAs, a fourth—the Puget Sound—had been recognized in 1995. Though white wines were still the majority, red wine production was growing steadily, accounting for 42 percent of the state's total. The commercial and critical success of the "cult" reds—Andrew Will, Leonetti Cellar, Quilceda Creek, and Woodward Canyon—had inspired a new generation of garagistes, wineries such as Cadence, Cayuse, DeLille Cellars, Dunham, Matthews Estate, McCrea, and Soos Creek. But the real growth had barely begun.

2000 TO THE PRESENT

In March of 2001, the Washington Wine Commission rolled out an exhaustive study (by Motto Kryla & Fisher) on the economic impact of the Washington state wine and wine grape industries. The report's most quoted statistic was its estimate of the full economic impact of the wine industry on the state. This included the sum total of revenues generated by vineyards, wineries, and their allied industries, the wages paid to more than 11,000 full-time employees in wine-related jobs, and even taxes and charitable contributions. The report concluded that, at the turn of the new century, the industry was generating $2.4 billion annually for the state.

Washington, though perhaps best known for its software, coffee, and airplane companies, is very much an agricultural state. Eastern Washington is farm country, and, by pointing out the enormous value of the wine industry, the Commission was saying to politicians, power brokers, and the state's citizens that this wine thing was not just some insignificant hobby business for rich guys. Wine grapes, the study noted, were already the fourth most important fruit crop in the state, behind apples, pears, and cherries (all of which were losing sales while wine grapes were gaining).

Not long after this report appeared, then-Executive Director Steve Burns issued his famous dictum (a sort of Moore's Law for wineries) that a new winery was bonded in Washington every 10 days. That is one of those great statistical sleight-of-mind statements that sounds more impressive than it really is. That translates to 36 new wineries a year—not bad, but nothing to beat a drum about. However, the actual growth was significantly higher. The 155 wineries counted in the 2001 report had jumped to more than 400 by the beginning of 2006, an average of roughly one new winery a week for five years straight. As we go to press, the 500th winery has been certified.

The great majority of these new wineries are so small as to be almost insignificant. A 2005 ranking of wineries by case production found that barely 25 produced more than 20,000 cases annually, and seven of those belonged to the Ste. Michelle Wine Estates group. What is significant is that Ste. Michelle Wine Estates is now the ninth-largest wine company in the country (according to *Wine Business Monthly*). For the past three decades, it has been principally responsible for establishing a market presence for Washington wines outside of the state. (Unfortunately, many out-of-state consumers continue to believe that Chateau Ste. Michelle and Columbia Crest, its two leading brands, are California wineries.)

Along with a tripling of the number of wineries, the first decade of the new century has brought a dramatic increase in the number of TTB-sanctioned Washington AVAs. The new AVAs (Red Mountain, Columbia Gorge, Horse Heaven Hills, Wahluke Slope, and Rattlesnake Hills) are all important grape-growing regions with distinctive soil, climate, and ripening profiles. They are home to many of Washington's most progressive vineyard owners and to more than a few of its best wineries.

For most consumers, the region that best embodies the spirit and style of the state's wine industry is Walla Walla. As recently as a decade ago, there were just eight wineries in Walla Walla; now there are 10 times that many. Knowledgeable locals expect that number to double again in the next five years. The valley has become a tourist magnet and is moving quickly to add the amenities (inns, restaurants, and wine-themed events) that will keep visitors coming.

Whether by accident or by design, the vintners of the valley have laid claim to syrah, making close to 200 different designated syrahs in any given vintage. They make broadly fruity, flavorful merlots, cabernets, and the country's best sangiovese and are now pioneering varietal bottlings of less well-known grapes, such as carmenère, cabernet franc, malbec, and tempranillo. The sheer physical beauty of the Walla Walla Valley, which puts the lie to the long-held notion that Washington wine country is all dusty desert, seems to have inspired others in the state to rethink their tourism possibilities as well.

New tasting rooms and visitor centers are opening in Prosser, on Red Mountain, along the Columbia Gorge, and in the Columbia Cascade country around Leavenworth, Wenatchee, and Lake Chelan. Both the Walla Walla Wine Alliance and the Washington Wine Commission hired new executive directors in 2006, and both have selected women with strong backgrounds in tourism. Tourism will clearly remain a priority in the decades to come.

Everything old is new again, just reinvented slightly. Riesling, which was Washington's original calling card to the wine world, was dumped like an ugly blind date in the rush to plant and promote red wines. But now a genuine riesling renaissance is under way.

Some years ago I sat in the office of Allen Shoup, then CEO of Stimson Lane. Shoup was on a roll, excitedly describing a "riesling renaissance" that he was attempting to promote. I thought he was nuts. At the time you couldn't give the stuff away. Riesling vineyards were being ripped out across Washington as fast as you could say "merlot." The idea of a riesling renaissance, fueled by the creation of the upscale bottling Shoup envisioned, seemed pie in the sky at best. In retrospect it looks brilliant.

Chateau Ste. Michelle's Eroica riesling, made in collaboration with Dr. Ernst Loosen of Germany, has become the gold standard for the country. All together, the Ste. Michelle family of brands is the biggest riesling producer in America (2003's production topped 478,000 cases, and production continues to climb). Shoup's new venture, Long Shadows, includes another riesling collaboration, this with Armin Diel of Schlossgut Diel. Dry riesling is also becoming a market driver as younger consumers turn away from the simple, sweet styles that were tasting room staples a generation ago. Overall riesling demand is so strong that there is now a shortage of grapes statewide.

As Washington stakes its claim to be recognized with other world-class wine regions, accolades and criticism from the press are coming in roughly equal proportion. This is to be expected and, on balance, is quite healthy. The challenges that face the state's vintners are in many respects exactly the same as those that face any emerging wine region, whether in Chile, South Africa, New Zealand, the Canadian Okanagan, or, for that matter, the south of France.

Winning the hometown fans is just the beginning. Washington must consistently define and explain itself to the rest of the world. Given that the state has no single "signature" wine or grape, it must consistently demonstrate quality and value across the board. It must take better advantage of the natural beauty and unjaded populace that make visiting wine country in this state such a pleasure. It must overcome the archaic, confusing, and expensive tangle of laws that regulate the distribution and sale of wine here and in every other state in the country. To put it bluntly, it must live up to its shiny new motto: "The Perfect Climate for Wine." In the next chapter, we begin to see how, where, and if it does.

2

THE AVAS

The American Viticultural Area (AVA) system was instituted by the Bureau of Alcohol, Tobacco, and Firearms (ATF) in the late 1970s in order to regulate the use of place names on wine labels. Though widely viewed as an American version of the tightly controlled appellation systems in place in Europe, it really is nothing of the sort.

In Europe the granting of an appellation generally brings with it specific rules regarding the grapes that may be planted, the sugar levels (and sometimes the actual picking dates) at harvest, prescribed (and outlawed) viticultural and winemaking practices, and other quality controls. In the United States, by contrast, there are few such requirements. Rather, the TTB (acronym of the Alcohol and Tobacco Tax and Trade Bureau, which took over from the ATF in 2004) wants to know your proposed boundaries, some soil and weather analysis, what you are planning to name your AVA, and how that name has historical significance for your area.

Apart from prescribed limits on chemical additions to wines, actual wine quality is the least of TTB's concerns. They are label approvers who want to regulate the verbiage on wine labels. Cigarette-style warnings are clearly a higher priority than meaningful quality guidelines. The use of the term *reserve*, for example, is completely unregulated and hence meaningless.

The TTB does expect an AVA to be "a delimited grape-growing region distinguishable by geographical features [in order to] allow vintners and consumers to attribute a given quality, reputation, or other characteristic of a wine made from grapes grown in an area to its geographical origin."

In order to qualify its role still further, the TTB explains that its goal in designating viticultural areas is "to allow vintners to better describe the origin of their wines, and to allow consumers to better identify wines they may purchase. Establishment of a viticultural area is neither an approval nor an endorsement of the wine produced in that area."

A recently approved Oregon AVA, named Red Hill Douglas County, illustrates the absurdity of this last statement. How many consumers can be expected to know that Red Hill Douglas County is completely different from the well-known Red Hills of Dundee, which has been the center of great Oregon pinots for decades? For that matter, Red Hill Douglas County might well be confused with Red Mountain (in Washington) or Red Hills Lake County (in California), both existing, approved AVAs.

In its official posting for the Red Hill Douglas County AVA the TTB went so far as to say that "the regulations pertaining to the establishment of viticultural areas do not require the existence of a substantial viticultural history, a production of unique wines, or a demand for wines originating in the proposed viticultural area. Therefore, in evaluating a petition, TTB does not consider as determining factors the questions of whether the viticulture of the proposed area is new or established, whether the area is producing unique wines, or whether wine from the area is in demand in the marketplace."

Any sane person might wonder exactly what they *do* consider or require, or, more importantly, what an AVA, once granted, actually signifies. This issue is especially relevant to Washington state, which has only recently begun to parse its mammoth Columbia Valley AVA into smaller, more crisply defined subappellations.

In purely legal terms, that a wine is AVA designated tells you that the named area was approved by the TTB under current regulations, that at least 85 percent of the grapes used to make the wine were grown in the named AVA, and that the wine was made ("fully finished") within the AVA.

The task of creating AVAs whose value extends beyond such pitifully weak guidelines falls, inevitably, on the wineries and growers whose land lies within the proposed boundaries. In Washington, the AVAs whose cachet has value beyond the official terms have created that value, quite simply, by producing exceptionally good wines.

When you grow good grapes and make good wines for a number of years, people begin to recognize your name. At that point, formal certification makes sense. The recently approved Washington AVAs (Red Mountain, Horse Heaven Hills, Wahluke Slope, and, to a lesser extent, Columbia Gorge and Rattlesnake Hills) have followed this path. Wineries may now begin to use these designations as marketing tools, and consumers can look to them as quality indicators. Beyond that, as smaller and more detailed AVAs continue to emerge (Frenchman Hills and Lake Chelan AVAs are in the application phase), the notion of a particular stylistic "terroir" associated with the AVA becomes more and more viable.

Washington, acting more timidly (or perhaps more thoughtfully) than either California or Oregon, has not yet given in to any wholesale petitioning for new AVAs. As of this writing there are just nine in the state (apart from the generic "Washington"). They have been developed rather slowly and in a fairly logical and meaningful progression.

When considered individually, they make sense; when taken collectively, they do a pretty good job (so far) of defining the emerging contours of the state's wine industry. It seems reasonable to hope that any future, smaller, more narrowly defined AVAs will contribute to an understanding of what differentiates their particular slice of Washington from its larger winegrowing regions. They should not only show you where the grapes are grown, but also convey some sense of the conditions of soil and climate that make them a candidate for AVA status. And, most importantly, you should be able to taste something in their wines that unites them by a common thread, a stylistic imprint that can be traced to the land, not to the hand of the winemaker.

WASHINGTON—"THE PERFECT CLIMATE FOR WINE"

In 2005 the Washington Wine Commission launched an ambitious advertising campaign with the tagline "Washington State—The Perfect Climate for Wine." Is it really? And if so, how so?

The search for answers to those questions leads to the research done by Dr. Alan Busacca. Recently retired from a teaching post at Washington State University and now a principal in Vinitas, a vineyard consulting firm, Busacca is a certified professional soil scientist and licensed geologist with a PhD in soil science from UC Davis. He and Dr. Larry Meinert, who also taught at Washington State University (WSU), have done exhaustive studies of soils and geology in eastern Washington. From these studies, a list of the most important and singular aspects of Washington's geology, soils, and climate has begun to emerge. It is an important first step on the road to defining a distinctive Washington style; especially useful because it is based on solid science rather than on poetic descriptions gleaned from winemakers' (and wine writers') tasting notes.

In Busacca's view, the Washington wine story begins with a series of cataclysmic floods that inundated the region at the end of the last ice age. As he explains, much of eastern Washington owes its present-day landscape and soils to these extraordinary events. To sum up briefly: Some 18,000 years ago, the Pacific Northwestern part of the North American continent was on the edge of a vast glacial sheet of ice. In a complicated series of events that took place repeatedly over centuries, the ice repeatedly dammed and completely blocked the Clark Fork River, which drains a large part of what is now Montana.

This created an immense lake—Lake Missoula—containing something on the order of 500 cubic miles of water. Periodically, the water overcame the blockage, unleashing the largest floods ever recorded on the planet. These cataclysmic Lake Missoula floods sent some 2500 cubic kilometers of water (think Lake Erie and Lake Ontario combined) rushing across the Columbia Plateau, 500 feet high and traveling at 60 miles an hour. The waters inundated a vast area of central Washington that corresponds, more or less, to what is now the Columbia Valley AVA.

Another lake briefly formed as the waters reached the Horse Heaven Hills and backed up, reaching as far west as Yakima and east into Idaho. Then, rushing through the Wallula Gap, a narrow canyon where the Columbia River breaches the Horse Heaven Hills, the floodwaters continued down the Columbia Gorge to present-day Portland, flooding the Willamette Valley before ultimately emptying into the Pacific Ocean.

A practiced eye can still see the scars and scabs left by these floods in the brutal, jagged landscapes of eastern Washington, with its profusion of coulees (huge channels eroded in the basalt rock), dry waterfalls, gravel bars, and massive boulders scattered across the desert. More importantly, the residue of the floods—the gravels and silts and sands that were deposited by the receding waters or, later, windblown over the land—comprise the basic soils that contribute to the distinctive flavors of Washington state wines. Busacca goes so far as to say that the floods and their aftermath are what created the potential for *all* agriculture in eastern Washington.

The soils that typically characterize Washington vineyards are derived from mixtures of glacial and postglacial materials. The base soils are the gravels carried down by the floodwaters and deposited over basalt bedrock. These are layered over with windblown sand from the postflood era and finished with up to several feet of loess, a mix of fine silt and volcanic dust.

LATITUDE

The next important piece of Washington's "perfect climate" assertion can be found in the state's climatic characteristics. Eastern Washington is largely sagebrush desert. It lies in the rain shadow of the Cascade Mountains, a volcanic chain that is anchored by Mount Baker near the Canadian border and runs south to include Mount Rainier (the highest, at 14,411 feet) and the well-known, still active Mount St. Helens.

The majority of Washington's vineyards lie between latitude 46 degrees (the Oregon border) and latitude 47 degrees (just north of the Wahluke Slope). Thus, they are roughly comparable to Bordeaux and Burgundy. Much has been made of this by marketers, but it doesn't really tell you a great deal about the state's aptitude for ripening grapes. Those same latitudes cross Mongolia and Minnesota, but don't look for Ulan Bator or Fargo to become the next Beaune anytime soon. It's also fun to point out that the Napa Valley is on a parallel with Algeria, but that doesn't really speak to the quality of either region's wines.

What *is* significant is that Washington's relatively high latitudes mean that the growing season is edgier and more prone to extremes than the long, relatively smooth conditions that apply to much of California. There are four quite distinct seasons here, and the temperature ranges in eastern Washington are far wider than those west of the Cascades. A hard freeze can occur as late as Mother's Day and as early as Halloween.

On the plus side, eastern Washington summers and falls are virtually guaranteed to be dry. The combination of that desert dryness and the deep winter chill means that many insect pests, mold, and rot are rarely significant problems for eastern Washington vineyards. Even phylloxera has not been able so far to establish any kind of foothold in the state. Consequently, wine grapes are almost always planted on their own rootstock.

The higher latitude also means that Washington vineyards receive an average of 17.4 hours of sunlight daily during the growing season, two hours more than the California average. The extra hours compensate for the rather late start to bloom in the spring; while the dry, warm September and October weather allows harvest to occur according to the optimal physiological ripeness of each varietal at each site. It's not unusual for a vineyard such as Klipsun on Red Mountain to begin picking its sauvignon blanc in late August and to finish up its cabernet at the end of October.

During harvest, diurnal temperature variations of 40–50 degrees (daytime highs in the low 90s and nighttime lows in the mid-40s) are common. So hang time is not just a buzz word in Washington; it is something that can be relied on to ripen pips and sweeten tannins, without the grapes reaching absurd sugar levels or sacrificing acids.

IRRIGATION

The average eastern Washington vineyard receives just eight inches of precipitation annually (many get even less). It falls almost entirely during the winter months, from November through March; summers are reliably warm and dry. A few dry-farmed vineyards exist in locations that are close either to the Cascades (the western edge of the Columbia Gorge) or to the Blue Mountains (the eastern edge of the Walla Walla Valley). But these are the exceptions; by and large, Washington vineyards are irrigated.

The use of irrigation, which is disparaged (and prohibited) throughout much of the wine-growing world, is not something that must be overcome in order to grow quality grapes in Washington. On the contrary, research has demonstrated the positive impact of timely and specific applications of water to the vines. In recent years, the proper management of irrigation has become an essential component of the quest for quality.

The improvement and refinement of standard irrigation practices evolved over several decades. The first step was to replace the early, wasteful applications of sprayed water with drip irrigation. Then it was learned that intentionally withholding all water (deficit irrigation) during the first weeks of growth would stress the vines and thereby control vigor. Controlling vigor early and then applying water to ripen the fruit brought dramatic reductions in the vegetative aromas and flavors of the Bordeaux varietals. Growing less canopy also saved money: Costly leaf-stripping, sucker pruning, and mildew treatments were eliminated or reduced. Properly irrigated grapes ripened earlier and more fully, with no reduction in overall quantity.

Much of this experimentation was carried out at Columbia Crest during the late 1990s. When test results proved positive, the winery's entire 2000 acres of vineyard were brought into the program. The winery reported that irrigation requirements were reduced by an average of 10 inches per acre per year, the equivalent of 374 gallons of water per vine.

Another breakthrough was the discovery that giving the vines a good soaking right after harvest, so the soil is moist down to about two feet, can protect the roots from severe damage (or death) during a particularly brutal winter freeze. As early as the 1950s some pioneering growers, many under the tutelage of Dr. Walter Clore of Washington State University, had begun trying significant plantings of vinifera vines in eastern Washington. But the problem was that every six years or so, along would come a particularly severe arctic blast, which would kill the vines back down to their roots.

Winter hardiness is somewhat variable, according to the age of the vines, the particular varietal, and the duration of the cold snap. Most vines can survive temperatures as low as −5 to −8 degrees Fahrenheit. But should it slip just a degree or two lower, damage begins to occur. At −15 degrees the vine will die to the ground. A prolonged period of extreme cold may freeze the ground itself as deep as several feet, killing the roots.

To help prevent this, growers are now advised to do a postharvest irrigation. This will afford an extra degree of insulation and root protection should a dry winter and deep freeze occur. In some locations, wind machines can also be used to raise temperatures by as much as 4 degrees, a critical difference.

The occasional incidents of extreme cold will continue. The most recent, during January 2004, hit the Walla Walla Valley especially hard and wiped out most of that year's harvest. But with each episode, something valuable is learned. Better vineyard sites are developed. In Walla Walla, for example, most new vineyard plantings are moving to higher ground farther south and east.

Despite these occasional setbacks, the once-common belief that Washington winters are simply too cold for vinifera grapes to thrive long-term has been proven wrong. With proper site selection, postharvest irrigation, and new techniques, such as burying canes, significant cold damage can be avoided, even in extreme years. And there is a plus side to Washington's cold winters. In all years, the vines go into full and complete winter dormancy, a rarity in warmer regions and a factor in vine health and the development of fruit flavor.

In an often-repeated anecdote that may or may not be apocryphal, the late André Tchelistcheff is quoted as having proclaimed, while touring a Washington vineyard planted with roses at the end of the vine rows, that the roses smelled more fragrant than those in his California garden. He believed it was because his roses never really went dormant.

FLAVORS

None of this would mean much if the unique influences that pertain to grape growing in eastern Washington didn't deliver unique, desirable, and identifiable flavors in the wines. Washington's rather bold claim to being "perfect" is not the sort of boast that should be taken to mean that other places are not as good. There are great wine-producing regions scattered across the globe. But those who live in Washington, grow grapes there, make wine there, and have spent decades, as I have, tasting thousands upon thousands of Washington wines have come to believe, with good cause, that Washington has earned the right to be considered in the same context as the rest of the world's great wine-producing regions.

In the range and overall quality of its wines it is the equal of California, though the wines are certainly not the same. Washington vintners are not trying to make California wine from Columbia Valley fruit. They are trying to make great Washington wines, and in many instances they are succeeding. The next challenge is to build on that success, to identify what works and why and how, and to focus on developing the potential that has been demonstrated but not yet deeply explored. One important part of that process is to identify and delineate newer, more specific, and more meaningful AVAs.

AVAs appear to be geographic, soil-based entities, but in truth the most important American AVAs are flavor based. Napa Valley has a flavor, Dry Creek Valley has a flavor, just as Walla Walla has a flavor and Red Mountain has a flavor. Those new to Washington wines will discover that the baseline flavors are built on vivid fruit, bright acids, and compact tannins. The defining character is intensity married to purity of varietal fruit. It is most identifiable in pure varietal wines and particularly in single-vineyard, single-varietal wines.

Taste, for example, a Dunham "Lewis Vineyard" cabernet sauvignon. Inky black, dense, and tannic, it has tightly layered, structured fruit tastes of mixed wild berries, black cherry, pomegranate, and mint. The tannins are ripe and firm, with black tea and graphite flavors. It's a big wine but not a jammy, palate-fatiguing, high-alcohol fruit bomb. It has the ripeness of a great Napa cabernet with the structure and polish of a French wine.

This clarity, intensity, and dense structure can frequently be found in Washington rieslings and semillons. It is occasionally true for chardonnay, sauvignon blanc, gewürztraminer, and viognier. It's too soon to tell for sure, but pinot gris and roussanne seem to have excellent potential also.

Nine AVAs are approved in Washington, and applications for others are already on file. Two of the current AVAs, Columbia Valley and Puget Sound, cover vast regions. The stand-alone Puget Sound AVA includes the waterways, islands, and shorelines west of the Cascade Mountains but is home to just a handful of wineries and 80 acres of cool-climate grapes. In eastern Washington, the Columbia Valley AVA includes almost all of the others, the exception being the Columbia Gorge, which borders it to the west. Here's a quick statistical breakdown.

Columbia Valley (est. 1984)
- Washington's largest AVA (covers a third of the state)
- 11.5 million acres (4.65 million hectares)
- Over 17,000 vineyard acres
- Includes Yakima Valley, Rattlesnake Hills, Walla Walla Valley, Red Mountain, Horse Heaven Hills, and Wahluke Slope AVAs
- Crosses the border into Oregon

Yakima Valley (est. 1983)
- Washington's oldest AVA
- 665,000 acres (269,115 hectares)
- Roughly 11,000 vineyard acres; over 50 wineries
- Includes Rattlesnake Hills and Red Mountain AVAs

Walla Walla Valley (est. 1984, amended 2001)
- Washington's second-oldest AVA
- 303,500 acres (122,822 hectares)
- Over 1200 vineyard acres; over 80 wineries
- Crosses the border into Oregon

Red Mountain (est. 2001)
- Washington's smallest AVA
- 4040 acres (1635 hectares)
- 710 vineyard acres; roughly a dozen wineries
- Top vineyards: Ciel du Cheval, Hedges, Kiona, Klipsun, Tapteil

Puget Sound (est. 1995)
- Western Washington's only AVA
- 4.75 million acres (1.9 million hectares)
- 80 vineyard acres; roughly three dozen wineries
- Cool-climate grapes; island wineries

Columbia Gorge (est. 2004)
- 179,200 acres (72,520 hectares)
- Roughly 350 vineyard acres
- 15 wineries
- Crosses the border into Oregon

Horse Heaven Hills (est. 2005)
- 570,000 acres (230,670 hectares)
- 6040 vineyard acres, including some of the state's oldest and largest plantings
- Five wineries, including the state's largest, Columbia Crest

Wahluke Slope (est. 2006)
- Washington's eighth AVA
- 81,000 acres
- 5200 vineyard acres, roughly 20 percent of the state's total
- One winery and two production facilities

Rattlesnake Hills (est. 2006)
- Washington's ninth AVA
- 68,500 acres (27,721 hectares)
- Over 1500 vineyard acres; 17 wineries

Among red wines, there is little argument that Washington makes some of the world's finest merlots, thick and dense and substantial. Washington cabernet sauvignon—especially old vine juice from one of the state's dozen or so 30+-year-old vineyards—straddles the line between the herbal elegance of Bordeaux and the sweet lushness of Napa. Syrah ripens beautifully all over the state and creates a wide variety of pleasing flavors, retaining enough acid and peppery character to stand up as a legitimate (though different) peer to wines from Australia and the Rhône. Some impressive wines (in very small quantities) are also being made from small plantings of cabernet franc, carmenère, counoise, sangiovese, and grenache.

THE WASHINGTON AVAS

Doug Gore, who oversees all winemaking and vineyards for Ste. Michelle Wine Estates, describes the baseline signature of the Columbia Valley as "its fruit intensity and varietally correct wines, first in the nose, then in the palate. Whether it is blueberry in cabernet franc, black cherry in cabernet sauvignon, raspberry in merlot, pear in chardonnay, melon in sauvignon blanc, or peaches and apricots in riesling," he concludes, "we seem to have it in spades."

That's as good a broad-brush overview as any, but it just begins to hint at the complexity and detail that can be found in the state's best wines. As those wines increasingly show, the exploration of specific vineyard sites has evolved rapidly, with dramatic quality improvements in a very short time. Now Washington vintners are embarking on the difficult, expensive, and time-consuming process of delineating meaningful subappellations.

Besides those profiled next, it is anticipated that new AVAs for Snipes Mountain, the Columbia Basin, the Frenchman Hills, and Lake Chelan will be added in the near future.

COLUMBIA VALLEY

The subappellations nestled within the vast Columbia Valley AVA are profiled individually here. The most important Columbia Valley vineyard areas not yet officially designated as AVAs lie north of the Yakima Valley, separated by long ridges of east/west hills—the Rattlesnake Hills, the Yakima Ridge, the Umptanum Ridge, the Wahluke Slope, the Saddle Mountains. Much of this sparsely populated midsection is rugged, isolated scrubland consisting of long stretches of desert, occasionally irrigated for hops or stone fruits or vineyards. The Columbia River meanders through the region on its way south and east, ultimately cutting through the Wallula Gap and jogging due west, becoming the border between Washington and Oregon as it runs into the Pacific Ocean.

A bit farther southeast the Columbia, Yakima, and Snake rivers meet at the Tri-Cities (Richland, Kennewick, and Pasco). North of the Tri-Cities the ridges flatten out into the broad Columbia Basin, where some of the state's oldest and largest vineyards are situated. Major vineyard developments first went in during the 1970s, when the Sagemoor vineyard (and its Dionysus and Bacchus neighbors) were established. Today Sagemoor Farms is still among the most prolific suppliers of grapes to Washington wineries.

But based on the significant number of vineyard-designates that are appearing, winemakers' interest seems to have shifted from the Columbia Basin to the newer vineyard plantings in the recently approved Wahluke Slope AVA, located on a bend in the Columbia just below the Saddle Mountains.

According to the application prepared by Dr. Busacca, the 81,000-acre Wahluke Slope already has roughly 5200 acres of wine grapes in production, a sixth of the plantings statewide. Three-quarters of it is planted to red grapes. The new AVA is set on a single alluvial fan that was created by the glacial floods. It receives less annual precipitation than any wine region in Washington and is also one of the state's hottest and windiest sites. Quality from vintage to vintage is remarkably consistent, due to the uniform soils, south-facing slope, low rainfall, and reliable sunlight.

Geographically isolated and containing no significant population centers, the Wahluke Slope has plenty of vineyard and some production facilities for winemaking but no tourist amenities. In contrast, the far northern and western reaches of the Columbia Valley AVA include some of eastern Washington's most heavily touristed locations. Until recently, there were almost no wineries in what has begun calling itself the "Columbia Cascade" region. But that is changing rapidly.

Clustered around Leavenworth, Lake Chelan, and the Wenatchee Valley, more than three dozen wineries have set up shop in the past five years. The most established vineyards are on the region's far eastern edge, near the Gorge at George (less famous than the Columbia Gorge AVA farther south but home to the world-famous outdoor concert venue).

Newer plantings are going in around Lake Chelan and Wenatchee, and a few hardy souls are trying to grow grapes around Leavenworth, though it is right on the fringe of viability. It is too soon to speak of any regional terroir. Most Columbia Cascade wineries measure their production in hundreds of cases, not thousands, and almost all of the wines are made from grapes grown outside the region.

To a visitor it is not immediately apparent what common thread might link these wineries. Those clustered around Leavenworth, Washington's self-styled Bavarian village, are on the eastern slopes of the Cascades, in rocky, heavily forested mountain terrain. Those on the panoramic hills above Lake Chelan seem to have more in common with Canada's Okanagan, while the wineries following the Wenatchee River east toward the basalt-sculpted sagelands abutting the Columbia River at the gorge seem to be more closely related to the Wahluke Slope, which lies 30 miles to the south.

Those who would create a Columbia Cascade AVA point out that the influence of the Cascade Mountains touches all three of these areas. The mountains offer protection from the worst of the winter blasts that periodically ravage eastern Washington vineyards. Cameron Fries (White Heron Cellars) planted his 18-acre Mariposa vineyard in 1990, just above a bend in the Columbia at the eastern edge of what may become the Columbia Cascade AVA. He maintains that he has never had a bad freeze.

Apart from the Wahluke Slope and Columbia Cascade, other, smaller subsections of the Columbia Valley are being explored, some of which will surely become AVAs unto themselves. Cold Creek is the most important, a single-vineyard site that is owned and used almost exclusively by Ste. Michelle Wine Estates. Still farther north, as new plantings reach farther out toward the real edges of viable vineyard land in Washington, failures will inevitably occur. But the successes in just the first three decades seem to have permanently boosted Washington viticulture into the proven category, after more than a century of being considered marginal at best due to the severe winters. Somewhere within the 11 million acres of the Columbia Valley lie as-yet-undiscovered vineyard locations that may well produce Washington's Hermitage or Pétrus.

YAKIMA VALLEY

Washington's first officially designated AVA, and its third largest overall, is the Yakima Valley AVA. It encircles the Yakima River as it winds from the Cascade foothills east toward the Tri-Cities. At the valley's eastern edge, and located completely within it, is the state's most prominent AVA, Red Mountain; along its northern rim is the newest AVA, Rattlesnake Hills. Established in 1983, the Yakima Valley includes roughly 11,000 acres of bearing vineyards, among them the Otis and Harrison Hill vineyards, which have some of the oldest bearing cabernet vines in the country.

Yakima Valley grape flavors are more climate- and temperature-driven than soil based. Modern viticultural practices—drip irrigation, tighter vine spacing, lower yields—have begun to replace the wasteful sprinkler systems, the wide spacing (for machine harvesting), and the overcropping that originally prevented most Yakima Valley grapes from achieving optimal ripeness. These days riesling is the valley's star grape, but pinot gris can also do well. Reds are improving steadily, and certain sites (Boushey in particular) are growing outstanding syrah. Old-vine Yakima Valley cabernet sauvignon expresses itself with a nuanced herbaceousness that is more true to Bordeaux than the ripe, sweet, jammy flavors found in California.

The cooler western half of the Yakima Valley is at its best in a warm year, such as 1998 or 2002. At the extreme western edge, on a high plateau in the Cascade foothills, sits the Red Willow vineyard, which has been for many years a sort of viticultural laboratory for grower Mike Sauer and (now retired) Columbia winemaker David Lake. Among many, many innovations, they were the first to plant syrah in Washington, back in 1985, with cuttings from Joseph Phelps.

At the time it was just one more experimental block, but it has succeeded beyond anyone's expectations. Today there are more than 2100 acres of syrah in Washington and at least 100 wineries making one or more versions of the grape. Some of the best cool-climate syrah is grown in the Yakima Valley, at vineyards such as Red Willow and Boushey. The cabernet and merlot are exceptional at DuBrul, Harrison Hill, Otis, Portteus, and Sheridan. Pinot gris has been a surprise success at Willow Crest, and riesling does well at many sites.

Despite their head start and many strengths, as a group the Yakima Valley vintners have not yet been able to establish a clear regional identity in the minds of consumers. They tend to be insular, proud, and even antagonistic, resentful of the success enjoyed by wineries in other parts of the state. To be brutally honest, a disheartening number of Yakima Valley wineries seem to have no awareness of wines other than their own. Those wines can be amateurish and deeply flawed, and they cast a pall, unfairly, over the reputation of the entire region.

In my view, an understanding of basic wine flaws (TCA, mercaptans, acetic acid, ethyl acetate, oxidation, brettanomyces, etc.) should be mandatory for anyone involved professionally in the growing and making of wine. Washington wines compete with wines from all over the world for a place in consumers' cellars. All too frequently, Washington wines are judged by the worst bottles, not the best.

The same things that have boosted quality elsewhere in Washington are just as effective when conscientiously applied in the Yakima Valley. Plant the right grapes in the right place. Don't overcrop; don't overwater. Get outside input from qualified experts who can give you honest feedback about your winemaking. Do not rely exclusively on your own palate or the comments of friends and visitors to your tasting room, not if you want to be taken seriously by critics and retailers outside the state.

Yakima wineries should work together to promote their genuine strengths. They need to put their best wines up against leading examples from more prestigious wine regions. Why not organize a tasting competition pitting a dozen top Yakima cabs against a dozen comparably priced Bordeaux from the same vintage? Done right, the Yakima wines would show extremely well.

Only when a higher percentage of the growers and vintners of the Yakima Valley commit to the relentless pursuit of quality will they be able to build a regional reputation that can compete effectively in the global marketplace. Meanwhile, consumers who do a little digging can certainly find superior wines made from Yakima Valley grapes, often selling for less than wines from better-known regions.

It is significant that until very recently almost all the best Yakima wines came from grapes purchased from dedicated growers such as Dick Boushey and Mike Sauer, men who do not make their own wines. Surprisingly, wineries that purchase Yakima grapes but are located outside the valley seemed to have a better feel for the terroir than many of those who live there and work exclusively with their own fruit.

There have always been exceptions, of course. Chinook has a 25-year track record of excellence. Wade Wolfe of Thurston Wolfe, is as knowledgeable about vineyards as anyone in Washington, and he sources brilliant fruit for his zins, syrahs, and sweet dessert wines. Willow Crest does a particularly good job with pinot gris from their vineyards. Portteus vineyards, first planted in 1981, grows fine cabernet.

Newer vineyards, such as Chris Camarda's "Two Blondes" and Scott Greer's "Sheridan," are producing well-crafted, estate-bottled wines with exciting, long-term potential. If these positive trends take hold, the Yakima Valley wineries should be able to dramatically upgrade their reputation as a viticultural leader in Washington state.

WALLA WALLA VALLEY

In the southeast corner of Washington, spilling over the border into Oregon, is the Walla Walla Valley. The area includes some of the earliest settlements in the Northwest. Lewis and Clark camped a few miles north of present-day Walla Walla on their way back home in 1806, Clark noting in his journal that "three young men arrived from the Wallah wallah Village, bringing with them a steel trap belonging to one of our party."

The name *Walla Walla* purportedly translates as "many waters." Records indicate that vineyards were thriving as early as the 1850s and that a commercial wine industry was being explored during the 1870s. But the modern era of Walla Walla winemaking didn't begin until 1977, when Leonetti Cellar was bonded and became the first local winery dedicated to producing varietal vinifera wines. Seven years later, with just four wineries and 60 acres of vineyard, the Walla Walla Valley was certified as the second official Washington state AVA.

It is shaped much like a cut diamond laid on its side, with the short, straight edge forming the western border. The AVA fans out as it follows the Walla Walla River east. A long ridge of windmill-topped hills runs along its jagged southern edge, which crosses the border into Oregon; the straight-line northern edge leads northeast into the rolling hills of the Palouse wheat country. The jagged eastern perimeter of the cut diamond runs along various waterways and ridges heading up into the Blue mountains that wrap dramatically around the town's eastern border.

Recognition as a premier red wine–producing appellation came quickly to Walla Walla, because the early releases of Leonetti, Woodward Canyon, L'Ecole N° 41, and a handful of others enjoyed remarkable success, winning gold medals and accolades from the press. The funny thing was that few were actually Walla Walla wines; the grapes came from Columbia Valley and Yakima Valley vineyards.

Leonetti had planted a trial acre of cabernet in 1974, but the first substantial planting in the valley was at Seven Hills in 1981. Though legally part of the AVA, Seven Hills was rather inconveniently located in Oregon. That matters not at all today, for vineyards are scattered all over the region. But in the early days it drove a marketing wedge squarely down the middle of the AVA. The Seven Hills winery, then located in Milton-Freewater, found itself isolated. Oregon was busy promoting the Willamette Valley pinot producers, while Washington was not about to include an Oregon winery in its marketing efforts.

Such shortsightedness may have contributed to the region's stalled growth. As recently as the mid-1990s, fewer than a dozen wineries called Walla Walla home. In an interview in the spring of 2000, Leonetti's Gary Figgins told me he had "always envisioned that Walla Walla would happen at some point. But it was just going so slow. There were only four or five of us, and we were doing well; but I had just about given up that it would happen within my lifetime. And about that time, within five years, it just went nuts!"

Virtually overnight the number of wineries doubled, doubled again, and doubled yet again. Most begin as microwineries making a few hundred cases of wine, and they tend to cluster around the Walla Walla airport, where cheap, industrial warehouse spaces are leased by the port.

Though it took almost two decades for the first dozen wineries to follow in Leonetti's footsteps, the momentum, once begun, built quickly and still shows little sign of slowing down. It's fueled by the region's bustling tourism, its stunning physical beauty, the genuine camaraderie and cooperation of the (mostly) young winemakers, a startling infusion of winemaking talent from France, and the maturation of sizeable vineyard plantings that have been added in the last 15 years.

In 1991 Norm McKibben and business partner Bob Rupar put in the first 10 acres of cabernet and merlot at Pepper Bridge; the vineyard now totals 200 acres. A few years later, they purchased 200 acres at Seven Hills and developed (with Leonetti and L'Ecole) Seven Hills east, an additional 170 acres. The most ambitious venture yet for the partnership is the development of 1700 acres surrounding the existing vineyard. This land includes an estimated 1000 plantable acres ranging from 900 to 1500 feet in elevation. Plans call for

Leonetti, L'Ecole, and Pepper Bridge each to keep a piece for themselves; the rest will be sold as 20- or 40-acre parcels for vineyard and winery development.

These and other recently established vineyards, scattered throughout the AVA, are as essential as water to the growth of the wine industry. The valley contains at least four quite different soil profiles. And as key vineyards in each have begun bearing fruit, different Walla Walla flavor profiles are crystallizing in the region's wines. Good examples of each can be found in the wines of Pepper Bridge, Cayuse, Leonetti, and Spring Valley.

In the December 2000 issue of *Geoscience Canada*, professors Larry Meinert and Alan Busacca identify these four fundamentally different substrates as slackwater terrace, loess, river gravel, and flood plain silt. Most Walla Walla vineyards currently are planted on slackwater deposits (residue of the great floods), loess (silty, wind-borne soils), or some combination of the two.

Pepper Bridge (profiled in Chapter 4) is one of the coldest sites, planted on loess over slackwater deposits. In some parts of the vineyard are big pockets of volcanic ash from the eruption of Mount Mazama (which formed Oregon's Crater Lake). "It's a totally different soil," McKibben explains. "We either pull the grapes or farm it differently." From Pepper Bridge fruit come broad flavors of strawberry preserves and black cherry. In cooler years it can show distinct herbal notes, but as vines mature these will diminish. The Pepper Bridge vineyard supplies grapes to dozens of wineries throughout the state, and the winery has attracted more than a dozen other wineries and vineyards to its location south of town abutting the Oregon border.

A string of vineyards farther south were first planted by Cayuse vigneron Christophe Baron beginning in the late 1990s; now others are following his lead. Extremely rocky, with large, round cobblestones that were once the gravel bed of a river, these vineyards are difficult to establish, labor- and time-intensive, and low-yielding. Baron, who also practices biodynamic farming, coaxes astonishing mineral, meat, truffle, and forest-floor flavors from his grapes and makes some of Walla Walla's best wines.

Leonetti's father–son team of Gary and Chris Figgins began planning to make all of their wines from 100 percent Walla Walla fruit more than a decade ago. In addition to Seven Hills east, they have 16 acres (11 cabernet, three merlot, one each petit verdot and sangiovese) at Mill Creek Upland, planted in 1997, and the 28-acre Loess vineyard (same grapes plus a bit of malbec and viognier), planted in 2001; they are establishing a 55-acre C.S. Figgins estate vineyard that will allow them finally to reach their goal of making all their wines from their own Walla Walla grapes.

The Mill Creek Upland vineyard, located east of town, has extremely deep (70 feet) loess soils and sits on a steep hillside close to the Blue Mountains. It is frost free and gets up to 25 inches of rainfall annually, triple the precipitation of most Walla Walla vineyards. Unlike most Walla Walla vineyards it can be dry-farmed, though some irrigation has been used to get it established. At night the temperature drops quite rapidly; Chris Figgins notes that it will fall from 90 degrees to 50 as soon as the sun sets. As a result, the grapes develop tremendously deep colors, naturally high acids, concentrated flavors, and firm tannins.

In its first few vintages, the vineyard has proved to be a major success, and Upland grapes have become the mainstay of Leonetti's Reserve blend and the backbone of the cabernet.

Spring Valley, located 12 miles northeast of town, is well into wheat-farming country. A trial two-acre block of merlot was planted in 1993 and immediately produced positive results. Soils are extremely deep and rich, and the vines are planted between 1100 and 1400 feet, set on steep south-facing slopes. After selling grapes for a few years, the owners established their winery in 1999, and the wines, all red, immediately drew rave reviews from the press. Today the 40-acre vineyard includes 18 acres of merlot, seven of cabernet sauvignon, eight of cabernet franc, four of syrah, two of petit verdot, and an acre of malbec. It is leased to Ste. Michelle Wine Estates, which will continue to make estate wines under the Spring Valley label. The wines are deep and powerful, with unique and fragrant aromas of grain, light herb, and red fruits.

These four widely scattered and quite different vineyards demonstrate that what currently falls under the umbrella Walla Walla AVA should ultimately be divided into several subregions. This will not happen anytime soon. Despite its deceptive history of success, Walla Walla is actually one of Washington's newest wine-growing regions. The vineyards that have been planted in the last 10–15 years are just beginning to reach maturity, and important efforts, such as the biodynamic viticulture practiced at Cayuse and the near-organic sustainable viticulture at Pepper Bridge and Mill Creek Uplands, are just getting under way.

What can be confidently stated at this point in time is that many Walla Walla vineyards are capable of ripening outstanding merlot, cabernet, and syrah. Very small amounts of sangiovese, cabernet franc, and other, still more obscure red grapes are also showing promise, and some white wines, notably viognier and gewürztraminer, have been exceptional. The future is extremely bright for this corner of the state.

RED MOUNTAIN

If you are looking for Red Mountain, Washington state's smallest and most exclusive AVA, don't expect to find something that is either red or particularly mountainous. Red Mountain rises like a brownish lump of unbaked bread at the eastern end of the Yakima Valley, just past the point where the Yakima River turns abruptly north.

Red Mountain was awarded its official AVA status in 2001. Hedges Cellars (now Hedges Family Estates) was a leader in that effort. Founder Tom Hedges describes Red Mountain as "essentially a southwestern-facing slope of homogenous soil types, with very high heat units and low-vigor, low-nutrient soils." What makes it unique, he believes, is the elevation, the slope, the way the winds are channeled from the north, and other factors that lend a dense minerality to its grapes, particularly the classic Bordeaux grape varieties. "Red Mountain produces a distinctive wine," says Hedges, "alcoholic, tannic, tight, very age-worthy, dark, dense, and lightly aromatic."

But Stags Leap it is not, at least on first glance. Dusty and hot, Red Mountain hardly seems like the sort of place that could grow grapes for some of Washington's greatest red wines. On a sunny late spring day you might notice a few green patches on the mountain's lower flanks, geometrically cut into the dusty sagebrush. But nothing that you can see from the highway far below would suggest that you are approaching the most prized vineyard land in the state.

What does underscore that point is the impressive who's who list of wineries that are using Red Mountain grapes to make their best wines. Historically they come almost entirely from one or both of the two biggest vineyards, Ciel du Cheval and Klipsun. Between them they grow around 280 acres of grapes: merlot and cabernet sauvignon, syrah and cab franc, and such exotica as counoise and mourvèdre.

Neither has a winery of its own. Instead, you will find their grapes in wines made by Andrew Will, Betz Family, Boudreaux, Cadence, DeLille, Januik, Mark Ryan, Matthews, McCrea, O•S, Quilceda Creek, Seven Hills, Soos Creek, Three Rivers, Waterbrook, and Woodward Canyon, among many others. Quilceda Creek and DeLille were so enamored of their Ciel du Cheval grapes that each has entered into a joint venture with Jim Holmes, Ciel's owner, to farm adjacent acreage.

Elsewhere on the mountain are roughly a dozen wineries, the biggest being Hedges and Kiona. Both use estate-grown fruit for their top wines and sell some to others. Small but impressive boutiques such as Hightower and Cadence have also set up shop on Red Mountain. But until 2005, significant growth was stymied by a lack of water. That year, two major events occurred, both with the prospect of altering forever the look and feel of the mountain.

On a sweltering afternoon in mid-July of 2005, Ste. Michelle Wines Estates CEO Ted Baseler stood alongside Italy's Piero Antinori and shoveled the first spadeful of dusty earth on land set aside for their new Col Solare vineyard and winery. The Col Solare project, a joint venture begun a decade earlier, had finally found a permanent home. The winery was functional in time for the 2006 crush, and the vineyard will be in full production within the next year or two.

The second event was a decision by the state Department of Natural Resources to lease roughly 600 acres of their Red Mountain land, with water rights included, for vineyard development. The first four leases were awarded in October of 2005, to several different partnerships that will build three new wineries and plant up to 86 acres of new grapes.

The state retains ownership of the land, and successful bidders must make their own wines rather than simply offering grapes for sale. But any new development on Red Mountain is expected to include new roads and to bring more visitors and more positive press for the region's wines.

The area was first developed in 1972, when Jim Holmes and partner John Williams bought 80 acres of what Holmes laughingly calls "worthless desert" and decided to plant 10 acres of riesling, chardonnay, and cab. "We paid two hundred an acre," Holmes recalls, adding "but the crook who sold it to us had paid only one hundred!" To say it was desolate country does not begin to do justice to the leap of faith that the initial purchase required. "It was like the frontier," says Holmes, "no roads, no water, no power, no people. Just sagebrush."

There was no wine industry either. In 1975 there were fewer than a dozen wineries in the whole state, and their mainstay grape was riesling. Holmes and Williams planted cabernet, in spite of the fact that "everybody knew you couldn't grow red grapes here in Washington."

In the next three decades the Washington wine industry grew to include over 375 wineries and 30,000 acres of vineyard. And from the first few harvests on, Red Mountain grapes have been a big part of the reason that the state's shiniest calling cards are its red wines, particularly its Bordeaux blends and syrah. It was Kiona cabernet, for example, that Alex Golitzin used exclusively in his Quilceda Creek wines in the mid-1980s. Red Mountain grapes—from some mix of Kiona, Klipsun, Ciel du Cheval, and the Tapteil vineyards—have been a major component of every Quilceda Creek cab made in the past 20 years.

In 2001 and 2002, Alex and son Paul Golitzin planted their own 17 acres on Red Mountain: 100 percent cabernet sauvignon, high density (2100 plants per acre). "We're trying to get more aroma, more flavor, and better textures," says Paul, who now oversees the winemaking. The first full crop from the new vineyard was harvested in 2004 and "made the cut" into the winery's flagship cabernet, the Golitzins report. That wine will be released late in 2007.

Red Mountain has been sculpted by repeated glacial floods ("a hydraulic massacre" is how Ciel's Jim Holmes describes it) that deposited massive granite boulders and layered its thin soils with an unusual mix of rock, clay, and mineral. It's a windy place, one of the reasons that cabernet and merlot grapes in particular develop thick skins and ripen at smaller sizes than elsewhere, creating concentrated, tannic wines. Tannins are plenty ripe, not harsh or green; but often, upon release, Red Mountain wines are hard, tough, tarry, and wrapped up tight.

Holmes also believes that what made Red Mountain wines good from the outset was the extremely high pH of the soils. It keeps nutrients tied up as insoluble minerals, so the vines must struggle. "Our vines never get big huge, bad canopies," Holmes remarks, "and our berry size is just 50–60 percent of standard berry size. Where Napa berries might weigh about 1.3 grams, ours weigh about 0.88."

Red Mountain red wines have a firm cherry core to the fruit, and they often show distinct mineral notes, much like iron ore. There are strong winds, which particularly impact vineyards on the west slope, thickening skins and, hence, tannins. During the last phase of ripening, the mountain's diurnal temperatures vary by 40 degrees or more, keeping acids up while sugars accumulate. Though considerably less is planted, the white wines are also well structured, with steely spines and semitropical fruit.

Most of the mountain's total vineyard is planted to cabernet sauvignon and merlot, but here and there are numerous small experimental plots of a couple of dozen other grapes. Kiona grows the appellation's only chenin blanc and riesling, which are most often used to make racy, densely concentrated late-harvest wines and the occasional ice wine. Owner Scott Williams has planted gewürztraminer at his other vineyard, higher up the mountain, named Ranch at the End of the Road. Klipsun and Artz have significant plantings of sauvignon blanc and semillon. Small plots of roussanne, pinot gris, viognier, and chardonnay are scattered about the mountain, making up the rest of the whites.

The focus on red Bordeaux grapes has expanded to include a fair amount of cabernet franc and smaller plots of malbec and petit verdot. Syrah is the third most popular red, especially at Terra Blanca, Klipsun, Ciel, Ranch, and the new Grand Ciel vineyard, belonging to DeLille Cellars. Driven largely by consumers' embrace of syrah, the rising importance of other Rhône grapes is beginning to be noticed. Doug McCrea (McCrea Cellars) makes varietal mourvèdre and counoise, both of which, along with grenache, were planted at Ciel at his request.

Keep looking around the mountain and you will also see a fair amount of sangiovese and even a bit of nebbiolo, tannat, zinfandel, a smattering of Portuguese grapes, and that old Washington warhorse lemberger. "We can pretty much grow anything," says Klipsun's Patricia Gelles, "which I know is very confusing for the wine consumer. We're very spoiled in that way."

HORSE HEAVEN HILLS

Washington state gained its seventh appellation with the official certification of the Horse Heaven Hills on August 1, 2005. Its borders lie entirely within the established Columbia Valley appellation but do not cross over into Oregon as do the Walla Walla and Columbia Gorge AVAs. It is bounded on the north by the ridge of the hills that form the southern border of the Yakima Valley and on the south by the Columbia River. Most vineyards are planted on south-sloping hills and sandy, well-drained soils.

When certified in the summer of 2005, the AVA included just five wineries but had 6040 acres of wine grapes planted, roughly a fifth of the state's bearing acreage. By some estimates as much as two-thirds of the region, which totals 570,000 acres, could eventually be planted to wine grapes.

The region's 20 vineyards already provide grapes for many of the region's premier wineries, including Andrew Will, Betz Family, Canoe Ridge, Chateau Ste. Michelle, Columbia Crest, Columbia, Long Shadows, Quilceda Creek, and Woodward Canyon. Major grape varietals for which it is best known are chardonnay, riesling, semillon, syrah, merlot, and cabernet sauvignon.

The growing season is fairly warm, but Horse Heaven's proximity to the river prevents the 100+-degree heat spikes that can shut down vines in summer. It also moderates the potential damage from winter's occasional deep freezes.

The largest vineyards are Columbia Crest (2314 acres), Alder Ridge (815 acres), Ste. Michelle's Canoe Ridge Estate (470 acres), Wallula (411 acres), and Coyote Canyon (310 acres). The first vineyard to be planted in the area was Mercer Ranch, in 1972. Now called

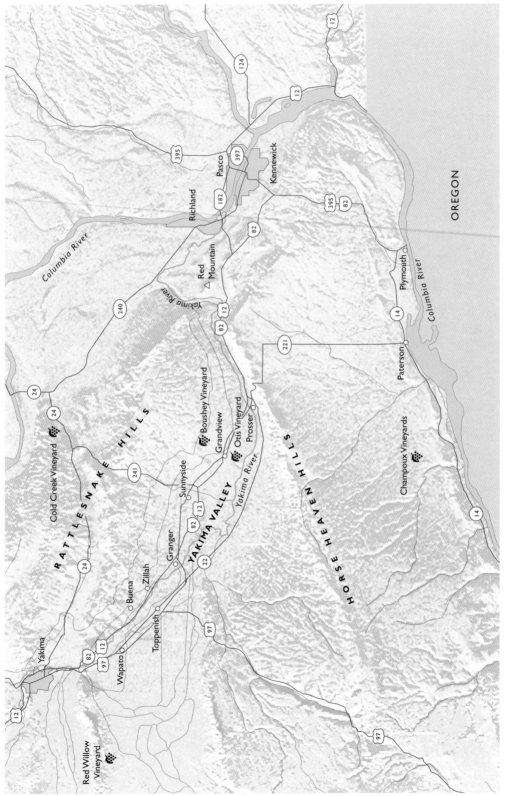

The Horse Heaven Hills, Yakima Valley, Rattlesnake Hills, and Red Mountain AVAs, the latter two situated within Yakima Valley

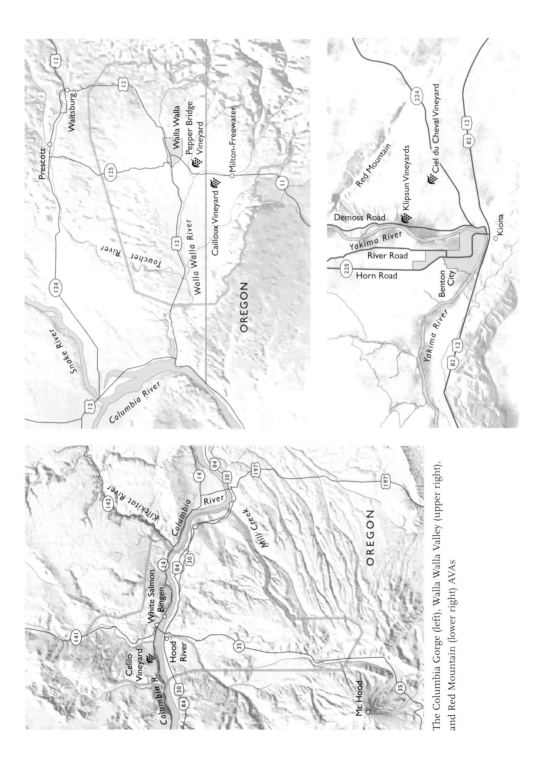

The Columbia Gorge (left), Walla Walla Valley (upper right), and Red Mountain (lower right) AVAs

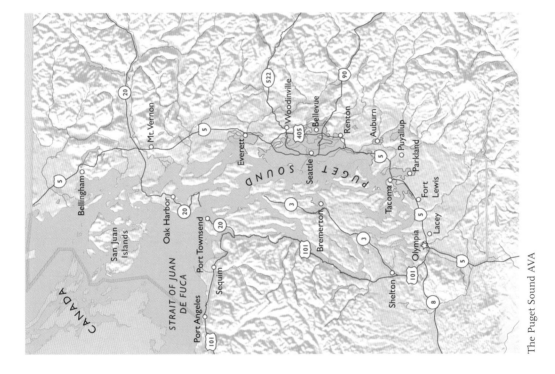

The Puget Sound AVA

yards and a famous outdoor amphitheater known as "The Gorge." But as far as the legally approved Columbia Gorge AVA is concerned, it refers only to the region bordering Oregon.

WAHLUKE SLOPE

On January 6, 2006, the 81,000-acre Wahluke Slope became Washington's eighth certified AVA, just 14 months after the application was submitted to the TTB. The name supposedly means "watering place," an odd choice for this amazingly dry stretch of rather scrubby desert. It lies in the dead center of the Columbia Valley AVA, bounded on the west and south by the Columbia River, on the north by the Saddle Mountains, and on the east by the Hanford Reach National Monument.

Geographically isolated, it has nonetheless proven to be an excellent grape-growing region, thanks to its uniform sand-and-gravel soils, its consistently smooth, south-facing slope, and its virtually rainless, reliably sunny, and quite warm climate. Vineyard elevations range from 425 feet along the Columbia River up to 1475 feet at the irrigated high point of the slope. The soils are coarse and well drained, and grapes ripen evenly and predictably well. "No other AVA in Washington state is contained on a single landform with large areas of uniform sandy and gravelly soils over a large area," notes Alan Busacca, a certified professional soil scientist and registered geologist who wrote the AVA petition in partnership with the Wahluke Slope Wine Grape Growers Association. Grower Butch Milbrandt describes it as "one big plateau that lays on a southerly plain."

As initially certified, the 81,000-acre region encloses over 20 vineyards, one winery, and two wine production facilities. Despite its forbidding isolation and lack of tourist facilities, plans for several new winery openings are on the drawing boards. Milbrandt vineyards, whose properties include Sundance, Clifton, Northridge, and Katherine Leone, plans to release its first estate wines this year.

With 5205 bearing acres, roughly comparable to Horse Heaven Hills, Wahluke Slope accounts for just under 20 percent of the total wine grape acreage in Washington. More importantly, it is in many ways the heart of the state's red wine production. Although Red Mountain and Walla Walla have much more notoriety, neither region actually grows significant tonnage. Wahluke Slope does.

Although the earliest plantings were white varietals such as riesling, chardonnay, and chenin blanc, red wine grapes (notably merlot, cabernet sauvignon, and syrah) now comprise 80 percent of the total. Among the largest vineyard holdings are Wyckoff Farms (925 acres), Jones (600 acres), Duck Pond (520 acres), Shaw (464 acres), and Milbrandt (453 acres).

More than 50 wineries purchase Wahluke Slope grapes, and many already use vineyard designations on their best wines. With the opportunity now to market the region with its own AVA, look for vineyard plantings to double in the next six to eight years.

RATTLESNAKE HILLS

Washington's ninth AVA, officially certified on March 20, 2006, is also its most controversial. Entirely contained within the Yakima Valley, Rattlesnake Hills began first as a loose association of wineries and vineyards hoping to establish a tourist trail that would lure cars off the interstate and into their tasting rooms.

Gail and Shirley Puryear (owners of Bonair Winery) were among the first to explore the wine potential of the region, purchasing five acres just outside of Zillah in 1979. It is their contention that the unique topography of the Rattlesnake Hills qualifies its status as a separate AVA, and they have successfully fought for its certification.

The 68,500-acre AVA encompasses an east–west ridge of hills along the northern border of the Yakima Valley. It begins at an elevation of 850 feet and tops out at about 3000, making it significantly higher than the rest of the Yakima Valley. Temperatures are moderate to warm, and winters average 8–10 degrees warmer than Red Mountain and Walla Walla, helping to protect the vines from freeze damage.

Some excellent wines are made in the region, but it is fair to say that no defining style or flavor has emerged that would elevate it to the status of a Red Mountain, for example. To put it bluntly, Rattlesnake Hills seems more like a marketing entity than a well-defined terroir. Some of the vineyards that have the greatest potential for doing that—Boushey, for example—have not been included, supposedly for geographical reasons.

PUGET SOUND

Puget Sound is clearly Washington's odd-man-out AVA, certified in 1995. It covers a big chunk of western Washington that includes the Puget Sound and San Juan Islands, parts of the Olympic Peninsula, and a wide swath of the mainland's western edge. Fewer than 100 acres of the AVA are planted to wine grapes.

Most of the 35 wineries that fall within the appellation purchase their grapes from eastern Washington, but some cool-climate white varietals are successfully grown, predominantly Madeleine Angevine, siegerrebe, and Muller-Thurgau. Early experiments with chardonnay, pinot gris, and pinot noir show some promise. As new clones and more appropriate sites are explored, the Puget Sound AVA may one day live up to the potential that its advocates proclaim. Excellent berry wines are also produced.

3

THE GRAPES

What is Washington's grape? Is it riesling, which has recently enjoyed a spectacular renaissance here, after being denigrated for decades? (Riesling—phew! Just a sweet, tasting room wine. Wine with training wheels. Or, the worst insult of all, one of the few wretched grapes that can be ripened in such a bitterly cold northerly clime.)

Moving right along: What about sémillon? Perfect for Washington, n'est-ce-pas? Sémillon is a grape no one else really claims as a varietal and that makes some very nice wines in Washington. Sadly, with one or two exceptions (notably the sémillons of L'Ecole N° 41), these are wines that consumers have steadfastly ignored.

Well then, how about merlot? Merlot actually shows some muscle and flavor in Washington, two things sadly lacking in merlots from most other places. Yes, Washington merlot had a pretty good thing going, until the movie *Sideways* came along. Now merlot makes a good sidekick, but it's lost its luster as this state's bomb.

Washington cabernet sauvignon, which one prominent critic has called "the best in the world," still has a long road to travel before public opinion ranks it the equal of Napa or even of classified Bordeaux. Putting on my homeboy cap, I'd say sure, we can compete with any cab in the world. But selling that story to the drinking public? That's a long shot.

Still thinking . . . maybe . . . syrah? Syrah is unquestionably off to a great start in its first decade in Washington (and so far vintners have resisted the temptation to call it shiraz). Unfortunately the French got there first, as usual, and then there's the Rhone Ranger thing that the Californians have working. The Australians have their shiraz, a name switch that further muddies the waters. But can Washington really stake an uncontested claim to syrah? Doubtful.

And yet it is one of the observable truths of the old wine world that the great wine-growing regions always have a signature grape, possibly two (one red, one white), or at most one or two signature blends. Among New World viticultural regions there are huge advantages when vintners can point to one particular wine they do better than anyone else outside of the Old World standard bearer, as Oregon did with pinot noir, Argentina with malbec, and South Africa with pinotage (ok, some work better than others).

Even in California, the land where everything grows ("plant a nail and you'll grow a crowbar" one old-timer told me), many wine regions have grabbed onto something to call their own. Napa has its cabernets, Dry Creek its zinfandels, Russian River its pinot noirs, and so on.

Washington, for better or worse, can do too many wines well. There are no obvious frontrunners for the grape that can become the icon for the state's wine industry. As Steve Burns (former executive director of the Washington Wine Commission) cogently notes in his commentary in Chapter 10 of this book, "Washington vineyards are capable of producing a large range of varietals on a high-quality and consistent basis. Is that a perceived weakness?"

The answer, at least from a marketing viewpoint, is clearly yes. If not actually a perceived weakness, this versatility is at the very least a perceived lack of strength. Any new region that is trying to stake out a hook for itself in the crowded coat closet of global wine needs a grape to call its own. Sadly, I see no such grape in Washington's immediate future. This state is what baseball managers call a utility player, the can-do, hustling newcomer who can play anywhere, fill any gap, step in and sub for the stricken star.

The marquee player who hits 60 home runs, strikes out 150 times, bats .285, and makes $6 million a year goes down with a bum knee and you plug in Joe Utility. He will hold down that spot in right field, get more walks than strikeouts, hustle his butt off, and cost you a tenth as much. And if the shortstop pulls a hamstring, he'll happily jump to the infield as soon as Sluggo can walk.

That's Washington. Name almost any frontline grape (ok, not pinot noir—yet) or wine region (ok, not Piedmont—I said *almost*), and Washington can put up a very good wine that offers exceptional quality at a better price. Is that a curse or a blessing? Time will be the final judge. But for now, a grape-by-grape survey of this state's extraordinary depth and breadth is the best, perhaps the only, way to really understand what Washington wines are all about. Here we go.

WHITE WINE GRAPES

ALIGOTÉ

Burgundy's "other" white grape is widely planted in eastern Europe but is virtually unknown in the United States. The Newhouse vineyard in Washington's Yakima Valley grows a couple of acres that date back to the 1970s. Once a popular wine for Quail (now Covey) Run winery, the Newhouse vineyard fruit currently goes to Jed Steele (for his Shooting Star aligoté), to FairWinds winery in Port Townsend, and to La Bete in Oregon. Steele barrel ferments his aligoté in neutral oak, making a high-acid, fruity wine that tastes of green apples, much like a pinot blanc.

CHARDONNAY

Chardonnay is grown in almost every corner of Washington, close to 7000 acres in all, making it the state's most planted grape. In the early days the wines were simple and fruity, with the best showing fresh green apple flavors and crisp acidity. There are (and have always been) those winemakers aiming to make a more buttery, tropical style, with flavors of banana and mango and buttered popcorn. But the most distinctive versions seem to combine elements of both styles, sometimes adding a mineral cut to the finish. These chardonnays can rival the best of California, and, given the tendency of many Burgundies to load on the new oak, the vibrant, polished fruit of Washington can stand up well against most anything up to Meursault quality.

BEST BOTTLES

Abeja

Apex II

Bonair Reserve

Boudreaux

Buty

Chateau Ste. Michelle (esp. "Ethos," "Cold Creek," and Reserve)

Columbia Crest (esp. Reserve)

Columbia "Wyckoff"

Forgeron

Januik (esp. "Cold Creek")

Mark Ryan

McCrea

Novelty Hill

Rulo

Saviah

Three Rivers

Woodward Canyon

CHENIN BLANC

Chenin has suffered a serious decline in Washington, as it has virtually everywhere else (outside of the Loire Valley). Consumers have moved on to more fashionable grapes. Harvest tonnage has been cut in half, just since the turn of the new century, and the 200+ acres of chenin left continue to be ripped out as it brings less dollars per ton than any other varietal, red or white. And yet there is no question in my mind that if market economics permitted vintners the luxury of treating their chenin with the care given to their other white wines, these old vines could produce wines of superb character. Washington could and should make world-class, bone-dry chenins, wines that show the complex, floral aromas and flavors of the dry chenins from the Loire. But as things stand, other than the occasional brilliant chenin-based late-harvest or ice wine, Washington chenins are destined to be fruity, off-dry, and entirely forgettable.

BEST BOTTLES (DRY OR OFF-DRY)

Covey Run

Kiona

L'Ecole N° 41 "Walla Voila"

Townshend

BEST BOTTLES (LATE HARVEST OR ICE WINE)

Kiona

Syncline

GEWÜRZTRAMINER

As author Leon Adams recounts in his *Wines of America*, it was a taste of a homemade Washington gewürztraminer in the mid-1960s that inspired visiting Beaulieu Vineyards winemaker André Tchelistcheff to proclaim it "the best in America." That bottle, and Tchelistcheff's timely comment, may well have sparked the modern-day Washington wine industry, which sprang to life shortly thereafter. The first commercially produced, vintage-dated varietal Washington wines (from Associated Vintners) included gewürztraminer. Tasted recently (at 35 years of age), the oldest, from 1967, was still showing (delicate) signs of life.

Gewürztraminer continues to do surprisingly well with consumers, who happily stumble over the name (get-smooched-traminer? get-worse-than-hammered?) and find many excellent and generally inexpensive versions made in a range of styles from bone dry to late harvest (or occasionally ice wine). Most typically, they are off-dry, sporting fresh flavors of grapefruit and citrus; occasionally the more distinctive, pungently floral Alsatian aromatics can be found—whiffs of blossom and fresh-cut fruit, hints of spice and honey—you get the picture.

Some have shown the ability to improve with a few years of bottle age, taking on flavors of fruit candy and softening the racy acids just a bit. But, in general, you're safest seeking out gewürztraminers from the most recent vintage. They take well to chilling and are particularly serviceable with spicy summer dips and picnic foods such as cold noodle salads. The great gewürztraminer vineyard in Washington is Celilo, and several vintners make wines from those grapes. Very good late-harvest gewürztraminer is also made by Kiona, from estate fruit, and by Three Rivers, from Biscuit Ridge vineyard vines.

BEST BOTTLES (DRY OR OFF-DRY)

Canoe Ridge "Snipes Vineyard"

Celilo Vineyard (all producers)

Columbia Crest "Two Vines"

Columbia

Covey Run

BEST BOTTLES (SWEET)

Bonair "Port"

Kiona

Three Rivers "Biscuit Ridge"

MADELEINE ANGEVINE

This northern French grape is one of the more successful to be grown in western Washington (Puget Sound AVA) vineyards. When done well it mixes dry, crisp citrus fruit flavors with herbal, spicy overtones, quite nice when served chilled with picnic foods.

BEST BOTTLES

Lopez Island Vineyards

Mount Baker Vineyards

Whidbey Island Vineyards

MARSANNE

The most important white wine grape of the northern Rhône, marsanne has only begun to be explored in Washington. Very small amounts are grown, usually to be blended with roussanne and/or viognier, adding ripe, round flavors of white peaches and lightly spiced pears.

MÜLLER-THURGAU

Müller-Thurgau is another grape whose adaptability to cool climate conditions makes it a natural for western Washington. It's best characterized by its aroma, which is both floral and musky. The flavors can be very fruity and refreshing when the wine is cleanly made. Bainbridge Island Vineyards makes both a dry and an off-dry ("traditional") version.

BEST BOTTLES

> Bainbridge Island Vineyards
> Mount Baker Vineyards
> Whidbey Island Winery

MUSCAT

Washington muscats labeled black, orange, or Canelli turn up at a surprising number of tasting rooms. The grape was often planted in the early days, at scattered locations around the state. Some of the best old-vine muscat still grows at Ste. Michelle's famed Cold Creek vineyard. (Morio muscat, which you may also encounter, is a different critter entirely, according to Oz Clarke's *Encyclopedia of Grapes*.) Distinctly marked by the grape's penetrating aroma of oranges, Washington muscats can be made in a range of styles from dry to ultrasweet, but most convey a definite hint of sweetness. Both Ste. Michelle (Moscato Frizzante) and Latah Creek (Moscato d'Latah) also produce light sparkling muscats reminiscent of the Moscato d'Asti of northern Italy.

BEST BOTTLES (OFF-DRY)

> Chateau Ste. Michelle
> Covey Run
> Latah Creek

BEST BOTTLES (LATE HARVEST)

> Kiona
> Thurston Wolfe "Sweet Rebecca"

PINOT GRIS/GRIGIO

Despite its enormous popularity in recent years, pinot gris is not easily turned into fine wine. If planted in a place too warm, its naturally low acidity becomes a liability, making fat, clumsy wines. If planted in a place too cool, it can be tart and tasteless. It's a varietal, one grower thoughtfully notes, "that dances or sags based on acidity."

Oregon's David Lett was the first to make pinot gris commercially in the United States, from cuttings that he hand-carried from Alsace in the late 1960s. Oregon vintners grabbed onto the grape in earnest in the 1990s, making rich, often buttery, oaky wines that seemed at times to have a yearning to be chardonnay. Then, dramatically, consumer tastes jumped on the Italian pinot grigio bandwagon, and that brisk, light, food-friendly, high-acid style became the new template.

Washington has only recently begun to grow pinot gris in any significant quantities. While plantings are limited—330 acres as of the most recent (2002) survey—demand is high. Only viognier commands a higher price per ton among white wine grapes. Though not as concentrated or fleshy as many Oregon bottlings, Washington's pinot gris and grigios are lively, fruit-forward wines, showing a zesty mix of tart green apple and Japanese pear flavors.

There are at least a dozen versions currently in the marketplace, and more seem to pop up with each new vintage. The Covey Run pinot grigio is a favorite, with its plump flavors of pear, peach, citrus, and green apple set against its persistent, mouth-cleaning tartness. Several of the vineyards and wineries springing up around Lake Chelan are also giving it a try, with promising early results.

BEST BOTTLES

Andrew Will ("Cuvée Lucia")
Benson Vineyards
Chateau Ste. Michelle
Chatter Creek
Columbia
Columbia Crest
Covey Run
Okanagon Estate
Pontin del Roza
Seven Hills
Whidbey Island
Willow Crest

RIESLING

When asked to name the greatest white wine grape in the world, most wine professionals will unhesitatingly say riesling. Then why is it perpetually tagged with a reputation for being simple and sweet, a wine for beginners?

In the early years, riesling was suggested as a good starter grape for Washington growers. They had no hope, it was believed, of ripening much else here in the far north. And, in fact, riesling did quite well here, so well that in the early 1980s a prestigious German company, Langguth, invested millions of dollars planting vineyards and building a magnificent winery in the stark, dusty middle of nowhere just outside of Mattawa, strictly dedicated to riesling.

The Langguth winery didn't last long, but time has proven them right about Washington riesling. The grape thrives here, and not just as a basic, off-dry, fruit-driven slurp. It can be bone dry yet retain amazing concentration and depth of flavor. It can be juicy, vibrantly off-dry, and tart, packed with ripe citrus fruits, as is perfectly expressed in the nation's best-selling version, Chateau Ste. Michelle's Johannisberg riesling. And it can make arguably the most dense, luscious, decadent, yet gloriously structured TBA-style wine in the country, the Single Berry Select from Ste. Michelle and Dr. Loosen.

Washington has marginally more acres of riesling than California, 2200 acres versus 2049 acres (as of 2002). Many Washington vintners release the new vintage in the spring, when the young wines are steely and fresh and still showing a bit of spritz. Pleasantly *frizzante*, they tickle the tongue on the way down and send up aromas that are loaded with the scents of spring blossoms and sweet citrus. The fruit-driven flavors mix oranges, tangerines, apricots, apples, peaches, and pears. Some of the very best dry rieslings also weave in textures of wet stone or light hints of herb, such as cilantro or fennel.

What ties them together stylistically is their vivacious mix of bright fruit, high acids, and the perception of sweetness (except in the most bone-dry versions). Riesling needs hang time to ripen properly and really show its stuff, and in Washington it gets plenty of extra hours of daylight throughout the growing season, which extends well into October. The significant day–night temperature variations during harvest also help to create the characteristic fresh, floral aromas, bright flavors, and acidic zip that buoys up the finish, sometimes laced with minerals and trace elements from the soil.

The dozens of rieslings that fall somewhere in between bone dry and the sweet, late-harvest dessert wines are often the best choices to match with food. But how sweet are they? One of the frustrations of all domestic riesling is that the labels rarely indicate the residual sugar, making it guesswork to match them with food. Here Washington's predictable levels of ripeness make it relatively simple to figure it out for yourself, by looking at the percentage of alcohol.

With rare exceptions, any Washington riesling with alcohol over 13 percent is bone dry; 12–13 percent is dry; 10.5–12 percent will be off-dry; under 10.5 percent will be quite sweet. Basically the lower the alcohol, the sweeter the wine. The very sweetest late-harvest rieslings may have alcohol levels of 8 percent or even less. These excellent late-harvest wines, which are sometimes but not always botrytis affected, maintain significant acidity, despite their high sugars, and are never cloying or syrupy. From time to time gen-

uine ice wines are also made (none of this cryogenic stuff) and offered at remarkably affordable prices.

BEST BOTTLES (DRY)

Apex

Chateau Ste. Michelle

Covey Run

Kiona

Woodward Canyon

BEST BOTTLES (OFF-DRY)

Avery Lane

Bonair

Chateau Ste. Michelle (esp. "Eroica" and "Cold Creek")

Columbia ("Cellarmaster's")

Columbia Crest

Covey Run

Dunham (Four Legged White)

J. Bookwalter

Kiona

Latah Creek

Poet's Leap

Snoqualmie

Townshend

BEST BOTTLES (LATE HARVEST AND ICE WINE)

Chateau Ste. Michelle "Single Berry Select"

Covey Run

Kiona

ROUSSANNE

Roussanne often complements marsanne and/or viognier in the handful of white, Rhône-
influenced blends being made in Washington. Even when bottled as a varietal there will
usually be a bit of viognier in the blend. Full-bodied and fleshy, roussanne in Washington

can taste like a real fruit salad mix, everything from apples, citrus, and lime to peaches, honey, and cream. There is very little planted: five acres at Ciel du Cheval, four at Alder Ridge, a few more at Destiny Ridge. The first experimental plantings were at White Heron's estate vineyard in 1990, though the winery's first commercial release of varietal roussanne wasn't until 2000. Some examples of varietal roussanne seem prone to early oxidation, though that may have more to do with the winemaking than the grape itself.

BEST BOTTLES

Alexandria Nicole
Doyenne
McCrea
Syncline
White Heron
Zefina

SAUVIGNON/FUMÉ BLANC

Sauvignon blanc is grown all over the world, yet it seems to be one of those wines that does everything possible to confuse people. First is the name. In France, the best sauvignon blanc–based wines are named for a place (Sancerre); in Italy they may be called fumé sauvignon or just plain sauvignon; in the United States it is sometimes labeled fumé blanc, a marketing gimmick that has outlived its usefulness. Wine writers often love sauvignon blanc, yet by using terms such as gooseberry, crushed nettle, and even *pipi du chat* to describe the stuff, they do little to convince consumers that it's worth trying.

Winemakers don't help much either. They often overripen, occasionally underripen the grape. Too ripe and the flavors turn soft and tropical; underripen and grassiness quickly turns to canned asparagus. Overcrop and the grape just gets sour and watery. But troubles don't end when the grapes are picked. Sauvignon blanc expresses itself best when made in stainless steel, but many winemakers, apparently imitating the seductive flavors of chardonnay, insist on barrel fermentation (sometimes in new oak) and a secondary (malolactic) fermentation, guaranteed to strip away any trace of varietal character.

Here in Washington, sauvignon blanc acreage has been fairly stable, and it ranks third among white wine grapes in terms of acreage. Some very good versions are made. You'll find some California-style chardonnay-wannabes, sweet, tropical, and toasty, the unsauvignon blancs. But you will also find many with the snap, the zip, the assertive flavors of (here we go) cut grass, lime, citrus peel, and a dozen different herbs and green fruits. These are sauvignon blancs that resonate with varietal character; they penetrate the palate and liven up the tongue. That's why they are so perfectly matched to food, especially goat cheeses, shellfish, and other light seafood and poultry.

Apex II

Arbor Crest

Balboa

Barnard Griffin

Chateau Ste. Michelle (esp. "Horse Heaven")

Columbia Crest

DiStefano

JM Cellars

Lone Canary

Matthews

Novelty Hill

Rulo "Combine"

Waterbrook

SÉMILLON

Like sauvignon blanc, with which it is often blended, sémillon can be made into a lightly grassy, dry white table wine, or it can be late-harvested, shriveled with botrytis, and turned into a sweetly honeyed dessert wine. Washington state does very well with the grape, and one producer (L'Ecole N° 41) makes several different versions each year. Best drunk young, sémillons taste of figs and melons, adding leafy notes as they age.

Sémillon has enjoyed a long and successful history in Washington, and if critics ruled the world I suspect it would become a genuine calling card for the state. It doesn't make truly distinctive wines in many places in the world, but it does in Washington. And it has a history there as well: Sémillon was one of a handful of varietal wines to be released from the watershed 1967 vintage—the first commercial vintage for both Ste. Michelle Vineyards (now Chateau Ste. Michelle) and Associated Vintners (now Columbia).

Sémillon has a lot going for it. The name is not impossible to pronounce, as is gewürztraminer. It's got a good French pedigree. It's a grape that can be used as part of a high-end Bordeaux blend (notably the Chaleur Estate Blanc, the Buty Semillon/Sauvignon Blanc, the L'Ecole N° 41 "Barrel Fermented" Semillon, and the Three Rivers White Meritage). It can be mixed with chardonnay, as the Australians do, to make a very nice warm-weather quaffing wine. What's not to like?

The best way to appreciate the flavors that varietal sémillon brings to the table is to drink wines labeled as such, which means that even if blended they must be at least three-quarters sémillon. The addition of sauvignon blanc may give the finished wine more acid backbone and lift and a pleasant whiff of grassy herb. When it is blended, barrel fermented, and aged in new oak, sémillon is usually aiming for the Bordeaux blanc model. But some of my favorite Washington versions are unblended and see more used than new oak yet still deliver stand-up flavors.

BEST BOTTLES

Amavi

Barnard Griffin

Bergevin Lane

Chateau Ste. Michelle

Chinook

Columbia

Columbia Crest

Dunham "Shirley Mays"

Fidélitas

L'Ecole N° 41

BEST BOTTLES (WHITE MERITAGE BLENDS)

Brian Carter "Oriana"

Buty

DeLille Chaleur Estate

Hedges

L'Ecole N° 41 "Barrel Fermented"

Three Rivers

Woodward Canyon "Charbonneau"

BEST BOTTLES (LATE HARVEST AND ICE WINES)

Chateau Ste. Michelle

Columbia Crest

SIEGERREBE

A cross between gewürztraminer and Madeleine Angevine, siegerrebe grabs the grape-fruity spice of the former and some of the lemony acid of the latter. It ripens well in the Puget Sound (western Washington) AVA, and you'll find some excellent, crisp, fresh versions being sold in the island and North Sound winery tasting rooms.

Bainbridge Island Vineyards

Lopez Island Vineyards

Whidbey Island Vineyards

VIOGNIER

Washington's viognier acreage is up 380 percent, from 60 acres to 230 in the most recent four-year statistical survey. As with so many other "oddball" grapes, viognier was first planted at Mike Sauer's Red Willow vineyard in 1983. By and large it remains very much a newcomer elsewhere in Washington, yet it sells for the highest price per ton of any white wine grape. It's in such demand because the wine has cachet, both with winemakers, who love the challenge, and consumers, who simply love the wine. A number of this state's most exciting young boutiques are making thrilling, vivid examples.

Best when fermented and aged in stainless steel, viogniers strike a neat flavor chord composed of citrus blossom, zest of lime and grapefruit, vivid peach and apricot stone fruit, and a tangy, sometimes-creamy, textured elegance. When it works, viognier really works. But this is not an easy wine to get right. Harlequin winemaker Robert Goodfriend bluntly notes that "a lot of winemakers don't like viognier because it really screws with your head." Goodfriend's viognier is a fragrant fruit bowl of a wine that delivers exotic scents of honeysuckle, peach, and Bosc pear.

Another outstanding version comes from Syncline, done in a creamier style, slightly spritzy, with citrus flavors outshining the floral notes. Syncline's James Mantone believes that it is viognier's tendency to ripen unevenly that gives winemakers such headaches. The vine does have an unusually tiny window of optimal ripeness at harvest time. If it is planted in a hot site and allowed to hang a bit too long, it makes a fat, oily, and alcoholic wine, a syrupy shadow of itself. If it's picked too early or planted in a site that's a touch too cool, it delivers bitterly tart lemon juice.

BEST BOTTLES

Abeja

Alexandria Nicole (the regular, not the reserve)

Bergevin Lane

Caterina

Cayuse

Chatter Creek

Coeur d'Alene

Columbia

Dusted Valley

Harlequin

K

Latitude 46° N

McCrea

Rulo

Syncline

Waterbrook

Zefina

WASHINGTON RED WINE GRAPES

BARBERA

Barbera has begun making an occasional appearance, always in very small quantities, as a handful of vineyards and wineries begin to explore the potential of Italian varietals (beyond sangiovese) in Washington state. Very small plantings of barbera are being tried at Cascade Cliffs, Ciel du Cheval, Morrison Lane, and Woodward Canyon, a bit more at Alder Ridge and Maryhill. Varietal bottlings come up rarely and, being from very young vines, do not show much of an identity beyond fresh and fruity, with a strawberry tang. It's still too soon to judge the long-term viability.

BEST BOTTLES

Cascade Cliffs

Lone Canary

Morrison Lane

Woodward Canyon

CABERNET FRANC

The first cabernet franc plantings in the state were part of Washington State University's experimental blocks that were established in the mid-1970s. In 1985 Red Willow put in a small block suitable for commercial use (in a red blend). A varietal cabernet franc was introduced by Columbia (the first in Washington) in 1991, followed by Ste. Michelle's Cold Creek vineyard bottling in 1992. Today cabernet franc is widely grown and generally admired, although at least one veteran winemaker refers to it half jokingly as a "generally noxious weed." Alder Ridge has a particularly large block of 100 acres.

Good Washington cabernet franc displays appealing scents of fresh-ground coffee and ripe, tangy, berry-flavored fruit, packed with berries, particularly blueberries. In all other respects it sits squarely alongside cabernet sauvignon, showing pretty floral and herbal nuances. Such light olive, cut leaf, or forest floor aromas are fine in cabernet franc when balanced against some riper fruit flavors.

Washington did not have cabernet franc planted in sufficient quantities to be statistically relevant until 1993, when a few wineries began using it in their Bordeaux blends. Slowly but surely plantings have increased, and today it ranks fourth for red grape production behind cabernet sauvignon, merlot, and syrah (though a distant fourth to be sure).

Despite its growing popularity with winemakers and consumers, cabernet franc tonnage peaked at 3300 tons in 2001 and has actually come down a bit since. So if you are looking for these wines in the marketplace, you'll find that, although overall quality is very good, quantities are low. Most often it is blended in modest percentages into varietal merlots and cabernet sauvignons, in order to boost the color or add some interesting aromas.

But some of the best red wines in Washington are more evenly distributed blends of these three grapes and are given proprietary rather than varietal names. A few of these red blends contain a very high proportion of cabernet franc and clearly reflect its varietal character.

Chinook gets credit for making not only one of Washington's most distinctive cabernet francs, but also a wonderful cabernet franc rosé, released each spring.

BEST BOTTLES (VARIETALLY LABELED)

Arbor Crest

Barrister

Camaraderie

Chandler Reach

Chateau Ste. Michelle "Cold Creek Vineyard"

Chatter Creek

Chinook

Fielding Hills

Matthews

O•S Winery

Red Sky

Sineann

Spring Valley

Tamarack Cellars

Walla Walla Vintners

Basel Cellars Red

Buty Merlot/Cabernet Franc

Cadence "Bel Canto"

Mark Ryan "Long Haul"

O•S Winery "Ulysses"

CABERNET SAUVIGNON

Because it has remained phylloxera free, Washington now has some of the oldest cabernet sauvignon vines in North America (see profiles of Champoux, Cold Creek, and Otis vineyards in Chapter 4). Better still, since they are planted on their own rootstock, the roots of these old vines go deep, and their flavors follow, deep and long.

Washington cabernets have been the signature wines of many of the state's most successful wineries, from Leonetti and Woodward Canyon to Andrew Will, Ste. Michelle, and Quilceda Creek. More than any other varietal, Washington cabernet sauvignon seems to capture the best of France and California in a single wine. Though they come in a range of styles, these cabs share an ability to walk the line between precision and opulence. They balance their bright, polished fruit with vibrant acid; they integrate their new oak slowly but surely, creating complete wines that are more than the sum of their components. Best of all, they make wines that are delicious young and yet have the capacity to age gracefully over decades.

Pure, 100 percent varietal cabernet sauvignon is relatively rare. Most often some percentage of merlot is included, and increasingly the other Bordeaux red grapes (cabernet franc, petit verdot, malbec, and even carmenère) are tossed into the blend. A developing trend is to mix cabernet, merlot, and syrah, a Washington take on a Super-Tuscan.

Cabernet sauvignon is grown in every Washington AVA except for Puget Sound, but it does particularly well on Red Mountain, in the Horse Heaven Hills, on the Wahluke Slope, and in a few Walla Walla vineyards. Yakima Valley cabernet can be thrilling when not overtaken by its herbaceous tendencies. The old-vine, vineyard-designated bottlings from Champoux, Cold Creek, Harrison Hill, and Otis are especially noteworthy.

BEST BOTTLES (VARIETALLY LABELED)

Abeja

Alder Ridge

Barrister

Beresan

Betz Family "Père de Famille"

Boudreaux "Reserve"

Champoux Vineyard (all producers)

Chateau Ste. Michelle "Cold Creek"

Columbia "Otis"

Columbia Crest Reserve

DeLille "Harrison Hill"

Dunham "Lewis Vineyard"

Feather

Fidélitas

Fielding Hills

Gamache

Gorman "The Bully"

Januik

J. Bookwalter

Leonetti Cellar

Matthews

Novelty Hill

Quilceda Creek

Reininger

Robert Karl

Rulo

Seven Hills "Seven Hills Vineyard"

Sineann "Baby Poux" and "Block One"

Soos Creek

Walla Walla Vintners

Woodward Canyon "Old Vines" and "Artist Series"

BEST BOTTLES (BORDEAUX BLENDS)

Andrew Will (esp. "Sorella" and "Ciel du Cheval")

Betz Family "Clos du Betz"

Cadence (esp. "Bel Canto")

Cayuse "Camespelo"

Col Solare

Columbia Crest "Walter Clore"

DeLille "Chaleur Estate"

Fidélitas Meritage

Hedges

J. Bookwalter "Chapter One"

L'Ecole N° 41 "Perigee"

Leonetti Cellar Reserve

Mark Ryan (esp. "Dead Horse")

Nicholas Cole ("Camille", "Michele", "Reserve")

:Nota Bene

Soos Creek "Artist Series"

Spring Valley "Frederick" and "Uriah"

Three Rivers Meritage

Woodward Canyon "Estate"

CARMENÈRE

Leonetti's Chris Figgins believes that he and his father secured the first carmenère plants to arrive in Washington. They were acquired in 1997 from Guenoc winery in California, bud wood off of a newly planted block that was, apparently, the first in California.

The very first plants went in at Leonetti's Mill Creek Upland vineyard, mixed in with some petit verdot. Figgins remembers referring to the whole adventure, tongue in cheek, as "Operation ABV, short for 'Ancient Bordeaux Varietal'!" The following year a larger amount of wood was purchased and planted to five acres at Seven Hills east. Some of those cuttings were shared with Mark Colvin and planted separately at Colvin, Seven Hills, and Morrison Lane. Colvin was the first Washington winery to make varietal carmenère.

Small amounts are now grown at scattered sites elsewhere, including Minnick Hills and Alder Ridge. It is generally introduced into Bordeaux blends as a grace note. The rare varietal carmenères have been a mixed bag. I've had just two that seemed to hint at long-term potential in a starring role: the 2002 Morrison Lane and the 2002 Reininger. Apart from those excellent bottles, Washington carmenère seems likely to remain a curiosity and a minor blending grape.

BEST BOTTLES

Morrison Lane

Reininger

CINSAULT

Morrison Lane grows a small amount, as do Minnick Hills and Alder Ridge; it's generally used sparingly in a handful of Rhône blends. Morrison Lane makes very small quantities of a varietal cinsault.

COUNOISE

Varietal counoise? Yes indeed, right there in the land of the pioneers, two wineries are making varietal counoise, from grapes grown at Ciel du Cheval on Red Mountain and at Morrison Lane in the Walla Walla Valley. Rhône Ranger Doug McCrea planted the Tablas clone (sourced from Beaucastel) at Ciel in 2000 and has made varietal counoise (blended with 10–12 percent syrah) since 2002. Morrison Lane also grows a small amount and does a fine job with their (very) limited bottling. A tiny bit is planted at Alder Ridge also.

Who knows what its future might be, but the existing examples are unique and fascinating. It makes quite a fragrant wine, scented and then flavored with blue plum, tart pie cherry, and blackberry. It shows the bracing acidity of sangiovese, with added notes of spice, cinnamon, and light chocolate and exotic suggestions of soy, cumin, and curry.

BEST BOTTLES

McCrea

Morrison Lane

DOLCETTO

Though they are still flying well under the critics' radar, several grower-producers are experimenting with Italian varietals in Washington. Very tart, leafy, pie-cherry flavors seem to characterize the early releases of Dolcetto, which is being tried at Cascade Cliffs, Willis Hall, and Woodward Canyon.

GAMAY NOIR

What little gamay noir is still grown in Washington winds up in blush wines with sweet, simple strawberry, raspberry, and cherry candy flavors.

GRENACHE

Grenache was one of the first successful vinifera grapes to be planted in the eastern Washington desert. Wine historian Leon Adams reported in his seminal *The Wines of America* that on a trip to the Yakima Valley in 1966 "the only fine wine I tasted . . . was a Grenache Rosé made by a home winemaker in Seattle."

Yet despite its head start, grenache has never been more than a bit player in the region's viticulture, for it is not especially winter hardy. Some old grenache vines survive at Cold Creek and Columbia Crest. Doug McCrea made a superb varietal bottling from 1989 until the mid-1990s, sourced from vines planted above the Columbia Gorge in 1965. McCrea also made a grenache–syrah blend called "Tierra del Sol," a pioneering effort that presaged the Rhône Ranger movement in the state.

Most of the old vines were wiped out in the freeze of 1996, and for a while that seemed to be the end of the road for grenache. Now it seems to be coming back, at least to a limited extent. Elerding vineyard was the first to replant grenache, in 1999, and since 2001 McCrea has gone back to making a spicy, brightly fruited varietal bottling. He also uses grenache in his southern Rhône blend called Sirocco. Additional new grenache plantings at Alder Ridge, Destiny Ridge, and Ciel du Cheval are now bearing, and the quality is inspiring winemakers such as Bob Betz (Betz Family), Charles Smith (K Vintners), and Gordy Rawson (Chatter Creek) to work with the grape. Consumers who manage to find one of the rare bottles are quickly converted.

It's easy to see why. Sappy, grapey, bursting with fruit, and nicely spiced, grenache is more approachable and purely fruity than syrah. These young vines do not (so far at least) show the kind of concentrated power that you find in old-vine grenache from Spain, France, and Australia. Give it another decade. This grape could become a real showcase for Washington.

BEST BOTTLES

Alexandria Nicole

Betz Family (Bésoleil)

Chatter Creek

K Vintners ("The Boy")

McCrea

Syncline (Cuvée Elena)

Willis Hall

LEMBERGER

Austria's Blaufränkisch, which translates as "the blue grape from France," goes by a number of names elsewhere, the least user-friendly being limberger. Here in Washington it is known as lemberger. When Washington vineyards were first being planted in the 1960s and 1970s, the grape was heavily endorsed by Dr. Walter Clore, the man who pioneered much of Washington's viticulture at the time. As a result, lemberger gained considerable appeal throughout Washington. At one time it could easily be found in a wide variety of styles, from grapey, rustic table wines to elegant, claret-style reserves to zinfandel-wannabes to lemberger "Ports."

The classic Washington lemberger is a blood red, lightly peppery picnic wine, bursting with the scents and flavors of ripe berries. When there was no Washington syrah or zinfandel to be had, it was the stand-in; good to guzzle by the glassful with thick cuts of greasy lamb or grilled sausage. These days lemberger is, quite fränkly, passé, perhaps feeling just a bit, well, blau. It's down to a couple of hundred acres, and relegated mostly to being an everyday tasting room red or tossed into mutt wine blends. Jed Steele's Blue Franc, which he makes as a joint venture with Ste. Michelle, is a more serious attempt to elevate its profile. Kiona and Champoux vineyards have some excellent old vines, and the classiest bottles are sourced there.

BEST BOTTLES

Alexandria Nicole

Covey Run

Hogue

Kiona

Shooting Star "Blue Franc"

Thurston Wolfe

MALBEC

Outside of Argentina, where it makes spicy, tart red wines that take well to aging in new oak, malbec remains a minor figure on the world stage. However, a number of important winemakers in Washington are betting that it will become a bona fide player in this state in the coming decade.

John Bookwalter, who has added it to his portfolio along with petit verdot, calls them "the most important wines to come along in some time." Malbec is easy to grow, he points out, ripens conveniently in between merlot and cabernet sauvignon, and adds dark colors and flavors to Bordeaux blends.

Casey McClellan (Seven Hills) planted some of the first malbec in the Walla Walla Valley, at the Windrow vineyard in the late 1990s. Seven Hills began producing 100 percent varietal malbec in the 2001 vintage, in very limited quantities. A few other varietally labeled malbecs are being made in Washington (Barnard Griffin, Camaraderie, Maryhill, Shady Grove, Terra Blanca, Willis Hall), but most of what little is grown here is used in Bordeaux blends. Alder Ridge has one of the largest plantings at 13+ acres; a couple of acres have also gone in at Destiny Ridge.

The best expressions of varietal Washington malbec capture the dark notes and peppery herbal qualities of the grape.

BEST BOTTLES

Alexandria Nicole

Barnard Griffin

Camaraderie

Reininger "Pepper Bridge Vineyard"

Seven Hills

Willis Hall

MERLOT

Merlot, it can be argued, put Washington state viticulture on the map. The state's first superstar winery, Leonetti Cellar, has always been a merlot specialist. Andrew Will's Chris Camarda made his mark a decade ago by producing up to six different single-vineyard merlots each vintage. And Columbia Crest, the state's biggest winery, sets the standard for the entire country for supple, succulent, affordable merlots. Until merlot proved otherwise, Washington was stuck with a "too cold to make good red wine" reputation.

Alas, despite all it's done for the state, merlot finds itself struggling for credibility once again. The fault is not with the wines, which are as good as (or better than) ever. But the global glut of thin, generic merlot has polluted consumer attitudes, and their disdain spills over, unfairly, into Washington.

Merlot, say the critics, is the chardonnay of reds: easy to pronounce, pleasant, and versatile but lacking any substantive character of its own. (The great exception, of course, is Bordeaux's Chateau Pétrus, where it comprises 95 percent of the blend.) Varietal merlot rose to popularity in the 1990s. But with insipid, watery, cheap, vegetal merlots now coming from all corners of the globe, the bloom is definitely off the rose.

It's time for Washington to reclaim the grape as its own. Here it ripens beautifully and creates fleshy, powerful wines that can age for a decade or more. Washington merlots start where most others leave off, with ripe flavors of sweet cherries, and then reach well beyond simple and fruity, adding plush, packed, textured flavors of mixed red and black fruits and berries. The best of them play out broadly across the palate, with smooth, supple tannins and plenty of lively natural acid. They happily embrace the flavors of new oak (toast, espresso, vanilla, and chocolate), but first and foremost they taste of rich, ripe fruit.

Despite its slumping cachet, merlot remains the most planted red wine grape in the state, accounting for roughly one-fifth (6000 acres) of Washington's total vineyard acreage. Rather than using merlot as a simple blending grape to soften their cabernets, Washington winemakers are just as likely to do the reverse, enhancing their merlots by blending in cabernet. Though Washington merlot has plenty of power, it is more broadly displayed across the palate. Cabernet adds verticality and a tighter tannic spine.

At least one high profile winery—Northstar, part of Ste. Michelle Wine Estates—was founded as a merlot specialist. Allen Shoup's Long Shadows project also includes a "superstar" merlot called Pedestal, made under the supervision of Michel Rolland.

Any list of the best Washington merlot vineyards must begin with Ciel du Cheval, Klipsun, and Kiona (on Red Mountain); Pepper Bridge, Spring Valley, and Seven Hills (in Walla Walla); both Canoe Ridges and Champoux (in the Horse Heaven Hills); DuBrul, Sheridan, Red Willow, and Boushey (in the Yakima Valley); and Ste. Michelle's Cold Creek.

It's true that Washington merlots won't age nearly as long as the state's top cabs. But the more muscular, dense vintages can certainly go for a good decade and will acquire soft, lush flavors of dried fruits, toast, honey, caramel, and cinnamon. By and large they are best consumed during the first few years after bottling.

BEST BOTTLES (VARIETAL LABELING)

Barnard Griffin

Barrister

Beresan

Bergevin Lane

Betz Family "Clos de Betz"

Boudreaux

Chateau Ste. Michelle (esp. "Cold Creek")

Columbia "Milestone"

Columbia Crest (esp. "Grand Estates")

Covey Run Reserve

Fidélitas

Fielding Hills

Forgeron

Hightower Cellars

Isenhower "Red Paintbrush"

Januik

J. Bookwalter

Kestrel

Latitude 46° N "Vindication"

Leonetti Cellar

L'Ecole N° 41 (esp. "Seven Hills")

Novelty Hill

Northstar

Pedestal

Pepper Bridge

Quilceda Creek (very limited)

Reininger

Seven Hills (esp. "Klipsun" and "Seven Hills")

Sineann

Snoqualmie Reserve

Soos Creek

Spring Valley Vineyards

Stevens

Three Rivers (esp. "Reserve")

Walla Walla Vintners

Waterbrook

Woodward Canyon

MOURVÈDRE

Mediterranean-influenced mourvèdre (from France and Spain, where it is known as monastrell) makes medium-bodied, lightly spicy wines with pretty, cherry-flavored fruit and occasionally a distinctive, gravelly minerality. Mourvèdre is found in the red and rosé wines of Bandol and blended into many Côtes du Rhône, Châteauneuf-du-Pape, and Côtes de Provence wines. In Washington the grape was first planted in 1983 at Mike Sauer's Red Willow vineyard. Recent plantings have gone in at Alder Ridge, Ciel du Cheval, Destiny Ridge, Grand Ciel (DeLille), and Willow Crest; most grapes go into Rhône-inspired blends. David Minick at Willow Crest and Doug McCrea at McCrea Cellars both began producing varietal mourvèdre at about the same time in 2001–2002. McCrea's is a big, smoky, meaty, gamey, chewy mouthful, enhanced with the addition of syrah.

NEBBIOLO

The principal grape of Barolo, Barbaresco, and Gattinara (all made in the Piedmont region of Italy), Italian nebbiolo unquestionably belongs with the great red wines of the world. Yet it remains, far more stubbornly than any other significant red vinifera grape, almost impossible to grow anywhere else.

A handful of Washington vintners are giving it a try, along with barbera and Dolcetto, its northern Italian stablemates. Nebbiolo has been planted at Red Willow since 1985 and was made into a light varietal bottling by Cavatappi beginning in 1987. Cascade Cliffs is also growing a bit of nebbiolo, as is Morrison Lane. Morrison Lane's is the best Washington nebbiolo I've tasted so far. Their premier release (from the 2003 vintage) included 10 percent Dolcetto and a splash of syrah in the blend, showed real varietal character, and seemed to have ripened well.

PETIT VERDOT

Columbia's David Lake recalls that in the early 1970s the agricultural research division of Washington State University established small experimental vineyard blocks in a number of locations around the state. These consisted of three or four vines each of up to 15 or 20 different varietals, but the project ran short of funding and was abandoned. However, one such block, at Mike Sauer's Red Willow vineyard, was kept up, and in 1985, at Lake's urging, Sauer planted small commercial-sized blocks of cabernet franc and petit verdot. Unfortunately, the petit verdot was UCD 1, a clone that failed to set a crop and had to be replanted (to cabernet franc) in 1991.

Different petit verdot cuttings from UC Davis were brought to Walla Walla by Gary and Rusty Figgins in 1990 and planted at Spring Valley vineyard in 1991. Additional plants went in at Mill Creek Upland vineyard in 1997 and Destiny Ridge a few years later. Petit verdot is a significant part (as much as 13 percent) of Leonetti's Reserve, and the 3.5 acres planted at Ciel du Cheval find their way into many of the state's best Bordeaux blends. A handful of varietal petit verdots are made; Januik and O•S Winery are the ones to look for.

PINOT NOIR

Pinot Noir may be the last major red grape to grab a toehold in Washington. It was also one of the first. Experimental vineyards scattered around the Yakima Valley in the 1960s and '70s often included a few rows of pinot noir. Salishan Vineyards, situated west of the Cascades in southern Washington, began making a pinot from their own grapes in 1976. Columbia (then Associated Vintners) also made pinots as far back as 1967, their first commercial vintage.

But despite occasional successes, the grape did not find a good home in Washington, a place where it could ripen reliably yet retain its natural elegance and feminine charm. That may be changing as new viticultural regions are opening up in the state. Of particular interest is the Lake Chelan area, which may have become Washington's tenth AVA by the time this book is published.

Bob Broderick (Chelan Estate) has planted eight acres to three different pinot clones, and he began making an estate pinot in 2002. As the vines mature his (and other) wineries in the region may well find that they have the right spot for pinot in Washington. If it can thrive much farther north, in Canada's Okanagan Valley (and it certainly does), it stands to reason that somewhere in Washington is the perfect mix of soil, sun, altitude, and protection from winter freeze damage.

Tom Bronkema at Lahar winery believes the Skagit Valley is the right place. There are a few scattered pinots coming from the Columbia Gorge, where some vines dating back to the 1970s still exist. At least one grower is trying it up in Washington's Okanogan, but at this time the vineyards sprouting up around Lake Chelan seem to be the state's best for turning the intractable grape into a delicate, Burgundian-style wine. It's already making some excellent sparklers, especially the budget-priced Domaine Ste. Michelle Blanc de Noirs and the nonvintage sparkling rosé from Mountain Dome.

BEST BOTTLES

Benson Vineyards

Chelan Estate

Lahar

Okanogan Estate

Salishan

Syncline

SANGIOVESE

Tuscany's mainstay grape has struggled in California, where it was barely a blip on the radar until recently. Washington may be better suited to grow sangio with true varietal character; parts of eastern Washington could visually pass for the heart of Brunello country.

Since many plantings are young vines in unproven locations, a fair amount of what is produced comes across as rather thin and insipid, but the best bottles clearly demonstrate good potential for the grape. When it's not overloaded with new-barrel flavors, fully ripened Washington sangiovese shows clear varietal notes of spicy cranberry, red currant, tart cherry, anise, and fresh-cut tobacco leaf. If the oak becomes more prominent, then the more subtle, lightly herbal side of the grape disappears.

There is no denying that sangiovese does take well to the warm, butterscotch flavors of new oak barrels, and its natural acids give a nice lift to the midpalate. Some especially rich versions are being made in the Walla Walla Valley. Leonetti Cellar, though best known for its Bordeaux reds, makes limited amounts of an exceptional sangiovese and prices it somewhat below its other wines.

BEST BOTTLES

Andrew Will (Cuvée Lucia)

Arbor Crest

Brian Carter "Tuttorosso" (three-fifths sangiovese blended with cabernet and syrah)

Leonetti Cellar

Morrison Lane

Three Rivers

Walla Walla Vintners

Walter Dacon

Willis Hall

SYRAH

At the beginning of this century, 18 Washington wineries were making syrah, which seemed, at the time, to be an explosion of interest in such an obscure grape. Bearing acreage was up tenfold and on track to double again within a year. At 12 years of age, the first commercial syrah ever made in Washington (from Columbia winery in 1988) was alive and still drinking well.

As I write these words, just six vintages later, I would conservatively estimate that at least 100 Washington wineries are making syrah, producing somewhere between 250 and 300 different bottlings annually. The first experimental block went in at Mike Sauer's Red Willow vineyard in 1985, cuttings from Joseph Phelps. The most recent figures indicate that syrah is a solid third among red grapes harvested and fifth overall, but there is every reason to believe that it will continue to climb as extensive new vineyard plantings come online.

The grape does well all over eastern Washington, showing a chameleon-like ability to reflect the specific growing conditions without ever being too green or too jammy. Winemakers such as Doug McCrea, Christophe Baron (Cayuse), and Charles Smith (K Vintners) use this to their particular advantage, offering different bottlings that seem genuinely distinct from one another.

Although many of the boutique-winery syrah bottlings suffer from a certain sameness, that can be attributed in part to the fact that a few large vineyards supply the lion's share of the grapes. To a lesser degree it is a function of the winemaking: Washington winemakers have been accused by a leading critic, with some justification, of making syrah as if it were cabernet.

His meaning, I think, is clear. In the vineyard, syrah behaves differently from Bordeaux grapes. A Bordeaux vine will do everything it can for the fruit to survive, including drop its leaves. Syrah will do the opposite. It will drop its fruit to save its leaves. The skins start to soften up, and the grapes do a kind of raisining. "Once those grapes start to shrivel up significantly, that's it for sugar," McCrea explains. "What you have to do is deficit irrigation. That's why we can make these wonderful wines; you can water and back off, and when the plants begin to fade a little, you give them a little more water, and it's kind of a dance really."

In the winery, syrah does not need to be soaked in oak to perform well; in fact, it shows far more interesting character when the oak is kept in check. Whether or not it is cofermented with viognier (some wines are, some are not), Washington syrah from slightly cooler sites shows a distinct citrus flavor, a streak of lemon-lime zest that adds lift and life to the wine. From warmer sites, such as the Wahluke Slope, the best examples get into a smoky, meaty, more tannic, and peppery flavor set without becoming fat, flabby, jammy, or horribly alcoholic.

As head winemaker for Penfolds from 1986 to 2002, John Duval was responsible for an enormous lineup of shiraz, including the iconic Penfolds Grange. Now, apart from running his own Barossa Valley label (John Duval Wines), he is making Sequel, a syrah marketed under Allen Shoup's Long Shadows Vintners umbrella. Duval immediately went searching for older vines, explains Shoup, hoping to get the character he wanted. Old vines in the Barossa (or the Rhône for that matter) generally clock in at 60–80 years of age. Old syrah vines in Washington are rarely older than a decade. So from a global perspective there's really no comparison . . . yet. "The exciting thing about syrah in Washington," Duval diplomatically notes, "is if the wines are as good as they are now, off such young vines, it augurs well for the future."

In fact, the state's syrahs seem to be improving by leaps and bounds, due to a significant degree to the aging of the vines. In a few short years Washington syrahs have gone from being a curiosity to being solid and interesting reds to knocking on the door of world class. Not only are the vines getting older, but the vineyard management is improving, and the winemakers are approaching their syrahs in particular with a youthful passion that is absolutely riveting.

Though made in quantities of just a few hundred cases, many of the new syrahs from some of Washington's most innovative wineries are absolutely dazzling. Note that not all are pureblooded syrah; the trend is to blend, especially with cabernet sauvignon and merlot. Washington's leading syrahs light up the palate with a mix of highlighted flavors that California (and for that matter Australia) can only dream of. These are wines that dance, that capture the bright, fresh, tangy berry fruit, the nuances of citrus and spice, and the sharp acids that provide the nerve structure, the definition, and the sheer vitality of this state's wines.

Winemakers are predicting that the 2005s will be the best yet. And the first early releases give every reason to believe they are right.

BEST BOTTLES

Abeja

Amavi

Andrew Will

Beresan

Bergevin Lane

Betz Family

Buty (Rediviva of the Stones)

Cayuse (all of them)

Columbia

Columbia Crest (Reserve and Grand Estates)

Doyenne

Dunham

Fidélitas

Fielding Hills

Gamache

Gorman "The Pixie"

Harlequin

Isenhower

Januik

K Vintners (many vineyard designates)

Kestrel

Latitude 46° N

Mark Ryan

Matthews

McCrea

Morrison Lane

Novelty Hill

Reininger

Rulo

Saviah

Seven Hills

Sheridan

Spring Valley

Stephenson Cellars

Stevens

Ste. Michelle (Ethos)

Syncline

Three Rivers

Walter Dacon

Waters

Woodward Canyon

TEMPRANILLO

Tempranillo is very likely to find a place for itself in the Pacific Northwest over the coming decade. The earliest attempts at growing and vinifying the classic Rioja grape have been very successful, though admittedly highly preliminary. Abacela Vineyards in central Oregon pioneered the varietal in the mid-1990s, having set out specifically to identify an area "somewhere in America" where they could plant and successfully grow the grape. Using books, climate studies, and geological maps they settled on the Umpqua Valley in Oregon, a region that had been relegated up until that point to making less-than-first-rank pinot noirs and cabernets.

Abacela's tempranillos are sturdy, dark, smoky, substantial wines that have quickly proved the point: The grape can thrive there. What about Washington? Here it is being tried in Walla Walla at Dunham's Double River Ranch vineyard, at Cayuse's Armada and En Chamberlin vineyards, and also at Spofford Station and Les Collines. Tempranillo plantings have also gone in at Destiny Ridge, Alder Ridge, and Tefft. Who is actually making varietal tempranillo? Casey McClellan at Seven Hills winery released his first tempranillo in March 2004; I have no record of anyone in Washington making one earlier. That wine was 100 percent varietal, dark and gamy and exotic. I found it fascinating, with a blend of scents mixing roasted meats, vanilla, licorice, clove, and black cherry.

New releases of varietal tempranillo from Alexandria Nicole, Cayuse, and Wind River will be appearing in coming vintages. A preview tasting of the 2005 Alexandria Nicole showed bright, blueberry-driven fruit flavors, tart acids, and earthy tannins. Whatever its future, tempranillo can be added to the list of European red grapes that demonstrate a remarkable ability to retain some of their Old World varietal character and styling here in New World Washington.

ZINFANDEL

For years I wondered why Washington produced no zinfandel. It was a phantom grape, reportedly not possible to ripen adequately up in the Far North. Lemberger, though often promoted as Washington's zinfandel, is really not the same at all. Vintners had many reasons for the lack of Washington-grown zin, but all it really takes is a great bottle or two to change their minds. That great bottle has arrived, and been validated in the past dozen vintages, from an obscure Columbia Valley vineyard called The Pines (located, rather inconveniently, in Oregon).

Though several wineries had made the occasional zin from these grapes, it was Sineann's Peter Rosback who really put the vineyard and indeed zinfandel itself on the Northwest map. Sineann's Pines vineyard zins (both regular and "Old Vine") are California-style blockbusters, ultraripe and bursting with flavors of ripe cherry, bourbon, espresso, and chocolate.

On the north side of the Columbia River things are finally stirring. New zinfandel plantings have begun going in: 10 acres at Alder Ridge, a few more in Walla Walla at Les Collines, and recently at a couple of other scattered sites. Some promising bottlings have been produced by Columbia, Forgeron, Maryhill, Thurston Wolfe, and Zefina but so far nothing that shouts, "I am Washington zinfandel!" Stay tuned.

CONCLUSIONS

In his 2006 keynote speech at Taste Washington in Seattle, addressing an audience liberally sprinkled with Washington growers, winemakers, distributors, and Wine Commission staff, the influential critic Pierre Rovani flatly stated, "Across the board, expensive to value [wines], Washington leads the pack. I think Washington's growers are at the peak of their profession. The vineyards are making incredible fruit. The future is unbelievably bright. We're not talking potential. You've achieved it."

Despite the welcome praise, Washington wines suffer, at home and elsewhere, from a reputation that they are too expensive. Somebody else leads the pack. This state's marketing mavens and wine writers dutifully trot out statistics proving that on the leading "Top 100" lists, Washington wines invariably sell at lower average costs than those from other regions. Makes no difference—the reputation for high prices lingers on.

Why is this? I believe there are two reasons. First of all, Washington has but a handful of wineries large enough to produce significant quantities of inexpensive wines. Many of the best deals (such as the wonderful dry rosés that are released each spring) are sold only in-state, so no one else sees them. Washington has no Central Valley vineyards kicking out 14 tons per acre over thousands of acres. Yes, there are some spectacular-value bottles, from Columbia Crest, Covey Run, and others. But the critical mass is not there, and may never be, because the state has just 30,000 acres planted to wine grapes. No one is coming in and planting big ranches with the goal of making the world's best jug wines. Water is too scarce, and, quite frankly, the land's potential for quality is too good.

The second reason for the bad rep is that most of Washington's 500+ wineries are tiny, and they are passionate about quality. They pay a very high price in order to obtain the very best grapes. Even if they cut their profits to the bone, they must charge premium prices for their wines. So consumers see a row of new and obscure Washington labels in the specialty shops, with price tags that all read $40 and up, and quickly get the impression that this is awfully expensive for some winery they've never heard of. The problem is further compounded when a new winery concludes that the way to be competitive is to spend a lot of money on heavy glass and the like (the my-cork-is-longer-than-your-cork mentality) and to slap a ridiculously high price on the bottle. It happens everywhere in the wine world, and Washington has its share. In my view, they do considerable harm, not just to themselves, but to the industry.

Nonetheless, I will say unequivocally that overall Washington offers better wines, at better prices, than any region in the New World. Let's leave Europe out of it; they have land that has been family owned for generations, generous tax subsidies from their governments, and other advantages. But comparing apples to apples—Washington to California to Australia to Argentina to Chile to South Africa—I would happily put the best under-$12 Washington rieslings, sauvignon blancs, pinot grigios, semillons, cabernets, merlots, and syrahs up against any others. Washington will shine.

Precept Brands' Andrew Browne asked me if I knew what percentage of Washington wines are sold below the $12 price point. Interesting question. Browne believes that the answer is close to three-quarters of the state's total production. Here is how he arrives at this figure.

Assume, he says, that Ste. Michelle Wine Estates sells 4 million cases a year and that at least 3.6 million are Washington state wines. Of that total, he estimates, roughly 300,000 cases were priced over $12, meaning 3.3 million cases were priced at $12 or below. Add another 250,000–300,000 cases of Domaine Ste. Michelle sparkling wines, all below $12. He goes on to list (speculatively, but with good insider knowledge) the following guesstimates:

- Hogue with 500,000 cases, 450,000 of them below $12
- Covey Run with 350,000 cases all below $12
- Columbia Winery with 125,000 cases below $12
- Silver Lake with 50,000 cases below $12
- Paul Thomas with 25,000 cases below $12
- Precept Brands with 200,000 cases below $12

All other brands (including low-cost wines from Waterbrook, Hedges, Barnard Griffin, Latah Creek, Preston, Claar, Six Prong, Bridgman, Bookwalter, Sagelands, and so on) would, Browne believes, add another 300,000 cases below $12, for a total of over 5 million cases. That would equate to 70,000 tons of grapes at a minimum, he concludes, which means that at least 75 percent of the volume in Washington is made into wine priced under $12.

The Washington Wine Commission's own research supports this idea and goes even further. The Commission's figures (based on grocery store wine sales) suggest that total sales of Washington wines priced under $12 account for 87 percent of all Washington wine sales, by total dollars, and as much as 92 percent of all case sales. Those ratios haven't changed significantly over the last three years.

Whether or not these statistics seem compelling, they do show that, relative to its total production, Washington certainly makes its share of affordable wines priced for everyday consumption. They come from a wide variety of grapes, and at least some wines are made in significant quantities and distributed widely. Will Washington ever "compete" with California box wines or the Australian Yellow Tail tsunami or the sea of cheap Languedoc wines? Doubtful. Washington doesn't have to. Quality, not quantity, is the focus here, and that is true at every price point.

4

THE TOP TEN VINEYARDS

Sometimes the French give us a wine word that is so appealing and so easy to pronounce that we can't help ourselves; we must have it. *Burgundy* is such a term. "We love this word," we think to ourselves. "In fact, we love it so much we'll just make it our own. Let's stick it on any bottle of red plonk that has a jug handle and a screw cap and confuse consumers for all eternity!" Voila! Generics are born.

Then again, sometimes the French give us a word that no one can pronounce, like *Fenouilledes*. So we just gargle our way through it and put an "eh" at the end, like Canadians, hoping no one will notice and it will just go away. And it does. When was the last time your spouse sent you down to the corner for a bottle of Fenouilledes?

But sometimes those wily French give us a word that no one understands, no one can pronounce—and no one can come up with anything better. That word is *terroir*.

Terroir, as anyone who reads the back labels of wine bottles will attest, is as common as, well, dirt. Some people think it *is* dirt, or the flavors that a wine picks up from dirt, or the "murmuring of the earth," as one writer has rhapsodized. Whatever it is, grape growers and winemakers all seem to agree that it's highly desirable, and therefore they are all pretty sure that they have it.

To simplify, let's call terroir the expression, through the grapes grown in a specific location, of the soil, climate, weather, elevation, latitude, and orientation of that place. It is the unique stamp of that particular site. If you apply that definition in the most generous and generic way, it's pretty clear that terroir in fact does exist everywhere. We all have terroir. Your garage has terroir.

But a grape-growing site whose terroir imparts extraordinary flavors and longevity to the wines it generates is rare indeed. Only the truly great vineyards, in truly extraordinary grape-growing regions, measure up to that standard. You'll get no argument from me that terroir is the foundation for all of the world's great wines, whether they are grand cru Burgundies, first growth Bordeaux, old-vine Priorats, single-vineyard Barolos, or Grosses Gewachs rieslings.

Therefore, the search for its own unique terroir(s) is an essential and defining attribute of an emerging wine region. Washington state vintners have already, in a very short time, begun to find it. Granted, many are called and few are chosen. All too often I come across a claim such as the following, taken directly from a bottle of Washington wine: "Our belief, a constant for all great wines around the world, is that quality starts in the vineyard. Through attentive viticulture management and passionate winemaking our goal is to create wines that are true to our vineyards [sic] terrior [sic]."

I've lost count of the number of back labels, press releases, and technical tasting sheets from wineries claiming to have found their "terrior" [sic] here in Washington. A good rule of thumb, if they think they have terrior, is that it's probably tied up in back, barking at the barrels, rather than lurking in the vineyard.

Apart from the inherent ability of the soil and site potentially to express terroir, the winemaking must be sensitive and extremely noninterventionist if the subtle scents and flavors of true terroir are to remain evident. Wines that are ripened to "hedonistic" jamminess, marinated in 200 percent new oak barrels, and finished at 15.5 or 16 (or 17) percent alcohol cannot rationally be expected to display tender nuances of site and soil. The sniffs and streaks of mineral, metal, rock, underbrush, herb, leaf, and spice that combine to create layers of flavor in great wines do not survive the sensory overload from fruit ripened to 27 or 28 brix, flavored with roasted barrels, and finished at liquorous, throat-burning levels of alcohol.

The Washington vineyards profiled in this chapter have demonstrated, over a significant period of time, that they ripen fruit that creates distinctive, characterful wines. Most of these vineyards are fought over. Their owners all tell the same story of having to choose from among dozens of winemakers eager for their fruit. When several of the state's best winemakers make a vineyard designate from the same site, it's a pretty clear indication that something special is there.

Certainly, stylistic differences exist in any lineup of wines, no matter how similar the source. Yet for these top sites a consistent thread can be found throughout; unique, site-specific flavors that speak volumes about the quality of the vineyard. Most of these vineyards have stood the test of time; they have proven over decades that they are special. Sometimes it is apparent when you walk the rows, and sometimes it is not. But it always comes through where it counts most: in the bottle.

There is no one formula for designing and tending these vineyards, but certain aspects do seem intrinsic to most of them. They are widely scattered across the state but most often on poor soils, at higher elevations than the easily tilled valley floors, and they are farmed sustainably. Some are mostly organic, one is certified biodynamic. But by and large they avoid the use of chemical pesticides, herbicides, and inorganic fertilizers.

Though several are well into their fourth decade, experimentation in all aspects of viticulture continues at a pace never before known in Washington. New plantings almost always are different clones, higher density, and often oriented differently from the original vines. Pruning, trellising, and water regimens are being fine-tuned. A few of the oldest sites make a good case for the advantages of mature, low-yielding vines, a hopeful sign in a state where most vineyards are less than a decade old.

The vineyards profiled here (and they are by no means the only ones deserving of acclaim) are very carefully attended throughout the year by vineyard managers and the individual winemakers who purchase their grapes by the row, not the ton. Although Washington may be criticized for having wineries located so far from the vineyards that supply them, the row-by-row attention that many boutique winemakers give to their purchased grapes seems to more than compensate. Working closely together, winemaker and vineyard manager decide exactly how each winery's rows will be tended. Overcropping, overripening, overextracting, overoaking, and the use of ameliorants (adding tannins and acids) is anathema to terroir. Again, the proof, as always, is in the bottle.

Unlike most great wine regions, Washington is unusual in that many of its best wineries built their reputations with purchased grapes. The brilliant wines of Andrew Will, Leonetti, and Quilceda Creek inspired dozens of others to try their hand at winemaking, even when they had no hope of owning a vineyard of their own. The Walla Walla AVA, which was federally certified back in 1984, had so few vines that it was essentially meaningless as an appellation until the late 1990s. Now wineries such as Cayuse, Leonetti, Pepper Bridge, Spring Valley, and others are growing enough grapes to bring meaningful quantities of Walla Walla–grown wines to market.

Still, it's fair to ask whether Washington can truly have world-class wines and wineries under these circumstances. Elsewhere in the world, it is a given that estate wines are going to be better than wines from purchased grapes. The meticulous care and the accumulation of small bits of vineyard knowledge over decades, which ultimately allows exceptional wines to be made, depends on ownership. Europeans, in particular, might look suspiciously on the many tiny garagiste wineries that have sprung up in Washington, owning no land of their own.

How can Washington vintners aspire to make great wine when they have no control over the vineyard and, worse still, have to truck the grapes over desert and mountains and (sometimes) large bodies of water just to get to the winery? The simple answer is that Washington wines made from purchased grapes have been winning global acclaim since the mid-1970s. This is not to say that schlepping tons of grapes in rented trucks over hundreds of miles of bad roads is a plus. But passionate, artisanal winemakers have made it work, simply because they had no other choice.

Animale, a 200-case micro boutique winery operating out of a home in Ballard, a north Seattle community, makes an amusing point. Owner Matt Gubitosa, a geologist by trade, has converted the basement of his Ballard home into a snazzy winery-laboratory and barrel room. Animale focuses on a few dozen cases of syrah, merlot, and cabernet franc, all sourced from eastern Washington vineyards. But in a gesture perhaps more philosophical than pragmatic, Gubitosa has planted and nurtured a few scraggly pinot noir vines in his tiny Ballard backyard.

In 2004, the entire vintage from the "estate" vineyard comfortably filled a single recycled beer bottle. When I suggested that it might qualify for some sort of world record, Gubitosa warned that it had not yet been racked and would eventually be moved into an even smaller beer bottle.

In the 1990s the leading boutiques began negotiating purchase contracts at favored vineyards that paid by the acre, not by the ton, so that grape growers would have the incentive to do green harvesting and put in the extra labor required to ripen superior grapes. The most savvy growers began assigning dedicated rows to individual wineries. A stroll through Klipsun vineyard on Red Mountain, for example, shows each row neatly labeled with the winery responsible for its care. The most quality-conscious boutique winemakers spend many days throughout the year on the road, checking up on "their" vines and making decisions about pruning, trellising, irrigation, green harvesting, and all the many other steps that lead up to harvest.

The next phase in this evolution, which is already well under way, is for the more successful boutiques to begin planting vineyards of their own. Unlike California, Washington has not been awash in moneyed vigneron-wannabes looking to join the elite winemaking country club. Zillah, Mattawa, and Benton City do not sing the same siren song as St. Helena or even Healdsburg. Washington's wineries are almost entirely small, shoestring ventures, and the quickest way to get started has been to rent a little hole-in-the-wall industrial space, buy some used tanks, and purchase enough grapes to make a few hundred cases of wine.

But those who do that successfully will usually, after a decade or so, begin to hunt around for vineyard land. Once they get that planted they may upgrade to a bigger, more carefully planned winery. Some, like Leonetti, plant their new vineyards close to the winery. Others, like Hedges, build their new winery next to their vineyards. And quite a few (Andrew Will, Cadence, DeLille, Quilceda Creek, and so on) will continue to endure the separation of vineyard and winery, which will always be a factor in Washington. The state's population centers are on the Puget Sound side of the mountains. That is where the tourists are. And one final consideration, as one candid winemaker recently explained: "The west side," he told me, "is where the good restaurants are."

BOUSHEY VINEYARD

Dick Boushey is right out of central casting. He looks the part of a Yakima Valley grape grower. Sturdy, plain-spoken, and self-effacing, his cool, weathered gaze and measured words convey an impression of solidity, calm, and fortitude.

His vineyards encompass roughly 80 acres, planted in five locations near his home, a few miles north of Grandview. The first grapes, merlot and cabernet sauvignon, went into the ground in 1980. Boushey admits to "not knowing a whole lot about what I was doing. I had grown them experimentally for three years," he explains, "because there was not a lot of merlot in the state at all. They seemed to ripen well on my site, so I jumped in."

Slowly and methodically he expanded his plantings, exploring the different soils and elevations (800–1400 feet) on his land and introducing syrah, cabernet franc, and sangiovese into the mix of red grapes. As more and more winemakers came knocking on his door he fine-tuned that mix also. Winemakers who are willing to work with him and whose wines he feels do justice to his grapes make the cut.

He is quick to admit that "the ideal situation is you own both the vineyard and the winery and manage them together to create the wine that you want. But Washington," he points out, "has a different dynamic. How do you make that all work? I make it work by staying in touch with the wines that are made from my grapes and the winemakers. Today I'm selling to a core group—17 different people—and we work well together. My vineyard matches their style."

Many of the leading wineries in the state are in this core group: long-time customers, such as Chinook, DeLille, McCrea, Ste. Michelle, Three Rivers, and Wineglass, and exciting newcomers, such as Betz, Doyenne, Forgeron, Long Shadows, Ross Andrews, and Fall Line. "We want to grow the best grapes we can," Boushey explains. "I'll do anything people ask, within reason, if it makes good viticultural sense. I'm always game, because I'm trying new things all the time. We've adjusted crop loads, changed canopies, dropped fruit just before harvest, changed watering regimes. Some people have a good viticultural understanding; I want to bounce ideas off them. What I get back is their ideas about flavor profile and the kind of wine they want to make."

At the request of winemaker Doug McCrea, Boushey was one of the first in Washington to plant syrah. He has demonstrated that the grape can do extremely well in his relatively cool, elevated Yakima Valley sites. Both McCrea and Betz make Boushey vineyard syrahs, and both are among the best in the state. At a time when some hotter Washington sites are having to fight extreme heat and a tendency for grapes to overripen, Boushey actually works to delay harvest. He times his pruning, suckering, and thinning according to the conditions of the vintage. The goal is uniformity, controlling growth and keeping smaller berries and clusters. Stressing vines, he believes, interrupts the whole ripening pattern. So he aims for a constant moderate. "By the time you see the stress," he says, "it's sometimes too late."

"In the Yakima Valley," Boushey continues, "I want to push harvest into late September and October, when you have the cool nights and the acids stay there. I pick three weeks later than the warm areas, but not at any higher sugar level. There's a big transformation in the flavor profile in that time window, and that's where I want to be. That way you get softer tannins, darker fruit but still retain some acid for balance."

Historically, many Yakima Valley vineyards have struggled to ripen grapes adequately. Boushey's fruit, particularly his syrah and merlot, shows what properly sited, fully ripened Yakima Valley fruit can achieve. Wines from his grapes show a tangy Bing cherry/tart berry character, sweet and spicy but not jammy, with elegant hints of light herb. Because he brings in his ripe grapes at still-moderate sugar levels (under 26 brix), winemakers often blend their lots of Boushey wine with others from warmer Red Mountain vineyards.

The best way to appreciate the quality of Boushey fruit is to taste a vineyard-designated wine, such as McCrea's Boushey vineyard "Grande Cote" syrah or Betz Family's "La Serenne" syrah. Bob Betz calls La Serenne his "wild child in the cellar." His tasting notes describe Boushey syrahs as "the most Rhône-like, meaty and smoky and with a hint of wild spice." These grapes are picked up to a month later than the Red Mountain grapes that go into Betz's other syrah. Boushey's cooler site and the extra month of ripening generate what Betz calls "these more undisciplined notes."

A recent vineyard expansion (25 new acres) is the largest Boushey has ever undertaken, a measure of the confidence he feels as he nears his thirtieth vintage. The experiments continue: changing the row orientation, high-density planting, different trellising, new Bordeaux clones, syrah from the Rhône, and small amounts of roussanne, marsanne, sauvignon blanc, and sémillon. "I'm responding to what my customers want," he explains. "If they want to grow, I'll grow with them. I'm hands-on, and I like working with smaller wineries. I like to have them feel that they actually own that vineyard."

CAILLOUX VINEYARD

His card reads, "Christophe Baron, Vigneron," and the thick French accent confirms the title. *Vigneron* is French for "winegrower"; the word perfectly expresses the idea that winemaking takes place in the vineyard. And 35-year-old Christophe Baron, born into a family of Champenoise (Baron Albert) whose winemaking history can be traced as far back as the sixteenth century, believes he's found one of the best places in the world to grow his grapes: Walla Walla, Washington.

He landed in Walla Walla in 1996, following brief winemaking stints in Australia, New Zealand, and Romania. Already he knew that he wanted to make syrah. At the time, very little syrah was planted anywhere in Washington, but he set out to explore the fields and orchards outside of Walla Walla, looking for a place to plant his vines.

The Walla Walla AVA crosses the state line into Oregon, and Baron was riding with a friend, on a quiet road on the Oregon side, when they passed an abandoned orchard, recently uprooted and newly plowed, and he saw what he was looking for. Round rocks, many the size of baseballs, littered the ground. He jumped out and dug into the earth. More rocks. An ancient riverbed cut through this part of the valley. The locals thought he was out of his mind, but he knew he had found the right place for syrah. "It definitely looks like Chateauneuf du Pape, this ancient riverbed where I've planted my grapes," he explains. "It's a mix of silty loam with a little sand and cobblestone for the first 18 to 20 inches; from there it's pure stone for 200 feet straight down."

The first 10 acres, painstakingly dug up and hand-planted, became the Cailloux vineyard. The winery, established in 1997, was named *Cayuse* after the native Americans who lived in the area. Some historians believe that the name *Cayuse* was actually derived from the French trappers and settlers who called the natives *Les Cailloux,* literally, "people of the stone." In 1998 Baron planted an additional 14 acres in two similar locations nearby. The En Cerise ("cherry") vineyard is 10 acres planted mostly to cabernet sauvignon and syrah, with a bit of merlot and cabernet franc as well. The Coccinelle ("ladybug") vineyard added another four acres of Syrah. En Chamberlin was next: 10 acres, planted in 2000 to equal parts tempranillo, cabernet, and syrah. Here, everything is 100% biodynamically farmed, and beginning with the 2004 vintage the vineyard became the first in Washington to be certified by the Demeter organization, an international body that regulates and approves biodynamic farms. Baron's most recent project, dubbed Armada, is 17 densely planted, stony acres of grenache, syrah, mourvèdre, and tempranillo. Baron calls it his southern Rhône/Spanish experiment.

Though each of the five vineyards fills a specific niche, the philosophy that underlies them is consistent. "Basically the goal is to handcraft wine that reflects the unique expression of each vineyard," Baron explains, "the quality and also the characteristic. In other words, the terroir." A self-proclaimed "freak about terroir," Baron declares, "I'm in love with the earth, with the ground, and I'm trying to express that in my wine. I'm French, after all!"

In pursuit of that goal, Baron is willing to go to extraordinary lengths and take extraordinary risks. Half of the vines at his five vineyards are on their own rootstock, a risky strategy that leaves them susceptible to the devastating root louse phylloxera. But he believes that the rocks will provide some protection and that own-rooted vines are healthier overall and more able to capture the subtle characteristics of the grapes.

High-density planting, frequent green harvesting, and the use of native yeasts are also part of his methodology. He drops half his crop on the ground long before harvest, stresses the vines further by denying them water, and goes so far as to send his workers through the vineyards days before harvest to pluck individual green berries from the ripe bunches.

In the winery, Baron is adamantly Old World, using no inoculation, no fining, and no filtration. In many wineries, he believes, purity, integrity, and personality are being lost. "I don't want to be part of globalization," he insists. "That is where biodynamic comes into the equation. It's an ancestral way of farming that creates a perfect environment for the vines."

Cayuse makes just 3000 cases of wine annually, sold mostly through a (now closed) mailing list. The winery has been making 100 percent estate wines since 2000, the first winery in Walla Walla to commit to exclusively estate-grown fruit. "I don't want to compromise Cayuse's reputation by sourcing elsewhere," says Baron. "To do everything right you've got to spend a lot of time in the vineyard."

Small wineries in Washington have learned the hard way that the state's frequent winter freezes can best be insured against by purchasing grapes from vineyards in widely separated locations. But in order to capture his terroir, Baron decided to do what vignerons have done for centuries: to work his land, nearby, and make only the wines whose grapes he has grown. This is especially challenging in Walla Walla, given its recurring history of truly ugly winter freezes. The last one struck early in 2004 and wiped out roughly 80 percent of that year's harvest. But Baron had been burying canes, a labor-intensive process ("it costs me about as much as a new car every year," is how he puts it) that paid off handsomely when he pulled in a full crop in 2004.

The labor-intensive commitment to finding and cultivating the right vineyard land meant putting off building an actual winery until 2005, when the winery he was sharing space with needed room to expand. He built his own spare but functional space in about six months and crushed his first grapes in his own space that fall. He calls it La Boîte ("the box"). "I refuse to call this building a winery," he says, with typical Gallic defiance. "To me it is a wine studio, a production studio. We're here to work, to create."

CELILO VINEYARD

Celilo vineyard, home to some of the oldest vinifera vines in the state, recently celebrated its thirtieth vintage, which makes it one of the oldest plantings of vinifera in Washington. Now recognized as one of the most unique sites in Washington, it is no overnight success. In fact, it has taken more than 30 years for the vineyard and region in which it is planted to receive its own appellation (Washington's seventh) the Columbia Gorge.

Celilo's 60-plus acres of vines occupy a southeast-facing slope on Underwood Mountain, an extinct volcano high above the Columbia River. It's well away from the Yakima Valley, Columbia Basin, and Walla Walla vineyards that have largely defined grape growing in Washington and considerably west of the Horse Heaven vineyards that are spread above the river farther east. Celilo is so remote that it even managed to fall outside of the massive Columbia Valley AVA.

The late Dr. William McAndrew, a Seattle surgeon, purchased the upper part of the property (about 35 acres) late in 1971, after doing extensive research on soil, temperature, rainfall, and elevation. "He was a dreamer and a doer," his widow, Margaret, recalls. His dream, say all who knew him, was to grow world-class wine grapes.

The land had once been an apple orchard; no wine grapes were grown on the mountain at that time. But there were some experimental vines just a few miles east, at Bingen, where Chuck Henderson had been having some success with gewürztraminer and pinot noir.

Dr. McAndrew took notice and began planting his land in 1972. Into the original 20 acres went a scattershot mix of vines obtained from California: chardonnay, riesling, gewürztraminer, chenin blanc, pinot noir, cabernet sauvignon, gamay Beaujolais, Müller Thurgau, and even a bit of malbec. As was generally true back then, no one had the slightest clue what, if anything, would survive.

A second property nearby was purchased and planted in the early 1980s. Today roughly half of the original vines remain; the rest of the vineyard comprises later plantings of chardonnay and gewürztraminer, with smaller amounts of pinot gris, viognier, Müller Thurgau, lemberger, pinot noir, and merlot.

Celilo is unusual in almost every way. It has no winery, relying on others to make wines from its grapes. All of the vineyard is dry-farmed (unirrigated). It is "subalpine," situated on a climatic cusp. Wet, maritime weather blows in from the west, while warm, dry air flows down the gorge from the eastern Washington desert. Celilo's proximity to the Cascade Mountains ensures that rainfall will be substantial, an average of 50 inches annually.

The view is a jaw-dropper. Spectacular vistas open in all directions, as you look upriver toward the desert, across the river to the verdant Hood River Valley and the looming presence of Mount Hood itself, or west to the flanks of the Cascade Mountains.

Celilo's perch above the Columbia River is more than a photo op; it also helps to mitigate the severe freeze conditions that can affect vines in many Columbia Valley, Yakima Valley, and Walla Walla Valley sites. The elevation (800–1200 feet) and slope prevent fog and cold air from sitting on the vines. No wind machines or smudge pots have ever been needed or used, no insecticides either.

The soil, too, is unique: a fine, porous powder that comes loaded with buckshot-sized pebbles. These are about the size and shape of ball bearings and ensure that the vineyard percolates well. This layer of volcanic soil runs as far down as 45 feet, where it hits lava rock, trapping the snowmelt and holding water during the dry summers.

As elsewhere in Washington, the drop in temperature at night during the final weeks of ripening preserves grape acids, while the warm days and southeast-facing slope give the vines the maximum amount of time in the sun, allowing the sugars to ripen fully.

Finally, there is the persistent wind funneling through the gorge. It toughens the skins, helps to control mildew and rot, and concentrates the juices. Not too surprisingly, given its unique location, Celilo experiences more variation in vintage conditions than most sites in Washington.

Thirty-five years after Dr. McAndrew scouted the territory, new dreamers and doers are catching on to the potential of Underwood Mountain and the area surrounding it. Tidy new vineyards are clustered all around Celilo. Like Celilo, they hope to catch the attention of the dozens of gifted winemakers, from both Washington and Oregon, who believe there is something special in this soil.

Winemaker Peter Rosback of Sineann calls Celilo gewürz "the best marriage of site and varietal in the state." Chardonnays from Woodward Canyon, Harlequin, and Ken Wright Cellars and especially the gewürztraminers of Sineann, Latitude 46, and Viento consistently prove that these grapes have something extra.

CHAMPOUX VINEYARD

It's pronounced shampoo. And if you ask any serious Washington winemaker where the state's greatest old vine cabernet is located, Champoux is the first vineyard they will name.

Owner Paul Champoux grew up in the hop industry. So the basic elements of a vineyard—trellises, wires, anchors, vine training, perennial crops, and so on—were quite familiar to him when Ste. Michelle came calling in the late 1970s. They were looking for someone to plant a substantial new vineyard overlooking the Columbia River, 2300 acres all together. He took the job, overseeing the initial planting (now part of Columbia Crest) from 1979 to 1983, and stayed long enough to see the first few vintages made.

He admits that he didn't know a whole lot about grapes when he started but had "great mentors," among them Wade Wolfe (Thurston Wolfe), Clay Mackey (Chinook), and Washington viticultural pioneer Dr. Walter Clore. He was hooked. And when he concluded his work for Ste. Michelle in 1986, Champoux moved up the road a few miles to manage the vineyard that would one day become his own.

The first wine grapes in what is now the Champoux vineyard had been planted in 1972. Seven acres of cabernet sauvignon went into a tiny corner of the 6600-acre Mercer Ranch, a vast agricultural enterprise producing corn, carrots, potatoes, and a wide assortment of other fruit and produce. Seven years later, more cabernet, along with riesling, chenin blanc, chardonnay, and lemberger, was added. By the mid-1980s 132 acres were devoted to wine grapes, and a winery was started, named Mercer Ranch Vineyards. The goal, owner Don Mercer grandly announced, was to grow grapes as good as Chateau Lafite.

The winery didn't last long. But under Paul Champoux's management, the vineyard continued to prosper. He began leasing the property shortly after the winery folded in 1989 and continued to expand it, planting nine more acres of cabernet in 1990. Finally, in 1996, he purchased the vineyard with a group of partners that included the owners of Woodward Canyon, Andrew Will, Quilceda Creek, and Powers.

There are now roughly 170 bearing acres: 84 of cabernet sauvignon, 30 of riesling, 16 of chardonnay, 13 of lemberger, 7 of muscat, 8 of cabernet franc, 2 of syrah, and 10 of merlot. There is also a tiny splash of petit verdot, recently planted for Andrew Will's Chris Camarda. Champoux is especially excited about his merlot, planted in 1998 and just now hitting its stride (it can be tasted in Quilceda Creek's limited-production merlot, where it makes up the bulk of the blend). Nonetheless it is cabernet sauvignon that is the star here, particularly the fruit from the original old vines, dubbed "Block One."

Though it is part of the recently approved Horse Heaven Hills AVA, the Champoux vineyard does not sit prettily on the bluffs overlooking the Columbia River, as do most of the region's vineyards. In fact it's rather flat and well back from the river. Paul Champoux rather candidly admits that if he should ever want to plant additional acreage, "there's other ground around Alderdale that would be a lot better to expand with." But "the Block One soil is a little different," he admits. "It's much older soil there. Not a whole lot of difference nutritionally, but it flakes better than some of the rest. I'm not a soil scientist by any means, but the flavors that vineyard puts off are second to none."

As with so many of Washington's remaining old vines, it was luck and happenstance that prompted the original site selection, nothing like the satellite imagery and hard soil science that motivates such decisions today. As Champoux tells the story, the original seven acres bordered the road, and the huge circle sprinklers that were used to irrigate the ranch crops didn't reach there. "Walt Clore needed to try planting some wine grapes, so here was seven acres that was available."

Champoux gets high praise from his partners and other winemakers who purchase his grapes, especially for his attention to vine nutrition. He says he hasn't used any synthetic fertilizers since 1989, believing that they are detrimental to microbial activity ("and that's the life of your soil"). To maintain what he calls "live soil," he uses cover crops and compost as feed. Vines are kept balanced by maintaining the optimal pruning–fruit ratio; nutritional balance is achieved by spraying directly on the leaves. "I'm trying to start my sugar building earlier with nutritional balances," Champoux explains. "Magnesium is the key nutrient for sugar building at véraison. So I'm trying to get the uptake of magnesium to start earlier." The bottom line for quality, he insists, is having the whole plant be nutritionally healthy. "That's what develops the flavors. That is what has made my vineyard stand out." As if to underscore the point, he finishes with one of the most disarming statements I've ever heard from a winegrower: "It's not a great vineyard site," he tells me. "It's a good vineyard site."

Part nutrient geek, part sun-baked farmer, Champoux likes to work closely with his partners on some of the thornier issues, such as how to ripen fully without sugars going sky-high. With Woodward Canyon's Rick Small, he is conducting an experiment to ripen grapes at lower sugars by delaying pruning. The idea is to set bud break back by as much as 10 days, thinking that the vine will still have basically the same heat units over the growing season. The jury is still out on the results.

A wine shop at the vineyard sells a wide variety of wines made from Champoux grapes. Woodward Canyon, Andrew Will, and Quilceda Creek are there of course, but so are vineyard designates from Three Rivers, Soos Creek, O•S, and Sineann. The old vine cabernet projects a sturdy muscularity, but more than that, a certain breed that comes of age. Lafite? Maybe not. But Mouton? Quite possibly. Turns out that Don Mercer wasn't boasting after all.

CIEL DU CHEVAL VINEYARD

No roll of the vineyard dice has paid a bigger jackpot in Washington than the decision by partners Jim Holmes and John Williams to plant cabernet sauvignon (of all things!) on Red Mountain (of all places!) back in 1975. Quixotic does not begin to describe their quest. "We needed electricity," Holmes recalled years later, "because there was no power at all. It was like the frontier: no roads, no water, no power, no people—just sagebrush."

What *was* there was great soil: a surface layer of sandy loam to hold water, then a good mix of calcareous chunks and more sandy loam, then an old riverbed, whose cobbles follow the contour of the mountain slope; quite possibly ancient Columbia River tracks. So they platted roads, brought in power from three miles away, and drilled and drilled and drilled. Running quickly out of funds, they hit a big aquifer at 560 feet. The first 10 acres of vines, planted at what is now Kiona, were a mix of riesling, chardonnay, and cabernet sauvignon, this last chosen simply because it was what the partners liked to drink.

In the early years, grapes were sold to wineries such as Preston, Quilceda Creek, and Oregon's Amity Vineyards; Kiona wines were introduced in the 1980 vintage. Over time, Kiona built a dedicated winery and expanded the plantings in their 80-acre parcel. Along the way, some friends interested in joining the grape-growing ranks asked Holmes for help planting their newly acquired 80 acres, dubbed Ciel du Cheval (the name is a French take on Horse Heaven, the name of the hills visible to the south). Holmes and Williams purchased it for Kiona in 1991. When the partners split amicably in 1994, the Williams family retained Kiona and its original vineyards, and Holmes took Ciel du Cheval.

In little more than a decade, he has turned it into what may well be the most prolific (in terms of variety) and distinctive site in the state. The vineyard now totals 120 acres. Thanks to its location farther east and a bit higher up the hill than either Kiona or Klipsun, Ciel has some of Red Mountain's most shallow soils, and it is somewhat better protected from the fierce winds that hammer the vineyards on the western slopes.

Holmes is a student of the vine and an eager collaborator with many of Washington's most gifted winemakers. Consequently Ciel du Cheval now boasts small blocks of roussanne, viognier, mourvèdre, counoise, grenache, nebbiolo, and Brunello-clone sangiovese, along with more substantial plantings of cabernet sauvignon, cabernet franc, merlot, petit verdot, and syrah.

Immediately adjacent to the home vineyard are two new 20-acre plots, joint ventures between Holmes, Quilceda Creek, and DeLille Cellars. Both wineries make top-tier red wines using Ciel grapes; they wanted more than Holmes could provide, so he offered unplanted acreage instead. Over two dozen other wineries currently purchase fruit from Holmes, who makes no commercial wines of his own (a Ciel winery is rumored to be under

CIEL/ANDREW WILL VERTICAL

In December 2005, Chris Camarda presented a vertical of Ciel du Cheval vineyard designates from his Andrew Will library. Here are my notes.

Andrew Will 1989 Ciel du Cheval Merlot

The first vintage for the wine and winery, one of two wines made (Champoux cab was the other). Holding up beautifully, with mature but not over-the-hill flavors of sour plum, earth, gunmetal, hints of smoke. There's just a whisper of light green herb through the finish; the wine is nicely pulled together and perfectly evolved.

Andrew Will 1990 Ciel du Cheval Merlot

This is lighter than the '89, with sour cherry and whiffs of tobacco. Noticeable VA. Loses focus in the finish but hints at the vineyard's gravelly terroir. Ultimately a bit lacking in weight and focus; drying out.

Andrew Will 1993 "R"

This is the reserve, and it's drinking well. Thick, heavy, full-bodied, and still in midlife. Shows noticeably more oak, scents of cracker, toast. Tight and dense, with some VA and a bit of mineral.

Andrew Will 1994 "R"

Tasted in Woodinville the day before the rest. Lean, acidic, and displaying significant VA. Comes across quite tannic, hard, and green. Tannins are chalky; the fruit is not keeping up.

Andrew Will 1994 Ciel du Cheval Merlot

Not one of Chris's favorite vintages, but it's in good shape. Tight, firm, with pure notes of berry, streaks of metal, a hint of reductive tartness.

Andrew Will 1995 Ciel du Cheval Merlot

The first bottle was off in an odd way (from VA?), but the second was much better. Rich, supple, firm, and full. Surprisingly hard, though decanted, it's an especially masculine style of merlot, again streaked with metal, gravel, and coffee grounds.

Andrew Will 1996 Ciel du Cheval Merlot

The freeze year; dramatically reduced crop. Opens at first smelling of silage, soy, slight decay. Appears light, well structured, but less concentrated than the '95. Opens up to show bright, fresh raspberry scents and fruit flavors and then a strong whiff of new barrel toast. There's a bit of heat in the finish, just on the edge of being intrusive. This is a fine bottle in a difficult year.

(continued)

Andrew Will 1997 Ciel du Cheval Merlot
The first vintage to include some cab franc in the blend. Lush and full, with a nose-ful of mixed fruits, a potpourri of berries with hints of chocolate, hay, cocoa, coffee, and even coconut. It's at a very nice age, the fruits just turning secondary but still fresh, good integration of new oak, and some interesting nuances from the franc. Airtime brings out more, mint, hay, etc.

Andrew Will 1998 Ciel du Cheval Merlot
One of the best '98s I've had. Sweet and bursting with intense blackberry and black cherry flavors. The fruit is softening, rounding out; it's a seductive wine that lingers on the palate. Drinking beautifully right now.

Andrew Will 1999 Ciel du Cheval Merlot
Still my favorite vintage of all. Dense, extracted, and compact, with black fruits, smoke, and coffee. Still quite young and tight, but also long and beautifully concentrated. This will age a long time. Would be a good bottle to linger over for several hours.

Andrew Will 2000 Ciel du Cheval Merlot
First bottle just slightly corked; second bottle much better. Here's where the pizza showed up, unfortunately. Scents of ham, iron, light herb, and a hint of pickle barrel. Getting hard to give these wines a fair shake, but 2000 has nowhere near the concentration of '99 or '01.

Andrew Will 2001 Ciel du Cheval Red
First blend year. Tannic, tight, well built. At first the tannins rule, with young wine notes of vanilla and green tea. Did not have time to savor this, unfortunately.

Andrew Will 2002 Ciel du Cheval Red
Young fruit again, primary flavors, spicy, grapey, and full. Has not noticeably changed in the past year. Did not have time for a good evaluation.

Andrew Will 2003 Ciel du Cheval Red
New release. Young, tart, spicy, and tannic. Shows new-barrel flavors of chocolate, smoke, toast. Tannic, and young.

consideration). What is most interesting is that no matter who is making the wine, the flavors of the vineyard shine through.

To cite just two recent examples: The 2002 Andrew Will Red reveals sculpted layer upon layer of citrus peel, plum, wild berry, red currant, and spice, set on a base of rich mineral and rock, with precisely cut tannins. The 2003 Ciel du Cheval Red from Cadence shows wonderfully aromatic scents of dusty coffee, cocoa, and mocha, streaks of chalk, limestone, gravel, and pencil lead, mixed fruits, and hints of expressive spice, all beautifully layered throughout. These are typical tasting notes for the vineyard, which seems capable of both power and refinement across all its grapes and vintages.

Why is it so good? Holmes, ever the scientist, points to the extremely high pH of the soils. It ties up nutrients as insoluble minerals, so the vines struggle. It comes back to the calcium carbonate, which controls the pH. The vines never get big canopies, and berry size is little more than half of standard berry size. Napa berries, Holmes says, weigh about 1.3 grams, while Ciel's average about point 88.

The unique site and soil is the starting point, but after 30 years on Red Mountain Holmes is not about to stop experimenting with every other component of his viticulture. About 10 years ago, he began to get new data, never before available, which allowed him to calculate how much water a vine would need based on the weather reports. His irrigation management evolved rapidly overnight; now there are soil moisture gauges and pinpoint controls on irrigation, varietal by varietal and block by block. One result is softer, rounder tannins than in the past.

Other data has led to a slight reorientation of the vine rows. New plantings no longer go exactly north–south; they're shifted 10 degrees off-axis, so the vines get more sun in the morning, when it's cooler, and less in the afternoon, when it's hot.

"It's more of a pioneering venture now than ever," Holmes modestly asserts. "The world's knowledge is expanding. We don't want Ciel to become stagnant; we want it to keep moving forward." In his mind, Red Mountain, despite its rather bleak, nonvineyard desert landscape, will be a tourist destination someday. He tracks scores of wines made with his fruit. "We score like Napa," he says. "Our products, our Bordeaux varieties run with the best that the country puts out. Why shouldn't people come here? We have 10 million people within a four-hour drive. Our biggest drawback is it's a desolate, hard place. OK; we can't put in mountains with trees on them, but we can put in parks, roads with vistas, and when people come we can give them a good time." Meanwhile, the wines are a pretty good destination all by themselves.

COLD CREEK VINEYARD

Despite its burgeoning investment in tourism, vast stretches of eastern Washington remain as primal and raw as any wine country in the world. Case in point: Cold Creek vineyard, the jewel in the crown for Ste. Michelle Wine Estates. Cold Creek fruit, especially its riesling, chardonnay, merlot, and cabernet, has been the lynchpin for many of the company's most prestigious wines: the Artist Series reserves, the Col Solare reds, the Northstar merlot, the new Ethos series, and some vintages of the Eroica riesling.

The first vineyard-designated wine made in Washington state was a Cold Creek cabernet sauvignon. The label reads: "1980 Ste. Michelle Chateau Reserve Cabernet Sauvignon

Benton County Washington Cold Creek Vineyards." Apart from its historical significance, what is noteworthy about the label is the inclusion of Benton County in the name.
Benton County never was, and still isn't, a name associated with fine wine, or with wine
in general for that matter. But back in the day, as they say in eastern Washington, there
was no Columbia Valley AVA or any AVA beyond Washington, which most people iden-
tified with the nation's capital. So the mar-
keting mavens at Ste. Michelle decided to
throw Benton County at the wall to see if
it would stick.

The drive to Cold Creek doesn't look
much different now than it did then. Heading east from Yakima on Highway 24, you
drive for about 35 miles, passing fields of
hops, cattle pens, and sheep ranches. The
Umptanum Ridge is to your left (north), the
Yakima Ridge runs along on your right
(south), and the Rattlesnake Hills are the
next ridge over. There are no wine grapes
anywhere along the drive. Suddenly, a broad
expanse of well-tended vines appears on the
left, draped across a gently sloping hillside: Cold Creek Vineyards. Ste. Michelle
Wine Estates owns the roughly 800-acre
parcel, of which almost 700 are planted. A
visitor to Cold Creek may or may not see the
creek, which is ephemeral (meaning dry
most of the time). Apart from the winter
months, it's not likely to be all that cold
either; in fact it is one of the warmest sites
in Washington.

Cold Creek, time has proven, is an ideal
grape-growing site, with 30+-year-old vines
planted in light, silty, well-draining soils. It
benefits from some of the warmest and
sunniest summer weather in the state, and
it sits on a slope that makes it impervious
to frost. As in much of Washington, the soils harbor no significant insect pests, one reason the original planting of cabernet, which went into the ground in 1973, is some of the
oldest in the country. The tough, rugged vines are planted on their own roots, the oldest
of them fan-trained, and the grapes go into a wide variety of the company's best wines,
along with up to half a dozen vineyard designates.

COLD CREEK VERTICAL

In November 2005 I sat with Doug Gore and Bob Bertheau of Ste. Michelle Wine Estates and tasted through a vertical selection of most Cold Creek vineyard cabernets. The first ever, a 1980 with the appallingly long moniker "Ste. Michelle Chateau Reserve Cabernet Sauvignon Benton County Washington Cold Creek Vineyards" was not in this tasting. Here are my notes on the wines that were.

1987 Cold Creek Cabernet Sauvignon (tasted twice)
The second bottle is more pruney, soy, and tobacco; the first bottle has more mushroom and was perhaps slightly corked. Both show Bordeaux-like character. Both are low pH and high acid, both drinking like aged Bordeaux. Lots of mushroom, roast beef, hints of soy, and strong acids. No trace of ripe, sweet, modern fruit, but this is an André Tchelistcheff-style.

1994 Cold Creek Cabernet Sauvignon
Low-crop, small-berry year. Concentrated with lots of smoke and dark notes. The pH jumped in the early 1990s. This is losing fruit, drying out, with more austere tannins and some finishing black tea flavors. Mike Januik made this wine. Time to drink up; this is showing end-game tannins and some minty herbs.

1995 Cold Creek Cabernet Sauvignon
Black cherry is the signature for Cold Creek. This tastes very much like black cherry soda; some banana; overall, lighter, riper, fruit-driven wine holding up, but time to drink. Missing the herbal components.

1996 Cold Creek Cabernet Sauvignon
Reduced crop from freeze year, concentrated and hard, with really dense flavors mixing cassis, blackberry, tar, smoke, leather; the best traits of '94 and '95 combined. Really a killer and at a beautiful spot right now.

1997 Cold Creek Cabernet Sauvignon
A lot of toasty oak and mushroom under; more cherry than berry. A big-crop year, the wine is broader by far than the '96 but still lush, showing pretty cherry, along with mature flavors and hints of chanterelle mushroom and vanilla, with a finishing hint of mint.

1998 Cold Creek Cabernet Sauvignon
Layered but not integrated; oak sticks out, fruit is fading; there are some bitter, edgy tannins; the flavors are more of the barrel than anything else. The youthful fruit shows some pie cherry and dried cranberry, but it's time to drink it up.

(continued)

1999 Cold Creek Cabernet Sauvignon
Smaller crop, smaller berries, moderate growing season. Wines just starting to unwind. Gore's comment: "If we didn't have an Indian summer, we felt we would be hosed on this season. Then September came and it really made the vintage." This is just beginning to pull itself together; it's still hard and tannic, but it's well integrated and shows dense layers of mineral, herb, tar, smoke, leather, and tight red currant/cassis. It will be a race against the tannins.

2000 Cold Creek Cabernet Sauvignon
Really fragrant, showing more youth by far. The fruit is moving beyond young and grapey, the tannins are less severe, the wine is in tenuous balance and drinking well. Some citrus shows up. But nothing like the concentration of the best vintages.

2001 Cold Creek Cabernet Sauvignon
Very fragrant, spicy, showing prominent herbs, tighter and younger fruit: cassis, black cherry, black tea. The tannins are a bit too prominent still, but the wine is better than at release, showing more herbal notes and integration.

2002 Cold Creek Cabernet Sauvignon
Softer, but still way too tannic; scrapey and chalky and rough. The tannin management is the problem; the fruit is soft and sweet and broad but lacks concentration. This might eventually turn into a lesser version of 2000.

2003 Cold Creek Cabernet Sauvignon (tasted prerelease)
Big, lots of black cherry in the nose. Like a very dense version of the '95. This is Bob Bertheau's first vintage; he says, "My goal is to keep all the power of Cold Creek but give it a sweeter midpalate than previous years."

It's hard to choose a favorite. The riesling is bright, intensely fruity, yet still razor sharp. The chardonnays are ripe and buttery yet retain the crisp acidity that characterizes the site. Merlots are thick and substantial, and the cabernets are dense, aromatic, tannic, and streaked with mineral and herb.

The vineyard receives just five inches of rain a year, but the soil holds moisture well enough so that irrigation can be postponed until late June and is tightly controlled after that. The vines grow their canopy without irrigation; when shoot growth slows down, drip irrigation is begun. The idea is to control canopy and berry size by waiting until the shoots really need the water and then giving them just barely enough to survive.

Over the years Cold Creek has been a training ground for learning the tricks of deficit irrigation. Along with the original (and newer) blocks of cabernet sauvignon and riesling, it is planted to chardonnay, sauvignon blanc, muscat Canelli, grenache, merlot, cab franc, and syrah. Each of these different varieties reacts differently to water.

The riesling vines, at the advice of Ernst Loosen, who collaborates on the Eroica rieslings, have lately been given more water to grow bigger canopies. This, Loosen believes, helps to avoid the bitter phenolics that come from overexposure to sunlight. Following véraison, irrigation throughout the vineyard is gradually reduced until it is cut off at harvest. Once harvest is complete, the water is turned on until the top two feet of soil are moist. This provides extra insulation for the roots against the winter cold.

In November of 2005 I tasted through a decade's worth of Cold Creek cabernets, from 1994 through 2003, along with a bottle of the 1987. This last was made back when the late André Tchelistcheff was a frequent visitor and advisor to Ste. Michelle. At nearly 20 years of age, the wine was surpassingly Bordeaux-like, the alcohol a moderate 12.9 percent, the flavors soft and mature, with streaks of mushroom, prune, soy, roast beef, and tobacco. In short, it was a lovely, well-aged bottle that had evolved along European lines.

The decade from 1994 to 2003 yielded a generous variety of Cold Creek wines currently at various stages of development. The best were the 1996, another freeze year that yielded dense flavors of cassis, blackberry, tar, smoke, and leather; the 1999, a cool summer with a glorious fall that made a tannic, well-integrated wine layered with cassis, currant, mineral, herb, and tar; and the 1997, still rather lush and pretty, though nearing maturity with dried cherry fruit, buttery chanterelle mushroom, light vanilla, and a hint of mint.

They demonstrated that Cold Creek fruit can go the distance and evolve, not just survive, in the bottle. The site shows vintage variation more than many Washington vineyards. That, along with ongoing, dramatic changes in vineyard management as well as winemaking techniques, will continue to occur. So any 10-year retrospective tasting will offer a record of experimentation rather than a series of fixed snapshots of a mature vineyard. But given its long (for Washington) history, unique flavor profile, and remote site, Cold Creek may well deserve its certification as an AVA in the near future. Benton County, on the other hand, will have to wait a while longer.

KLIPSUN VINEYARD

If you visit the Klipsun vineyard on the right sort of day, when a gentle breeze is blowing and the perfume of the grapes in bloom scents the air, it is quite lovely. There's a pergola near the top where you can sit and look out in all directions. Straight west the hill slopes steeply down toward the snaking line of green trees that hug the meandering Yakima River. Two ridges of mountains are in view: the Rattlesnake Hills to the north and the Horse Heaven Hills to the south. Behind you, to the east, is Red Mountain itself. Looking neither red nor particularly mountainous, it unfolds in large squares of well-manicured vineyards, an occasional stand of trees, and patches of dusty desert.

Patricia (Trish) and David Gelles began planting Klipsun in 1984, following the lead of their friends and neighbors Jim Holmes (Ciel du Cheval) and John Williams (Kiona), who had pioneered the Red Mountain area a decade earlier. Already Holmes and Williams had proven that excellent cabernet and merlot could be grown in this then-desolate place, and winemakers such as Alex Golitzin (Quilceda Creek) and Gary Figgins (Leonetti Cellar) had been eagerly purchasing their grapes.

But it was still relatively unexplored and risky. Unlike most of the Yakima Valley vineyards that were going in at that time, Red Mountain was virgin land. Nothing had ever been grown there. The soil had gone untouched since the great floods had recontoured all of eastern Washington 10,000 years earlier. "I think we are lucky nothing was grown here before," Trish Gelles states emphatically. "There were no mistakes to correct. It's always better to farm on virgin land. And sagebrush is a good indication that the soil is good for growing. It's just amazing that no one did it before we did."

Though Red Mountain is best known for its Bordeaux reds, the site and soil can ripen almost anything—almost. "We used to have chardonnay," says Trish Gelles, "until we found that Red Mountain is really too hot (chardonnay doesn't like extended high heat). But it's unusual to be able to grow whites and reds both as well as we do."

Initially Klipsun was two-thirds white and one-third red; now it is about 85 percent red and 15 percent white. Cabernet and merlot dominate, along with syrah and even a bit of nebbiolo. Semillon and sauvignon blanc are the remaining whites. But the cab and merlot bring three times the price, and production costs are equivalent, so the remaining white grapes are more or less a gift, left there simply because they make excellent wines and because the Gelleses like to drink white wines from their own vineyard.

The red wines, from a who's-who list of Washington's top boutiques, are what built the vineyard's reputation. Klipsun vineyard Bordeaux blends, whomever the winemaker may be, consistently show massively concentrated black fruits, hard tannins, a stiffness to the spine, and a steely minerality. "They're just huge wines," says Trish Gelles, "and long-lived wines, as far as you can tell. There's always a strong cherry and blackberry fruit component. They're just really big."

You'll get different theories as to the importance of Red Mountain soils. Some growers point proudly to the many variations and the mix of glacial rock and wind-blown volcanic dust; others say there is no particular difference from elsewhere. "Our soils were laid down because of a series of huge floods that occurred every hundred years during the Ice Age," David Gelles explains. "I'm beginning to realize that we have the same soils up and down the Yakima Valley, the Walla Walla Valley, and the Willamette Valley. We're all basically dealing with Canadian topsoils."

Red Mountain does get more heat units than virtually anywhere else in Washington, with summer temperatures commonly peaking over 100 degrees, the tipping point at which vines shut down. But it makes up for the extreme heat with strong winds, which keep the grapes free of rot and eliminate most pests. And its elevation (grapes are planted between 600 and 1100 feet) means that once the sun goes down, things cool off considerably. The diurnal temperature swing, especially during harvest, is 40 degrees or more, so the grapes never lose their firm acids, though harvest is earlier here than in most parts of the state.

Klipsun's location, on the lower, most west-facing slopes of the mountain, exposes it to more wind than most of its neighbors, toughening the grape skins, concentrating the juice, and thickening the tannins. Klipsun grapes, especially cabernet and merlot, are in high demand; they have the reputation (the Gelleses will neither confirm nor deny) of being the most expensive in the state. Roughly 30 different wineries purchase Klipsun grapes, and many have their own designated rows. Many happily label the wines "Klipsun Vineyard," for they know that the name brings with it a lot of respect from consumers.

As the vineyard moves into its third decade, the Gelleses maintain that they are happy with the mix and have no plans for expansion. A couple of acres of malbec were added in 2005; that's it for a while at least. "We may do more clonal stuff as the vineyard ages and we have to replant," Trish Gelles confirms, "but we're still a little way off."

OTIS VINEYARD

Standing in the Otis vineyard on a crisp, cloud-studded Yakima Valley spring day, I find myself surrounded by beautiful old cabernet vines. Gnarled, sculpted, and twisted by time, their shaggy trunks as much as six or eight inches in diameter, they corkscrew skyward, forming row upon row of fan-shaped dancers. Trellised shoots are just beginning to push new buds.

Otis recently passed the half century mark, a remarkable age for cabernet in Washington state or anywhere in this country. Because the original vines are planted on their own rootstock and head-trained, they will outlive cabernet grafted onto phylloxera-resistant rootstock. Should the vineyard get whacked by one of eastern Washington's periodic winter freezes, you can train a new trunk up from the roots, rather like a rose bush.

So these Otis vines are survivors, pioneers from a distant time when the Washington wine industry was protected by strict trade tariffs and the economics of wine were based on laws that allowed so-called "high ferment" wines to be the strongest drinks sold in taverns across the state. These wines, made from high-yielding, heavily irrigated grapes such as sultana, palomino, alicante, and salvador, were augmented at fermentation with bags of sugar and turned into high-octane "sherry" and "port." A leading producer of the day was Alhambra. The owner, Otis Harlan, was a savvy businessman who knew that Washington's state-protected wine industry would eventually have to compete on more equal terms. He began keeping an eye on the new wine styles being made in California and decided to plant a few experimental acres of vinifera wines in his Otis vineyard.

The first six acres of Otis cab went into the ground in 1957. Harlan recalls that it was initially used to make an inexpensive rosé, a "Burgundy" blend designed to imitate the Hearty Burgundy of California, and a "Port." "We were even thinking of using corks for

In April 2005 I sat down with winemaker David Lake and reviewed almost every vintage of Otis Vineyard cabernet sauvignon he has made, beginning with his inaugural wine, the justly famous 1979 Millennium (1982, 1984, 1987, and 1990, Lake explains, have been "retired/discarded"). The earliest vintages were recoopered American whiskey barrels; the first new French oak was in '85. Here are my notes.

1979 Columbia Millennium Cabernet Sauvignon

Still a remarkable wine, showing brick edge but still dark, black cherry color in the center. It's Barolo-like, with tar and leather, rose petals, and tobacco scents mingling. Not a trace of exhaustion, it's a mature, confident, spectacular wine, with fruit still nuanced with hints of cherries, raspberries, tobacco leaf.

1981 Columbia "Otis Vineyard" Cabernet Sauvignon

Strongly herbal, peppery, mineral. This is not vegetal, no green bean or asparagus, but quite distinctly peppery and woody, not from barrel but from stem. Fruit is faded but elegant, tasting perceptibly of raspberries. Evolves beautifully in the glass; as the fruit fades, it shows more green tea in the tannins.

1983 Columbia "Otis Vineyard" Cabernet Sauvignon

Dark, with bricking; powerful scents of meat, herb, smoke, again that pepper, this time bell pepper. Perhaps a bit less complex than the '81, but still holding up and in good shape.

1985 Columbia "Otis Vineyard" Cabernet Sauvignon

Cedar, tobacco, leather; still sweet on the palate, with generous fruit and a classic, Bordeaux structure; some mint-menthol sneaks in also.

1986 Columbia "Otis Vineyard" Cabernet Sauvignon

Perhaps showing more brown than the others so far; not generally a good vintage in Washington (the even-year curse). But here another glorious bouquet, with pepper and cinnamon and hints of meat; characteristic structure with acid under soft tannins; good length and still plenty of tart pie cherry fruit.

1988 Columbia "Otis Vineyard" Cabernet Sauvignon

Raisined, pruney nose, with assertive wood aromas and sweet butterscotch too; also the typical pepper/gravel tannins. This has more youthful fruit, a sweeter flavor all around, and a rounded, simple, pleasant character without strong Otis markers.

1989 Columbia "Otis Vineyard" Cabernet Sauvignon
Scents of untoasted wood; it's drinking well with sweet oak and soft fruit; nicely rounded out, but lacks the texture and depth of the best vintages. Finishes with a cracker/toast note.

1991 Columbia "Otis Vineyard" Cabernet Sauvignon
Another beautiful nose, more typical Otis aromatics. Pepper (jalapeño), a sweeter spice note, smoke, gravel; there's a beautiful elegance to this wine, graceful and lingering; nuanced.

1992 Columbia "Otis Vineyard" Cabernet Sauvignon
Interesting mix of meat, smoke, herb, with a strong spine of cardamom; open and sensuous; drinking really well right now; just starting to show the tea tannins. The fruit is carrying through but maturing, with some butterscotch and sour cherry mixing; smooth and elegant.

1993 Columbia "Otis Vineyard" Cabernet Sauvignon
This has 10 percent merlot; the first time it was blended. Complex aromas of herb, tobacco, leaf. Broad, full, lush; fat fruits underscored with herb and a hint of mint. It falls off a bit in the mouth; the nose is the best part. Finishes with lingering flavors of barrel, fat and fading fruit. Lacks intensity, but quite pleasing.

1994 Columbia "Otis Vineyard" Cabernet Sauvignon
Definitely more youthful, with scents of pure cherry and good concentration. Shows some of the same tobacco and tar as the Millennium wine; deep color and more mass and weight than most other Otis. Black cherry, liquorous with some heat.

1995 Columbia "Otis Vineyard" Cabernet Sauvignon
Back to the more standard Otis elegance, with plenty of acid and the tannins still sticking out a bit; fruit is soft, and some pepper is showing; not an outstanding vintage but plenty of finesse, elegance. Drinking quite nicely right now in its tenth year.

1997 Columbia "Otis Vineyard" Cabernet Sauvignon
Lightest in color; just 13 percent alcohol. Some creosote in the nose; the vines recovering from '96 freeze; "maybe not yet firing on all cylinders," says Lake. Light, tart, elegant, but complex, with unresolved tannins, green herbs, and speckles of pepper.

1998 Columbia "Otis Vineyard" Cabernet Sauvignon
Ripe fruit highlighted with hay, alfalfa. This is real peppery; there is almost a bit of cayenne heat to the finish. Rounding out, spicy with good acid and texture.

(continued)

OTIS VINEYARD VERTICAL *(continued)*

1999 Columbia "Otis Vineyard" Cabernet Sauvignon
This is very young, with black currant aromatics. Concentrated bush and berry aromas; dense, thick, tough, chewy. Still plenty of acid, and very young, with great potential.

2000 Columbia "Otis Vineyard" Cabernet Sauvignon
Young, round, fruity, approachable wine with good cherry/plum flavors. Nice spicy highlights and round, pretty fruit, but not as substantive as the '99.

2001 Columbia "Otis Vineyard" Cabernet Sauvignon (prerelease)
The oak is overwhelming the fruit right now, but the spice and intensity come through. Should be an excellent Otis vintage, though maybe not typical.

2002 Columbia "Otis Vineyard" Cabernet Sauvignon (prerelease)
The first Otis to hit 14 percent alcohol. Young, grapey, and lush, with mixed red fruits and lovely Asian spices. Generous, broad, and sweet; truly delicious.

that wine," he says, a radical departure from the screw-capped wines of the day, "until we found out that not many people had corkscrews!"

David Lake came to work at Columbia winery (then called Associated Vintners) in September of 1979. The previous winter had seen a deep freeze; many vineyards were wiped out, and Otis lost two-thirds of its crop. Associated Vintners, scrambling for grapes, arranged to purchase a small amount of Otis cabernet and merlot. Lake, who had never visited the vineyard, was so impressed with the quality of the fruit that he created a special "Millennium" cabernet and predicted that the wine would live long enough to be enjoyed two decades later, when the new century began.

He was too modest. Tasted most recently in mid-2005, the 1979 Millennium was still a remarkable wine, showing brick edges but quite dark, the color of black cherries. Barolo-like, it smelled of tar and leather, rose petals, and cut tobacco. Showing not a trace of exhaustion, it was a mature, confident, spectacular wine, nuanced with hints of cherries, raspberries, and tobacco leaf.

Columbia got no Otis fruit in 1980. But beginning in 1981 Lake made a vineyard-designated Otis cabernet sauvignon in every vintage, until his retirement in 2006. The wine is always 100 percent Otis and usually pure, unblended cabernet sauvignon, and it is generally the last wine of the vintage to be released in the entire state.

Despite the extra bottle age, it is not always an easy wine to love. Except in the very warmest years, Otis cabernet will not romance you with sweet, succulent fruit or toasty new oak. In fact, newly released vintages can be rather hard, unyielding wines, occasionally quite tannic, and marked by a distinctive peppery, herbal nose. They are in many respects the antithesis of the sweet, superripe California cabs that have been so much in vogue for the past couple of decades.

Otis makes old-school, European-style wines (Lake, one of Washington's three Masters of Wine, has a very European palate), wines that are structured to age, balanced to accompany meals, and designed to show more of the varietal herbaceousness of the cabernet grape than is usually found in American versions.

It has often been noted that the Washington style of making red wine straddles (or defines) an imaginary border between Napa and Bordeaux. Otis cabs clearly fall on the Bordeaux side of that fence; they display the classic herbal aromas of the cabernet varietal, the sort of lightly vegetative scents prevalent in even the best young Bordeaux, along with fairly hard tannins and tightly knit layers of tart red fruit.

These same qualities make them remarkably cellar-worthy. It is not just because the vineyard is so old that it merits inclusion in this chapter. It is because these wines pass the gold standard for greatness: They evolve as well as survive. They develop the nuances of bottle bouquet that Bordeaux lovers will rarely find in New World wines.

Until his untimely departure, Lake had doggedly stuck with the vineyard and its unique imprint, despite the fact that Otis wines are slow and late and, quite frankly, not to everyone's taste. "A lot of people don't want to see any herbaceous character," he told me. "I'm troubled by that, because that is the classic cabernet character of the Bordeaux varietals. I guess you could argue that it isn't necessary to the birthright of cabernet, but I personally feel that without it, it makes a less interesting wine."

Today, the entire Otis vineyard comprises 120 acres, with many newer plantings, including Washington's first pinot gris and Dijon-clone chardonnay vines. It continues to evolve and since 2000 has been managed by Terry Herrmann, who is introducing sustainable viticulture practices, revitalizing the soil, and, in collaboration with Lake, ripening the fruit a bit further than in the past. "In the recent years we've been getting a better handle on the bearing of these older vines," said Lake on my last visit. "The styles [of future Otis cabs] will tend to be perhaps more mainstream. Some of the warmer years probably will be less acidic and won't last as long. We're not immune to the tendency to let things hang, but in the case of Otis it's more about controlling the yields a bit more."

Owner Otis Harlan rather sadly notes that he sees a lot of his grapes dropped on the ground these days, a yield-reducing practice called *green harvesting*. "I'll bet they look just like dollar bills," I suggest, and he nods. Such is the price of greatness. It is also an indication that for old vines that are this good, life begins at 50.

PEPPER BRIDGE

Until very recently, the only vineyards in Walla Walla that added up to any significant acreage were Seven Hills and Pepper Bridge. These days there is expansion everywhere, especially at the higher elevations (across the state line) south and east of town. Prices for raw land with "vineyard potential" have gone through the roof. Diversity is becoming the hallmark; Walla Walla is already an AVA in need of subdividing. But if one vineyard can stand in for the most typical soil, style, plantings, and sense of innovation that characterize the region, it is Pepper Bridge.

The original property was an old wheat ranch, and most importantly it had water rights, when partners Norm McKibben and Bob Rupar first decided to purchase it for a joint venture growing apples. Tom and Kent Waliser, who had an apple-packing business, were brought in as junior partners, and the first Pepper Bridge orchards—not grapevines—were planted in 1989 and 1990.

McKibben had previously been trying to grow pinot noir and chardonnay at his 40-acre Whiskey Creek vineyard, some miles north of town. He soon convinced his Pepper Bridge partners to try some wine grapes on their land also. In 1991, the first five acres each of merlot and cabernet sauvignon went into the ground.

In retrospect the timing could not have been better. Though there were only a half dozen wineries in Walla Walla, several had already established national reputations. The odd thing was that they couldn't really make Walla Walla wines; only about 40 acres of grapes were planted in the entire valley. So virtually all these Walla Walla winery wines were made from Columbia Valley and Yakima Valley grapes.

The pent-up demand for true Walla Walla fruit was so great that even before the first crop was picked, Pepper Bridge had signed up Woodward Canyon, Leonetti, and L'Ecole N° 41 (among others) as its customers. It was win–win; the wineries were desperate for local grapes, and the new vineyard quickly benefited from the excellent reputations that the wineries had already built.

Currently, the 200-acre Pepper Bridge vineyard includes 162 acres of bearing vines, mostly split between cabernet sauvignon and merlot, with 11 acres of syrah and smaller amounts of sangiovese and malbec. A different set of partners owns the Pepper Bridge winery, which maintains control over specific blocks of grapes. Since the eighth or ninth vintage, says McKibben, the cabernet in particular has become more and more consistent. "The vines," he says with characteristic modesty, "seem to pretty well self-regulate, and it's harder for us to screw them up."

Pepper Bridge sits in one of the valley's colder sites, and the vineyard was hit pretty hard by winter freezes in 1996 and 2004. After the loss of most of the 2004 crop, Pepper Bridge, along with many other low-lying Walla Walla vineyards, began to bury canes for protection. In at least some freeze years that strategy will ensure a decent crop the following summer.

Drip irrigation is used, regulated by buried soil sensors that read moisture levels at 12 inches, 18 inches, and four feet. If moisture reaches the four-foot depth, it is more than the vine needs; like many leading vineyards in the state, Pepper Bridge is using less and less water. Theories of stressing the grapes are changing also. "We don't grow our grapes to stress any more," says McKibben. "Everybody's backed off that now." Too much stress, and pH's "go wild and flavors fall off."

The movement toward sustainable viticulture is gaining momentum in Washington, though the state still lags far behind Oregon and California. There is justifiable doubt about the practicality of being certifiably organic, but many of the underlying principles of organic farming are being incorporated into regular practice.

At Pepper Bridge, compost (mostly ground logs along with some winery must and timothy hay), compost tea (applied through the drip lines), and other treatments (molasses, fish compound) are all being used in efforts to rebuild soils sterilized by a century of wheat farming. "We're about as close to organic as we can get without being organic" says McKibben. After two years, he proudly notes, the organic content of the soil is already up about 50 percent. "I'd like to think that my grandkids will thank me someday for the quality," he beams. "The vineyard is where we're going to be able to increase our quality the most; and it's largely a function of rebuilding the soil."

RED WILLOW

On a glorious midspring morning some years ago, I found myself on the road with then-Columbia winemaker David Lake, driving south through the Yakima River Canyon, following along beside the lazy, winding river. The steep hills surrounding us were softly draped in subtle tones of sage green, delicately spotted with the yellow blossoms of the balsam root plant. We passed through Union Gap, a break in the Ahtanum Ridge, and burst into the sun-drenched Yakima Valley, with its apple and cherry orchards, fields of mint and alfalfa, and endless rows of hops and vines.

Virtually all of the valley's vineyards follow the river as it bends east, but we turned sharply west, directly toward the foothills of the Cascade Mountains. Here, at the extreme northwestern edge of the Yakima Valley, is one of the prettiest and most unusual vineyards in Washington state. Red Willow, surrounded on all sides by the Yakama Indian reservation.

The land was purchased by the Stephenson family from the Yakama tribe back in the 1920s. Initially it was farmed to potatoes and alfalfa, with cattle let to graze on the higher slopes that were unsuitable for row crops. In the early 1970s, Mike Sauer, who had married the granddaughter of the man who pioneered the property, planted a 30-acre Concord vineyard, along with a few experimental rows of chenin blanc and sémillon. Ironically, he notes, the vinifera grapes didn't survive where the Concords were planted; the soil was too rich.

The Red Willow Vineyard got its real start in 1973, and, as with so many of Washington's old-vine locations, it was Dr. Walt Clore who instigated it. Clore wanted a weather station installed so that he could compare temperature data with other areas around the state. At the same time, he and Sauer put in a small experimental vineyard. But Sauer already had commercial aspirations, and he decided to go ahead and plant three acres of cabernet sauvignon as well. The trials and tribulations of this early planting would test the patience of Job: weeds, rabbits, grasshoppers, drought, and more. But Sauer typically looks on the bright side, recalling those early days with some fondness. "We were trying to figure out how to pronounce the varieties, let alone grow them," he grins. "The climate was different then. We had several pretty cold winters. The emphasis was on trying to figure out which varieties would survive. Walt put an experimental plot on our land with about 20 different varieties; and it sparked this interest. From about 1983 to 1991 we tried nebbiolo, sangiovese, syrah, cab franc, tempranillo, mataro, malbec, and viognier."

By the early 1990s, a lot of people were jumping into these varieties, but Red Willow was often first. An exceptional partnership between grower Sauer and winemaker Lake had formed, one that would last for almost three decades. "David was always very encouraging," says Sauer today. "If we would grow it, he would make the wine from it." New vineyards were added regularly, usually on steep hillsides that required weeks of bulldozing. Each new plot, each new grape revealed more and more about this unique site, which sits between 1100 and 1300 feet, above the ancient floodplain that created most eastern Washington vineyards. A wide variation of soils—calcareous, sandstone, clay, sand, loam, and silt—were uncovered. And the combination of these poor, ancient, well-drained soils, the east-, south-, and west-facing slopes, and the desert climate (just six inches of precipitation annually) provided perfect laboratory conditions for Lake's and Sauer's ongoing trials.

The emphasis shifted somewhat during the 1990s as new sections of the vineyard were developed. The focus then was matching soils to varietals, hoping to find the true Red Willow terroir. Then came another round of changes as Columbia Winery, the winery purchasing the vast majority of the grapes, was being acquired by Canandaigua. "We spent a lot of effort on landscaping at that time," says Sauer, "sprucing the place up. Canandaigua brought quite a few people through during the summers." Today the Columbia Winery brand is part of Icon Estates, the high-end portfolio of wines from Constellation, and Sauer feels as though his 35-year-old vineyard is going in a new direction once again. "We're getting a lot of technical input," he says, "and when you've been doing it for so many years, at first it's a little tough on your ego. But we're realizing there's a lot of different ways that things can be tweaked again. We're getting input from some of the top people in the country, so all at once our emphasis is on utilizing what we've built on for all these years, and things seem to be coming together."

Though the partnership between Lake and Columbia Winery was a productive and prolific one, Red Willow has not had the benefits, as have most of the other vineyards included in this chapter, of receiving input from a wide variety of winemakers. That is now changing. A new 60-acre vineyard, located three quarters of a mile west of Red Willow, has been planted to even more unusual grape varieties, among them aglianico, barbera, carmenère, and malbec. Rolling hills rather than steep slopes, newer clones, and creative trellising also help to differentiate the site from Red Willow.

Named Les Vignes de Marcoux, it is already selling grapes to Andrew Rich, Betz Family, Long Shadows, Owen Roe, Wineglass, and several other new wineries. For now, Columbia Winery will continue to have exclusive rights to Red Willow grapes and the use of the name on its labels (the only exception being Cavatappi, a tiny Seattle-area producer making Red Willow nebbiolo).

In some ways the history of Red Willow encapsulates many of the challenges that impact Washington as a whole. It sits on land that can grow almost anything, but after 35 years it is still searching for what it can grow best. Indeed, what can Washington grow best? Ask Mike Sauer and he will tell you that he believes the answer is syrah. But he isn't about to stop experimenting. "This spring [2006] we're planting another dozen acres: three of sangiovese, five of syrah, two of cab franc, a dash of petite sirah, and a touch of Dolcetto. Last year we put in a bit of Barbera. We're trying to ripen things later in the season, especially merlot and syrah. We've been experimenting with clones. Certain clones may give you better flavors at lower brix, but it's too soon to tell for sure," he admits.

Trying to even out the ripeness is his current "big challenge," he explains. "You get into these vineyards on the hillsides with ancient soils; you move down the hill 200 feet and you're in a different world. On the one hand you want things evenly ripened, but on the other you want these more interesting terroirs. So we are breaking out the vineyard into smaller blocks, looking for ways to even out the ripeness of that fruit so you're not mixing 28 brix and 24 brix to equal 26 brix. That's the challenge."

It's a challenge that Sauer, at 60, seems ready and even eager to accept. "I'm enthused right now with the direction we're going," he grins. "My three boys are back on the farm, and that gets the old man going again. You've got another generation coming and that pushes you, but you don't have to deal with all the minutiae."

PART 2

WINERY PROFILES

5

THE LEADERS

Rather than do a catalog-type listing of every winery in Washington, I elected early on to focus this book on the top 25 percent. By historic and global standards, that is a generous slice. Look at any country or wine region in the world and you will find that the list of recognized, globally significant wineries is but a tiny fraction of the total number of producers.

When I wrote my first guidebooks to Washington wines some years ago, it was enough merely to list everyone making wine in Washington and to make a few comments about perceived quality. The region was so new and unknown that it would have been presumptuous to do a selection, and, besides, it would hardly have qualified as a book-length project had I done so. But things have changed. Many Washington wineries now have meaningful track records. Vertical tastings of older wines are within the realm of possibility for more than a handful; two wineries can pull out wines that are 40 years old! Most importantly, consumers are far more knowledgeable and demanding than ever before. They want to know who is doing the best work.

Making a critical evaluation of a region's producers is a mark of respect, and Washington's leaders have earned that respect. Bordeaux, to cite the obvious example, has some 22,000 growers, at least 6000 distinct chateaux, and several hundred cooperatives. They get parsed down all the way to five First Growths and a handful of Super Seconds that dominate the market. Even so exhaustive a reviewer as Robert Parker evaluates roughly only 10 percent of the region's labels. A 25 percent slice of Washington is downright generous by comparison. But then, Washington is still young, and fully a third of the wineries listed here are so new as to be unrated. They are the wineries to watch in the coming years.

It would be foolish for anyone to propose that Washington state is made up entirely of notable wines and wineries. But in making my selections and further winnowing them down in this and the next three chapters, I have found what I consider to be Washington's First Growths and Super Seconds. In this chapter I examine each of them in turn and discuss why they have elevated themselves to this level.

Does this mean they are perfect? A few brush up against perfection; all strive for it. But Washington is still just barely past the pioneering stage, as any vintner will tell you. Most of this state's wineries are less than a decade old. Much of the vineyard is still some years away from its prime. This makes it even more remarkable, in my opinion, that these wineries have been able to achieve so much so soon.

ANDREW WILL CELLARS

Founded 1989
12526 SW Bank Road
Vashon, WA 98070
206/463-9227
www.andrewwill.com
E-mail: info@andrewwill.com

Score: 90 (28/26/28/8)

Andrew Will's winemaker-founder, Chris Camarda, pioneered single-vineyard varietal wines (merlots and cabernets) before deciding to reverse the priorities; he is now focusing almost exclusively on blended wines from favored single vineyards.

Chris Camarda honed his palate during his years as a Seattle maitre d' before turning winemaker. The first Andrew Will wines (the winery was named for his son Will and nephew Andrew) were made at a tiny rented space on Seattle's Elliott Avenue. From this hole-in-the-wall outpost came some astonishingly good wines that generated immediate acclaim. Running the business on sheer talent and a relentless work ethic, Camarda and his late wife, Annie, were soon able to build a house and winery on bucolic Vashon Island, a half hour's ferry ride from West Seattle.

Chiefly responsible for Andrew Will's early successes were Camarda's extraordinary merlots, which arrived just as Washington merlot was attracting the attention of the national wine press. He was one of the first in the state to explore and carefully define the specific flavor characteristics of individual vineyards. He did this methodically, by eliminating all winemaking variables other than the vineyard site. His single-vineyard, single-varietal merlots and cabernets were all treated identically in the winery. When tasted horizontally, the vineyards themselves could be compared and contrasted. Tasted vertically by vineyard, vintage variations were made clear.

Camarda's gift was to endow each wine with a unique personality. He steadfastly labored *not* to put his own stylistic stamp on them. "I wanted people to see one person making wine the same way, with the same barrels, the same techniques," he later explained, "so what you were left with was the flavor of vineyards. We're interested in the differences between vineyards, not the similarities. Otherwise you might as well make beer."

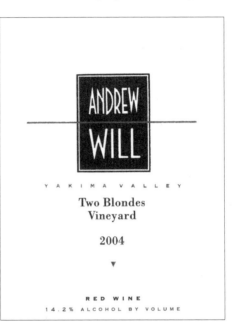

The vineyards chosen (Ciel du Cheval and Klipsun on Red Mountain, Pepper Bridge, and Seven Hills in Walla Walla, Champoux in the Horse Heaven Hills, and Sheridan in the Rattlesnake Hills) were selected specifically for their ability to express some unique terroir. With the benefit of hindsight, it is clear that Camarda knew what he was doing; he included representatives of the Red Mountain, Walla Walla, Horse Heaven, and Rattlesnake Hills AVAs, though at the time only Walla Walla was officially designated.

By the late 1990s Camarda was making plans to develop his own vineyard in the river rock region of Walla Walla. Then he discovered the newly planted Sheridan vineyard in the Rattlesnake Hills subregion of the Yakima Valley. "When I made the '99 Sheridan cab franc," he recalled, "it was really outstanding, soft and plush. So when the land next to it came up for sale I went ahead and bought it." He named his 36 acres Two Blondes, immediately planting most of it to cabernet sauvignon and cabernet franc, with small amounts of merlot, petit verdot, and malbec. He believes (and points to a $20,000 study as proof) that it compares analytically to Howell Mountain.

Camarda is brusque and animated, a graying, elfin figure who seems to operate in a perpetually caffeinated condition. In winter, when the unblended wines fill the winery with the scent of newly fermented grapes, he races from barrel to barrel, splashing the inky contents into sparkling glasses and evaluating the strengths of each with a practiced precision.

At one such moment, the light went off, and he decided it was time to swap variables. His wines are no longer varietally labeled as merlot or cabernet sauvignon. Instead, they are red Bordeaux blends, whose identity is anchored by the vineyard. A dedicated audiophile, he draws an analogy between tasting blends and listening to music. An unblended cabernet sauvignon, no matter how brilliant, is like listening to a monaural recording of a beautiful song, he asserts. But a blended red from the same vineyard is like hearing the same recording in stereo.

Andrew Will's 4500-case annual production now includes vineyard-designated wines from Ciel du Cheval, Champoux, Klipsun, Two Blondes, and Sheridan. If forced to choose, I would rate them in that order. The winery's reserve is the Sorella red, produced from the oldest (Block One) Champoux vineyard vines.

A recent sadness was the passing of his much-loved wife and partner, Annie Camarda, whom he honors with an "Annie Camarda" syrah, made from Ciel du Cheval grapes. Camarda also makes a lower-priced line of wines called Cuvée Lucia, for barrels that don't fit into the Andrew Will portfolio. Among the offerings are some real treasures, such as a recent Ciel du Cheval sangiovese and a Celilo vineyard pinot gris.

Camarda has demonstrated an artist's touch from his first vintage. Many of his oldest wines have aged quite well, despite his protestations that he didn't really know what he was doing. He has always found great vineyards and has consistently pushed past his own limitations and errors. By doing so, he elevates all of this state's wines.

BETZ FAMILY

Founded 1998
PO Box 39
Woodinville, WA 98072
425/861-9823
www.betzfamilywinery.com
E-mail: info@betzfamilywinery.com

Score: 91 (29/25/28/9)

Bob Betz, one of two Washington state winemakers holding an MW (Master of Wine) degree, traveled the globe on behalf of Ste. Michelle and its brands during almost three decades with the company. His own winery is focused on a small portfolio of red wines, made with meticulous attention to detail.

Key in "overachieving workaholic" at Wikipedia.com, and a picture of Bob Betz pops up. From 1976 until 2003, he worked for a single company—*the* company as far as Washington wine is concerned—Ste. Michelle Wine Estates (then called Stimson Lane).

Betz held many titles over the years, but mostly what he did was educate, himself first, his coworkers second, and then the trade and the wine world at large. He traveled endlessly as the company's point man for education and research, spoke on hundreds of panels, and walked the great vineyards of Europe with some of its leading winemakers.

Along the way he studied for and obtained the highest credential in the wine world, a Master of Wine degree, and developed a palate equally adept at analyzing wine from any perspective: grower, lab rat, winemaker, marketer, retailer, collector.

Betz Family Winery began as a weekend project, an escape from the corporate life that was beginning to grind on him. During these formative years, with the winery jammed into a tiny, no-frills Woodinville warehouse, Betz maintained a tight focus, keeping total production around 800–1000 cases. He made up for his limited time and financial resources with his superb technical knowledge, his business acumen, and his wealth of vineyard contacts. But he knew from the start that it would require a full-time commitment to make the wines he could already taste in his imagination.

In 2003 he "semiretired," determined, he told me, "to reclaim parts of my life . . . my garden . . . my wife needs hugging, all those things that time has just eaten away at." Over the next couple of years he gradually weaned himself away from the corporate world while developing plans to build a new winery. "The goal was to make a winemaker's winery," he explains, "to move, interact, and control those things most important to us."

That dream winery opened just in time for the 2005 crush. As expected, Betz Family's new quarters are expansive and supremely well thought out. Betz points out feature after feature designed somehow to help improve the wines. It could be something as simple as a floor that is built to slope and drain properly, a luxury that many small wineries, tucked into tiny warehouse spaces in generic office parks, are denied. Yet on such small decisions are great wines built. A clean floor allows for better sanitation practices, which Betz calls "the core issue to good winemaking."

Ease of mobility, constant temperature and humidity control, and the ability to avoid ever having to pump the wines are other defining features of the new winery. Production is up to 2500 cases, where Betz and his wife Cathy intend it to remain. The most important wines are a pair of Left Bank/Right Bank-styled Bordeaux reds, and a pair of syrahs.

The Père de Famille cabernet sauvignon is a stunning wine packed with a rainbow of fruit flavors. Cassis, blueberry, black currant, black cherry, and more reveal themselves in layers as it opens up from its compact, dense entry into a seamless, fragrant, beautifully proportioned wine. The scents and flavors just continue to unfold, running the gamut from citrus peel to clove to soy to chocolate, espresso, and beyond.

The Clos de Betz, which gets the same care as the cabernet, features considerably more merlot in the blend and is more open and generous on release. The vineyard mix ranges from Red Mountain to Horse Heaven Hills to the best of the Yakima Valley. Intensely fragrant, beautifully integrated, toasty, and lush, it offers layers of caramel, butterscotch, and creamy oak around black cherry and plum.

The two syrahs are La Cote Rousse, a dark, dense, tannic wine produced from Red Mountain grapes, and La Serenne (a northern Rhône nickname for syrah), an elegant and tart, cool-climate style sourced from the Boushey (Yakima Valley) vineyard. Betz wines are always carefully structured and beautifully proportioned, and the winemaker does not overreach, overextract, or overfuss with things. The newest Betz Family wine is the Bésoleil, a grenache-dominated, southern Rhône red, limited to fewer than 200 cases and sold exclusively through the mailing list. It's a juicy, delicious tangle of red fruits and berries, highlighted with a spicy finish.

As his wines demonstrate, Betz is a painstaking blender, an MW-level taster, a "complete" winemaker who intimately knows how to work the vineyard, the laboratory, the barrels, and the blending to make superb wines. A cleanliness fanatic, he keeps the barrel room at 50 degrees, does individual monthly SO_2 adjustments, maintains a natural 72 percent humidity, and scribbles a tasting note on every barrel. The blending, done over the course of three months, is, he admits, the most difficult and most artistically satisfying part of the entire process.

Constant improvement is the goal. "There's a chance," he says, "that we haven't planted the best vineyard in Washington yet. That's really exciting! To make wine this good at this stage and still have all these sites to explore. I always go back to what we have here: high light intensity, ample heat during the growing season, dramatic day/night temperature differences during ripening, a general high-stress situation for vines, a long growing season, and a relatively pest-free situation. This is a great area to grow grapes."

CAYUSE VINEYARDS

Founded 1997
17 East Main Street
Walla Walla, WA 99362
509/526-0686
www.cayusevineyards.com
E-mail: info@cayusevineyards.com

Score: 94 (29/27/28/10)

Christophe Baron, profiled elsewhere in these pages, has dramatically impacted the prevailing ideas about where and how to grow grapes, and what grapes to grow, in the Walla Walla Valley. A brilliant vigneron, he was the first in Washington to achieve biodynamic certification. His quirky but intensely flavorful wines mystify some and dazzle others.

—————————

Cayuse Vineyards has one of the prettiest little tasting rooms on Main Street in the heart of Walla Walla's downtown, but don't bother going there. It's only open two or three days a year. Winemaker Christophe Baron sells every bottle of his wine long before it is released, and he has closed the waiting list to get on his mailing list. Flying Pig is one of several humorous labels done by Cayuse. So if you want to taste a Cayuse wine, you will have to find it at a restaurant, beg it from one of the handful of retailers who get a case or two, or attend one of the local wine events where his wines are poured. It's a pity, because Cayuse wines are among the most distinctive in America; distinctive because Baron

brings with him a classically French perspective on grape growing and winemaking; distinctive because he is as hardheaded as he is hardworking, as opinionated as he is opportunistic.

Baron's family ties are in the Marne Valley, where they own the Champagne house Baron Albert. With a father, two uncles, and several other family members lined up in front of him, young Christophe realized that he would have better luck pursuing his winemaking dreams elsewhere. After studying viticulture and enology in Champagne and Burgundy, he traveled to Oregon and worked briefly at Adelsheim, then interned at Waterbrook in Walla Walla, and spent some time commuting to winemaking assignments in Australia, New Zealand, and Romania. He returned to Walla Walla for good in 1996.

Once he discovered his vineyard sites (profiled in Chapter 4), he knew he'd found the right place to make wine his way, free from restraints. His first couple of vintages were made at Waterbrook, in borrowed space with purchased grapes. The estate vineyards began producing in 1998, and since 2000 Cayuse wines have been entirely estate grown. But still there was no winery; Baron made his wines at Pepper Bridge until he could afford to build what he calls "a simple metal box" in time for the 2005 crush.

For the past decade, Baron's energy, attention, and limited funds have been firmly fixed on vineyard development. He is a passionate man, never more so than when speaking of his biodynamic principles. "When you use forces of death in your vineyard—nasty chemicals—you end up with nasty strains of yeast and you deal with the risk of stuck fermentation," he explains. "*Biodynamie* is dealing with forces of life, not forces of death. So when I bring the fruit and crush it into my fermenters I have no worries; it may take some time but it will finish. Three months, so what? You have to wait, and you bottle it when it's finished. That's ok. It's being low-key and not forcing steps. There's life in each bottle, liquid life. You have to respect that."

Baron's focus has paid off. His wines are the best expression so far of unique Walla Walla flavors, derived entirely from the land itself and from strictly applied Old World winemaking techniques. Cayuse makes about 3000 cases annually of these vineyard-designated, biodynamically raised wines. Small amounts of an excellent Cailloux vineyard viognier are produced, but Baron's license plate, which reads WWSYRAH, gives a good indication of his priorities. Cayuse releases individual syrahs from the Cailloux, En Chamberlin, En Cerise, and Armada vineyards as well as from the most unusual of them all, which Baron calls the Bionic Frog.

That wine, from the Coccinelle vineyard, comes "straight from the soil, from the earth to your table, in honor of my mentor, Noel Verset of Cornas," he explains. Tasted at four years of age, the 2001 Bionic Frog smelled like a charcuterie, with bacon fat, soy, seaweed, and other organic aromas. This is a wine you either like or don't like; it does not resemble any other syrahs, not even Baron's. Aromatic and uniquely flavorful, it constantly jumps through flavor hoops, now showing green tea flavors and aromas, now smoked meat, chocolate, mocha, and cherry.

Camaspelo, Cayuse's Bordeaux blend, smells of earth, undergrowth, and autumnal fungus. Fragrant and floral, wild and gamey, it's spiced with thyme and herbs de Provence. The Widowmaker Cabernet Sauvignon, from En Chamberlin, is another intensely aromatic, sexy wine, with bright, spicy cranberry and cherry fruit. Extremely concentrated, massive, pure, and explosive, it sports California-style jammy, ripe concentrated fruit.

The Armada vineyard is home to what Baron has named his southern Rhône/Spanish project. The ground here is littered with baseball-sized rocks that go down hundreds of feet below the surface, according to Baron. Planted to grenache, syrah, mourvèdre, and tempranillo, he says it is his most challenging venture to date. The grenache he calls "my beetch," explaining that it is at least as hard to grow as pinot noir. "It's fickle," he continues, "but I am pitiless. I like to make them suffer!"

The first wine to be released from the vineyard, a 2003 Armada Syrah, is a stunning wine of amazing complexity. It has layers of depth rarely found in any Washington wines, beginning with dense black fruits, black licorice, smoke, pepper, and charcoal. The trademark Cayuse herbal–green tea–pot-bud elements are there also, more as hints than as layers. The extra time aging in big, neutral barriques has buffed it out; as it breathes in the glass, the wine opens beautifully, gaining flesh and density. It's a tour de force, deeply aromatic and fascinating, and it's a sure sign that, good as Cayuse is already, the best is yet to come.

CHATEAU STE. MICHELLE

Founded 1967
14111 NE 145th
Woodinville, WA 98072
425/488-1133
www.ste-michelle.com
E-mail: info@ste-michelle.com

Score: 88 (25/25/28/10)

This seminal brand, whose roots extend back to the post-Prohibition era, is one of just two in Washington (Columbia is the other) that has produced an unbroken string of varietal wines dating back to 1967. Despite its size, its clout, and its history, Chateau Ste. Michelle continues to be the archetype for all Washington brands and a leader in everything from clonal research to the development of wine tourism.

The Chateau, as it is universally known, traces its origins back to the 1930s, but the modern-day winery was founded in 1967, when the Ste. Michelle label was created for a new line of wines based on French varietal (vinifera) grapes. The name is attributed to the daughter of founder Vic Allison, who, the story goes, was particularly fond of the Mont St. Michel abbey in northern France.

UST purchased the Ste. Michelle winery and brand in 1974 and has been expanding its vineyard and winery holdings ever since. In the mid-1980s the parent company launched Stimson Lane as its wine and spirits holding company. Under the direction of CEO Allen Shoup, Stimson Lane became the corporate parent to a worldwide portfolio of wineries and winemaking alliances. Shoup retired in 2000, and Ted Baseler took over as president and CEO, restructuring the company and tightening its focus on Washington state.

Stimson Lane was renamed Ste. Michelle Wine Estates in 2004. The company now includes in its portfolio six of the seven largest Washington wineries, along with smaller, prestige properties, such as Northstar, Spring Valley Vineyards, and wineries in California and Oregon. Chateau Ste. Michelle, though not as big as sister winery Columbia Crest, remains the flagship brand, producing 1.3 million cases annually. Its releases cover a broad portfolio ranging from inexpensive varietal wines, to limited single-vineyard chardonnays, merlots, and cabernets, to showcase reserve wines and high-profile collaborative ventures such as Eroica and Col Solare.

Ste. Michelle's signature wines continue to be its immensely popular rieslings (it is the biggest producer of riesling in America); its Cold Creek vineyard whites and reds, and its Artist Series meritage. If any single winery can represent the style, the history, and the potential of Washington state viticulture, it is Chateau Ste. Michelle. As Baseler has repeatedly emphasized, "This company is always going to be a Washington wine company. That's what we have passion about, and that is what makes us unique."

Generous with their talent and resources, inclusive in their marketing, and always with an eye on the larger goal (to create an image of world-class quality for the entire region), Ste. Michelle has benchmarked the best wineries in the world, determined to join their ranks. Their extensive lineup of wines is portrayed, more or less accurately, as the products of numerous smaller wineries within the big winery. Ste. Michelle is proud of the fact that it uses its overall size as an asset to make the best grapes and resources available for each individual project.

In recent years, the winery has weathered some significant changes. Following the departure of the multitalented Mike Januik, the winery's red wines stumbled, and the early twenty-first-century vintages were disappointing. Tannic and herbal in 2001, stripped and excessively filtered in 2002, they began to return to form in 2003 as new winemaker Bob Bertheau, working closely with head of vineyard operations Doug Gore, took over the final blending.

Bertheau, brought in to make the white wines following the departure of winemaker Erik Olsen, had an immediate impact. His five different chardonnays are beautifully crafted and distinctive, with better integration of the oak and more softness and complexity in the mouth than their predecessors. The top of the line "Ethos" chardonnay has intriguing streaks of orange peel and citrus zest, along with buttered nuts, toast, and hazelnut flavors, all threaded through the long, silky finish. The Cold Creek chardonnay, which has always delivered extra intensity, drills down into the heart of the palate with refreshing acids and crisply defined fruit.

From the early 1970s on, rieslings have been one of Ste. Michelle's strong suits. The winery makes more than 550,000 cases of what it calls its "everyday" riesling, the Columbia Valley bottling, and it's a gem, loaded with fresh fruit flavors of peach, pear, and melon, lightly spiced, and perfectly framed by vibrant acids. A newly designated Indian Wells vineyard riesling showcases ripe, tropical flavors from a new AVA, the Wahluke Slope. The latest vintages of Eroica, a riesling collaboration with Ernst Loosen of the Mosel's Dr. Loosen estate, continue to evolve and add refining touches. Eroica single-handedly has elevated Washington riesling out of the cheap tasting room wine category into the realm of more serious, German-style wines, briskly walking the line between crisp apple-citrus and off-dry honeyed sweetness with tremendous grace and length.

Bertheau was made winemaker for reds as well in 2004 and has vowed to restore to those wines a proper balance of tannin with acid, better separation of programs, proper barrel selection, and new percentage(s) of oak. These are well-thought-out goals that seem designed to correct the harsh tannins and herbal rusticity that had crept into even the Cold Creek and Artist Series wines. Given that Bertheau's reign is just beginning, it is not yet possible to evaluate the results.

But in 2006 a look back at the winery's history, at a pair of tastings of some of the cabernets made during its first decade, provided solid evidence that Washington fruit, even then, had the guts and tenacity to age. The early Ste. Michelle cabernets, from vintages 1969, 1970, and 1973 through 1978, were all still drinkable; several were standouts.

When Bertheau speaks of "a better separation of programs," he is acknowledging that for some time the winery's Artist Series meritage, its Col Solare, and some of its reserves have been difficult to tell apart. Even before the troubling, tannic wines of 2001 and 2002, these high-end reds seemed to draw on many of the same vineyard sources and were chiefly differentiated by their labels.

Col Solare, now the centerpiece of a new vineyard and winery on Red Mountain as well as the cornerstone of a joint marketing alliance between Ste. Michelle Wine Estates and Marchesi Antinori, seems likely to benefit as much as or more than any other single wine.

At the moment, Ste. Michelle's white wines are as good as ever, in some cases better. The single-vineyard wines from Cold Creek, both white and red, are world-class, and the Canoe Ridge and Indian Wells designates are beginning to express identifiable regional styles. The Eroica riesling is among the best in the country, and the Horse Heaven vineyard sauvignon blanc merits its vineyard-designated status. The excellent Ethos chardonnay now has several companion reds: Ethos merlot, cabernet sauvignon, and syrah. Though Bertheau had only a limited hand in making the 2003s, the syrah is a real success, a seductive, spicy wine whose tart fruits tumble out in a pile of mixed berry, cherry, chocolate, baking spices, and nicely integrated oak.

Given its historic importance and dominating role in the development of Washington wine and the dynamic leadership and winemaking talent now running the company, it seems certain that all of Chateau Ste. Michelle's affordable wines will once again be textbook examples of soundly made, varietally correct Washington fruit, while the single-vineyard and reserve bottlings will stand comfortably beside the much more limited offerings from the state's leading boutiques.

COLUMBIA CREST

Founded 1984
PO Box 231, Highway 221
Paterson, WA 99345
509/875-4302
www.columbia-crest.com
E-mail: info@columbia-crest.com

Score: 92 (26/26/30/10)

What began 25 years ago as a massive vineyard project offering a blush riesling as one of its first wines has become a nationally recognized leader in delivering wines of exceptional flavor at value prices. Merlots are the principal calling card, but Columbia Crest, now the state's largest brand (1.7 million cases and climbing), competes favorably in every category.

It's startling to recall that back in 1984, when its first wines were introduced, Columbia Crest was a one-wine brand that offered just a nonvintage blend of riesling, gewürztraminer, and muscat. From such humble origins has grown Washington state's largest winery.

Varietals, at first all white, debuted with the '86 vintage. Chardonnay, sauvignon blanc, sémillon, riesling, gewürztraminer, and chenin blanc were offered, soon joined by merlot and cabernet sauvignon. These days the winery makes three separate tiers of wines. Eighteen of them are distributed nationally, and a few others are sold exclusively in the Pacific Northwest. Roughly 60 percent of its sales are of the low-priced Two Vines line, and all but a tiny percentage of the rest is the midpriced Grand Estates.

Columbia Crest Reserve wines account for less than 1 percent of the total production, which has passed 1.7 million cases a year and continues to climb. Recent AC Nielsen data ranks Columbia Crest sixth among all domestic table wine brands, with a bullet, as we used to say in radio. Overall sales are growing at better than three times the national average, fueled principally by its cabernet sauvignon (the number two best-selling national brand), its merlot (number three), and its chardonnay (number six). The Two Vines shiraz has also been a huge success, and it is now the nation's top-selling domestic shiraz.

Retailers love this brand. Typical are these comments from one of the largest southern California wine outlets, which frequently features Columbia Crest wines in its newsletter: "If we were going to put something from the USA in a world value competition, Columbia Crest would probably have the best chance of any entity." No surprise then that the winery consistently finds its wines, particularly the merlots, cabernets, and chardonnays, listed in leading wine publications as best buys, top 100, and so on.

Along with the sheer volume of the Columbia Crest portfolio, its high quality and bargain pricing make it the only Washington winery that can compete on a national level with behemoth California brands such as Kendall-Jackson. Credit the 2500-acre Columbia Crest vineyard, first planted in the early 1980s, which contributes fruit from vines more than

20 years old. Access to so much mature fruit allows winemaker Ray Einberger to pick and choose carefully, so the winery's size becomes more of an asset than a liability.

Einberger, whose background includes time as Maître de Chai (cellar master) at Mondavi's Opus One, came to Washington in 1993. He worked at Columbia Crest under then-winemaker Doug Gore for a decade, developing its reserve wine program, before being elevated to the winemaker position in 2003. Einberger is one of those guys who seems to have been blessed with the fun gene. His eyes twinkle, his voice sparkles, even his mustache looks like it's winking at you when he speaks.

He set up the reserve operation as a separate boutique winery within the larger winery, applying French grand cru–style winemaking techniques he had learned at Mouton with the Opus One team. That means hand-picked fruit, small open-top fermentation, secondary fermentation in barrel, blending shortly after fermentation, and long aging in new oak. "From grape to finish, it's done by a separate crew; we're going for a small Opus or a small Mouton," he explains with some pride.

Each of Columbia Crest's three tiers has a distinct style and marketing niche. The "Two Vines" wines, priced around $8, are soft, immediately drinkable wines powered with good, ripe fruit and no-frills winemaking. The usual cheap wine tricks of the trade (excessive use of oak flavorings and residual sugar) are not needed here. The "Grand Estates" wines, priced around $11, offer a significant step up in concentration, weight, and the use of new oak. "We want to make a $20 bottle of wine that sells for 10 bucks," says Einberger, and by and large he succeeds.

The reserve wines, though very good, face stiffer competition. Priced between $30 and $35, they cross swords with many boutique wines from Washington as well as some of the entry-level reds from top Napa Valley estates. It may confuse some consumers to see a $30 price tag on a wine from what they believe is an $8 "value" brand. But in the long run, wine marketers agree, it is smarter to elevate a value brand by adding superpremium wines than to risk devaluing a superpremium brand by tacking on a low-end line.

Ultimately, it's the connection between the consumer palate and the consumer wallet that measures success. Columbia Crest is so successful that Ted Baseler, CEO of parent company Ste. Michelle Wine Estates, calls it "the growth engine driving the company." One could easily conclude that this brand is the engine driving the global aspirations of every winery in Washington state.

Twenty years ago, when Columbia Crest was first introduced, few would have imagined such success. But in retrospect it seems inevitable, if you agree that the key to success for Washington vintners is to express intense and pure varietal fruit flavors enlivened by vivid acids. A state known for its apples should and does produce brilliant rieslings and other white wines, just as the globally recognized quality of Washington cherries and berries presages similar flavors in its red wines.

It's often stated that the benchmark Washington wines are a perfect synthesis of California ripeness and French elegance. Credit Columbia Crest, more than any other brand, for showcasing that style to the broadest possible segment of the wine-drinking world.

DELILLE CELLARS

Founded 1992
PO Box 2233
Woodinville, WA 98072
425/489-0544
www.delillecellars.com
E-mail: contact@delillecellars.com

Score: 88 (28/25/27/8)

DeLille's founders, Charles and Greg Lill, Chris Upchurch, and Jay Soloff, embody the ideal mix of marketing magic and winemaking savvy. Trace the arc of DeLille's development from a tiny start-up modeled on the best chateaux of Bordeaux (right down to its second label, named D2 for the highway running through the Médoc) to its present-day portfolio of brilliantly conceived, unique wines. Encapsulated is the history of Washington's evolution from a state dominated by farmer-growers to one dedicated to the highest goals of the true garagiste.

DeLille Cellars occupies a picture postcard setting, from the restored 1890s farmhouse to the meadow dotted with lazily grazing sheep and the occasional peacock. The lovely 10-acre site, high above the Woodinville Valley floor, overlooks Chateau Ste. Michelle and Columbia winery.

The partners who founded the winery—Charles Lill (now retired), Chris Upchurch, Greg Lill, and Jay Soloff—have turned it into one of the most dedicated party palaces in Woodinville, complete with a 40-foot dining table that has hosted many a fine dinner. The dinners, a fixture at DeLille since its first wines were released, feature a visiting celebrity chef, a sampling of DeLille wines, and wines from a guest winery. "At first it was all about association," Soloff explains. "In 1995, no one knew who DeLille was. But that first year we had Quilceda Creek, Andrew Will, Chateau Ste. Michelle, and Columbia as guest wineries." Attendees couldn't quite grasp why a brand-new winery was promoting other people's wines, but the tactic worked perfectly. DeLille, by association, gained instant credibility.

Now one of the state's premier producers of Bordeaux blends and Rhône-inspired wines (under their Chaleur Estate and Doyenne imprints), DeLille finds itself the name brand that up-and-coming wineries want to be associated with. In contrast to the elegant tasting room and offices, the wines are made in a humble warehouse, nothing charming about it. But what emerges from the pristine racks of French oak barrels is pure magic.

Magic is what winemaker Chris Upchurch speaks about when describing his newest project, the 18-acre Grand Ciel vineyard on Red Mountain. Beautifully sited (adjacent to Ciel du Cheval), it was planted in the spring of 2001, following two years of extensive (and expensive) clonal research. "The one thing all vineyards face," says Upchurch, "is the potential for uneven ripening, when it doesn't

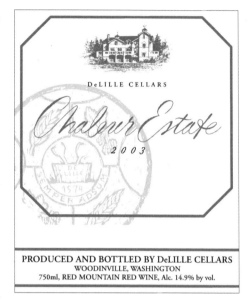

PRODUCED AND BOTTLED BY DeLILLE CELLARS
WOODINVILLE, WASHINGTON
750ml, RED MOUNTAIN RED WINE, Alc. 14.9% by vol.

happen in that magic moment that great Bordeaux gets. The idea we had from the start was to get grapes to ripen evenly. Everything was done with the idea that it is possible to get even ripening here in Washington."

Clonal research is the new viticultural frontier in Washington state, and Upchurch and his partners believe that their pioneering mix of cabernet and syrah clones at Grand Ciel will give them a five- or six-year jump-start on their competitors. The first couple of vintages so impressed the winemaking team that they have separated out specific blocks in both 2004 and 2005 and designated them for a new, superpremium DeLille bottling, to be called Grand Ciel. Grand Ciel will be 100 percent cabernet sauvignon, made from one or more of the new clones. Early barrel tastings of both the 2004 and 2005 vintages make it clear that their excitement is well founded.

In a sense, Grand Ciel brings them full circle. DeLille Cellars began with the goal of producing exceptional, Bordeaux-quality, cabernet-based wines. The flagship wine, Chaleur Estate, is now in its fifteenth year. At a retrospective tasting of the first decade's releases, the 10 wines on display were balanced and silky, most still quite juicy and youthful. The wines from the mid-1990s were in particularly fine condition, the '95 a standout for me, showing early hints of cinnamon, cedar, incense, and tobacco, with concentrated raspberry fruit at the core.

The blend of the Chaleur red is consistently about two-thirds cabernet sauvignon, one-quarter merlot, and the rest cabernet franc, mostly from Red Mountain vineyards. There is also a Chaleur Estate blanc made from sémillon and sauvignon blanc. Vinified in a rich, buttery style, at times just this side of unctuous, it is smoothly wrapped in lingering layers of citrus oils, stone fruits, melon, and nuts.

The winery also makes a vineyard-designated Harrison Hill Red wine, a Bordeaux blend showcasing the second-oldest vinifera vines in the state. A graceful mix of old-vine bramble, Yakima Valley herbs, and other peppery spices, with dry tannins redolent of Earl Gray tea, this supremely elegant wine wears its flavors like an immaculately tailored suit.

D2 is DeLille's second wine, and in terms of quality there are few wineries in the state whose best wines exceed it. Merlot-driven and blended from barrels not used in the Chaleur Estate, it is more likely to express vintage variation. Depending on the year, it can be ripe or herbal, hot or soft; on occasion it may even resemble a somewhat funky Bordeaux, replete with truffles, leather, and earth.

Upchurch spends a lot of time visiting wineries in France, and his is one of the most experienced and globally savvy palates in the state. He and assistant winemaker Chris Peterson are both Rhône wine lovers, and DeLille's initial experiment with syrah ("only 100 cases") has blossomed into a full-fledged winery of its own (see Doyenne in Chapter 8, "The Rookies"). Total case production for both wineries should reach 10,000 in 2006, about two-thirds of it DeLille.

HEDGES FAMILY ESTATE

Founded 1987
53511 N. Sunset Road
Benton City, WA 99320
509/588-3155
www.hedgesfamilyestate.com
E-mail: info@hedgesfamilyestate.com

Score: 86 (25/26/25/10)

Tom and Anne-Marie Hedges began their family's wine odyssey with a brilliant business plan, marketing Washington wines from a "virtual" winery to buyers in Scandinavia. They parlayed that early success into an audacious vision for establishing vines, a magnificent chateau, and (most unlikely of all) tourism on Red Mountain.

Hedges has always been a smartly run business operation, from its early focus on a single, vivid, fruity blend of cabernet sauvignon and merlot, to its substantial investment in building its vineyards and winery on (then) little-known Red Mountain, to its efforts to gain legal approval of Red Mountain as an official American viticultural area. Along with marketing savvy and consistently well-made, affordable wines, from both purchased and estate-grown fruit, Hedges has kept a tight focus on Bordeaux blends and varietals and avoided the temptation to expand past its core competence.

In 2005, with an eye toward both changing market conditions and the need to plan for the next generation, owners Anne-Marie and Tom Hedges elected to change the name to Hedges Family Estate. Hedges remains the largest family-owned winery in Washington (just slightly ahead of Barnard Griffin), with brother Pete Hedges heading up the winemaking team and son Christophe and his wife, Maggie, doing sales and marketing.

The workhorse wines are the value-priced CMS red and CMS white (a small amount of CMS rosé is marketed locally), which account for 50,000 cases annually. The red came first, a cabernet-merlot-syrah blend that has always tasted like a more expensive wine. It has a European polish to it, mixing plum, berry, and cherry fruit with darker streaks of tar, coffee, and smoke. You'll find it offers unusual complexity for a budget red, and it clocks in at a reasonable 13.5 percent alcohol.

The companion CMS white was introduced in 2004; it's mostly "C" (chardonnay) and "S" (sauvignon blanc), with a splash of marsanne providing the "M." It continues the brand's winning streak, with each of the three grapes adding something special and the whole seemingly more than the sum of its parts. The sauvignon blanc lifts it, giving it vivid acid and bright herb, the chardonnay fills in round apple and pear flavors, and the little bit of marsanne adds a hint of peach.

Apart from CMS, Hedges Family Estates makes 11,000 cases of red blends and single-vineyard wines from the three estate vineyards that surround the chateau-like winery atop Red Mountain.

The Hedges Estate vineyard opens out toward the west in front of the grand chateau. It was first planted in 1991, to 18 acres each of cabernet sauvignon and merlot and a single acre of cabernet franc. In 1998 and 2000 a two-acre block of Portuguese Port varietals was added, along with a bit of petit verdot and malbec.

The 40-acre Bel'Villa vineyard is the highest-planted vineyard on Red Mountain. Most of it is devoted to cabernet and merlot, along with three acres of cabernet franc and six of syrah. The Red Mountain vineyard completes the trio. Managed and farmed (though not owned) by Hedges, it is considered a part of the estate.

Almost all of Hedges Family Estate's non-CMS production consists of its "Three Vineyards" Red. Broad-shouldered and powerful, it's a supple, meaty, and tannic blend of 56 percent merlot, 40 percent cabernet sauvignon, and a smattering of cabernet franc and syrah.

The rest of the winery's production is sliced into very fine and pricey slivers. The "Two Vineyards" Red Mountain blend is a limited (350-case) selection of Bel'Villa and Hedges vineyard fruit, four-fifths cabernet, and one-fifth syrah. Focused, young, tight, and full of promise, it's got bright cranberry, cherry, and currant fruits married to light chocolate and black tea and showing some of the gravelly minerality that characterizes Red Mountain fruit. Less successful is the "Two Vineyards Reserve," a bit bigger than the regular bottling but lacking the same level of complexity and finesse.

The "Single Vineyard Cabernet Sauvignon," "Single Vineyard Merlot," and "Single Vineyard Syrah" are new projects, designed to occupy the very top of the Hedges pyramid. They will all be priced at $100 and produced in miniboutique quantities. Tasted prior to release, they had not had sufficient time in bottle to be fairly evaluated.

L'ECOLE N° 41

Founded 1983
PO Box 111, 41 Lowden School Road
Lowden, WA 99360
509/525-0940
www.lecole.com
E-mail: info@lecole.com

Score: 86 (25/26/25/10)

What began as their parents' little retirement project has become an international force. Daughter Megan and son-in-law Marty Clubb have taken the winery in the converted schoolhouse and grown it to a sizeable 35,000-case operation by tirelessly marketing their wines from London to Hong Kong and all across the United States. Along the way, L'Ecole has earned a reputation as the nation's leader in making and promoting sémillon.

If sémillon is Washington's least appreciated great grape, then L'Ecole N° 41 might arguably be the state's least appreciated great winery. Named for the old Frenchtown schoolhouse in which it is headquartered, L'Ecole began as a retirement project by the late, much-loved Baker and Jean Ferguson. Improbably, the Fergusons, who were well into their sixties when the winery was begun, struck gold with their first wines, a broad, chocolatey merlot and an oily, honeyed sémillon. Medals and critical acclaim came immediately, helped by the unusual story, the colorful label (a watercolor drawing of the schoolhouse done by an eight-year-old cousin), and the fact that L'Ecole was just the third modern-day winery to open in the Walla Walla Valley.

The winery still makes plenty of merlot, but it is its sémillons that push it ahead of all competitors. Daughter Megan and son-in-law Marty Clubb met while both were working on graduate degrees at MIT's Sloan School of Management. They returned to Walla

Walla in 1989, Marty gamely taking over as both winemaker and general manager at the winery while Megan pursued a career in banking (she is president of the region's oldest institution, Baker-Boyer Bank).

The Clubbs have expanded smartly, building steadily on L'Ecole's early strengths and ramping up quality across the board. "Baker really set the thinking that sémillon was a varietal to pursue in Washington," notes Marty, and no winery in the country does more to pursue it than L'Ecole.

There are three different dry sémillons and from time to time a late-harvest version as well. The "Barrel Fermented" cuvée blends in up to 20 percent sauvignon blanc; the "Seven Hills Vineyard" bottling (from the estate vineyard) is also barrel fermented and displays lush, ripe, rich, round, peachy-citrus fruit. The "Fries Vineyard" sémillon is often the biggest, creamiest, and oakiest of all, thanks to extended barrel aging on the lees. Deep, rich, and golden, it is bursting with ripe and delicious fruit flavors of green apples and pears, with bright, toasty tropical notes.

L'Ecole's red wines account for about 70 percent of the 35,000 cases made annually. All are instantly likeable, offering ripe, luscious black fruits wrapped in smooth, chocolatey tannins. They may at times be criticized as two-dimensional, with flavors of fruit and barrel taking precedence over soil, but no one would ever say that these wines are not delicious and full.

"Merlot is still King at L'Ecole," Clubb maintains. There are two made, both blends that may include significant amounts of cabernet sauvignon and cabernet franc.  The "Columbia Valley" bottling is a Right bank–styled Bordeaux blend, 80 percent merlot, 12 percent cab franc, and a smattering of cabernet sauvignon, petit verdot, and/or carmenère. Berries and spice, chocolate and herb, and many other lightly applied nuances make this a pleasure to sip. The estate-grown "Seven Hills Vineyard" merlot is another fine effort, tannic and sculpted, with cedary, silky black cherry fruit.

The 200-acre Seven Hills vineyard, in which L'Ecole is a partner with Leonetti and Pepper Bridge, grows exceptional sémillon, merlot, cabernet sauvignon, and syrah. Originally planted in 1981, it is the cornerstone of L'Ecole's recently launched estate Bordeaux blend dubbed "Perigee." A big, chewy wine, its nose suggests violets, truffle, fresh-turned earth, sweet spice, hay, and leather and continues on with a panoply of exotic, well-matched fruit flavors, hints of stone and pepper, and a finish of broad, chocolatey oak.

Its companion is the Pepper Bridge vineyard "Apogee," a more supple, lighter wine with flavors of cherry and blackberry fruit, hints of dill and herb, and a sprinkle of coffee. L'Ecole also makes a pair of cabernets: the Columbia Valley cabernet, a pure varietal bottling from vines averaging over 25 years of age, and the Walla Walla Valley cabernet, a vibrant mix of boysenberry, blueberry, black raspberry, and black cherry. There is also a Seven Hills vineyard syrah, spicy and powerful, with layers of citrus and tart berries, with a green tea streak through the substantial tannins.

Much of L'Ecole's purchased Columbia Valley fruit comes from name vineyards, such as Klipsun, Milbrandt, Bacchus, and Dionysus. L'Ecole has the reputation and buying power to source from the best for its non-estate chardonnays, cabernets, and merlots. One final wine, not to be missed, is its "Walla Voila" chenin blanc, made from 25-year-old vines in a lively Vouvray style. Good chenin blanc (as opposed to tasting room plonk) is a rarity in this country, and L'Ecole's is one of the best.

LEONETTI CELLAR

Founded 1978
1875 Foothills Lane
Walla Walla, WA 99362
509/525-1428
www.leonetticellar.com
E-mail: info@leonetticellar.com

Score: 98 (30/28/30/10)

For most of the past three decades, Leonetti has been the iconic Washington red wine producer. Despite his enormous success, founder Gary Figgins, now working closely with his son Chris, refuses to rest on his laurels. Leonetti's 30-year commitment to ultimately make its wines exclusively from Walla Walla grapes is at last coming to fruition.

As we sat on the porch of his modest ranch home in the summer of 1986, Gary Figgins, whose Leonetti Cellar was already enjoying quite a bit of acclaim for its elegant, oaky cabernets and creamy merlots, pointed to the little shed where his press, fermenting tanks, barrels, and case storage were jammed. Soon we'll have a real cellar, he told me, explaining that he was about to embark on a construction project that would enable him to ramp up production from 1200 to 2000 cases. The new winery, a sturdy building with 18-inch walls of native basalt and cellars dug deep into the earth, was completed in time for the 1989 crush. "I'll be able to heat it with a candle and cool it with an ice cube," he told me proudly.

Figgins first sampled wine at his grandparents' home. Frank and Rose Leonetti, who moved to Walla Walla from Calabria in the early 1900s, ran a 20-acre truck farm, which included an acre of vineyard. On visits to his grandfather's wine cellar in the 1950s, Figgins would taste homemade wines from the family vines, a grape called Black Prince. In 1968, Figgins began his own home winemaking experiments, and in 1974 he planted an acre of cabernet and riesling in his backyard. It's now the oldest vinifera vineyard in the valley. He bonded Leonetti Cellar in 1978, the first vinifera winery in Walla Walla since the repeal of Prohibition. Eleven years later, just as the new winery was nearing completion, he retired from his full-time work as a machinist at Continental Can to devote himself completely to winemaking. His goals, which are now almost fully realized, were to focus his efforts on producing just three or four red wines a year while gradually moving away from using Columbia Valley grapes.

He dreamed that one day Leonetti wines would come exclusively from estate-grown, Walla Walla fruit.

Leonetti cabernets were among the first in the state to use cabernet franc in the blend. Along with the winery's merlot and the occasional reserve cabernet, they were notable for their plump, ripe fruit coated with layer upon layer of rich, fat, succulent oak. Figgins worked tirelessly on his barrel regimen, creating a unique mix of Hungarian, Oregon, other American, and various French oaks that imparted decadently rich flavors of toast, chocolate, espresso, and licorice to the wines.

Throughout the 1990s Leonetti enjoyed a growing national reputation as Washington's first (and only) "cult" winery. Production climbed toward 5000 cases, and another new winery, including a striking underground barrel room, was constructed in time for the 2001 crush. During these same years, a series of land purchases brought substantial vineyard holdings into the fold.

A partnership with L'Ecole's Marty Clubb and Pepper Bridge's Norm McKibben in the Seven Hills vineyard provided the grapes for Leonetti's reserve wines and contributed to the regular cabs and merlots also. In 1997, the 16-acre Mill Creek Upland vineyard was planted to cabernet sauvignon, merlot, sangiovese, and petit verdot. Now a decade old, Mill Creek Upland grapes have dominated Leonetti's reserve blend in recent vintages and serve as the backbone of the cabernet.

The 28-acre Loess vineyard, located directly behind the winery, was added in 2002. It has the same basic mix of grapes as Mill Creek, along with a tiny bit of malbec and viognier (made strictly for home consumption). Loess began bearing in 2005, with grapes going to Northstar, Pepper Bridge, L'Ecole, Long Shadows (Sequel syrah), and Waters as well as Leonetti.

The 55-acre C.S. Figgins estate is just now being planted. First into the ground (in 2005) were 11 acres of merlot, destined for Leonetti. These grapes will be the final piece of the puzzle that allows the winery to convert its varietal merlot bottling exclusively to Walla Walla Valley fruit. The expectation is that Leonetti wines will be entirely estate grown by 2008 or 2009.

The newest vineyard project is a partnership (again with Norm McKibben, Marty and Megan Clubb, and McKibben's partner, Bob Rupar) that recently purchased 1700 acres above the existing Seven Hills vineyard. As much as 1000 acres is plantable, deep loess soils over fractured basalt, ranging from 900 to 1500 feet in elevation. Leonetti, L'Ecole, and Pepper Bridge winery will each keep a prime chunk of vineyard for their own use and develop the infrastructure (pumps, ponds, mainlines, roads, and so on) for the whole property. Once the county approves their proposal to divide the remainder into smaller (20- or 40-acre) parcels, they will sell them off, hoping to create a very high-end community of boutique vineyards and wineries.

Leonetti's own production has climbed past 6000 cases; roughly half is merlot, and most of the other half is cabernet sauvignon. In the best vintages a small amount of a Walla Walla Valley Reserve is produced. The only addition to the original lineup is a sangiovese, beautifully crafted, aromatic, and high-toned, with plummy, pretty cherry fruit. Much of it comes from the original estate vineyard, now planted to a half acre each of merlot, syrah, and sangiovese, and an acre of cabernet franc.

No great winery stands still. If there was a knock on Leonetti throughout its first decades, it was that the wines didn't age all that well. In some vintages, the seamless, gorgeous, buttery mix of ripe fruit and rich oak cracked up after a few years. Rare indeed was the Leonetti wine that tasted better at 10 years of age than it did on release.

As son Chris Figgins has assumed more and more responsibilities, especially in the area of vineyard management, there have been subtle changes in Leonetti wines, becoming more pronounced with each passing year. The newer vintages seem more fruit-driven, more classically styled. The oak is more laid back than laid on, and the wines seem less buttery and fat than before, better structured for aging.

As we tasted through the new releases in March of 2006, Chris Figgins shared with me his ideas about Leonetti's ongoing evolution. "We try to think long term," he began. "One thing you'll notice across our wines, we're going towards being entirely estate grown, and all of that pushes me philosophically towards showing off our vineyards. The crux of the matter is I'm going for less oak and better integration of that oak." He went on to describe a "slow evolution" in his and his father's thinking about where and how to institute changes. The development of estate vineyards has been Gary's goal from the beginning, and Chris has a degree and a particular interest in soil science. He believes, and I would certainly agree, that the most significant future improvements in Washington winemaking will be centered in the vineyard. "In terms of the winemaking, we're very much a team," he continued, "with Dad standing back and making sure I don't screw things up. There was never a conscious decision to cut back on oak; I like where we're at now. I want to show off our vineyards. I want to make terroir-driven wines. Let's have hints of vanilla as a background spice and let the fruit shine through."

The "new" Leonettis are more contemplative, more subtle wines. They are just as innovative as in the past, but moving toward a more contemporary style. Just as Gary Figgins explored the many nuances and uses of oak barrels, working with the best grapes he could purchase at the time, Chris Figgins is now focused on what can be done with newly available estate-grown fruit. The trade-off, for the time being, is that the estate vines are young, and the decadently rich barrel flavors have been pulled back to accommodate their somewhat lighter flavors. "We've never fallen into the trap of resting on our laurels," says Gary. "There's the double emphasis on staying ahead of the pack. It's so much better to make dust than to eat it!"

It's a bit startling to realize that as Leonetti moves into its fourth decade, it is a winery in transition. But change is inevitable, essential, and even desirable when it is handled this well. The new Leonetti wines respect the winery's rich legacy and point to an even brighter future.

MATTHEWS ESTATE

Founded 1993
16116 140th Place NE
Woodinville, WA 98072
425/487-9810
www.matthewswinery.com
E-mail: info@matthewswinery.com

Score: 89 (28/25/27/9)

Besides crafting his own superlative lineup of stylishly blended reds and creamy, delicious white wines, Matt Loso has become a virtual one-man mentor-incubator for a burgeoning crop of Woodinville wineries.

Matt Loso has never been to Europe, didn't study enology at UC Davis (or anywhere else), and by his own assessment breaks most of the generally accepted rules of winemaking. He picks late, blends early, uses native yeasts, racks infrequently, and generally raises hell with his growers. He also makes two of the best red wines in the country. "I really watch Dominus, Cain Cellars, and Spring Mountain Vineyard," he explained as we sampled the new wines from barrel. He practices what some call minimum-intervention winemaking: Bring in the grapes, ferment them, blend them, and let them sit pretty much undisturbed until bottling.

Loso's winemaking ideas have been gleaned from years of formal and informal apprenticeships, beginning with frequent visits to Chateau Ste. Michelle and Columbia winery and continuing with a year at long-gone French Creek Cellars. "I was scraping mold off of tanks of lemberger," he remembers. Thus a star was born.

He next worked for Doug McCrea, making the first few barrels of his own Matthews wine in 1993. "The last time I had a real job," Loso says with a certain amount of glee, "was in 1995, driving a forklift in the R.E.I. warehouse. That's where I learned my forklift skills." He gypsied around for the next few years, making wines in a number of locations, until a silent partner's investment enabled him to buy eight acres just outside of

Woodinville, where he built his functional, unpretentious winery just in time for the 1999 crush.

Matthews wines have been excellent all along, but business success has come in fits and starts. Up until 1999, Loso was making fewer than 1500 cases of wine a year. Following the sizeable new investment in property and winemaking equipment, he bumped production up to 3000 cases. Those wines were offered to his mailing list customers on September 10, 2001. "I usually sold out everything within 60 days," he recalls. "But the next day was 9/11. I didn't receive a single order until the following January." Scary times for a young winemaker stretched to the financial breaking point.

Loso prevailed, aided by a large order from Gary McLean, for whom he now makes the Barons V wines. He also began consulting and took on his own apprentices, many of whom have now set up their own warehouse wineries in the neighborhood.

In 2005, Loso hired Erica Orr (since departed) to be his assistant winemaker. Loso outfitted a state-of-the-art laboratory to serve as her playground. A return to prosperity has also allowed him to purchase an oak upright fermenting tank, used once, from Harlan Estate; it will handle his cabernet from now on. Recently arrived are a pair of egg-shaped, French concrete fermenters, especially designed for sauvignon blanc. "It's the new old thing in winemaking," he explains. "There's a special shape for each type of wine, sort of a giant Riedel fermenter." Loso is determined to make great sauvignon blanc, and he believes that this is the ticket. On the drawing board are still bigger plans, for a chateau, a tasting room, and underground wine caves, Leonetti style, to be built in the coming year on his eight-acre site.

Loso is never afraid to depart from generally accepted winemaking practices. He judges when to pick his grapes by taste, as many others do. But where standard practice is to consult the lab numbers for brix, which measures sugar, Loso disagrees. "The number one thing I watch is for is pH," he says. "Most wineries pick by sugar level; I believe it's the wrong way to pick. People should look for physiological maturity."

He blends his red wines shortly after fermentation is complete, rather than waiting until just before bottling. He believes this gives the finished wines more time to integrate their various components. I can't argue with him. Matthews Estate wines are dense and saturated, some almost jet black, and tightly packed with layers of flavor. They are big and potent, yet they retain perfect balance, are wonderfully harmonious, and convey a surprising impression of elegance.

Sauvignon blancs are yeasty, bone dry, and richly textured; Loso aims for Dagueneau-like intensity. Of his 4000-case total production, one-quarter consists of an excellent Claret, his declassified Bordeaux blend. Very limited amounts of syrah and petit verdot are offered, mainly to mailing list customers. These are wines well worth having; a recent vintage of a Hedges vineyard syrah, as black as the night sky, exploded from the glass with blueberry-blackberry fruit, streaked with anise, bitter chocolate, soy, and espresso. A tour de force.

Matthews Estate's flagship Columbia Valley Red is being broken out into three different premium wines: Red Mountain, Wahluke, and Horse Heaven blends, 400 cases of each. "I'm always looking back to whatever roots we want to follow," Loso explains. "I want to follow either a vineyard or a small area. That creates up-and-down vintage variation. But picking AVAs I know I can ripen gives me a bit more peace of mind."

Once a year he takes samples to his growers and shows them how their wine compared with others. "I tell them I made these exactly the same way; what happened to yours?" he confides. Loso is good enough and his push for quality unassailable, so most growers take it in stride. Those that can't, or won't, make the changes he requests are quickly replaced.

McCREA CELLARS

Founded 1988
13443 118th Avenue SE
Rainier, WA 98576
360/458-9463
www.mccreacellars.com
E-mail: mccreawine@aol.com

Score: 87 (27/25/25/10)

Doug McCrea, Washington state's leading Rhône Ranger, has both pioneered and dramatically elevated the quality of the state's syrahs. His early work with grenache was visionary, and he continues to expand the reach of the state's vintners with fascinating wines such as his varietal counoise.

If we didn't have Doug McCrea making wine in Washington, we'd have to invent him. No one has been more focused or tireless when it comes to exploring wines made from Rhône Valley varietals. And now that it seems half the winemakers in the state have jumped on the syrah bandwagon, McCrea, who planted some of the very first Washington syrah 15 years ago, remains way out in front of the pack, making such unusual varietal bottlings as roussanne, counoise, and mourvèdre.

When I sat down with him some years ago to talk syrah, McCrea enthusiastically spoke of its "animal side." "Some people call it gamey, some call it road kill," he grinned, going on to explain that in his estimation those animal aromas, combined with an earthy element, add olfactory appeal to the natural juicy robustness of the grape.

When he first decided to explore Rhône grapes in Washington, only David Lake had planted syrah, and few winemakers even in California were doing much of anything with grenache. McCrea's first grenache–syrah blend was named "Mariah" and then changed to "Tierra del Sol." It was an explosively fruity, forward wine that quickly won him a devoted following. McCrea literally begged growers to plant more, and he convinced Dick Boushey and Jim Holmes (Ciel du Cheval) to give it a try just as he rolled out his first varietal syrah in 1994. A blockbuster of a wine, it was the one that put syrah on the Washington map. "That really launched it," McCrea recalls. "We got some very high scores, and did two versions, one with American oak, one with French oak. 'AD' was the French and 'BC' was the American oak."

The Boushey and Holmes plantings bore their first crops in 1997, followed by the Elerding vineyard in 1998, and suddenly the grape seemed to find some traction in Washington. "We're on the launchpad," McCrea enthused. "The rocket's gearing up, and the engine's just fired. They've just said minus one and you can see the smoke coming out. We've got a lot of miles to log before we're gonna know what syrah's all about."

We're still logging miles, but we've definitely left the launchpad. McCrea's early experiments with American oak and French oak versions of syrah have blossomed into a full range of bottlings, each designed to express a different style. Unlike many wineries that go on a single-vineyard binge, each of McCrea's wines is identifiably unique, thoughtful, and relevant.

The lineup begins with a southern Rhône–style blend named Sirocco (for the hot wind that blows from Africa across the Mediterranean Sea). Peppery, tannic, and bursting with mixed fruits and barrel toast, it's a potpourri of fruit flavors, a zesty, insouciant wine that comes on bright, toasty, forceful, and always interesting. Next up is a blended "Washington" syrah, juicy and tart, with plenty of pucker and tannin. Then the "Amerique," from Klipsun and Ciel grapes, polished, ripe, and forward, with lots of vanilla cookie scents and flavors. It aims for an Australian shiraz style.

The single-vineyard "Boushey Grande Côte" is a masterful example of McCrea's belief that syrah reflects its terroir—the soil in which it is grown. Forward and opulent, it's packed with flavors and scents of smoked meat, herb, gorgeous red fruits, and pretty chocolate. Despite its heft, it remains precise, focused, and beautifully defined.

The other single-vineyard syrah, "Ciel du Cheval," exhibits deep, succulent black fruits underscored by tart acid, bone-dry tannins, and the vineyard's typical mineral streak. Finally there is the "Cuvée Orleans," a reserve-style tribute to his musical past. Dark and jammy, it's loaded with minced pie–fruit compote flavors of baked apple, cherry, and plum. The blend includes 12 percent mourvèdre and a touch of viognier.

McCrea makes just 3500 cases of wine a year, nothing in large quantities. His white wines can appear to be a bit of an afterthought; in fact he made a bold, buttery chardonnay for many years but quit after 2002 to focus exclusively on Rhône whites to complement the reds. The viognier and roussanne are flavorful, appealing wines, but they will never take center stage away from the reds.

Moving past the simplicity of syrah, McCrea has been exploring a wide variety of other Rhône red grapes. In 1999 he cajoled the ever-agreeable Jim Holmes into planting mourvèdre and counoise at Ciel du Cheval. The intent was to use them exclusively in McCrea's "Sirocco" blend. But in 2002 and again in 2003, they were also bottled as separate varietals, unique wines that offered consumers a rare chance to taste these two grapes straight up (almost—a bit of syrah is blended into each). The mourvèdre is a forward, fruity, spicy-sweet red wine with plenty of charm. Flavors of berry pie, cracker, and vanilla cream swirl through the mouth; it's a bit like drinking pie. The counoise is more jagged but also more interesting, showing tart pie cherry fruit and a long, tangy finish.

A new winery opened in time for the 2005 crush, and in 2006, McCrea promised, he would do fermentations with several more new varietals, including grenache blanc, picpoul, marsanne, cinsault, and the syrah "Clone C" from Tablas Creek. This is one Rhône Ranger who isn't heading for the pasture any time soon.

Like all true explorers, Doug McCrea has had his share of hits and misses. But on balance, the essential, dogged, backbreaking, and groundbreaking work he has done for the good of the entire Washington wine industry has earned him a place with the state's best.

QUILCEDA CREEK VINTNERS

Founded 1979
PO Box 1562
Snohomish, WA 98291
360/568-2389
www.quilcedacreek.com
E-mail: info@quilcedacreek.com

Score: 100 (30/30/30/10)

The father–son team of Alex and Paul Golitzin are making, by anyone's standard, as fine a cabernet sauvignon as anyone in the world. Their single-minded focus, their ability to make brilliant wine in virtually every vintage, and, most impressively, their unbroken track record of excellence are unparalleled. Nobody does it better.

From the very earliest days, when Alex Golitzin was making wine in his garage, buying used dairy tanks for his fermenters, and relying on occasional visits from Uncle André (Tchelistcheff, the late, famed enologist and winemaker for Beaulieu Vineyards) for advice, he had a vision. And that was to make a perfect, world-class cabernet sauvignon.

A full-time process engineer at Scott Paper, he coupled his mechanical skills to an intuitive, artist's sensitivity about handling the fermenting grapes. He began modestly, making a barrel a year from 1974 through 1978, using grapes purchased from the Otis vineyard. These were exceptionally good wines, but his reputation was secured with the release of his first commercial vintage, the 1979, which won the Grand Prize at the prestigious Northwest Enological Society judging.

Much like Gary Figgins at Leonetti, Golitzin hung on to his day job for many years before retiring to make wine full time. The Quilceda cabernets of this first decade were all the more astonishing because they were being made in a simple shed, in rural Snohomish County, with largely scavenged equipment.

An important sea change began to occur in the late 1980s and early 1990s, when Quilceda Creek experimented with the idea of making a reserve wine. Paul Golitzin, then barely into his twenties, was the driving force behind the project. Among the many changes he instituted, the use of much more new French oak was the most striking. His father, who had been using four-year-old barrels purchased from Jordan, was dubious at first. "I don't want to overoak," he told me at that time. "I like it as a flavoring, not as a main course."

The few reserves that were made (in 1988, 1989, 1990, and 1992) convinced him that Paul was on to something important. They were so good and represented such a clear leap

forward that the father–son winemaking team decided, beginning in 1993, to make them the standard. One cabernet, of reserve quality, was again the focus.

Quilceda Creek cabernet has always had a unique personality, never more so than in the very early years of the Washington wine industry, when there were precious few cabernets of any quality being made here. Black, dense, and tannic, with deep, compact flavors of cassis, anise, and spicy oak, these were wines that seemed to open up somewhat grudgingly over very long periods of time. And they had a Dorian Gray quality about them; they retained their youth and color for unusually long periods of time—decades. At a Quilceda retrospective in 2004, the wines made from 1979 through 1991 (missing only the '82 and '83) displayed Bordeaux-like scents of sandalwood, cedar, licorice, and light herb matched to brilliantly ripe fruit. Several of these wines, though almost 20 years old, were still displaying plenty of berry highlights and purple-blue shades in the glass.

With the success of the experimental reserve wines, the Golitzins had moved away from André Tchelistcheff's influence, though he continued to visit and offer advice. They set themselves a new goal, the attainment of a perfect 100-point score from Robert Parker's *Wine Advocate*. Parker had tasted the 1988 and 1989 reserve wines during a rare visit to Seattle and showered them with praise. As much as anything, that challenged Quilceda's winemakers to do even better.

Vineyard sources changed, but they were always the very best grapes the state could offer: Otis Vineyard in the early years, Kiona through the first half of the 1980s, and then a blend of Kiona, Mercer Ranch, Klipsun, and Ciel du Cheval. When Mercer Ranch was sold and renamed Champoux in 1997, the Golitzins acquired a 21 percent share; it now provides some of their oldest cabernet.

Red Mountain vineyards (Ciel du Cheval, Klipsun, and Tapteil) have historically contributed the rest. And in a move to solidify their control over grape sources, the Golitzins purchased and planted their 17-acre Galitzine vineyard, adjacent to Ciel du Cheval, in 2001 and 2002. Additionally, the 10-acre Discovery vineyard is being leased and planted in the Horse Heaven AVA, near Champoux, as a safeguard against winter freeze. "It should be fairly frost free," says Paul. "That's why we did it. A little defensive move." "We play a lot of defense here," notes Alex. "You have to."

The Galitzine vineyard produced its first crop in 2004. The winemakers plan to release 500 cases of a vineyard-designated cabernet sometime in 2007 (it would be their second; a 1997 Champoux vineyard cabernet was made to celebrate that new acquisition). If all goes as hoped, a portion of the 2005 Galitzine fruit will find its way as a blending component in the Quilceda Creek.

In 1993 they made their first merlot, 50 cases from Ciel du Cheval grapes. Limited amounts of a varietal merlot have been made from 1997 on, and beginning in 2002 Champoux has been the sole source, with production doubling to 400 cases. Their second-tier Columbia Valley Red Wine, a blend much in the mold of the second wines of Bordeaux's First Growths, is up to about 1300 cases, though it depends on which wines make the cut for the cabernet. The Columbia Valley Red offers exceptional value, especially given the skyrocketing demand for the Quilceda Creek, which has now been awarded consecutive 100-point scores by Robert Parker.

The achievement of so far-fetched a goal might seem to signal the end of the road. How much better than perfect can you get? But the Golitzins, a remarkably low-key team (who always credit son-in-law Marv Crum as their co-winemaker), take it in stride. "The wine can always get better," says Alex. "Worldwide, everybody is getting better at what they're doing." Paul continues: "We've never made our best wine. We can always do better. A 100-point wine today won't be a 100-point wine in five years. The bar is getting raised."

No one has raised it higher than Quilceda Creek, and their success has enabled them to build a 5300-square-foot, architect-designed showplace winery, which opened early in 2004. Given the frequent changes of vineyard sources, the evolving blend of grapes (now almost always pure cabernet sauvignon), and the innovations introduced by Paul Golitzin, it is astonishing that Quilceda Creek Cabernet has sustained both its quality and its brooding, potent style over the decades. In their own words, the Golitzins are "ruthless" about every aspect of the winemaking. Blending the (still-unreleased) 2004, for example, they thought they had it made and then went back and declassified another 1300 cases before finally deciding they had it right. "I'm looking for a stand-alone wine from each fermenter in its own right," Paul explains, "massive fruit, wonderful balance, silky tannin. It's a textural phenomenon that we look for." "*Texture* is a good word for it," his father agrees. "You've got all these multiple flavors, but on top of that you've got all these different textures."

Because they are so meticulous and have settled into a comfortable working relationship, their wines are consistent from vintage to vintage yet reflect the specific variables of each year. The most recent release, beautifully colored and aromatic, offered a mix of plum, berry, dust, mint, and menthol; spicy and youthful, it seemed surprisingly light on its feet. The concentration and texture of Quilceda cabernets is different from the cult cabernets from Napa; the fruit has a pleasing elegance, the acids are firm but unobtrusive, the tannins are ripe, smooth, and substantial, giving the wine some weight and power.

Roughly 3400 cases of Quilceda Creek cabernet are made, and that might climb slightly to about 4000 cases, but the wine will inevitably become ever more difficult to obtain now that its success has been globally recognized. Having tracked their remarkable progress over the past two decades, I'm left wondering why dozens of Washington boutiques aren't trying to replicate their success. The focus, the intensity, the dedication to consistency that has always characterized this winery should be a model for many, many others. Yet the discipline required to focus on a single great wine seems completely to elude the young, start-up winemakers of this state. Until someone else takes up the challenge, Quilceda Creek will remain a unique and uniquely important property.

WOODWARD CANYON

Founded 1981
11920 West Highway 12
Lowden, WA 99360
509/525-4129
www.woodwardcanyon.com
E-mail: info@woodwardcanyon.com

Score: 91 (28/26/27/10)

Rick and Darcey Small founded Woodward Canyon, Walla Walla's second modern-era winery, and their initial success, particularly with cabernets and chardonnays, generated much of the early interest and outside investment in Washington viticulture. The Smalls fought for (and won) official recognition for the Walla Walla AVA when there were just three wineries and 40 acres of vines in the valley, and they continue to be tireless proponents for the region's wines.

Rick Small's family farm was located in Woodward Canyon, and he and Darcey Fugman-Small chose that name for their winery. The humble winery facility is located in Lowden, a whistle-stop on the road to Walla Walla, and its tiny tasting room, in a nineteenth-century cottage, retains the feeling of the good old days when Rick and his close friend Gary Figgins first had the wild notion to make wine.

But where Figgins and his Leonetti wines have enjoyed a fairly smooth, consistent ride at the top of the state's quality pyramid, Woodward Canyon's course has been more of a roller coaster ride, with a few loop-the-loops thrown in for good measure. For most of the 1980s, Woodward Canyon set the Northwest standard for seductive, intensely flavored chardonnays. They were rich, thick, and buttery, in the California style of the day, and at one time the winery produced up to four different bottlings. The best of them, from Celilo vineyard fruit, is the only one that remains in regular production (an estate bottling, very limited, is made from time to time).

Vertical tastings going back a decade or more have demonstrated that, despite their awesome power, heady new oak, and immediate appeal, these chardonnays will age and often improve in the bottle. A 1994 Celilo vineyard bottling, tasted at 11 years of age, was beautifully evolved, softly nutty with long hazelnut and butterscotch flavors. In most years the wine, labeled simply Columbia Valley chardonnay, includes a portion of the estate-grown fruit, from vines planted in 1977.

Limited amounts of an austere, searingly tart estate-grown sauvignon blanc and a gorgeous dry riesling (from DuBrul vineyard fruit) are offered, mainly to tasting room and mailing list customers. But the bulk of Woodward Canyon's 15,000-case production is devoted to a portfolio of intense, age-worthy red wines. At the top stand the winery's Dedication Series cabernets, which go back in an unbroken succession to WWC's first vintage. They can age wonderfully: A bottle of the 1981, tasted at 20 years of age, had developed into a dead ringer for a fine Pauillac. Since 1995, the wines in this series have been designated "Old Vines." They are made primarily from Champoux and Sagemoor vineyard cabernet vines that date from the early 1970s, placing them among the oldest on the West Coast. (Woodward Canyon is a joint partner in the Champoux vineyard.)

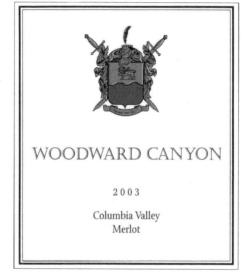

The winery hit a rough patch with its red wines between 2000 and 2002, vintages that were almost impenetrable on release, with extremely hard, tough tannins. Wines from those years may require hours and hours of decanting before they grudgingly begin to open up. But with a new winemaker, Kevin Mott, on board as of 2003, things have taken a turn for the better. The latest Dedication Series cabernet requires no strenuous effort to appreciate; it is instantly fascinating, a rich mix of fruits, ripened to compote intensity, with subtle streaks of herb, leaf, and wet hay. The old-vine complexity shines through in both the power and the detail of this wine.

Woodward's Artist Series cabernets were introduced in 1992. Made in much larger case quantities and priced at slightly more than half the cost of the Dedication series wines, these are blended from top vineyards such as Champoux, Canoe Ridge, Klipsun, Tapteil, and Pepper Bridge. Stylish and tight on release, with compact flavors of cassis, black cherry, and berry, these muscular cabs are served up in a wrap of baby fat.

The Estate Red is a classic Right Bank Bordeaux blend, predominantly cabernet franc and merlot. It's a barrel selection from the estate vineyard fruit, which is always low yielding to begin with—two tons an acre in a good year, less than a ton an acre in a "recovery" year, such as 2006. Complex and fragrant, the Estate Red puts forth a varied mix of fruit and leaf flavors, from dried cranberry, cherry, and raisin to tobacco leaf, soy, and spice.

Filling out the lineup are a chewy and substantial Columbia Valley merlot and a DuBrul vineyard syrah, wonderfully concentrated and flavorful, with smoked meat, tar, iodine, pepper, and clove. On very rare occasions (just three times in 25 years), a Special Selection über-reserve red wine is produced, offered to tasting room and mailing list customers exclusively.

Small is a wiry, boundlessly energetic man whose motor never ceases to rev. He is unusually candid about his winemaking trials, the experiments that went sideways, and the hard lessons he has learned. "When I'm done and out of this I want to say I never held anything back!" he says, quite happily, and no one would ever doubt him. But he does not give himself enough credit for his many triumphs, choosing rather to focus on the contributions of others, the many new projects in the works, and his ongoing efforts to establish the estate vineyard.

Set on a hilltop a few miles north of the winery, in rolling wheat land, it's a dry, windy site on very rocky soil. Vines struggle mightily to get established, and the topography offers little protection from the occasional arctic blasts. Small is the third generation on the land, which has been both cattle ranch and wheat farm in past decades. "It was never good soil," he admits; "where a lot of the cabernet grows is very shallow and rocky."

Sustainable viticulture is now being introduced, to amend soil badly depleted from the years of growing grain. Roughly 41 acres are planted; seven to merlot, six and six to cabernet sauvignon and cab franc, two and a half to chardonnay, and a smattering to sauvignon blanc. Some of the vines are now 30 years old. Small's experimental projects, which include a few barrels of barbera and Dolcetto, come from these estate vines.

Under the Charbonneau label, Small releases a Bordeaux-style red from the vineyard of the same name. The Charbonneau blanc, a sémillon–sauvignon blend, has been discontinued in favor of the estate sauvignon blanc. Finally,s the Nelms Road label represents Woodward Canyon's second-tier wines, which include a pleasant, forward merlot and a somewhat herbal cabernet sauvignon.

6

THE SPECIALISTS

I call the 30 exceptional wineries discussed in this chapter specialists, not necessarily because they make just one or two wines (many make a full range), but because they have a focused excellence. They have risen to this book's second tier because the rating system I've developed rewards longevity, consistency, and style. The longer a winery has been in business, demonstrating a clear and distinctive style vintage after vintage, the higher its ranking will be.

In practical terms these are wines and wineries you can rely on virtually 100 percent of the time. They may not always be the newest, the priciest, the most trendy, or rare, but they deliver the goods, and they do it well. Why list just 30? It's an arbitrary number, to be sure, but keeping each of these chapters to a limited number of wineries has forced me to make the critical selections that ultimately let the cream rise to the top. Rest assured that every winery in this group is a proven star, for the reasons listed.

ABEJA

Founded 2001
2014 Mill Creek Road
Walla Walla, WA 99362
509/526-7400
www.abeja.net
E-mail: info@abeja.net

Score: 82 (28/20/26/8)

Though Abeja (pronounced ah-BAY-ha, it means "bumblebee") is one of the newest wineries to make this list, its winemaker, John Abbott, has long-established credentials. Straight out of college, he went to work for Napa's Pine Ridge and, later, Chalone's Acacia winery. In 1994, he moved to Walla Walla to make wine for Canoe Ridge Vineyard, then a new Chalone venture.

Abbott's years at Canoe Ridge produced some of this state's most breathtaking merlots and seductive chardonnays. The experience left him eager to pursue winemaking on a more personal scale, and, having conquered merlot, he turned his focus toward perfecting Washington state cabernet sauvignon. Happily, Abbott's quest matched up nicely with Ken Harrison's own plans for a new winery (and B&B) just outside of Walla Walla. Ken and Ginger Harrison, John Abbott, and Molly Galt formed their business partnership in 2002, dedicating themselves to producing largely estate-grown cabernet, made to the highest standards, at the property now called Abeja.

Harrison had already begun by planting his 17-acre Heather Hill vineyard, just east of Seven Hills, in 2001. Heather Hill grows mostly cabernet sauvignon, with an acre and a half of merlot and a shy acre of cabernet franc. The seven-acre Mill Creek vineyard, which adjoins the winery, was extensively replanted in 2006 and grows four acres of merlot and smaller amounts of chardonnay, viognier, and syrah.

This eastern section of the Walla Walla Valley has much to recommend it. The elevation is over 1300 feet, and the proximity to the Blue Mountains brings with it considerably more rainfall than elsewhere. The older vines at Abeja have been successfully dry-farmed for the past three vintages. The late-summer temperatures are cooler here, and the vines benefit from a longer window of time during which the afternoon heat is balanced with crisp, autumnal nights.

All of Abbott's wines avoid the high-extract, high-alcohol, heavily oaked style in favor of a more elegant, more European approach. Many wineries ferment with custom yeasts designed to maximize the buttery microwave popcorn flavors; Abbott uses a strain that minimizes that buttery character. The chardonnay, he explains, is "a labor of love," especially given the widely separated vineyard sources, the expensive Louis Latour barrels, the limited (700-case) production, and the modest (by global standards) $28 selling price.

Cabernet sauvignon remains Abeja's raison d'être (should I perhaps say *raisin* d'être?) and accounts for roughly 80 percent of the total production. "My benchmark," says Abbott, "is to be true to the varietal. I don't worry about its tasting like Washington; the wine will taste like where it's grown, which *is* Washington. I knew that wouldn't necessarily bring me massive scores. These are wines for food, not meals in a glass. I want to make wines that I personally feel comfortable drinking."

Though Washington chardonnays rarely rise above the mundane, the exceptions, such as Abbott consistently crafts, make you wonder why not. Rich and voluptuous, these gorgeous wines retain enough acid and balance to deliver their big-time flavors with finesse. Silky, ripe, lush, yet sculpted, they play out deliciously through an extremely long and deeply fruity palate.

Abeja's cabernet sauvignons, supple and dense, lack nothing in terms of power, muscle, or complexity. Tar and smoke and gravel run right down the spine; tannins are substantial and have not been "smoothed" to death. Everything about the wines feels classy, and their compact confidence rewards patient tasters with layers of ripe, varietal flavor, perfectly matched to the new oak.

Abeja also makes the Beekeeper's Blend, a cabernet-based red table wine, and small amounts of estate viognier, estate syrah, and (very rarely) a reserve cabernet.

BARNARD GRIFFIN

Founded 1983
878 Tulip Lane
Richland, WA 99352
509/627-0266
www.barnardgriffin.com
E-mail: info@barnardgriffin.com

Score: 79 (22/26/23/8)

"We're too available to be cultish," says Barnard Griffin's Rob Griffin. (Writers of wine lists, please note, there is no such person as Bernard Griffin! Deborah Barnard is married to Rob Griffin.) It's just the sort of wry, self-effacing, slightly cynical and pointed remark that makes him the king of no spin among Washington winemakers. Griffin is exceedingly bright, disarmingly honest, and stubbornly dedicated to a firm conviction that "quality and price are almost unrelated in the wine business." And he sets out to prove the point with each new vintage, determined to make wines that perform far above their modest prices.

Barnard Griffin debuted with just a few hundred cases of three wines: a riesling, a chardonnay, and a fumé (sauvignon) blanc. For some years it served as Griffin's artistic outlet, allowing him to do everything absolutely his own way while working as a winemaker for Hogue Cellars.

When Griffin left Hogue in 1992, the Barnard Griffin really began to take off, and it is now producing better than 45,000 cases annually. "Right in that awkward area where everyone says you shouldn't be," says Griffin; "too big to be small, too small to be big." Production covers the gamut of prices and styles.

Reserve wines (cabernet sauvignon, merlot, syrah, and chardonnay) are drawn from Griffin's best vineyard sources and get first-class treatment: extra barrel time, up to 100 percent new French oak, fancy labels, and very limited production. Still smaller quantities of experimental wines, such as a pungent, raisiny petit verdot, and prestigious, limited-edition vineyard-designates, such as the Ciel du Cheval merlot, are sometimes available through the tasting room.

But it is the widely available, sensibly priced sauvignon (fumé) blancs, sémillons, chardonnays, and reds that have won the winery a wide and grateful following. They deliver consistent, flavorful renditions of ripe Columbia Valley grapes. Griffin is not shy about oak, but he does work quite hard to keep his alcohol levels in check, and he makes wines that not only are delicious young but may be cellared for some years as well.

The wine industry needs more Rob Griffins. And brand-new wineries, many of which seem to think that a quality statement necessarily begins with a high price tag, might want to consider what sort of a message such hubris sends to consumers. These days, consumers value value, and that is what will continue to make Barnard Griffin one of this state's most successful brands.

J. BOOKWALTER

Founded 1983
894 Tulip Lane
Richland, WA 99352
509/627-5000
www.bookwalterwines.com
E-mail: info@bookwalterwines.com

Score: 81 (25/25/23/8)

2005
RIESLING
COLUMBIA VALLEY • WASHINGTON

Jerry and wife Jean Bookwalter opened their winery in 1983, making mostly off-dry riesling, chenin blanc, and chardonnay. Jerry worked in vineyard management; the winery was a sideline, and it puttered along until problems with other business ventures led to a bankruptcy filing in the early 1990s. When son John Bookwalter returned home a few years later after a successful business career of his own, he did a full-blown SWOT (strengths/weaknesses/opportunities/threats) analysis, in PowerPoint no less, and rolled it out to the folks. The prognosis was not so good. The patient was on life support, and John proposed a complete reinvention of the business. "I could see the explosion of Washington wines in the market and all the new, upscale packaging," he recalls. "I wanted to take advantage of my father's skill sets, his contacts and knowledge. And I knew all the players on the distribution side."

The first year brought with it some challenges. A lot of sweat equity went into learning enough about the winemaking side of the business to see what specifically needed to change. "I remember sitting down with Gary Figgins (Leonetti Cellar) early in 1998," Bookwalter recalls. "We started tasting through barrels, and suddenly the light went off in my head. There's a difference between these barrels and the barrels we have in our cellar! It was what I call the 'Aha!' phase."

Winemaking consultant Zelma Long was contacted, and her assessment of the Bookwalter wines rang true. The 2000 vintage marked their first vine-to-wine collaboration, and snazzy new packaging was introduced when the wines were released two years later. The transformation was startling; virtually overnight, Bookwalter had leaped to the front ranks of Washington red wine producers.

The winery is now a $2 million company, with ambitions to grow to $10 million. Quality improvement is more incremental but steady. The Bookwalters' long history in vineyard management means that exceptionally practiced eyes are on their vines. Grapes come from a nice assortment of older vineyards (the youngest is their own estate vineyard, established in 1993), many of which are well beyond 20 years of age.

J. Bookwalter rieslings are spectacular, fragrant with blossoms, sweet peach, mango, and pear, beautifully ripened and concentrated. Gewürztraminer, chenin blanc, and a chardonnay–viognier blend are also offered, all well made. Long's influence is particularly apparent in the reds, which go from strength to strength. The merlots are dense and deeply saturated, inky to the eye and thick against the glass. The cabernet, 100 percent varietal, perfectly captures the uniqueness of great Washington fruit, showing power and structure without the jammy thickness of California cabs.

Finally, J. Bookwalter's first meritage, named "Chapter One," set the bar extremely high, with layered and complex black fruits, streaks of pencil lead and licorice, and a finish of sweet tannins. I'm eagerly awaiting Chapter Two.

BUTY

Founded 2000
535 East Cessna Avenue
Walla Walla, WA 99362
509/527-0901
www.butywinery.com
E-mail: info@butywinery.com

Score: 80 (28/20/25/7)

When I encounter a new winery, what I look for is consistency, steady improvement, and an emerging sense of a polished style. I have found all three in the wines of Buty. This small Walla Walla winery (it's pronounced "beauty") is on the cutting edge of quality and innovation. Caleb Foster and Nina Buty Foster founded their family business in 2000, but Caleb's winemaking résumé includes eight years working with Rick Small at Woodward Canyon, winemaking positions at Mount Baker winery and Glen Fiona, and further experience working crush in New Zealand and South Africa.

Nothing has been easy. Woefully underfunded, they made their wines at five different locations in their first six years, using borrowed or rented equipment and trading their labor and expertise in return. What lim-

ited resources they had were used to purchase the best possible grapes and to hire the best consultant they could find: Zelma Long.

Long, who also consults for J. Bookwalter winery, was asked to help Buty build a better chardonnay. She and the Fosters began to explore ways to maximize flavors and textures without using new oak barrels, not just in chardonnay but in their sauvignon blanc–sémillon blend and recently in their red wines also.

The proof, as always, is in the bottle. Buty started out at a very competent level, but they have consistently ramped it up from there. Each year the wines gain something in terms of detail and precision; it's clear that the focus on specific vineyards and fermentation techniques is paying off. Buty wines, both white and red, consistently show the sort of nuance and depth that mark the world's best. They keep alcohol levels in check, striving for balance, elegance, and extract. Seamless flavors blend subtle mineral, herbal, and spice components, in a style that is clean, a bit lean, polished, complex, and powerful.

Total production is up to 3000 cases, and as the Fosters have finally moved into their own, tiny space, their star is on the rise. Buty wines are being aggressively sought out by restaurants and retailers around the country; they may be better known in New York than in their own home state. Every wine is a gem, but the Sémillon–Sauvignon blanc is exceptional. Smooth, round, rich, and toasty, it stands with the very best white Bordeaux blends made anywhere in the country.

The Conner Lee vineyard chardonnay consistently features plush fruit flavors of apples and white peaches shot through with butterscotch and caramel. The red wines (Columbia Rediviva, Rediviva of the Stones, and Caballo Blanco) are blends of syrah–cabernet sauvignon or merlot–cabernet franc. They have a European elegance, along with a concentration and brightness that speaks specifically of Washington state.

CADENCE

Founded 1998
9320 15th Avenue South
Unit CF
Seattle, WA 98108
206/381-9507
www.cadencewinery.com
E-mail: info@cadencewinery.com

Score: 80 (28/20/25/7)

Ben Smith and his wife, Gaye McNutt, launched their tiny Cadence winery in 1998. Smith's years in the Boeing Wine Club had brought him a handful of first-place medals and the confidence to launch a professional winemaking career. Cadence began by contracting grapes from a handful of carefully selected sites, most of them on Red Mountain. Production has gradually ramped up from 700 cases toward a goal of around 3000 cases. But the road has proven challenging at every step.

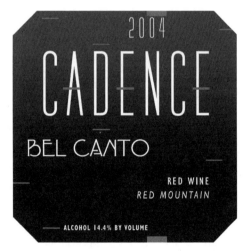

In 2004 the 10-acre Cara Mia vineyard was planted on Red Mountain under the supervision of Ciel du Cheval's vineyard manager, Ryan Johnson. The land was purchased in 1997, but establishing the vineyard required water, time, money, more time, studies, and, well, lots more money. The well alone cost upwards of six figures. But extensive soil studies at 31 discrete sites scattered around the vineyard convinced the owners that they had struck gold. "We have perhaps the most unique and varied soil profiles of any vineyard site on Red Mountain," they write. Of three major soil types in the vineyard, two (cobblestones and clay) have not been uncovered in any other Red Mountain vineyard sites. They appear to be quite similar to the cobbles and clay found in Pomerol and St. Emilion in Bordeaux.

Cadence wines have been admired by several critics, including this one, yet inexplicably ignored by others. What I find that distinguishes Ben Smith's winemaking is the nuanced complexity of the aromas he coaxes out of his young wines. Bouquet is something that great wines develop over time, and young wines, even the best ones, rarely show more than a glimmer of what lies ahead. But sniffing through Cadence releases, I am struck by their complexity. The Ciel du Cheval vineyard red blend is elegant and refined, showing scents of dusty coffee, cocoa, and mocha, streaks of chalk, limestone, gravel, and pencil lead, mixed fruits, and hints of expressive spice. The Bel Canto red, a Bordeaux blend, is muscular and detailed, showing mixed Asian spices, supple fruit, and beautiful fine-grained tannins. The winery also makes excellent vineyard designates from other prestigious Red Mountain sites, such as Tapteil and Klipsun. Coda is the inexpensive red blend and is always well made and charming.

As the Cara Mia vineyard begins bearing (the first crop was harvested in 2006), the next phase of Cadence's decade-long quest to make Washington wines with the structure of great Bordeaux should click into high gear. The owners say that henceforth grapes will come exclusively from just three Red Mountain vineyards: Ciel du Cheval, Tapteil, and the estate.

CHINOOK

Founded 1983
Corner of Wittkopf Road and Wine Country Road
Prosser, WA 99350
509/786-2725
www.chinookwines.com
E-mail: info@chinookwines.com

Score: 76 (21/26/20/9)

Kay Simon and Clay Mackey are the wife-and-husband winemaker–vintner team behind Chinook (the name references a warm wind that blows through the area, not the famous salmon). This much-loved winery was among those that pioneered the suddenly fashionable Prosser area more than two decades ago. Before that, Simon spent some years making wine for Ste. Michelle, one of the first women in the country to work for such a large winery.

The Chinook style is tight, controlled, and precise. "Compatibility with food is an ever-present winemaking goal," says Simon. "All of our wines are fermented to dryness and then aged in barrel and bottle until we feel that they are ready to enjoy with a meal." Made in a converted red barn on the outskirts of Prosser (the tasting room is in the old farmhouse), Chinook wines are technically exact and infallibly consistent. They are the classic expression of Yakima Valley fruit.

Chinook's chardonnays show crisp, melony fruit and very light notes of barrel toast. The sémillons are tart and sharp, with a pleasing tang and snap. Their complex, clean, and crisp flavors layer fig, citrus rind, and clove with high notes of candied orange and citrus blossom. Sauvignon blanc completes the white wine lineup, all of them varietally true to their cool-climate fruit.

Turning to the Chinook reds, you will find the merlot light and slightly green, with blueberry and fresh herbal flavors. A small amount of cabernet franc is planted at the winery. Along with purchased grapes, it is made into both a dry rosé and a sort of Washington Chinon, firm and tart, with spicy apple, plum, date, fig, and even golden raisin flavors. The Chinook cabernet franc rosé has become something of a cult favorite among Seattle restaurateurs.

COLUMBIA

Founded 1967
14030 NE 145th Street
Woodinville, WA 98072
425/488-8164
www.columbiawinery.com
E-mail: contact@columbiawinery.com

Score: 84 (27/26/21/10)

The eccentricities of this seminal Washington winery can both confound and delight, but its place in the history of the Washington wine industry is secure. Columbia began as Associated Vintners, the weekend pastime of a group of University of Washington professors. In 1967 they bonded the winery and produced their first commercial wines, a riesling, a gewürztraminer, a pinot noir, and a cabernet sauvignon.

Over the years the business has weathered the sale of its vineyards, a change of names (from AV to Columbia), several changes of owners and of venue, and an absolutely bewildering array of labels. The guiding light throughout most of Columbia's history was the palate of (now-retired) winemaker David Lake, an MW whose distinctly European tastes were wedded to the mind of a (slightly) mad scientist. In the spirit of the amateur wine lovers who pioneered the AV brand, Lake experimented tirelessly. His longstanding collaboration with grower Mike Sauer of Red Willow vineyard most famously pioneered syrah in Washington state, which they planted in 1985 and first vinified in 1988. They were also the first to do a Washington pinot gris and have been among the first for a dozen other varietals, including viognier, cabernet franc, barbera, malbec, mourvèdre, sangiovese, nebbiolo, and tempranillo.

But breaking new ground is rarely easy, and Columbia has faced its share of hurdles. Confusion with Columbia Crest, the state's largest winery, still haunts the brand (the two have no connection). A profusion of wines, labels, and special, limited bottlings makes it difficult for consumers to get a solid fix on Columbia's strengths. And Lake himself acknowledged that the style of wines he favors (wines that are "not too high in alcohol, not overtly oaky, truly drinkable wines that work nicely at the dinner table with food") are "not necessarily the wines that win the top awards. The pressure is very much to try to get the big awards, the high-percentage-point scores."

Historically, Columbia has not often gotten the big scores. Its white wines were too steely and tart, and its red wines too tight and unyielding. But as several recent tastings have proven, Lake's wines can age remarkably well, and they reveal hidden depths over time. They are wines that complement a meal without dominating it, and they are wines that have done a lot of pioneering work to demonstrate Washington's ability to display terroir, that elusive, individual expression of soil, season, and climate that characterizes the world's greatest vineyards.

Columbia's white wines are elegant, crisp, and shellfish friendly, especially the sauvignon blancs, sémillons, and pinot gris. There is a fine off-dry gewürztraminer and an equally lovely Cellarmaster's riesling, and the Wyckoff vineyard chardonnay can be a dead ringer for a French white Burgundy from a lesser appellation. Many of these wines sell at bargain-basement prices.

The single-vineyard cabernets (from Red Willow and Otis) stand stylistically with classified-growth Bordeaux and show a similar capacity to improve with age. Columbia celebrated its fortieth commercial vintage in 2006, a remarkable milestone. With the retirement of David Lake (due to declining health) that same year, this seminal, pioneering, irreplaceable Washington winery (now part of Constellation's Icon Estates portfolio) faces an uncertain future.

COVEY RUN

> Founded 1982
> 14030 NE 145th Street
> Woodinville, WA 98072
> 888/659-7900
> www.coveyrun.com
> E-mail: info@coveyrun.com

> Score: 77 (22/23/26/6)

In 1999, Covey Run, which began life as Quail Run in the early 1980s, brought in winemaker Kerry Norton from Oregon's Eola Hills Wine Cellars. Though it might seem to be a big switch, in terms of both climate and wines, Norton was one of Oregon's most eclectic winemakers. During his eight-year run at Eola Hills, he produced flavorful, herbaceous sauvignon blancs, roundly fruity chardonnays, and spicy cabernets along with good budget versions of pinot gris and pinot noir.

He continues in the same selfless, quiet, steady mode with his wines for Covey Run, a 300,000-case winery that is now part of Constellation Brands. I say selfless because the bright lights ain't gonna shine on the winemaker for a big, commercial winery making $7 wines in Sunnyside. And yet, such wines are the bedrock of the Washington wine industry. They are affordable for the average consumer, they are widely available, and, most importantly, they are good tasting, varietally correct, and steadily getting better.

Norton remembers that when he first arrived, in time for the 1999 crush, Washington vineyards all looked the same. "I couldn't tell what was good and what was bad," he admits. "I had to learn to recognize how the different soils in Washington produce different regional flavors." Norton won't say it, but my hunch is that he was given some marginal raw material to work with and had to make the best of it.

In 2001 Constellation bought the winery and, fortunately for Norton, the sale did not include vineyards. Suddenly he found himself with the freedom to chase down new vineyard sources. These new sources of quality fruit, from all across the Columbia basin, have contributed significantly to the ongoing evolution of the Covey Run brand. "Every year is an experiment," notes the winemaker. "We never make huge changes; we want continuity. Washington's best card is fruit; fruit is what we really do well. I want that fruit to be right out there in the wines."

Covey Run makes about 300,000 cases a year in three tiers. The Quail Series wines, priced between $7 and $9, showcase bright, expressive fruit flavors. The bottles feature the quail label, a graphic reference to the original winery name. Among the white wines, the pinot grigio, dry riesling, and chenin blanc are standouts; but everything from the muscat to the gewürztraminer to the chardonnay (partly barrel fermented in real barrels, not tank staves or chips) is a winner.

In the summer of 2005 Covey Run introduced the Winemaker's Collection, line-priced at $13 and aimed primarily at the restaurant trade. Included are a chardonnay, a merlot, a cabernet sauvignon, a syrah, and a late-harvest riesling. A reserve series, which debuted a year earlier, includes a chardonnay, a merlot, and (occasionally) a sémillon ice wine. A new winery is planned for the near future in the heart of the Prosser wine community.

DUNHAM CELLARS

Founded 1995
150 East Boeing Avenue
Walla Walla, WA 99362
509/529-4685
www.dunhamcellars.com
E-mail: wine@dunhamcellars.com

Score: 82 (27/24/23/8)

Eric Dunham, though still in his mid-thirties, has already acquired full renaissance man credentials. An accomplished chef, painter, and winemaker, he traces his interest in wine back to his early teens, when he perfected a variety of techniques for breaking into his father's cellar. "It went from unlocked to locked," he recalls, "to bolted, to welded shut with the screws reversed, so there were no screws on the outside to take off. So I went through the sheetrock."

Dunham speaks in a quiet monotone, which belies the passion he brings to everything he touches. The colorful abstract paintings that adorn his wines are his own, and many of the originals hang in the winery tasting room. When he started the winery, his back-

ground consisted primarily of a Hogue internship and four years as an assistant winemaker at L'Ecole. Dunham Cellars' first vintage, 200 cases of 1995 cabernet, was made while he was still working there.

Though it's little more than a decade old, Dunham Cellars was just the eighth (or ninth, depending on who is telling the story) winery bonded in Walla Walla. The region's explosive growth followed shortly thereafter. Walla Walla is now approaching 100 wineries within the borders of the AVA, so Dunham's timing could not have been better. The wines were exceptional right from the start, and the cabernets, numbered with Roman numerals, were the first from Walla Walla to achieve national notoriety from a brand-new producer since the early days of Leonetti and Woodward Canyon. One hundred percent varietal, with dense, sappy, supple, silky flavors of wild berries and black cherries, these early Dunhams showcased that mix of power and precision that Washington fruit can deliver so well.

In 1999 a Lewis Vineyard syrah was introduced, from an exciting new vineyard high in the Rattlesnake Hills. From the start it has been a dazzler, packed with fleshy blackberry fruit and sweet, toasty oak. Big, peppery, and profound, the Lewis syrah proved that Dunham was no one-trick pony. More recently, an equally profound Lewis vineyard cabernet sauvignon has been added. Though Lewis stands at the top, all the Dunham syrahs are exciting wines, purple at the rim, black at the core, spicy, and penetrating, the flavors a fine and textural mix of citrus oil, raspberry, cassis, cinnamon, and toast.

The winery's white wines, dedicated to Eric Dunham's grandmother Shirley Mays, include a rich, toasty, full-flavored sémillon, and a ripely tropical chardonnay

Dunham Cellars's annual production has climbed to 17,000 cases, but more than half is devoted to a popular budget wine (declassified) called "Three Legged Red." It's dedicated to Eric Dunham's dog Port, so named because he is missing a leg on his right side. A companion, dubbed "Four Legged White," was introduced in 2006. There are 3000 cases made of Trutina (Latin for "balance"), a Bordeaux blend that was originally bottled under the Trey Marie label but is now folded into the Dunham lineup. The Columbia Valley cabernet and Columbia Valley syrah account for another 3500 cases, and the rest is divided among the single-vineyard wines.

There are three estate vineyards. Frenchtown (10 acres) was planted in 2000 to cabernet sauvignon, syrah, and cabernet franc. Double River (27 acres adjacent to Basel Cellars) was planted in 1999 to cabernet sauvignon, merlot, sémillon, tempranillo, syrah, and cabernet franc. Buckley Terrace (two acres next to L'Ecole N° 41) is a leased site planted to cabernet sauvignon and syrah.

His goal, says Eric Dunham, is focusing on the three estate vineyards and maintaining current production levels. "I never thought we would be this big," he writes, "but now that I am here it's great. Being able to whittle down from 99 acres of vineyard helps make our ultrapremium wines top notch as well as provide great wine for the Three Legged Red."

FIDÉLITAS

Founded 2000
46415 E. Badger Road
Benton City, WA 99320
509/521-4433
www.fidelitaswines.com
E-mail: info@fidelitaswines.com

Score: 75 (25/20/23/7)

Winemaker Charlie Hoppes came to Washington via a stint at Ste. Michelle, where he worked closely with head winemaker Mike Januik for eight years. Under Januik's supervision, Hoppes was in charge of day-to-day winemaking operations at the winery's Canoe Ridge facility during its formative years. As such he was one of the unsung artists who helped to define the Washington winemaking style of red wines during the crucial decade of the 1990s, when merlot staked a claim to fame as the state's leading red grape.

In 1999, Hoppes left the Chateau to become the winemaker for Three Rivers winery in Walla Walla. I first met him there one fine summer day in 2000 as he was hanging out with Januik, who had stopped by to say hello. I remember the day because the two old friends were so excited to see each other that Januik backed his brand-new truck off the crush pad behind Three Rivers and T-boned it, breaking an axle.

Hoppes made some terrific wines during his three vintages at Three Rivers, and then he set off on his own. He has since pursued a high-profile career as a consulting wine-maker to a growing number of Washington start-ups and as master of his own project, named Fidélitas. It means, he explains, faithful, loyal, and true. "Faithful to Bordeaux grape varieties, loyal to classic winemaking techniques, and true to Washington state's Columbia Valley terroir" is the Fidélitas mission statement. It's not just a slogan, but a way of doing business and a roadmap to the style of these wines. "My goal," he adds, "is to try to get the very best fruit that I can and put some blends together. I like to think that there's always a better vineyard out there, and I like to try some new ones every year. Ultimately, I would like to build a winery on Red Mountain. If there's a destination place in this area, I think that's it." (As we go to press, he's building it.)

Hoppes knows where to hunt for good fruit and for sources from established name vineyards, such as Conner Lee, Champoux, Gamache, Klipsun, and Windrow, mixing flavors from all over the state in his expert blends. "I like the diversity that it gives me," he confides. "I feel real comfortable blending. It adds a lot of complexity to what you're doing."

In late 2005, Fidélitas acquired a five-acre parcel of land on Red Mountain, with plans to build a winery there in time for the 2007 crush. Until that time, Hoppes will continue to make his wines at nearby Cañon del Sol winery. All of his wines exhibit very smooth, seamless, beautifully integrated fruit, and Hoppes is not shy with the new oak barrels either. He makes a fine sémillon, ripe and scented with wheat, clover, lemon, and apple. His syrahs are immediately drinkable, with jammy berries and fruit preserves, light touches of toast, and a nice finish of butter and caramel.

Merlots are sweet and tangy, with clean, pretty cherry and blackberry fruit; and the cabernets are silky and saturated, with flavors of ripe berries complemented with buttery oak. Newly introduced is OPTU, a red meritage from Champoux, Conner Lee, and Milbrandt grapes. It's fair to say that I have never had a wine made by Charlie Hoppes that didn't stand out a bit from the pack, representing a clear stylistic vision, pure fruit flavors, and good value in its quality range.

HARLEQUIN WINE CELLARS

Founded: 1999
1211 Sand Pit Road
Touchet, WA 99360
509/394-2112

www.harlequinwine.com

E-mail: pinotboy@hotmail.com

Score: 75 (25/20/24/6)

Named in homage to Picasso, Harlequin Wine Cellars is the handiwork of Robert Good-friend and Elizabeth Cook. Goodfriend brings a chef's sensibility to his winemaking. He was a self-confessed "science geek" in college and then went into restaurateuring in Santa Fe. His next stop was California's central coast, where he worked for a time at Wild Horse, in charge of the crush pad. It was the first time, he remembers, that he had ever tasted pinot noir grapes. It was an epiphany. "I put them in my mouth," he told me some years later, "and it made sense. I realized this is what the fruit tastes like. It all worked for me, from a culinary stand-point."

Harlequin's winemaking facility is in Touchet, about 20 miles west of Walla Walla, but Goodfriend sources grapes from all over the Northwest. His pinot noir comes from Oregon's Hoodview vineyard, his chardonnay from the Celilo vineyard in the Columbia Gorge, and his viognier from the Wahluke Slope. That viognier gets him talking—Goodfriend is nothing if not voluble, and his opinions are strongly held. "I love aromatic whites, but viognier has a very brief window of ripeness," he points out. "It's green, green, green and then raisins, overnight. It's like walking a tightrope. But when it's right, I get honeysuckle, peach, Bosc pear."

Harlequin's viogniers are in fact full, ripe, and intense, 100% barrel fermented in neutral oak and given no malolactic. Harlequin's chardonnays are done in a Burgundian style (many claim to be, but in this instance it's a fair claim to make). "Here in Washington we choose between Burgundian- and Bordeaux-style winemaking," says Goodfriend. "Burgundians are not afraid of lees. We embrace lees. They add mouthfeel and texture through autolysis. But lees can get really stinky if you go through fermentation without the right nutrient levels."

The syrahs are wonderful wines, sourced from Wahluke Slope and Yakima Valley vineyards. The Minick vineyard bottling is done in an Australian shiraz style. Goodfriend describes it as "IHOP boysenberry syrup on new car leather." (I can't do better than that.) Its companion, designated Sundance Vineyard–Wahluke Slope, is 100 percent syrah, 30 percent whole cluster fermented in 20 percent new French oak. Juicy and quite tart, the snappy cranberry-raspberry flavors are nuanced with wet earth, black tea, and soy.

Completing the portfolio is the Cuvée Alexander Bordeaux blend, with grapes from vineyards such as DuBrul, Sundance, and Ciel du Cheval and a wonderfully smooth, soft, lush mouthfeel. From time to time a Jester's Red (syrah–zinfandel or some other interesting combo) is also offered. Prices across the board are moderate for wines of this quality.

ISENHOWER CELLARS

Founded 1999
3471 Pranger Road
Walla Walla, WA 99362
509/526-7896
www.isenhowercellars.com
E-mail: winemakers@isenhowercellars.com

Score: 76 (25/20/25/6)

Brett and Denise Isenhower are both pharmacists by trade but farmers by birth. "Wine represents a place better than any other agricultural crop," says Brett. "When it's made with respect from vineyard to the bottle, it represents that slice of earth better than anything else."

Winemaking began as a hobby but quickly turned into a passionate pursuit. They arrived in Walla Walla just as the second wave of new wineries was breaking. There were 11 wineries in town when they arrived; a year later they were bonded as number 23. It was a good time, and the newcomers found willing help and advice from Christophe Baron, Casey McClellan, and Rusty Figgins. They made their first two vintages at the original Glen Fiona facility (now Abeja) and then at Rulo in 2001 and built their own plain, functional winery in 2002, right next door to Rulo. Production has ramped up to about 3300 cases, a good comfort point for them, and is largely devoted to a dizzying variety of syrahs.

Isenhower wines are attractively packaged and cleverly named for different wildflowers. The Snapdragon white is a blend of roussanne and viognier. Creamy and fresh, it tastes of light citrus, grapefruit, pineapple, and a hint of honey. Among the syrahs and syrah blends have been some lovely successes: a plump, floral 2003 River Beauty Red blended with a generous percentage of mourvèdre and an all-syrah 2002 River Beauty dense with black cherry fruit and laced with graphite and gravel. Other bottlings of syrah, merlot, and cabernet sauvignon are named Wild Alfalfa, Red Paintbrush, Looking Glass, and Bachelor's Button. A new Bordeaux blend is called Wild Thyme.

At this juncture it is fair to say that Isenhower is probably having a wild time, making very good wines at fair prices. But as with many newcomers, it's hard to know where their focus will ultimately lie. Under the circumstances, consistency from vintage to vintage is impossible to achieve. Their wines change dramatically from year to year as different vineyards, grapes, and blends are tried. The names and labels provide a sort of faux continuity.

As this is written a small trial vineyard is being planted, but it's just an acre and a half, not enough to provide the sort of stability that could elevate Isenhower to the next level. It's a pragmatic decision, says Brett Isenhower. "I figure if we're digging a bunch of holes in the ground, I don't want to bury money in them too." Still, Isenhower is clearly a winery to watch, and the best vintages are yet to come.

JANUIK

Founded 1999
19730 144th Avenue NE
Woodinville, WA 98072
425/481-5502
www.januikwinery.com
E-mail: mike@januikwinery.com

Score: 84 (27/27/22/8)

Soft-spoken and shy, Mike Januik is not a swashbuckling figure in the world of wine. But his wines more than compensate for his natural modesty. Lush and confident, they combine power and grace. His impeccable vineyard sources range across the best in the state, from Cold Creek and Elerding chardonnay, to Seven Hills and Champoux cabernet, to Klipsun merlot, Ciel du Cheval petit verdot, and Lewis syrah.

Januik has a long history in Washington, and he knows its vineyards as well as anyone. He began his wine career as a retailer with a wine shop in Ashland, Oregon. After

doing some amateur winemaking, he studied at UC Davis and took his first winemaker job at Stewart vineyards in the Yakima Valley, where he turned out some thrilling rieslings. From there he went to work at Snoqualmie, and became Ste. Michelle's head of winemaking from 1990 until he left to start Januik Cellars in 1999.

Januik's white wines, graceful and elegant, are remarkably consistent. When he first started making his own Cold Creek chardonnay (he had made it for years at Ste. Michelle) the new-oak influence seemed a bit excessive, but he has ramped it back down and takes full advantage of the vineyard's strengths. Firm in structure, with green apple and spiced pear fruit, it's got a very lively finish, with a lick of light butterscotch and hazelnut crème. His Elerding vineyard chardonnay expresses that site's unique flavors equally well.

Januik's red wines are every bit as good as his whites, detailed wines made in small lots with exacting care. The merlots, blended with cabernet sauvignon, cabernet franc, and petit verdot, are tight, textured, vertically integrated wines, with more character and snap than the usual broadly fruity Washington merlot. The syrahs are saturated, sappy, and brilliantly detailed wines that combine the audacious power of perfectly ripened fruit with the zest of fresh-squeezed citrus and defining notes of pepper, tar, and graphite.

Januik cabernets are the best of the best. The Columbia Valley cab uses Champoux, Klipsun, Red Mountain, Seven Hills, and Ciel du Cheval grapes, an all-star lineup for Washington vineyards. Deep, concentrated, and tannic, it mixes its dense and earthy black fruits with barrel notes of smoke and char. The vineyard designates from Champoux and Seven Hills are textbook examples of the best flavors to be found in the Horse Heaven Hills and Walla Walla appellations, respectively.

Januik is building a showcase facility in Woodinville, due to open in 2007. After decades of doing brilliant work for others and then making his wines in a charmless warehouse, he is finally getting the winery he has long deserved.

K VINTNERS

Founded 1999
820 Mill Creek Road
Walla Walla, WA 99362
509/526-5230
www.kvintners.com
E-mail: charles@kvintners.com

Score: 78 (28/20/24/6)

The wine business often makes you ponder life's inscrutables. Why is gasoline at four bucks a gallon considered horribly expensive, while beer at $64 a gallon (been to the ballpark lately?) is worth a half inning's wait in a long line? Why do wineries spend tens of thousands of dollars designing labels that don't last for three vintages, when a guy like K Vintners' Charles Smith can doodle one on a napkin and come up with something so instantly brilliant that you have to slap your head and say, "Why didn't I think of that?"

The label in question is the House Wine that Smith marketed through his Magnificent Wine Company (now a joint venture with Precept Brands): blocky black type on plain white paper; that's it. But it reads "House Wine," and all of a sudden you want it in your house. So does everyone else. House Wine sold 92,000 cases in its first year. Precept is rumored to have spent millions just for the rights to expand and market the brand.

If Smith were simply a marketing genius, it would be enough to be a success in the wine business. But in truth he's got a terrific palate, honed during more than a decade of living in Copenhagen, touring with and managing a number of Danish rock bands. You might imagine that a few bottles of good wine were consumed during that run.

The idea for K Vintners germinated after a chance invitation to a dinner party in Walla Walla led to a friendship with Christophe Baron of Cayuse. Baron encouraged Smith, who had left Copenhagen to open a small wine shop on Bainbridge Island, to try

his hand at making wine. Walla Walla seemed like the right sort of place, "a town that thrives on the production of sustenance for people" says Smith. The region's mix of wine and agriculture held enormous appeal. And besides, he adds, "California doesn't need any new wines. You wouldn't move to Little Italy to open up a pizza place. There's a great deal of opportunity here in Washington. You can carve out your future just like in pioneer days."

Carve it out he has. K Vintners makes more different syrahs than any winery in the state, perhaps in the country, and to a bottle they are succulent, delicious, and distinctive wines. His arrival in Walla Walla was timed perfectly, his palate is seemingly infallible, and his friendship with Baron blazed the trail to the best grapes from the best vineyards in the valley, not the least of which were Baron's own pampered plots.

Smith is thoughtful and outspoken, generous and egotistical, innovative and combative. His mind races at full throttle at all times; during a brief conversation he will lay out ambitious plans for new labels, new businesses (he owns a growing portfolio of vintage properties in Walla Walla County), and expansive vineyards.

Above all, his wines have style. The kanji-inspired labels—a stark black slash reads "K" on a plain white background—the silly puns (K syrah indeed!), the quirky, slightly boastful names ("The Beautiful." "The Creator"), and the distinctive, nonmainstream flavors reflect the man himself. "The idea [of my label design] was to communicate the language of wine to people who don't speak wine," Smith explains. "Back in the old days they'd have a brand for their livestock; this is like a brand, 'K.' Once you get it, it's like stepping in gum. It speaks in a language that you can understand."

Smith is quite clear in his vision of what wines, particularly Washington state wines, should be. "All my wines taste like the varietal; they taste like the place they were made from," he opines. "And they are beautifully balanced. That's everything. It's a sensory thing; I'm sensitive to what I want these wines to be like. It's not formulaic. Because year in and out grapes don't give you the same things." Neither does Charles Smith, but you may be sure that whatever he is selling, it will grab you by the throat and it won't let you go.

MOUNTAIN DOME

Founded 1984
16315 East Temple Road
Spokane, WA 99217
509/928-BRUT
www.mountaindome.com
E-mail: info@mountaindome.com

Score: 75 (21/26/20/8)

There is nothing in the wine world harder to make competitively than *méthode champ-enoise* sparkling wine; Champagne is arguably the most time- and labor- and money-inten-sive target any winemaker can take aim at. Mountain Dome has been at it since 1984, slowly building up to the current production of about 6000 cases annually, roughly half of it non-vintage Brut.

Michael Manz, who passed away suddenly in the fall of 2006, founded the brand and in recent years shared the winemaking chores with his son Erik. They worked with con-sultant Raphael Brisbois (Iron Horse, Piper Sonoma). The winery, set next to a striking geodesic dome, was built by the Manz family on 85 acres of land a half hour from downtown Spokane.

Vineyard sources have changed over the years. Currently the nonvintage Brut, two-thirds pinot and one-third chardonnay, is sourced principally from Columbia Gorge vineyards. About 300 cases of vin-tage Brut is made in the best years, from selected barrels given an extra three years en tirage. Ten have been made so far ('88, '90, '91, '92, '93, '94, '95, '97, '98, and '99). Mountain Dome makes an excellent rosé and on rare occasions a Cuvée Forté reserve.

First produced in 1995 and released for the millennium, the Cuvée Forté reserve is half pinot and half chardonnay, made from the best of the best grapes and vintages. It is the winery's most elegant sparkling wine, and it has a fine, textured mouthfeel and nicely nuanced flavors of pear, apple, and light citrus. The over-the-top fruitiness of the regular brut is tamed; this has the grace and texture of a genuine Champagne.

Before his death Manz had acquired a new, 350-liter, French-designed, Portuguese-built alembic copper still, and he was designing and building the brick furnace that would fire it, in hopes of producing a Mountain Dome brandy. We wish the very best for this hard-working family and hope that the unique winery that Michael Manz founded will continue under the guidance of the next generation.

Founded 2000
19728 144th Avenue NE
Woodinville, WA 98072
425/481-8317
www.noveltyhillwines.com
E-mail: info@noveltyhillwines.com

Score: 76 (25/20/24/7)

Seattle attorney Tom Alberg, whose venture capital firm specializes in technology start-ups, is the owner of Novelty Hill. The winery's future is centered on two key strengths: its estate vineyard, called Stillwater Creek, and its winemaker, Mike Januik. Stillwater Creek, a steep, south-facing site on the Royal Slope of the Frenchman Hills, was purchased more than two decades ago but not planted until 2000. No expense has been spared, and innovative clonal selection has been chosen, with the goal of creating superior chardonnays, cabernet sauvignons, merlots, and syrahs.

Januik makes both his own wines and those of Novelty Hill in a shared, no-frills warehouse space in Woodinville, and now the two wineries are building a magnificently architected, ultramodern winery and tasting room near Columbia and Ste. Michelle.

With Januik's help, Novelty Hill has been able to source grapes from excellent Red Mountain and Columbia Valley vineyards, and the young winery has made excellent sauvignon blancs and chardonnays from the get-go. Inevitably, the Novelty Hill wines, especially the cabernets and syrahs, are quite similar to Januik's own, not that there is anything wrong with that, since he is one of the state's most talented winemakers.

The first Stillwater Creek wines came out strong, including a rich, creamy chardonnay loaded with pineapple and banana fruit and flecked with peppery spice and nutmeg. The sauvignon blanc is crisp and authoritative, with flavors of melon and mineral limned with lime and citrus and pineapple. Even better is the merlot, powerful and sappy, its tarry core

packed with plummy fruit and whiffs of anise. Finally, the cabernet sauvignon is a high-quality Bordeaux blend, nicely fleshed out with malbec, merlot, and cabernet franc components. Mixed fruits and fine spices come to a focus in the core of raspberry and black cherry, with a suggestion of cola running through the finish.

I may be jumping the gun a bit with the high rating for such a young venture, but given the talent and money behind it, I have to believe that Novelty Hill is going to be a major player in the state. Production is up to 11,000 cases and heading quickly to 20,000. Still-water Creek will need a few years to settle in, but all indications are that this is a fine site that will anchor the brand.

OWEN ROE

Founded 1994
8400 Champoeg Road
Saint Paul, OR 97137
503/678-6514
www.owenroe.com
E-mail: winery@owenroe.com

Score: 80 (26/25/22/7)

As vineyards and winemaking styles have matured, Washington and Oregon have split into quite separate winemaking regions, yet Owen Roe is most accurately described as a Northwest producer, with a foot in both camps. Owen Roe winemaker David O'Reilly, much like his business partner, Peter Rosback of Sineann, makes stylish and intense wines from both Washington and Oregon vineyards. For the purposes of this book, I am focused primarily on the Washington state offerings. A certain amount of confusion ensues from the dual Sineann–Owen Roe brands. David O'Reilly is the winemaker and a partner in Owen Roe. Peter Rosback is the winemaker and a partner in Sineann. Both partnerships also include different members. Each has his own winemaking facility and different grower relationships.

The name Owen Roe, says O'Reilly, originally belonged to a seventeenth-century Irish patriot. "We share his dedication to principle in our work to produce the wines of Owen Roe," O'Reilly writes. "At Owen Roe we do not compromise: Only the best is good enough." In this instance, it's not a boast so much as a calling card. I can't decide if O'Reilly does a better job with his whites or his reds; both are superb. There are three tiers offered: the O'Reillys, value-priced Oregon wines, which feature an Irish wolfhound on the label; the midpriced Owen Roes, with a woodcut label; and the most expensive wines, limited-production, vineyard designates, which come in massive, weighty bottles and sport artsy, iconic photographs of Irish monuments.

The best of the O'Reilly wines is the excellent pinot gris; there is also a pleasant chardonnay and an herbal pinot noir. The Owen Roe lineup is highlighted by the Abbot's Table Red, a popular blend of up to nine different grapes that outclasses many more costly varietal bottlings. A Bordeaux blend called Yakima Valley Red belies its plebeian name with sophisticated and lively herb and spice details. Perfectly balanced, elegant, and stylish, it's the textbook example of how Washington reds can express the best of Old and New World styles.

The winery's vineyard designates are selected to be best of type. The DuBrul vineyard, a high-elevation Yakima Valley site, is the source for many of them, including a powerful riesling with a firm grip and striking minerality; a succulent, dusty merlot, lightly scented with rose petals and chocolate powder; a dense, almost syrupy cabernet sauvignon, loaded with concentrated blueberry fruit, balsamic vinegar, moist earth, and black tea; and a fine "Lady Rosa" syrah, dark, sensuous, hard, and a bit chunky.

There is also a "Rosa Mystica" cabernet franc, stiff and herbal, with unusual cola and root beer flavors, and other gems, such as a Lewis vineyard zinfandel, a Seven Hills (Walla Walla) cabernet, and a syrah called "Ex Umbris" (out from the shadows). Anything from the top tier at Owen Roe is going to be memorable, hand-crafted, and intense.

O•S

Founded 1997
1501 South 92nd Place, Suite B
Seattle, WA 98108
206/243-3427
www.oswinery.com
E-mail: mail@oswinery.com

Score: 75 (24/22/22/7)

Formerly known as Owen-Sullivan (a threatened lawsuit, as usual, prompted the name change), O•S is the project of Bill Owen, a wine industry veteran (in wholesale and retail), and Rob Sullivan, a retired banker. From an initial run of just 80 cases, they've ramped up production to more than 2000 cases, most of them big, full-throttle reds.

These are not wimpy wines, and critics are divided. Much as I admire what O•S has achieved, I have too often felt that their red wines have been pushed to (or just past) the limits. There is no question that the vineyard sources are well chosen, and they include such novelties as a Champoux riesling, a succulent, lush bottle loaded with lemon-drop flavors.

But red wines are the stock in trade. Also from Champoux comes an excellent cabernet franc, with raspberries, strawberries, melon, tobacco, and espresso in the nose and a rough-and-tumble finish. BSH is a blend of cabernet sauvignon, merlot, and cab franc; R3 and M are different red blends from previous vintages.

The Sheridan vineyard provides grapes for the winery's archetypical "Ulysses," which in the best years is a blockbuster, voluptuous red dominated by cabernet franc with a good portion of merlot and cabernet sauvignon. Extracted and volatile, "Ulysses" is certainly not a bashful wine, but it has many layers of expansive scents and flavors, filling the nose and mouth with dried herbs, mineral, leaf, coffee, and scorched earth.

The nearby Dineen vineyard is the source for the O•S syrah, a silky smooth wine, floral and bright with fresh berry juice and lightly toasted chocolatey barrel flavors.

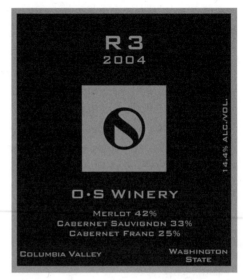

This seems to be the style: Push fermentations to the edge of volatility, for maximum extraction of color, aroma, and sheer alcoholic power, and finish with loads of chocolatey oak. In some instances, to some palates, the wines can taste scorched and raw, with burning, volatile aromas. But at other times, they stop just short of that and deliver the kind of dark, smoky, earthy layers of flavor that make big reds so fascinating. Though I would love to see Owen pull back on the reins just a bit, obviously there are many fans of this style who wouldn't change a thing.

But taste one of the more interesting experiments, such as the winery's Meek vineyard petit verdot, with its flavorful mix of blue plum, cassis, black pepper, black coffee, and smoke, and you can see what O•S can accomplish when everything is working in harmony to create a truly balanced wine.

PEPPER BRIDGE

Founded 1998
1704 JB George Road
Walla Walla, WA 99362
509/525-6502
www.pepperbridge.com
E-mail: info@pepperbridge.com

Score: 77 (27/20/20/10)

Norm McKibben and his partner, Bob Rupar, acquired the Pepper Bridge property in 1989, determined to turn the old wheat ranch into an apple orchard. Wine grapes began to go into the ground in 1991 (five acres of merlot, five of cabernet) and now comprise some 250+ acres.

The first small crop was picked in 1992. McKibben cleverly saw that there were only about 40 acres of grapes planted in the whole valley, so his fruit, however young, would be in demand. The first grapes were sold to Rick Small, Chris Camarda, Gary Figgins, and Marty Clubb. "That kind of marketing," says McKibben, "got people to notice Pepper Bridge."

An estate winery was founded in 1998, and the spacious, gravity-flow winery and tasting room opened in 2000. Jean-Francois Pellet was hired to be the full-time winemaker beginning, with the 1999 vintage, and has done a masterful job of coddling the wines along as the vineyard slowly matured. J-F, as he is called, believes that a winemaker that doesn't show his terroir is not doing the right job. McKibben says he is "not so sure the general public cares that much about it, but to him [Pellet] it's a big thing to show consistently that terroir. You're going to get a little more variation vintage to vintage, because you're not trying to mask it."

Pellet's prediction that he needed at least five vintages to learn the vineyard has proven quite accurate. His fifth vintage of both the merlot and the cabernet was clearly the best yet from Pepper Bridge. The fruit flavors are classic Walla Walla, broad and suggesting strawberry preserves, blackberries, and cassis. New oak is generously applied, and the wines on release are heavily flavored with toast, sweet cocoa, and whiskey barrel. Pepper Bridge also makes a pair of vineyard reserve wines (Pepper Bridge and Seven Hills) that carry the same flavors up a notch or two in intensity.

The winemaking and dedication to superior vineyard practices are what set Pepper Bridge wines apart from many of those who purchase grapes from the vineyard. That vineyard has recently been placed on an aggressive program of organic management, an effort to rebuild soil deadened by decades of wheat farming. As these measures take effect and the vines mature, the impact of the new oak barrels on the finished wines will hopefully be less evident, and the flavors of terroir that are so eagerly sought after will become the defining characteristic of the Pepper Bridge wines.

REININGER

Founded 1997
5858 West Highway 12
Walla Walla, WA 99362
509/522-1994
www.reiningerwinery.com
E-mail: info@reiningerwinery.com

Score: 78 (26/24/22/6)

Chuck Reininger, like Rob Newsom of Boudreaux, began life as a mountaineer, working as a climbing guide in Argentina, Alaska, and Washington. He learned winemaking by working a few vintages at Waterbrook before opening his modest winery, dubbed "Shackteau Reininger," in 1997. It was just the tenth winery in the Valley and among the first to be located at the airport, now home to a thriving, incubator-style community of garagistes.

Reininger himself has moved his wine-making six miles west of town on Highway 12, where he has renovated two old potato sheds into an impressive 15,000-square-foot winery and tasting room. Nearby is the Ash Hollow vineyard, in which he is an investor and from which he receives cabernet, merlot, and syrah.

The winery's production has climbed steadily, from a few hundred to 3500 cases over the first decade. For the Reininger label, quality has been remarkably consistent, thanks to great grape sources and a confident touch with the barrels, and the winery is now sourcing Walla Walla grapes exclusively.

In 2004 a second label, Helix, was introduced. It is designed for larger-production, lower-priced Columbia Valley wines, a way to expand without cannibalizing the founding brand. Named for a town in eastern Oregon where his grandparents once farmed, Helix is making about 5500 cases annually. The early vintages of Reininger were sourced from Pepper Bridge, Seven Hills, and Spring Valley vineyards (no slackers there), but Chuck Reininger's style surmounts vineyard and vintage variation; his wines are supremely smooth and supple, creamy and delicious in the way a thick milkshake is delicious.

Both the merlots and the cabernets are elegant, light, and nicely nuanced; the young fruit from Ash Hollow is not over-manipulated or overwhelmed with too much new oak. Syrahs are done in a classy, confident style showing the dense, tannic, peppery fruit first and foremost. "My entire philosophy with syrah," Reininger explains, "is to show off the grape. She's

such a pretty lady, she needs to be dressed in simple, elegant clothes." In other words, neutral oak. Good call!

There is a sangiovese-based blend called Cima ($45) that Reininger calls his "Super Wallan." The Helix wines, from purchased Columbia Valley grapes, are also off to a good start. First releases include a very nice chardonnay–viognier blend named Aspersa, a Clifton Hill syrah, and a meaty, substantial merlot.

ROBERT KARL CELLARS

Founded 1999
115 W. Pacific Avenue
Spokane, WA 99201
509/363-1353
www.robertkarl.com
E-mail: info@robertkarl.com

Score: 80 (26/20/27/7)

Robert Karl Cellars hit a home run with its first release, a 1999 cabernet sauvignon, and has been knocking it out of the park ever since. Sleek, compact, and polished, its Bordeaux blends and varietal wines consistently score at the top of my tastings.

It's a bit of a schlep from Spokane to the Horse Heaven Hills, where owners Rebecca and Joe Gunselman (another of this state's physician-winemakers) purchase their grapes. That's not a whole lot easier than the kind of travel required to make grapes on Vashon (Andrew Will) or the Olympic Peninsula (Camaraderie), for example. But the Gunselmans are happy to be there. Beginning with their 2003 vintage, all their wines are being made from their designated Horse Heaven vines at Phinny Hill and Andrews. "To me Horse Heaven has a magic to it," says Joe. "It just hit us the first time we traveled there. We didn't know there were a lot of vineyards already there; we just knew it was the place. We learned about Champoux, Phinny Hill; we looked around Alder Ridge. We were awestruck to see all that vineyard."

I can't help but find a studied, precise, clinical, physician's approach in these wines, but I mean that as a sincere compliment. They are clean and polished: Gunselman is to reds what Rulo's Kurt Schlicker is to whites. These red wines, when first released, are locked up tight; they must be decanted.

Robert Karl makes one white wine, a gorgeous sauvignon blanc, toasty and stylish, 100 percent varietal, 90 percent barrel fermented in new French oak. The flavors pile on: toasted coconut, melon, custard pie, light tropical, hints of buttered toast. At 12 bucks a bottle, I don't think you can find a better sauvignon blanc in the country.

The place to start diving into the reds is the Robert Karl Claret, a minimeritage that is a lighter version of the winery's reserve. You get meritage quality at a mutt-wine price, jammed with mixed berries, plums, spice, hints of pepper and clove, plenty of natural acid, and no obvious oak; its flavors unwrap luxuriously in a series of gradient layers. Joe Gunselman modestly calls it "a deviation" because it breaks the winery's commitment to staying varietally focused. But he found they had too many blending grapes to make only a cabernet. The Claret sops up the overflow. "Malbec," he notes, "comes in really ugly, juicy, sloppy, and big, but it adds such midpalate. It adds gusto."

I don't know when I've had a pure merlot any better. Despite its high alcohol content (listed at an honest 15.5 percent), the wine is smooth and supple, and, amazingly, it retains the fresh herbal highlights that are usually obliterated in high-octane wines. The cabernet is better still. It's not easy to make 100 percent varietal cabernet such as this; the fruit must be perfect, because you can't use other grapes to fill in the holes. Compact, extremely firm, and muscular, it barely hints at layers of cassis, berry, cherry, cranberry, and more. The stiff, tart fruit gives it up grudgingly; the tannins too are ripe, but hard as nails. Give it a good airing, and it begins to show itself: a dark, rich, and thick wine, layered with red and black fruits, the tannins fine-grained and mouth-coating, the fruit intense with streaks of smoke, anise, herb, soy, baking chocolate.

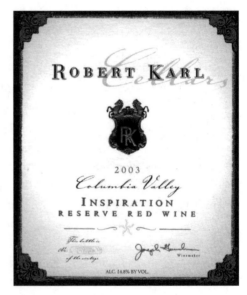

A tiny amount of reserve cabernet (fewer than 100 cases) is also made. Dubbed "Inspiration," it is everything a reserve should be: wonderfully concentrated, with sweet, stiff, sappy fruit. Juicy in the mouth, but tightly wound, it is fleshed out with buttery oak flavors of vanilla, toast, and caramel. Young, hard, and a little bit hostile, this needs major decanting; or stick it away and let it blossom for a decade or more. In fact, I would be very surprised if all these young reds did not have a lifetime measured in decades.

RULO

Founded 2001
3525 Pranger Road
Walla Walla, WA 99362
509/525-7856

www.rulowinery.com

E-mail: schlick@pocketinet.com

Score: 82 (28/20/28/6)

Because Kurt and Vicki Schlicker choose to self-distribute their Rulo wines (to save their customers money), they are rather hard to find outside of Walla Walla. Rulo's owners do not seek out, nor do they need, high praise from influential critics; they sell every bottle and have a growing legion of admirers. So you may not be familiar with their wines. But if you love clean, bracing flavors, flavors that seem to crystallize the essential components of wine—fruit and acid—and capture the sparkling clarity of grapes in a style reminiscent of great Friulan producers such as Schiopetto, Marco Felluga, and Venica & Venica, well, Rulo is the Washington winery for you.

Kurt Schlicker took the name Rulo from the side of a grain elevator he recalled from his childhood. He and Vicki moved to Walla Walla from California, where he attended medical school and worked as an anesthesiologist, a practice he continues to this day, even as he runs his meticulous winery.

Built in 2001, Rulo is in a Spartan building next to the owners' home and next door to Isenhower Cellars. Viognier, chardonnay, and syrah are the focal points. It cannot be overstated: These wines offer extraordinary clarity and focus. They profile superclean fruit with bracing acid and tread lightly on the new oak. Kurt Schlicker takes full advantage of his degrees in microbiology, pediatrics, and anesthesiology and runs a tight ship.

For some tasters, wines that smell like old saddles or silage or barnyard stalls may have character, but I wish that more young wineries followed Schlicker's lead and got fanatic about showing superclean fruit. His wines are immaculate, though never boring or stripped. There is nothing clinical about them, but you get the feeling they have been well cared for.

Rulo's sauvignon blanc–viognier blend, named Combine, is vivid and bracing, like a dash through a cold mountain spring. All stainless fermentation, no malolactic, it's cool as ice, clear and leesy, the tart fruit edged with citrus rind flavors mixing orange, lemon, and lime.

Rulo's crisp, laserlike viogniers also feature flavors of citrus rind rather than ripe peach. There is sometimes a powerful herbal note, tasting of juniper and quinine, that lays down a spicy spine in the wine. Chardonnays are barrel-fermented but never oaky. Green-gold in color, they marry pretty peach flavors to a mix of cinnamon and Asian spices.

Rulo's nonvintage red blend called Syrca is roughly three-quarters syrah and one-quarter cabernet, bright, tart, peppery, and smoky with lifted scents of mint. The reserve syrah, called Silo, is spectacular, as fine as any syrah I've ever tasted from Washington state. This is classic styling: firm and fruity, with spanky acids and a finish that runs and runs, annotated with caramel and roasted nuts.

Schlicker pulls no punches when asked how he can keep the price on such a great bottle so much lower than anything comparable. "I think our syrah is a good value; it'll stand up to anything the Rhône or Australia can throw at it for around that price. We buy a lot of those wines and we drink a lot of those wines; I know what's out there. We probably pay as much for our grapes as anyone; and we're still able to sell our wines for these prices. We're not making a lot of money, but we're keeping the lights on. If I see one more $40 or $50 bottle of syrah out of this valley from some newbie, I'm gonna kill them." No need to kill them, Kurt, you've already left them in the dust.

SAVIAH CELLARS

Founded 2000
1979 JB George Road
Walla Walla, WA 99362
509/520-5166
www.saviahcellars.com
E-mail: info@saviahcellars.com

Score: 75 (25/20/24/6)

Richard Funk's Saviah Cellars is situated in grand company, across the road from Beresan and a stone's throw from Va Piano, Pepper Bridge, and Northstar. He studied microbiology at Montana State and began home brewing, briefly considering a career in beer. A move to Walla Walla in 1991 led to an interest in the growing wine industry.

His work as an environmental health specialist with the Walla Walla County Health Department brought him in close contact with the wineries, as he helped them untangle complicated water quality and wastewater management regulations. He now makes wine his full-time occupation.

Saviah started small, with just 300 cases the first year, and has leapt quickly up to over 4200. The wines are fairly priced for the company they keep. Saviah's chardonnays deliver leesy, creamy, butterscotch flavors around green apple fruit; they carry themselves with crisp authority and keep the structure firm.

A red blend called "The Jack" has been a huge success and accounts for almost half the total production. Priced around $15, it uses great fruit (most recently Seven Hills and Canoe Ridge vineyard merlot mixed with Pepper Bridge and Cold Creek cabernet). It sports one of the cleverest labels to come down the road in a long while, a sepia-toned jack of clubs that references Funk's grandfather Jack Hutchens. Saviah was the name of Anita Funk's great-grandmother, a schoolteacher, artist, and author who settled in western Montana a century ago.

All of Saviah's red wines deliver sweet, tangy, ripe red fruits; "The Jack" is all about berries and cherries and hints of mango and apricot, then rolls into a silky smooth middle, finishing with a lick of licorice. The "Big Sky Cuvée," a Columbia Valley Bordeaux blend, shows some muscle and cabernet strength, with black cherry, cassis, and plenty of chocolatey oak. Funk's Walla Walla Valley red, called "Une Vallée," is even better, with plum, spicy cherry, oak, and chocolate nicely layered into finishing notes of tobacco and tea tannins.

Those are the stars of the show, but there are also limited-edition bottles, such as the Red Mountain and Stillwater Creek vineyard syrahs. Steady and smooth, Saviah is on track to make a real name for itself in the crowded Walla Walla field.

SEVEN HILLS

Founded 1988
212 North 3rd Avenue
Walla Walla, WA 99362
509/529-7198
www.sevenhillswinery.com
E-mail: info@sevenhillswinery.com

Score: 79 (23/25/23/8)

Seven Hills began as a vineyard and is still one of the most-sourced and oldest suppliers of Walla Walla grapes. Both Leonetti and Woodward Canyon leaned heavily on Seven Hills grapes in their early vintages, and Leonetti was the first winery to bottle a Seven Hills vineyard reserve (in 1987).

Casey McClellan's family established the vineyard in the early 1980s, and, because it was situated on the Oregon side of the appellation, the winery was initially located in the Oregon town of Milton-Freewater. This left McClellan the odd man out for a number of years. The Washington winery associations viewed him as an Oregon winery and did not include him in their promotional efforts; the Oregon winery associations barely knew that the Walla Walla appellation existed. In fact, during its first decade, Seven Hills was eastern Oregon's only grape-growing winery.

McClellan sold the vineyard some years ago, and the Seven Hills winery joined the Washington team, relocating to a fine old brick building in Walla Walla (it also houses the excellent Whitehouse-Crawford restaurant). The original Seven Hills vineyard is now called Windrow; the current Seven Hills vineyard is under separate ownership and more recently planted. McClellan's new estate vineyard is nearby, a field planting of half cabernet and the rest divided among petit verdot, merlot, and malbec.

Though it is widely regarded by its peers as one of the region's founding fathers, Seven Hills winery remains somewhat underappreciated by the critics. I suspect that it retains a bit of its original odd-man-out persona, despite the steady, consistent quality vintage after vintage. Perhaps it is the unassuming style of the wines or the quietly modest personality of the winemaker. Neither shouts out, "Recognize me!," and in such a crowded field, that can be a liability.

Among the white wines is a fine Oregon pinot gris, a Columbia Valley riesling, and a Columbia Valley viognier. All are made in a fruit-forward, crisp, no-frills style. Cabernets and merlots first established the reputation of the brand, back when all of the fruit was estate-grown, and these wines, now sourced from a wide variety of Columbia Valley vineyards, still form the core of the portfolio.

Purchased Seven Hills grapes go into the winery's Seven Hills vineyard designates. McClellan also purchases top-quality Red Mountain fruit for his Klipsun and Ciel du Cheval designates, the latter a classic show of tart black cherry, plum, and cranberry fruit along with gravelly stone.

Seven Hills syrahs are always well balanced. The Walla Walla Valley bottling, cofermented with viognier, sports an invigorating, lifted nose that combines lemon and lime and orange peel with raspberry syrup and mocha. A rare Walla Walla Valley–grown tempranillo is dark and gamy and exotic, a beguiling blend of roasted meats, vanilla, licorice, clove, and black cherry.

The winery's top wine, in terms of price, is the Pentad Red, an estate-grown, cabernet-dominated Bordeaux blend that includes a generous portion of carmenère. Its smoky oak aromas and flavors are out in front; the fruit is ripe and silky.

I don't believe you will ever be disappointed with any wine from Seven Hills, but you may very well be surprised by the power and polish tucked away inside these graceful, unpretentious efforts.

SINEANN

Founded 1994
PO Box 10
Newberg, OR 97132
503/341-2698
www.sineann.com
E-mail: sineann@pcez.com

Score: 83 (28/24/22/9)

SINEANN
Old Vine
Zinfandel
2005
Columbia Valley
14.8% Alcohol By Volume

Sineann began as the brainchild of Peter Rosback and David O'Reilly (Owen Roe), created while both were working at Oregon's Elk Cove winery. Rosback was an amateur winemaker helping out during crush, and O'Reilly was Elk Cove's marketing director. Both partners have Irish roots and wanted an Irish moniker. Sineann (pronounced shuh-NAYN), says Rosback, was the mythical princess of the little people. She fell in the river and drowned (in wine, we presume).

From the start, Rosback was Sineann's winemaker, O'Reilly its marketer. When Owen Roe was created, O'Reilly became that brand's winemaker, and for a time both operated out of the same facility. Today they source completely different vineyards and have separate wineries. Sineann's is located at the Medici vineyard, and Rosback makes the Medici wines as well as his own.

Sineann debuted with a stunning old-vine zinfandel, sourced from an almost-forgotten, century-old vineyard near Hood River called The Pines. "I had tasted a great 1985 zinfandel from Hood River Vineyards," Rosback later recalled, "absolutely bursting with deep, rich fruit, but with a contaminated old-oak flaw." Rosback figured that by using better barrels he could make a better wine. That first old-vine zin became the paradigm for all of Sineann's wines, which quickly gathered momentum as the brand rapidly expanded. Rosback, a manic, wiry, long-haired, hockey-playing sushi addict, relentlessly searches out fruit from great, often-undiscovered sites. He then meticulously sets up the specific rows and viticultural practices he will require, cutting tonnage down to levels as low as one ton per acre in some instances, and sets about crafting his intense, brilliant wines.

It is rare for any winery anywhere to show a lineup of wines as varied, powerful, and impressive as these. Sineann's website lists 30 or more current vintages for sale at any given time, and nothing is backed up; everything is released very young and sells out quickly. Pinot noirs are sourced from up to a dozen different Oregon sites, including some in the new Columbia Gorge AVA, which straddles the Washington–Oregon border. Sineann's gewürztraminers come from three different vineyards; the best is the Celilo, a spicy mix of stone fruits set against crisp citrus and mineral.

Another highlight is the Champoux vineyard "Block One" cabernet sauvignon, from some of the oldest vines in Washington. Deeply concentrated and Bordeaux-like, the wine layers black fruit, cedar, and streaks of iron ore with sculpted, refined tannins. From young Champoux vines Sineann makes a firm, full-bodied "Baby Poux" cabernet along with a dense, intense cabernet franc.

In 2006 Rosback began sourcing old-vine grapes from the Cold Creek vineyard, the jewel in the crown of Ste. Michelle's expansive properties. The mouth waters in anticipation of what will come from that perfect pairing of vintner and vineyard. Sineann is also a leader in packaging trends, one of the first wineries in the country to use the glass stoppers marketed by Vino-Lok.

I have never had a wine from Sineann that did not rise well above average; many are extraordinary. Pricing is all over the map but mostly reasonable, particularly in view of the labor-intensive winemaking, the fanatic devotion to small crop loads, and the miniscule quantities produced. Were Rosback operating out of Spring Mountain or some other Napa cult spot, these wines could sell for triple their cost, if you could find them at all. Odds are that there would be a waiting list to get on Sineann's waiting list.

SOOS CREEK

Founded 1989
20404 140th Ave SE
Kent, WA 98042
253/631-8775
www.sooscreekwine.com
E-mail: winemaker@sooscreekwine.com

Score: 83 (28/25/26/4)

No one can accuse Soos Creek's Dave Larsen of impatience. The first of a growing number of Boeing Wine Club alumni to make it to the big leagues, Larsen crushed his debut commercial vintage in 1989. Fifteen vintages later he finally retired from his day job as a Boeing financial planner to take on wine-making full time.

A new winery building at his home in south King County was the early payoff. Soos Creek has been able to ramp up its production to 1200 cases annually: a pair of single-vineyard cabernet sauvignons, a merlot, and a couple of Bordeaux blends. "I have no grandiose plans of getting too big," Larsen insists. "I like being small; I like doing everything myself."

The winery is named after a little creek located nearby, and its wines are easily spotted on retail shelves by their distinctive label graphic of a horse outlined in thick, black ink. Larsen was able to line up impeccable vineyard sources (Ciel du Cheval, Champoux, and Charbonneau among them) early in the going. He remembers seeking out their fruit because, he says, "Woodward Canyon, Leonetti,

ARTIST SERIES #4

2004

SOOS CREEK

COLUMBIA VALLEY
RED WINE

ALCOHOL 14.1% BY VOL.

and Quilceda Creek were already doing great things with it." At the time, he wondered why more people weren't after the same stuff he was.

Now they are, and such exceptional grapes are hard to come by. Soos Creek does well by them. Currently Larsen makes two standout single-vineyard cabernet sauvignons. The Champoux vineyard bottling is a broad bruiser of a wine, friendly as a lapdog and loaded with black cherry fruit, cocoa, and toast; the Ciel du Cheval is better still, with earthy scents of barn and fur wedded to licorice, black cherry, and cassis.

In 2003 Larsen released his first merlot, a happy accident when he discovered that his other blends were better off without it. He may or may not continue to make merlot in the future, but he says it's selling well. Sundance is his inexpensive red blend, but its blend of cabernet sauvignon, merlot, cab franc, and 25 percent petit verdot gives it the substantial tannins and dense, black cherry fruit of a far more expensive wine.

At the high end is the winery's Artist's Series Red, a tight, slaty Bordeaux blend. It's got firm, hard, but certainly ripe tannins wrapped around concentrated cassis and mulberry fruit. Compact and very well made, it needs years to soften up and express itself fully.

All Soos Creek wines are excellent values. Across the board these are wines with wonderful density and concentration, ripely balanced, plummy, mixed red fruits, and elegantly astringent tannins. Larsen gets wonderfully layered, elegant flavors without anything harsh, sharp, or rough. His wines are thoroughly professional, never a hint of volatility or other technical flaws. In short, real winemaking craft is on display here, every detail beautifully rendered, substantial but not out of whack in any way. Soos Creek is one of the great, under-valued, stellar performers in the state.

At a recent visit to the winery, Larsen kindly opened a 1995 Soos Creek cabernet when I asked him how well these wines cellared. Three days later, when I finished the last of it, it was still smooth, plummy, and detailed with evolved fruit, spice, and floral components.

SPRING VALLEY VINEYARD

Founded 1999
1682 Corkrum Road
Walla Walla, WA 99362
509/337-6915
www.springvalleyvineyard.com
E-mail: info@springvalleyvineyard.com

Score: 80 (28/20/24/8)

For over 100 years the Corkrum family has farmed wheat at their Spring Valley ranch, 12 miles northeast of Walla Walla. In 1993 they planted two acres of merlot, a successful experiment that has grown to include 40+ acres of merlot, cabernet sauvignon, cabernet franc, petit verdot, malbec, and syrah. The lush vineyard is still surrounded by wheat fields and is truly one of the most picturesque sites in Washington wine country.

Almost immediately Spring Valley grapes were in demand, going to Cadence, Walla Walla Vintners, Reininger, and Tamarack, among others. Sparked by the interest being shown, the Derbys launched their own winery with the help of Gordon Venneri and Myles Anderson of Walla Walla Vintners. They produced 1000 cases of a merlot-dominated blend and named it "Uriah" to honor Shari Corkrum Derby's grandfather. His photograph is on the label.

The new winery's lineup quickly expanded to include several additional wines. Frederick is primarily cabernet sauvignon, Derby is all cabernet, Nina Lee is pure syrah, and Muleskinner is all merlot. Small amounts of a cabernet franc are sometimes made also. The wines named for the family pioneers have interesting labels featuring old photographs and brief biographies,. The Muleskinner is a tribute to farmer Frederick Corkrum's skill with mule teams in the early twentieth century.

All of the Spring Valley wines share a common terroir, quite distinct from any other Walla Walla Valley vineyard. Intense, almost syrupy berry flavors are augmented by streaks of herb, grass, leaf, and bark—grace notes if you will—that characterize this unique site. The fruit is ripened to fairly high alcohol levels and buoyed with powerful acids.

Tragedy struck Spring Valley late in 2004, when winemaker Devin Derby died following a one-car accident. It sent the winery into disarray, created discord among family members, and ultimately led to the sale of the brand, though not the vineyard, to Ste. Michelle Wine Estates.

The dust from that sale is yet to settle, but Ste. Michelle is unlikely to make any sweeping changes with such a unique property. Given the extent to which Devin Derby and his wife, Mary, were responsible for the quality of the brand, this sale may be the best possible outcome.

Serge Laville, a Frenchman who joined the winery as Devin Derby's assistant in 2002, has been promoted to winemaker. Devin's widow, Mary Derby, had been instrumental to the winemaking also; but she is no longer involved in the winery. For the remaining members of the Derby family, the sale solves the problem of what to do with a successful small wine operation that they had no intention of running. "Maybe 20 years ago we might have taken it on," says Devin's father, Dean Derby. "But we're 70 years old; this takes a load off us."

SYNCLINE WINE CELLARS

Founded 1999
PO Box 761
Bingen, WA 98605
509/493-4705
www.synclinewine.com
E-mail: info@synclinewine.com

Score: 81 (27/20/26/8)

Syncline's James Mantone may just be the Billy Beane of Washington winemakers. Beane, the celebrated general manager of the Oakland Athletics, was famously profiled in *Moneyball* as a guy who found value in ballplayers who didn't fit the mold, ballplayers he could sign for little money and turn into champs.

Mantone does that with wine grapes. He's in his mid-thirties, bookish, and intense, with wide-set, open, inquisitive eyes—not shy, but not demonstrative either. A native Midwesterner, he was studying organic chemistry at Purdue when a professor gave him a bottle of Oregon pinot noir. The wine bug bit, hard.

In the summer of 1995 he backpacked through Oregon, living in a tent and working crush, and eventually hooked up with a custom crush facility making small batches of wine for a wide range of clients. "It was like working at 10 or 12 different wineries, all at the same time," he recalls.

He tasted some early Rhône Ranger efforts from McCrea and Glen Fiona, wines so good that he started driving up to visit eastern Washington wine country and meet the growers. "I started to see some great potential in the land. Everybody was still chasing merlot, which they picked in the first weeks of September, and they didn't get a frost till November! So I asked myself, 'Well, what's wrong with the rest of the growing season?' And I started looking into some late-ripening varietals." A marriage and a move north brought him to the Columbia Gorge to start Syncline Wine Cellars with Poppie Mantone, who now serves as assistant winemaker. Though Syncline's first wine was a pinot noir, it is the Rhône varietals that really constitute the heart of Syncline's portfolio: viognier, roussanne, grenache, and syrah.

On a visit to Condrieu to research viognier, Mantone was told that sand—lots of it—is the key for growing it. At Butch Milbrandt's Clifton vineyard, he found three feet of windblown sand on top of hundreds of feet of fist-sized river rocks. Bingo! Syncline's viognier is penetrating and ripe, big but, not blowsy, with nuances of orange peel, citrus, and apricot and hints of peach, mango, and honeysuckle.

Also from Milbrandt grapes comes a sweet, spicy, pungent syrah with meaty, bright berry scents of white pepper, blueberry, and violets. Syncline makes other vineyard-designated syrahs from McKinley Springs and Destiny Ridge, along with small amounts of a reserve. The winery's very newest releases include roussanne, a rosé of grenache, and the most recent vintage of the Subduction red, this time a syrah–mourvèdre blend with a splash of viognier. "There's a bit of the underdog aspect in me," says Mantone. "If I wanted to do the easy thing I would have just made the big three [chardonnay, cabernet, and merlot]. But look, I'm making grenache rosé, viognier, roussanne! Underdog grapes."

Syncline's success with such an unusual lineup is proof that you can be a boutique start-up with big aspirations but not much cash and hit the mark with stylish wines that have something important to say while still keeping your pricing realistic. "The buzz phrase," Mantone explains, "is that wine is made in the vineyard. But you talk to growers and they say a lot of winemakers sign the contract and are never seen again till harvest. Washington is such a tremendously great climate that it's really quite forgiving. You can get away with a few sloppy things and still make good wines. I want to see what we can get if we cut out the sloppy things. I think it's how we manage our vineyard rows, not how much money we spend on oak, that will differentiate us."

Founded 1995
225 Vineyard Lane (off Mill Creek Road)
Walla Walla, WA 99362
509/525-4724
www.wallawallavintners.com
E-mail: mjanders@bmi.net

Score: 78 (26/23/21/8)

Myles Anderson, who serves as the director of the Walla Walla Institute for Enology and Viticulture, founded Walla Walla Vintners with Gordon Venneri in 1995, about the same time as Dunham Cellars. (There is some disagreement about who was eighth in the region and who was ninth.) WWV's focus is making hand-crafted, premium red wines, specifically cabernet franc, cabernet sauvignon, malbec, merlot, and sangiovese. These are succulent wines in the Leonetti mold, voluptuously ripe and decadently oaked.

Venneri and Anderson had been amateur winemakers for a decade before turning commercial. "We experimented with oak chips, used oak barrels, beer kegs, food-grade plastic buckets, plastic apple juice containers, Coca-Cola syrup stainless steel containers, and glass carboys," they write. "Some tasted bad and some blew up in wine racks." They persisted, and, ultimately, they prevailed.

Once they turned pro, success came quickly, and Walla Walla Vintners has steadily grown from an initial production of 675 cases to more than 5000 cases currently. Their wines are seductive, fruit forward, soft, and round, sometimes called "baby Leonettis" by critics. In fact, Venneri and Anderson are good friends with Leonetti founder Gary Figgins, and their winery is adjacent to his Mill Creek Upland vineyard.

What gives these wines their hedonistic flavors is aging in several different types of new oak. Anderson and Venneri enjoy experimenting with different barrels, an ongoing effort to understand the complex synergy between barrels and grapes. Their merlot is richly aromatic with mocha and chocolate, tastes of spiced plum and cherry fruit, and feels deliciously soft and round in the mouth.

The cabernet franc has scents of tea leaf and black cherry and flavors of bright berry and cassis, with smoke and licorice woven through. It finishes firm and chewy, with the roasted-coffee character of the cab franc beautifully evident. The cabernet sauvignon is classy from the get-go, with an appealing mix of strawberry preserves, anise, licorice candy, smoke, and cedar. The fruit and oak are beautifully matched and laced together, and the flavors unfold with a slightly salty, mineral edge.

In 2003 a Vineyard Select cabernet sauvignon was made, for just the second time in a decade. A cut above the regular cab, it is loaded with sweet-tart berries and flavors of coffee liqueur and chocolate-covered espresso beans. WWV has also begun making some vineyard designates: a Cordon Grove vineyard Cuvée Red and a Sagemoor vineyard Cuvée, both Bordeaux blends. The sangiovese, though not as rich as its stablemates, is very pleasing, a ripe bowlful of berries, finishing soft as silk.

WATERBROOK

Founded 1984
31 East Main Street (tasting room only)
Walla Walla, WA 99362
509/522-1262
www.waterbrook.com
E-mail: info@waterbrook.com

Score: 80 (24/26/22/8)

Until its sale to Precept Brands in 2006, this 42,000-case winery was one of the largest family-owned operations in the Northwest. It was Walla Walla's fourth winery when it was founded in 1984 by Eric and Janet Rindal, and it quickly established itself as the value brand in the region, a mantle it can claim to this day.

Grapes come from Red Mountain vineyards, Columbia Valley vineyards, and the winery's own Blackrock and Waterbrook estate vineyards. The Blackrock vineyard, near Red Mountain in the Columbia Valley, was planted in 1997; it includes 18 acres of cabernet sauvignon, seven of cabernet franc, and eight of merlot. New plantings will soon add another 20 acres of syrah, petit verdot, malbec, tempranillo, mourvèdre, and carignane. Waterbrook's Walla Walla Valley estate vineyard was planted in 1998 and grows 12 acres of chardonnay.

Solid, rarely spectacular, but genuinely flavorful and very reasonably priced, Waterbrook wines have kept up with the times and then some. The viognier is luscious, tart, and snappy, perfectly ripe without excessive alcohol or any hint of bitterness. The mainstream whites, particularly the chardonnay and sauvignon blanc, show plenty of toasty new oak but balance it nicely against broadly flavorful fruit.

When Washington was first becoming known for its exceptional merlots in the early 1990s, Waterbrook consistently offered the best budget bottles, wines that could stand up with those costing three times as much. Cabernets are more tannic and substantial, their flavors laced with herb, pepper, and green tea. Syrahs are light but clean and refreshing, with surprising tenacity. Their Mélange, a blend of merlot, cabernet sauvignon, cab franc, sangiovese, and syrah, is a restaurant favorite that has become iconic. It mixes well-sourced grapes and substantial flavors of Washington-grown fruit at a modest cost. The most recent vintage shows dark tar and licorice, along with plum and black tea and teasing hints of chocolatey oak.

Though many more prestigious Walla Walla wineries have captured consumers' attention with a combination of charm, accolades, and product scarcity, what Walla Walla has not had in abundance are budget wines. In tasting after tasting, the really standout bottles, whether white or red, have price tags ranging from the mid-$20s up to $60 or more, not exactly everyday wines! Waterbrook's invaluable contribution is to offer widely available, well-made, true-to-varietal wines at far more affordable prices.

7

THE BENCH

In baseball, the bench consists of players who have some special skill that can help the team in certain situations. These are not your "five-tool" players, but they have at least one valuable and exceptional strength: They hit left-handed pitching, or they steal bases, or they don't commit fielding errors. The 30 wineries in this chapter are all candidates to move up in this book's pecking order in the future. They have all made the cut. I have indicated particular strengths and in some instances areas in which I think there is room for improvement. The thing to remember is that these are all winners, with at least five vintages released.

ANDRAKE CELLARS

Founded 1998
6315 Boston Harbor Road NE
Olympia, WA 98506
360/943-3746
www.andrakecellars.com
E-mail: bobandrake@msn.com

Score: 56 (18/20/14/4)

Bob Andrake learned the practical side of winemaking by helping out at McCrea Cellars and Andrew Will. He's a big man, and he makes big wines—about 2500 cases annually.

Early releases showed massive, raisiny fruit, thick oak, and rough tannins. Recently Andrake has toned it down somewhat, although the wines still deliver outsized style and flavor. The regular cabernet sauvignon is deeply colored and age-worthy, while the Reserve Cuvée is notable for its wild black cherry aroma and red licorice flavor. A pair of merlots (Washington State and Red Mountain) are full bodied and full flavored. Tiny amounts of sangiovese, syrah, malbec, and cabernet franc are also produced and sold to mailing list clients. More work is needed to elevate them to the quality of the mainstream reds. The second label is called Hurricane Ridge.

Prices are relatively high, starting around $30 and running as high as $40 or more for the big reds.

Best bottle: Cabernet sauvignon is the star here, especially if you like it thick and meaty and dark.

APEX CELLARS AND APEX II

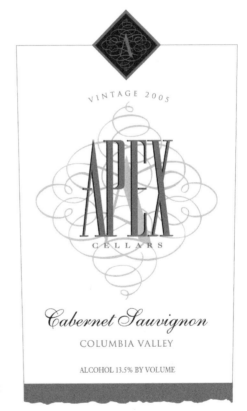

Founded 1988 and 2001
111 East Lincoln Avenue
Sunnyside, WA 98944
509/839-9463 or 1-800-814-7004
www.apexcellars.com
E-mail: winery@apexcellars.com

Apex Score: 58 (16/20/16/6)
Apex II Score: 57 (18/15/18/6)

Apex was originally the superpremium label for a group of wineries that also included W.B. Bridgman and Washington Hills. In 2004 the Washington Hills brand was sold (to Precept), and the Bridgman wines are marketed regionally, mostly on the east coast. Apex II, which was introduced a few years ago, is a big improvement on both of those brands and has delivered solidly made wines at lower price points than the regular Apex.

Apex does best with its cabernets. A recent tasting of almost every vintage from 1990 to 2002 was impressive; the wines were all evolving well, drinking well, and showing vintage variation. The core fruit for Apex comes from the winery's Outlook vineyard, a cool Yakima Valley site. The cabs are more Bordeaux-like than many in Washington, and they age gracefully, with subtle flavors of leaf, herb, forest, and light toast. That said, I have found significant bottle variation among them, and vintages for both Apex white and red wines seem to be backing up.

Brian Carter, who has been making wine in Washington since the 1970s, has been winemaker since 1990. The extensive Apex lineup includes such unusual wines as a dry, barrel-fermented gewürztraminer and a late-harvest riesling.

When owner Harry Alhadeff sold the Washington Hills brand to Precept, he and Carter embarked on a two-pronged strategy to reinvigorate Apex and to offer consumers a well-made alternative, priced for everyday consumption: Apex II. The Apex II lineup includes eight different varietal wines, all made with Yakima Valley grapes. A stricter selection now goes into the Apex line, while Apex II benefits by receiving some of the discarded Apex barrels.

Best bottles: Apex cabernets and syrahs are the best of that lineup, with the syrah showing dense fruit flavors mixing blackberry, blueberry, raspberry, and black cherry. Apex II does especially well with its white wines; the sauvignon blanc is creamy and seamless; the chardonnay is a lip-smacking mix of tropical fruit and sweet crème brulée.

ARBOR CREST

Founded 1982
Cliff House
4705 North Fruithill Road
Spokane, WA 99217
509/927-9463
www.arborcrest.com
E-mail: info@arborcrest.com

Score: 65 (18/22/18/7)

Brothers David and Harold Mielke founded Arbor Crest in 1982. The family history as Inland Empire fruit growers dates back to 1910. When David retired a few years ago, Harold's daughter Kristina Mielke van Löben Sels took charge of the winemaking (roughly 20,000 cases annually), following six years as associate winemaker at Ferrari-Carano. She and her husband, Jim, have revitalized the winery, putting more attention on vineyard management, and they are working hard to bring consistency to all of the winery's releases.

Recently they became part owners in the Wahluke Slope vineyard, with Jim serving as the managing partner. Arbor Crest also carries long-term contracts with other favored sites, such as Dionysus, Bacchus, Conner Lee, Milbrandt-Katherine Leone, Milbrandt-Sundance, Stillwater Creek, and Klipsun. In all of these vineyards Arbor Crest has designated rows and remains active in year-round management.

From the beginning the winery has produced exceptional sauvignon blancs that showcase intense, creamy, ripe, and sometimes tropical fruit flavors. The Conner Lee and Sagemoor vineyard chardonnays are also done well. More recently the winery has put its efforts into improving its red wines, particularly its cabernet and syrah. These wines show a tendency for high-toned aromas and occasionally volatile flavors; otherwise they are robust and well crafted. Small amounts of malbec, sangiovese, cabernet franc, and petite sirah are also made.

Cliff House, a national historic landmark set high above the Spokane River, is one of the state's most spectacular tasting rooms. A satellite tasting room in downtown Spokane has also opened in the Riverpark Square Mall.

Best bottles: Their excellent track record with sauvignon blanc still makes this the standout Arbor Crest wine. A very good cabernet franc and a ripe, rich merlot are the best of the red wine lineup.

CAMARADERIE CELLARS

Founded 1992
334 Benson Road
Port Angeles, WA 98363
360/417-3564
www.camaraderiecellars.com
E-mail: corson4@tenforward.com

Score: 72 (22/22/22/6)

Camaraderie began, as have so many Washington boutiques, as a weekend hobby. One hundred pounds of grapes were purchased in the fall of 1981, five gallons of cabernet sauvignon were produced, and that first wine won a gold medal at the Puyallup fair in 1983. The hook was set.

"The best things in life are meant to be shared," says winemaker Don Corson. For him and his wife Vicki, and business partner Gene Unger (who keeps all things mechanical humming along), that means wine and food and friendship. Hence the winery name. An intense, dynamic man with a natural gift for teaching and an inspirational zest for wine, Corson has navigated the hurdles of his first decade of commercial winemaking and steadily grown the enterprise, which now produces around 3200 cases of reds and another 600 of white.

Camaraderie lays claim to being the farthest northwest winery in the continental United States. That tells you something about the winemaker. Moving grapes 300 miles over desert, mountain passes, and the Puget Sound in the midst of crush doesn't faze him. And it doesn't hurt the wines either. "I'm thinking of putting up a billboard saying 'Washington State is Wine Country, not just where the grapes are grown,'" jokes, Corson.

Camaraderie's white wines have been a mixed bag; the winery's forte is clearly its cabernet-based reds. Top vineyards such as Champoux, Artz, Milbrandt, and Chandler Reach provide the raw materials, which Corson fusses over relentlessly. He wants his wines to be ranked among Washington's best, but he keeps his prices affordable and is adamantly non-elitist.

Camaraderie's top blended red, named Grâce (pronounced grahhss), is full, seamless, and rich, its satiny fruit layered on chocolatey oak, with the underlying acid-driven structure of Washington grapes. The merlots are substantial and loaded with smoke and cedar, and Camaraderie also makes one of the best cabernet francs in the state. New is a white wine blend called Trinquer ("to clink" in French), a pleasing mix of sauvignon blanc, sémillon, and viognier.

Best bottle: Grâce claims the honor here, though the regular cabernets and merlots are not far behind.

CANOE RIDGE VINEYARD

Founded 1994
1102 West Cherry Street
Walla Walla, WA 99362
509/527-0885
www.canoeridgevineyard.com
E-mail: info@canoeridgevineyard.com

Score: 56 (16/15/18/7)

Canoe Ridge Vineyard (this is not Canoe Ridge Estate, which is part of Ste. Michelle Wine Estates) was founded by Chalone and a small group of shareholders from Washington state in the mid-1990s. The timing was good, because the AVA now known as the Horse Heaven Hills was just beginning its expansive growth and development.

The name was coined by explorers Lewis and Clark, who first spotted a five-mile-long, canoe-shaped geological formation running east–west about 900 feet above the Columbia River. The 163-acre vineyard is planted primarily to merlot and cabernet sauvignon, with chardonnay, cabernet franc, and syrah filling in the rest. The moderating influence of the river helps minimize the risk of winter damage, and the steady winds prevent rot or mildew problems.

Chalone's first winemaker, John Abbott (now at Abeja), was a meticulous and talented craftsman who made some of the best merlots and chardonnays in the state. During his tenure, production climbed steadily toward its current level of 40,000 cases annually. When Abbott left in 2002, Canoe Ridge quality slipped dramatically (hence the relatively low score). The further changes wrought by an ownership shuffle slowed down the timing of a recovery.

But a recovery is now under way, for Diageo runs the show and a very talented Frenchman, Christophe Paubert, has been brought in (as of late 2005) to make the wines. Paubert studied enology at the university in Bordeaux while making what he calls his "practice wines" at Chateau d'Yquem (his résumé also includes consulting stints in Chile and Spain and winemaking at Chateau Gruaud-Larose and Montana in New Zealand). "I am a terroir winemaker," he says, and since he is French he knows what he's talking about. "I want to express the terroir. You will never express terroir if you overripen, overoak, and keep your wine two years in barrels. First you need to want to express it; then you need to know how." Paubert believes it is the ripeness of the skin rather than the pulp or the seeds that is most important. "Red wines are made with the skin. The idea is to ripen the skin and harvest at the best moment for that. If you wait to ripen the seeds, you overripen the skin."

Whatever the process, the influence of Paubert should be felt in Canoe Ridge wines from the 2005 vintage on. They have the grapes, the deep-pocket ownership, and once again the winemaking talent. Look for good things to happen.

Best bottles: Chardonnay, merlot, and gewürztraminer have been successes in the past and should be again.

CASCADE CLIFFS

Founded 1990
8866 Highway 14
Wishram, WA 98673
509/767-1100
www.cascadecliffs.com
E-mail: cascadecliffs@gorge.net

Score: 59 (16/18/18/7)

This 4000-case producer in the Columbia Gorge AVA is tackling a most unusual lineup of wines, with an emphasis on estate-grown Italian varietals. The vineyard was begun 20 years ago, but the winemaking was amateurish until a change of ownership in 1997 put ex-banker Bob Lorkowski in charge as managing partner and winemaker.

Lorkowski notes that his grandfather was a moonshiner and wine was drunk frequently. "I was fascinated by fermentation," he adds. Experience gained at Paul Thomas, Cavatappi, and Chinook also contributed to his knowledge, but his focus on Piedmont varietals is strictly his own.

The high-acid barberas and nebbiolos show some promise. There is also a good Dolcetto and a mix of non-Italian reds, including merlot, petite sirah, syrah, zinfandel, and cabernet sauvignon. Everything is estate grown. Though its location in the Columbia River Gorge Scenic Area is one of the most breathtaking in the state, the winery remains off the beaten track for most consumers, and my tastings have been limited and somewhat inconclusive.

CHANDLER REACH

Founded 2000
9506 West Chandler Road
Benton City, WA 99320
509/588-8800
www.chandlerreach.com
E-mail: chandlerreach@comcast.net

Score: 62 (20/18/18/6)

The 42-acre Chandler Reach vineyard, which overlooks (but does not occupy) Red Mountain, not only provides fruit for owner Len Parris's wines, but also sells to a growing number of producers outside of the Yakima Valley. The estate wines are showing steady improvement, as the vines age and the use of new oak becomes a bit less heavy-handed.

The winery fancies itself a Tuscan villa (Washington has more than a few of these, oddly enough), and the vineyard grows a bit of sangiovese, but the strengths are the Bordeaux grapes: cabernet sauvignon, cabernet franc, and merlot. One of the hallmarks of really good Yakima Valley cabernet such as Chandler Reach grows is that it comes closer to Bordeaux-grown grapes in its flavors than any cabernet in Washington. Alcohol levels can be kept below 14 percent while achieving full ripeness, with a pleasing herbal quality and tannins tasting of green tea.

Best bottles: The "Parris"-designated cabernets (the winery reserves) are the wines to search for. The Parris cabernet sauvignon is sweet and plump, with well-ripened fruit balanced against supple tannins, and the Parris cabernet franc is minty and muscular. The winery's lower-priced red blend, called Monte Regalo, offers especially good value and sells out quickly.

CHATTER CREEK

Founded 2000
18658 142nd Ave NE
Woodinville, WA 98072
425/485-3864
www.chattercreek.com
E-mail: email@chattercreek.com

Score: 72 (22/22/22/6)

Ask Chatter Creek winemaker Gordy Rawson how many hats he wears, and he quickly replies, "All of them." Not that a lot of small, start-up wineries aren't essentially solo operations. But at 1500+ cases, Rawson's Chatter Creek winery is not all that small; nor, given his two decades of winemaking experi-ence, is it a typical start-up.

Rawson is one of those people who wants to make anything he likes. He tried his hand at apple wine and won best of show at both the Island County Fair and Woodinville Wine Festival; made his first zinfandel and riesling in 1984; and followed with gamay, Müller-Thurgau, merlot, and sparkling wine in 1985. Book learning and relentless experimentation guided him, along with plenty of generous advice from wine sellers and winemakers, including Columbia's David Lake, for whom Rawson served as cellarmaster from 1985 until mid-1998, when he briefly served as winemaker for Cascade Ridge, a second label for Columbia.

Rawson launched his own winery, making sparkling wines (from 1996 to 1998), which he bottled and sold under the Alexia label. They were quite good, but, sadly, a trademark infringement lawsuit, brought against Alexia by the makers of Alexi vodka, closed the door on that venture. "How anyone could have gotten a cheap Russian vodka confused with a $20 bubbly I have no idea," Rawson says with more than a hint of exasperation. He began making cabernet in 1998, and, needing a new name and a new label for his wines, he hit on Chatter Creek, a favorite fishing spot from his childhood. "I was looking for something that wouldn't get me sued," he explains.

Chatter Creek debuted in January 2000, as Rawson's run at Cascade Ridge ended. Production has slowly climbed to about 1500 cases annually, and the winery makes an interesting mix of white and red wines, including pinot gris, viognier, grenache, syrah, cabernet sauvignon, and cabernet franc. Most are produced in quantities of just a couple of hundred cases. Grapes are mainly sourced from Yakima Valley, Horse Heaven Hills, and Wahluke Slope vineyards. In 2005 a small winery and tasting room were opened in the burgeoning Woodinville warehouse district.

Best bottles: Especially good are Chatter Creek's single-vineyard syrahs, the supple, generous cabernet franc, the viognier, and the pinot gris.

COL SOLARE

Founded: 1995
50207 Antinori Road
Benton City, WA 99320
509/588-6806
www.colsolare.com
E-mail: info@colsolare.com

Score: 70 (19/23/21/7)

Ste. Michelle Wine Estates and the Antinori family of Tuscany established their joint-venture partnership and began making wine with the 1995 vintage. Col Solare, which means "shining hill" in Italian, is a blended red wine made predominantly of cabernet sauvignon and merlot, with small amounts of malbec and syrah as well. Oddly, despite the name and the partnership, no sangiovese is included in the blend.

Renzo Cotarella, winemaker and enologist for Marchesi Antinori, has been working on the Col Solare project since its inception, and he visits from Italy several times a year. He sees "huge opportunities" in the climate and soils of Washington, explaining (in a translation from his original Italian) that "this permits the possibility to obtain stylistically very particular wines also endowed with a soul." The goal of the Col Solare project, he explains, is "to try to make a wine that represents two different worlds."

On the occasion of Piero Antinori's 65th birthday, which he celebrated in Seattle, a tasting of the first five vintages of Col Solare (1995–1999) was held, along with a vertical of Antinori's famed Tignanello. Smooth, silky, and stylish, the Col Solare wines seemed to have more muscle and perhaps even a bit more staying power than the Tignanello. The '96 and '99 vintages were particularly good, with plenty of life ahead.

Until 2006, all vintages of Col Solare were made at Chateau Ste. Michelle's Canoe Ridge Estate winery on the Columbia River. A dedicated Col Solare winery opened on Red Mountain just in time for 2006 crush. When complete, the winery will have wine caves built into the mountain, a tasting room for visitors, and a European-style barrel room adjoining the winemaking cellar. There will also be estate vineyards, on some of Red Mountain's highest ground. All of this promises good things to come.

Despite its early success, more recent vintages of Col Solare have seemed a bit aimless; the wine is yet another superpremium red wine among a confusing profusion of such wines being poured out by Ste. Michelle Wine Estates. What it has lacked is a unique and separate identity. Once that is achieved, Col Solare may well live up to its shining hill name.

DiSTEFANO

Founded: 1984 (as Newton and Newton)
12280 Woodinville Drive NE
Woodinville, WA 98072
425/487-1648
www.distefanowinery.com
E-mail: mark@distefanowinery.com

Score: 58 (16/21/15/6)

"Making wine seems to be at the core of my soul," says DiStefano owner and winemaker Mark Newton. "There is not much I'd rather do than smell a new oak barrel, taste a fresh pressed lot of cabernet, or walk the vineyards." He began as a sparkling wine producer in the early 1980s, went through a series of changes both evolutionary and revolutionary, and lost the rights to the original winery name (Newton and Newton) in a lawsuit with a California winery.

In 1990 he dropped the sparkling wines and began the production of Bordeaux-inspired still wines under the DiStefano label (DiStefano is his wife's maiden name). The lineup includes sauvignon blanc, done in a toasty, oaky style, and a number of varietal reds, including a merlot, a cabernet sauvignon, a meritage, and a wine named Sogno, which is almost pure cabernet franc.

Recently added to the repertoire is an excellent syrah, done in a smooth, oaky style (as are all these wines) but with more substantial fruit holding down the center. Though well into his third decade making wines in Washington, Newton has somehow managed to maintain a high-profile Microsoft career throughout, and he recently opened a fully equipped wine analysis laboratory in Woodinville for both himself and others in the trade. It would be wonderful, one day, if he would say goodbye to the 'Borg and dedicate his talents full time to his winemaking.

Best bottle: A super cabernet, called Ottimo, made in minute quantities (47 cases in 2003), provides a glimpse of this winery's ultimate potential. Structured somewhat like the famed Osoyoos Larose, it is firm, tight, almost severe, with compact fruit and dense tannins. It is brooding and magnificent, and one hopes there will be more like it.

DONEDÉI—GIBBONS LANE WINERY

Founded: 1999
PO Box 7755
Olympia, WA 98507
360/264-8466
www.Donedei.com
E-mail: donedei@aol.com

Score: 57 (20/15/18/4)

Donedéi is the brand name for the wines of Gibbons Lane Winery, founded in 1997 in Tenino, just south of Olympia. According to winemaker and co-owner Carolyn Lakewold, the name translates as "gift of God." No one can accuse this tiny winery of lacking in confidence!

Beginning in 1999, a few hundred cases have been produced each year, roughly one-third of them merlot, the other-two thirds cabernet. Production now hovers between 750 and 1000 cases annually, "depending on the whims of nature," says the winemaker.

Lakewold seems to have a natural talent for winemaking. Her first wine, a sublimely textured, merlot-dominated blend was reminiscent of fine Pomerol. The 2003 Donedéi cabernet sauvignon (the most recent vintage tasted) included a bit of merlot and cabernet franc in the blend. Grapes came from several Red Mountain vineyards. Another good effort; it showed firm, muscular fruit and ripe layering of flavors. The 2003 merlot is a well-matched companion.

FIELDING HILLS

Founded 2000
1401 Fielding Hills Drive
East Wenatchee, WA 98802

509/884-2221
www.fieldinghills.com
E-mail: mike@fieldinghills.com

Score: 74 (26/20/23/5)

Growers Mike and Karen Wade began
planting their RiverBend vineyards in
1998. They harvested their first crop and
made their first commercial wines two
years later. They grow 23 acres all together,
a mix of cabernet sauvignon, merlot, cab
franc, and syrah.

Mike took a class or two at UC Davis
but mostly learned his winemaking by
working alongside Charlie Hoppes (Fidélitas) and Gordon Venneri (Walla Walla
Vintners). A third-generation apple grower,
he is a naturally gifted winemaker with
a knack for crafting elegant, expressive
wines. His early releases have been stunningly brilliant.

Production during the first few vintages was a miniscule 425 cases a year; it has now
doubled, but Fielding Hills' owners seem in no hurry to capitalize on their success by crank-
ing out more wine. The winery is headquartered in an orchard in East Wenatchee, on a
spectacular site overlooking the river. In repeated tastings, I have been extremely impressed
by the balance, clarity, definition, and complexity these young wines show. This winery
is a superstar in the making.

Best bottles: Where to begin? Across the entire lineup Fielding Hills merits superlatives.
The merlots are brilliant, polished, beautifully nuanced wines that can stand alongside the
best I've ever tasted from this state. The syrahs, which include a bit of cabernet and merlot in the blend, are supple, silky, and plump, with luscious fruit wrapped in powerful, toasty
and buttery new oak. The winery's cabernet sauvignons, cabernet francs, and RiverBend
Reds (a blend of the three grapes) all follow suit; across the board these are supple, juicy,
firm, and generous wines.

GORDON BROTHERS FAMILY VINEYARDS

Founded: 1983
671 Levey Road
Pasco, WA 99301

509/547-6331
www.gordonwines.com
E-mail: info@gordonwines.com

Score: 55 (16/15/16/8)

These longtime grape growers, with a spectacular 100-acre vineyard set 620 feet above the Snake River, have enjoyed some tremendous success over the years. The vineyard is fertilizer free and planted to cabernet sauvignon, merlot, syrah, chardonnay, sauvignon blanc, and gewürztraminer. There are also small experimental rows of tempranillo and malbec.

The Gordons also farm apples and cherries; those orchards are certified organic. In 1998 Jeff Gordon's brother Bill retired, and a new wine production facility was built to centralize and modernize the winemaking process. For a time in the late 1990s, with the talented Marie-Eve Gilla in charge of the winemaking, Gordon Brothers Family Vineyards was making a serious run at top-tier status in Washington. A series of missteps followed, and along with winemaker changes came an aborted sale and a couple of damaging winter freezes. For a time, vintages were backed up, and some strange wines, seemingly flawed, somehow got released.

The newest wines are a significant improvement and suggest that once again Gordon Brothers is back in the groove. After all, this is a winery that has some of the oldest estate grapes in Washington, and it remains family owned and operated. You want them to do well. Best to stick with the tried-and-true varietals, especially the chardonnay, done in a clean, high-acid style, and the no-frills cabernet sauvignon.

HIGHTOWER CELLARS

Founded: 1997
19418 E. 583 PR NE
Red Mountain, WA 99320
509/588-2867
www.hightowercellars.com
E-mail: handsorted@aol.com

Score: 58 (18/18/16/6)

Like many young couples with a winemaking dream, Kelly and Tim Hightower started small, working day jobs while making a few hundred cases of "handpicked, hand-sorted, handmade" wine in a funky warehouse in Woodinville. They were fortunate (and determined) enough to find 15 acres of undeveloped vineyard land on Red Mountain, where water rights are as rare as trees, and moved from Woodinville to Benton City in the summer of 2001. They began planting their estate vineyard in the spring of 2004.

A total of 12 acres are now bearing, primarily cabernet sauvignon and merlot, with small amounts of cabernet franc, petit verdot, and malbec. Grapes for their high-toned, polished red wines will continue to be sourced from a variety of vineyards, including Alder Ridge in the Horse Heaven Hills, Pepper Bridge in Walla Walla, and Artz and Shaw up on Red Mountain.

Until the estate vineyard gets some years under its belt, Hightower will continue to be a winery that has more potential than actual achievement. The wines are competent but unremarkable, and the impression is that they are getting fruit from the younger vines, even at prestigious sources such as Pepper Bridge.

Best bottles: One exception to the young-vine syndrome are the grapes sourced from Red Mountain, where the Hightowers are now making their home. The Red Mountain Red, though overoaked for my palate, shows nice dark streaks of mineral, espresso, and caramel, and the core cherry/cassis fruit is ripe and focused. The most recent merlot, from a mix of Columbia Valley vineyards, was also a standout.

JM CELLARS

Founded: 1998
14404 137th Place NE
Woodinville, WA 98072
206-321-0052
www.jmcellars.com
E-mail: info@jmcellars.com

Score: 67 (23/20/20/4)

John Bigelow began making wines in 1998, in the basement of his Seattle home. He and his wife Peggy moved their winery to its current location in 2001. "Bramble Bump," as they have named it, is a wooded knoll above Chateau Ste. Michelle in Woodinville.

Brother-in-law Mike Januik (Januik Winery) has been an inspiration and role model for JM, whose production is roughly 2500 cases annually. Winery equipment is first rate, the fruit they obtained is world-class, and from the beginning their wines were skillfully rendered. JM produces mostly red wines, including syrah, cabernet sauvignon, and a blend called Tre Fanciulli. (Pronounced tray fan-chew-lee, it means "three good lads" in Italian, a reference to the Bigelows' three sons.)

JM's Red Mountain cabs and the Tre Fanciulli hit the same chord consistently: big, choco-latey, tannic wines with plenty of consumer-friendly flavors and wide appeal. There is also an excellent sauvignon blanc, made from Klipsun vineyard grapes, that makes you wish they did more with white wines (a tiny amount of viognier was added to the lineup in 2004).

Best bottle: The winery's signature "Tre Fanciulli" red features Klipsun cabernet blended with merlot and syrah sourced from a variety of top sites. The most complex and complete effort in the lineup, it displays interesting cherry, tobacco, and chocolate streaks and ripe cherry fruit. It's got the extra length you look for in the $35 price range.

KIONA VINEYARDS AND WINERY

Founded: 1979
44612 North Sunset Road
Benton City, WA 99320
509/588-6716
www.kionawine.com
E-mail: info@kionawine.com

Score: 70 (16/26/20/8)

Kiona was a founding winery on Red Mountain. John and Ann Williams, parents of Kiona winemaker Scott Williams, were original partners with Jim Holmes (now proprietor of nearby Ciel du Cheval vineyard) and developed the area jointly. Kiona-grown grapes have, at one time or another, provided the core fruit for some of Washington's finest caber-net sauvignons, among them Leonetti Cellar, Quilceda Creek, and Woodward Canyon.

The path that Kiona has followed on its own, however, has been a rather rambling one. The vineyard holdings are extensive (65 acres) and include some of the finest land in the state. The range of wines produced is equally large (25,000 cases annually), and quality can range from remarkably good to simply so-so. The problem, if you want to call it that, is that after three decades the winery has not been able to define itself clearly and consis-tently. Its wines only occasionally live up to the quality of its own fruit.

Kiona has made a good showing with its lembergers. They planted the first commer-cial lemberger vineyard on the West Coast in 1976, but that hardly qualifies as a trump card. When the stars are in alignment, Kiona has made outstanding cabernets of its own, the 1999 reserve being perhaps the finest example. But the winery's attempts with other red grapes, such as zinfandel and sangiovese, have been very disappointing, and the dry white wines are spotty also.

One promising development: a brand-new winery building, adjacent to the old facil-ity, has recently been constructed, adding much-needed underground barrel storage

(10,000 square feet) and a new tasting room, along with office space, a meeting room, and a catering kitchen. A covered deck offers panoramic views of the Horse Heaven Hills, Mt. Adams, Rattlesnake Mountain, and Red Mountain itself.

Best bottles: Kiona's late-harvest and ice wines (chenin blanc, gewürztraminer, muscat, and riesling) are often superb and very attractively priced.

LATAH CREEK

Founded: 1982
13030 East Indiana Avenue
Spokane, WA 99216
509/926-0164
www.latahcreek.com
E-mail: mconway@latahcreek.com

Score: 68 (18/22/22/6)

Washington State
MERLOT
Wahluke Slope Vineyards

Mike Conway earned his winemaking stripes under California's John Parducci in the late '70s and then moved to Washington to make wine at Worden and at Hogue before starting Latah Creek in 1982. His wines have always been value-oriented, everyday, everyman wines, and the white wines in particular show a confident, veteran hand at work.

Modestly priced and meticulously made, Latah Creek's rieslings and muscats offer excellent value vintage after vintage. A Prosecco-styled, light sparkling wine called Moscato d'Latah offers sweet, pure flavors of lime and orange liqueur. It would make a lovely dessert all by itself; unfortunately, it is sold only at the winery. Recent releases of the red wines have been somewhat disappointing.

Best bottle: Unquestionably the Johannisberg Riesling, classy and classic, with just enough sweetness to offset the zippy acids. Bright, fresh, crisp, and clean, there's a wash of honey-eyed sweetness underlying the ripe peaches and apple-flavored juice. All for seven bucks a bottle.

MARK RYAN

Founded 2000
19501 144th Avenue NE
Woodinville, WA 98072
206/910-7967
www.markryanwinery.com
E-mail: mark@markryanwinery.com

Score: 74 (26/20/22/6)

Mark McNeilly is a tall, disheveled, gregarious, and instantly likeable winemaker, and his wines follow suit. They ride big in the saddle, with jammy fruit and plenty of oak and alcohol, and they sport names such as "Dead Horse" and "The Dissident," names with attitude. McNeilly got into the wine business as a salesman for a Seattle distributor and then went to work for Matt Loso (Matthews Estate) to apprentice himself and learn the winemaking trade. From his first vintage (2000) he has focused on using Red Mountain (Ciel du Cheval) grapes to make a Left Bank and Right Bank Bordeaux blend.

These signature wines are his "Dead Horse" and "Long Haul" reds. The Dead Horse (the name is a play on the Horse Heaven hills, which can be seen from the Ciel du Cheval vineyard) is the cabernet-dominated wine, a big, lush, full-bodied Bordeaux blend. The Long Haul, a Right Bank–styled merlot–cab franc blend, seems to show more heat, more oak, and broader shoulders. "I'm dropping anchor on Red Mountain," McNeilly elaborates. "I'm a structure guy, tannin and acid. I want to make sure everyone knows that Red Mountain is the Côte Rôtie of Washington."

To this end, he has added a Red Mountain–sourced "Wild-Eyed" syrah. There is also a red blend called "The Dissident," crafted from barrels that didn't make the cut for the "Dead Horse" and "Long Haul"; a "Gun Metal" red showing classic herbal cabernet notes along with bacon and smoke, cedar and plum; and a "Bad Lands" red blended from Red Mountain syrah and petit verdot.

Best bottle: The Dead Horse, despite the unappealing name, is the epitome of the Mark Ryan style. Inky and thick, with black cherry fruit, wrapped in smoke and iron, it captures the essence of the brilliant Ciel du Cheval vineyard.

MARYHILL

Founded: 1999
9774 Highway 14 West
Goldendale, WA 98620
509-773-1976
www.maryhillwinery.com
E-mail: info@maryhillwinery.com

Score: 51 (16/14/14/7)

Maryhill makes a dizzying assortment of wines, and quality is all over the map. The winery is located in a spectacular setting near the Maryhill Museum, overlooking the Columbia Gorge, and apart from the scenery it draws visitors for its summer concerts at the outdoor Maryhill Winery Amphitheater.

The Proprietor's Reserve wines, priced from $25 to $40, include the best and the worst from this puzzling producer. Too many of the wines seem to have overpowering aromas of tack room leather (brettanomyces?); others are ripened to the point of tasting pruney or clobbered with oak. But some come through with flying colors, especially the two cabernets. Maryhill is experimenting with many different and unusual grapes: malbec, sangiovese, barbera, zinfandel, and so on. But too many of these wines are interesting only on paper; they do not (so far) differentiate themselves in any meaningful way. Maryhill is a bit like a kid in kindergarten with too many crayons in his desk. Gotta try them all.

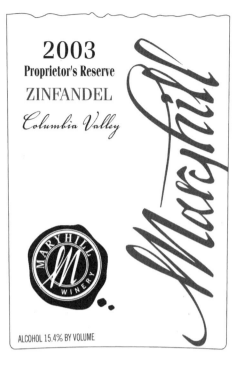

But experimentation can lead to good things, and once the winery figures out which crayons to work with, and tightens up the winemaking, Maryhill could well become one of the best in the region, especially with its strong emphasis on attracting visitors. The Maryhill Winery Amphitheater, which has hosted stars such as Willie Nelson, Bob Dylan, BB King, Don Henley, and ZZ Top, skipped the 2006 summer concert series in order to add private box seats, a permanent stage, and other improvements. If all goes according to plan, the amphitheater will be back in action in 2007.

Best bottles: The Proprietor's Reserve Cabernet Franc is structured and supple, its dense, dark, black fruits laced with licorice and streaks of tarry tannin. The companion Cabernet Sauvignon is every bit as good, classically structured, dense, and dry, with cedary, black tea flavors circling black cherry and blackberry fruit.

NORTHSTAR

Founded: 1994
1736 JB George Road
Walla Walla, WA 99362
509-525-6100
www.northstarmerlot.com
E-mail: info@northstarmerlot.com

Score: 70 (24/22/18/6)

Northstar began as a winery devoted solely to merlot, when merlot was king and Washington was angling for the producer crown. The brainstorm of California winemaker Jed Steele and former Ste. Michelle Wine Estates CEO Allen Shoup, it was to be an "icon" project for the company. When Ted Baseler took over as CEO in 2000, he too announced that it was his intention to make Northstar "the best merlot on the planet."

Things have been a bit bumpy on the road to stardom. Following a few good but unspectacular early releases, the wine took a huge quality jump forward in 1998 and 1999. In 2001–02, a dedicated winery was built just across from Walla Walla's Pepper Bridge vineyard. But then Northstar wine-maker Gordy Hill declined to make the move to Walla Walla. Rusty Figgins (Glen Fiona, Cave B) was hired, but he barely lasted through the 2002 crush before moving on.

The original Northstar style—smooth and satiny, with a lot of expensive-tasting French oak—owed a lot to the thinking of Jed Steele. At first there was just a single bottling, sourced from top Ste. Michelle vineyards; then, a few years ago, Northstar began offering both a Columbia Valley and a Walla Walla Valley bottling. The former now comes from a confusing array of vineyard sources; the latter is more focused but quite light, to the point of being insubstantial. There was no Walla Walla bottling in 2004, because the freeze took out virtually all of the valley's grapes.

A few hundred cases of an excellent Northstar syrah and a so-so cabernet sauvignon are also being made (for tasting room sales only); so much for the merlot-only concept. Stella Maris is the second wine, and the Stella Red can be almost as good as the frontline wine at half the price.

Will Northstar come through its growing pains and find its way back to its original focus, making a soft, satiny, and sexy wine? The voluptuous black cherry and blackberry fruit, the layers of chocolate, the spices suggestive of cinnamon, mint, and other exotic flavors—this is what it was on the road to being and hopefully will be once again.

RYAN PATRICK

Founded: 1999
S. 4th Street and Rock Island Drive
Rock Island, WA 98850
509-667-9861
www.ryanpatrickvineyards.com
E-mail: info@ryanpatrickvineyards.com

Score: 67 (22/20/21/4)

Ryan Patrick owns 58 acres of vineyards on the eastern edge of the Columbia Cascade wine region. The winery produces about 5000 cases annually of chardonnay, sauvignon blanc, an everyday "Rock Island Red," and a more substantial Reserve Red.

The no-frills winery and tasting room is located on the northern flank of the Columbia River at Rock Island, east of Wenatchee. Though not the state's prettiest picnic spot, the winery offers some of north central Washington's best value wines.

Retired racecar driver Terry Flanagan founded the winery, named for his son Patrick, who was tragically killed in a one-car accident in the summer of 2004. Patrick was the winery's assistant winemaker and a truly likeable, high-energy young man. After his death the assistant winemaking duties were taken over by Craig Mitrakul, who previously worked at Three Rivers Winery in Walla Walla. Mitrakul has since been installed as the winery's full-time winemaker and made the winery's first reserve wine, a 2004 cabernet sauvignon with the power and precision to age for some years.

Best bottles: The sauvignon blanc is a full-flavored, spicy bottle showing off tart pineapple and citrus fruit lightly dusted with cinnamon. The addition of 11 percent sémillon punches up the core, and barrel fermentation adds some lovely, spicy highlights. The Rock Island Red (named for the town, not the railroad) is a gem of a budget bottle, a Bordeaux blend roughly three-fifths merlot, the rest cabernet sauvignon and cab franc. Sleek and well made, it sports highlights of light spice and herb, graphite and slate.

SANDHILL WINERY

Founded: 1998
48313 North Sunset Road
Benton City, WA 99320
360-887-5629
No website as of April 2007
E-mail: sandhillwinery@aol.com

Score: 57 (16/16/19/6)

Sandhill winery owns a 40-acre vineyard on Red Mountain, planted by hand beginning in 1989. "A result," says managing partner John Dingethal, "of my midlife crisis." More than half of the acreage is dedicated to cabernet sauvignon; a third is merlot, and the remainder consists of an acre or two each of pinot gris and cab franc. The vineyard sells three-quarters of its grapes to Waterbrook, Hedges, Januik, JM Cellars, Fidélitas, and Willis Hall, among others.

Sandhill made its first estate wines in 1998, focusing on pinot gris, cabernet sauvignon, and merlot and a nonestate table red called Cinnamon Teal, bottled under the Ridgefield label. Production is about 3000 cases annually.

The location of the vineyard, between Hedges and Ciel du Cheval on the east side of Sunset Road, and the impressive list of client wineries purchasing its fruit would suggest that there is terrific potential for the estate wines. But in my experience they have fallen a bit short of that potential, delivering rather light, ordinary flavors for such a favored terroir. These are not bad wines by any means, and they are attractively priced. But on Red Mountain, expectations run high; the bar has been set very high.

SNOQUALMIE

Founded: 1984
660 Frontier Road
Prosser, WA 99350
509-786—2104
www.snoqualmie.com
E-mail: info@snoqualmie.com

Score: 70 (20/21/23/6)

The full and complete history of Snoqualmie could fill this book, so we'll skip right to the present and simply say that it has become one of the top half dozen wineries in the state making value-priced wines. Winemaker Joy Anderson has been the unsung heroine of the rise in quality.

To this observer it always seemed as if Snoqualmie got the last, worst fruit from the long list of parent company Ste. Michelle Wine Estates' vineyards. The red wines in particular were unripe, vegetal, and charmless. It is no accident that the sole successes during the first half of the 1990s were the winery's muscat and gewürztraminer, grapes that no one else was eager to claim. But the tide seemed to turn about the time the century did, and quality has been consistently good and sometimes even better ever since.

There are several different tiers of wines. The Columbia Valley bottlings have a new look, with labels promoting the small-town appeal of Prosser. Small-town appeal notwithstanding, they have jumped significantly in price, from $7 to $11, making them less of a steal but still fair value. The Rosebud vineyard designates are priced in the midteens and the reserves in the mid-$20s. A pair of organically grown and vinified gewürztraminers and rieslings are sold as Snoqualmie "Naked," an unnecessary gimmick because the wines speak for themselves.

There are many strengths here: the sauvignon blanc, as light and clean as a spring breeze; the Winemaker's Select riesling, sweet and penetrating, with deep flavors of spicy pear, dried apricots, and candied citrus; and the reserve syrahs, dark, tannic, and earthy, with surprising depth.

Best bottles: Some years it's the reserves (especially the syrah), but the sure-fire, everyday-go-to-Snoqualmie wines are the rieslings, naked or fully clothed.

TAMARACK CELLARS

Founded: 1998
700 "C" Street
Walla Walla, WA 99362
509/526-3533
www.tamarackcellars.com
E-mail: ron@tamarackcellars.com

Score: 58 (17/17/19/5)

Tamarack, named for a short-needled species of larch, has done quite well with its Firehouse Red, an unusual blend of syrah, merlot, cabernet franc, sangiovese, and carmenère. The winery's other reds, all varietals, include a soft, leafy sangiovese, a tart and tannic cabernet franc, and well-made examples of merlot, cabernet sauvignon, and syrah. White wines are a bit of an afterthought, but the winery's chardonnay is well made, with an appealing mix of green apple, pineapple, and butterscotch.

Not to pick on Tamarack, but what has not yet happened here is the ability to show an extra something that would set its wines apart from the pack. Its syrah, for example, could stand in for any good Walla Walla syrah from a couple of dozen different producers. On the one hand you can say that it is a testament to the overall high quality of Washington fruit (this particular syrah is from the Sagemoor vineyard). But on the other hand, Tamarack's wines suffer a bit from the flavor sameness that plagues many Walla Walla syrahs. The fruit starts with a nice streak of boysenberry, and then the barrels kick in with roasted coffee, bitter chocolate, and toast. It's a good recipe, but it's one that is becoming a little tired.

Best bottle: For the money, it's got to be the Firehouse Red, a lush, fruity, and forward wine that's got a little bit of everything going for it: berries, cherries, cassis, coffee, chocolate, vanilla bean, and cinnamon.

THREE RIVERS

Founded: 1999
5641 West Highway 12
Walla Walla, WA 99362
509/526-9463
www.threeriverswinery.com
E-mail: info@threeriverswinery.com

Score: 74 (26/20/23/5)

You can't miss this imposing winery, which sits just off the main highway leading into Walla Walla from the west. It's the result of a three-way partnership formed by retired telecom executives Steve Ahler, Bud Stocking, and Duane Wollmuth. They planned Three Rivers as a destination winery, complete with conference rooms, a spacious deck, a 14,000-square-foot cellar and barrel room, a large gift shop and tasting room, and a three-hole golf course.

The golf course seemed a bit over the top to the locals when it was announced, with some fanfare, back in 1999. But as it turns out it was merely ahead of its time, for Walla Walla is now bursting with grandiose plans for golf course development.

Since its somewhat ostentatious debut, Three Rivers has consistently delivered excellent wines. Charlie Hoppes made the inaugural vintages and then passed the winemaking baton over to Holly Turner, who has demonstrated a deft sensitivity, particularly in her white and red Bordeaux blends and her exceptional syrahs. Fruit is sourced from a range of first-rate vineyards, including Champoux, Boushey, and Pepper Bridge.

For reasons unclear to me, Three Rivers seems to have escaped the notice of the out-of-state critics; the winery rarely turns up on anyone's best-of-Washington lists. And yet, reviewing my notes on its releases over the past half decade, I find that scores are consistently high, and my comments typically praise Turner's finesse with virtually everything she touches.

She is one of a relatively small number of winemakers who seem to have a built-in gift for achieving balance and complexity. "For me it's all about balance," she explains. "I don't want too much wood or alcohol; I want everything to flow on the palate. My wine should be juicy in the mouth but not too toasty, with no burn. Everything I do with wine is based on tasting and balance."

The modestly priced River's Red (an everyday mutt blend of merlot, cabernet sauvignon, malbec, and grenache) shows layers of ripe (but not sweet or jammy) red fruits, hints of fresh herb, stiff but not obtrusive tannins, and firm acids. The cabernet is harmonious and balanced; the tannic, chewy merlot is dark and scented with cocoa, coffee, cherry, and a dash of vanilla. For tasting room visitors and members of the mailing list, the winery offers limited-production gems, such as a Clifton vineyard grenache and a Chinon-style cabernet franc.

Best bottles: The Meritage White, along with comparable wines from Buty and DeLille's Chaleur Estate, can stand with California's best. The regular syrah is a good value, smooth, bright, and juicy, with a nice mix of berries and chocolate, cassis and coffee. And for your sweet tooth, Three Rivers offers the Biscuit Ridge vineyard late-harvest gewürztraminer, decadent, rich, and irresistible.

TOWNSHEND CELLAR

Founded: 1998
16112 North Greenbluff Road
Colbert, WA 99005
509/238-1400
www.townshendcellar.com
E-mail: don@townshendcellar.com

Score: 65 (22/18/21/4)

Don Townshend was (and still is) a seller of commercial cooling equipment. Bitten by the wine bug on a sales call to a winery, he began home winemaking just a decade ago. It seems he has a natural gift. His first commercial vintage was 1998, and he gives his self-described "big red wines" up to 30 months in new oak and a year in bottle before release.

After a spotty start with the early releases, Townshend Cellar's quality has improved dramatically across the board, from the off-dry perfectly balanced riesling to the viscous and gloriously peachy chenin blanc, the stylish syrah, the tight, muscular cabernet, and the nonvintage Vortex Red, an especially fine value.

Most unusual are the winery's huckleberry wines, including a sparkling Brut, a spirituous "Port," and a sweet, summery blush wine. Though his early focus was on the reds, he has more recently branched off into a rambling mélange, including some whites, some

Port, some sparkling, some pinot noir, and late-harvest viognier and chenin blanc. Obviously, with such a curious mix, there will be some hits and misses, but when he hits it's mighty good.

Best bottles: Townshend's off-dry white wines are his most impressive and reliable; the riesling is one of the best in the state.

THURSTON WOLFE

> Founded: 1987
> 588 Cabernet Court
> Prosser, WA 99350
> 509/786-3313
> www.thurstonwolfe.com
> E-mail: whwolfe@bentonrea.com

> Score: 69 (19/21/20/9)

Thurston Wolfe, which will soon be celebrating its 20th anniversary, has carved out a unique path, even in a state laden with pioneers. Wade Wolfe, a lean, square-jawed man in his late fifties, holds a Ph.D. in Plant Genetics from UC Davis. Soft-spoken and unassuming, Wolfe arrived in Washington in 1978, hired by Chateau Ste. Michelle to be its Technical Viticulturalist. Back in the day he encouraged growers to follow basic viticultural practices: cut back on irrigation, rein in crop loads, etc. He made it his personal mission to inves-

tigate alternative red grape varieties for eastern Washington (at the time, cabernet sauvignon and pinot noir were the two most commonly planted).

The Thurston part of Thurston Wolfe is his mother's maiden name. It was chosen because, as his practical-minded wife and business partner, Becky Yeaman, explains, "Yeaman Wolfe or Wolfe Yeaman just didn't sound right." When he left Ste. Michelle to start his own winery, the focus was dessert wines: a black muscat, a late-harvest sauvignon blanc named Sweet Rebecca, a pair of Ports. Table wines began to enter the mix in the mid-1990s, when the winery moved from downtown Yakima to Prosser. At first a grenache and several lembergers were produced, then

THURSTON WOLFE

2005 DOCTOR WOLFE'S FAMILY RED
WASHINGTON STATE TABLE WINE

one of the state's first zinfandels, and later a bit of sangiovese, syrah, and even a petite sirah. White wines have been fairly limited, but a pinot gris–viognier blend called PGV is a welcome recent addition.

Wade Wolfe's somewhat quixotic pursuit of esoteric table and dessert wines presented a bit of a financial challenge to the winery in its formative years. But nonmainstream varietals (so-called "sport varieties") are quite trendy now. As it enters its third decade, Thurston Wolfe may finally be right in sync with the times.

Recent releases have been very fine, priced below most Washington boutiques. The wines are never flashy; they reflect the quiet confidence of the winemaker, his deep knowledge of grapes and vineyards, and his focus on the clean, intense expression of pure varietal fruit. They can hit some pretty high alcohol levels, however; the Doctor Wolfe's Family Red, a proprietary blend of primitivo, petite sirah, and lemberger, clocks in at 15 percent.

Best bottles: The JTW Port, a blend of touriga, souzao, petite sirah, and cabernet sauvignon, is remarkable, as is the Sweet Rebecca, pungent and spicy, with dense aromas of orange, lemon, and lime peel, rose petals, and tropical fruits. Among the red table wines, the Burgess Vineyard syrah is the standout.

WILLOW CREST

Founded: 1995
135701 West Snipes Road
Prosser, WA 99350
509/786-7999
www.willowcrestwinery.com
E-mail: wilowine@bentonrea.com

Score: 72 (22/20/22/8)

Willow Crest scores well on the strength of its excellent vineyard practices and its pioneering efforts with pinot gris. Owner-grower-winemakers such as David Minick are still something of a rare commodity in Washington. Many of the top vineyards sell all their grapes and do not make wine. Some that do have dedicated, independent winemakers. Minick does it all and does it well.

The vineyard part of the operation dates back to 1982. Located six miles north of Prosser, it sits at 1300 feet, one of the higher sites in the Yakima Valley. Currently there are 185 acres planted to pinot gris, riesling, chardonnay, gewürztraminer, cabernet sauvignon, cab franc, merlot, mourvèdre, and syrah. A testament to the quality of Willow Crest grapes is the long list of wineries that purchase them, including Ash Hollow, Chateau Ste. Michelle, Columbia Crest, C.R. Sandidge, Harlequin, Hogue Cellars, Seven Hills, Sorenson Cellars, and Snoqualmie.

The winery, started in 1995, has ramped up production to 5000 cases. A new tasting room, next door to Thurston Wolfe, is located in Prosser.

Minick has got a streak of the mad scientist in him, hence his three different syrahs (table wine, sparkling, and Port) and his cabernet franc ice wine (don't tell the Canadians!). But he is a dedicated pioneer who also was among the first to make Washington pinot gris and Washington mourvèdre, and he does them quite well. Since he is both grower and producer, he is able to offer all of these wines at modest prices.

Best bottles: The pinot gris and the estate syrah are exceptional.

WHIDBEY ISLAND VINEYARDS AND WINERY

Founded: 1991
5237 South Langley Road
Langley, WA 98260
360/221-2040
www.whidbeyislandwinery.com
E-mail: winery@whidbey.com

Score: 63 (18/21/19/5)

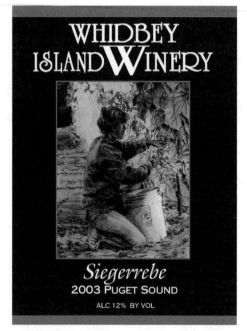

Quite a few tiny wineries are scattered among the islands of Puget Sound, but Whidbey Island winery consistently rises to the top of the heap, not only for its homegrown Madeleine Angevine and siegerrebe, which are crisp and stylish, but also for many of its Yakima Valley and Columbia Valley wines.

Getting ripe grapes from eastern Washington to Whidbey island is not an easy task, but Greg and Elizabeth Osenbach, winery owners, seem to have it figured out. Current releases include a pleasantly light, bright strawberry and cherry candy–flavored sangiovese and a fragrant and ripe, brightly colored cabernet franc, along with the more standard chardonnay, lemberger, and merlot offerings. The syrah has won some positive notice as well.

Whidbey Island Winery's good prices, balanced winemaking, interesting varietals, and food-friendly alcohol levels merit praise. Not everything is a success, but it does an especially nice job with the Puget-grown grapes.

Best bottle: You've got to try the siegerrebe, to get a taste of the Puget Sound appellation. An off-dry white wine rich with citrus, spice, honey, pear, apricot, and pine tar, it leaves an overriding impression of fresh-squeezed grapefruit.

Founded: 1994
260 North Bonair Road
Zillah, WA 98953
509/829-3011
www.wineglasscellars.com
E-mail: sales@wineglasscellars.com

Score: 58 (17/19/17/5)

Linda and David Lowe produce roughly 3000 cases annually of sturdy Yakima Valley whites and reds. There are moments of real brilliance here; the 1998 and 1999 vintages in particular seemed to bring out the best in their wines. Credit grape sources that include top vineyards such as Elerding and Boushey. When the right ingredients are there, Wineglass can do quite well, for example, the Boushey/Elerding vineyard sangiovese, a pretty wine, with a good core of cherry fruit, nicely accented with leaf and spice, or the Boushey vineyard syrah, sappy, snappy, and loaded with bright, tart red fruit flavors.

On the downside, recent bottlings of the reserve wines have been hit or miss, and the winery seems to be backing up on its vintages. Perhaps the focus has shifted to simple tasting room wines, such as the Fran's rosé and the nonvintage Capizimo red. That may be a perfectly logical business decision, but I would hope to see more of the early promise fulfilled.

Best bottles: The vineyard designates from Elerding and Boushey are the stars.

8

THE ROOKIES

The number of Washington wineries has increased fourfold in the past decade and now has moved past 500, with few signs of slowing down. As impressive as this number may seem, it is important to realize that almost all of these wineries are producing fewer than 1500 cases of wine annually. Three-quarters of them have been through fewer than five vintages. Only a handful actually own their own vineyards. Though quality is surprisingly high, many of these wines are, for all practical purposes, unavailable, unless you visit the tasting room, sign up for the mailing list, or own a wine shop in Seattle.

In the preceding three chapters I have named and rated roughly 15 percent of the state's wineries, those that I consider to be outstanding. A major factor in their selection was longevity. The ability to do quality work over the course of many vintages is one of the hallmarks of a first-class winery and winemaker. Anyone can get lucky once or twice.

The young wineries listed in this chapter have released fewer than five vintages, but the early results are exceptional. Some, such as Barrister, Beresan, Bergevin Lane, Boudreaux, and the Long Shadows group, seem destined to become superstars. Others, such as Gamache and Sheridan, own great vineyards that have been sourced by other first-class wineries for some time; there are no doubts about their ability to grow quality fruit. All of these young wineries should be on the radar of anyone who wants to taste the cutting edge of Washington state winemaking; however, given their very limited track records, I have elected not to apply the rating system to them until a few more vintages have made it to bottle.

ALDER RIDGE AND ZEFINA

Both founded 2001
Vineyard:
101 Columbia Ridge Road
Prosser, WA 99350
509/786-9116
www.winemakersllc.com
E-mail: alderridge@hotmail.com
Winery:
600 University Street, #2500
Seattle, WA 98101
206/728-9063
www.zefina.com
E-mail: kenm@zefina.com

Alder Ridge is a large (800+-acre) vineyard in the Horse Heaven Hills, set high above the Columbia River. The oldest vines are approaching tenth leaf; the newest have yet to begin bearing. Much of the vineyard is planted to cabernet sauvignon, cabernet franc, merlot, and syrah; but the rest includes a wonderful mix of grapes, most of them new to the state. Alder Ridge barbera, carignane, carmenère, cinsault, counoise, grenache, malbec, marsanne, mourvèdre, petite sirah, petit verdot, roussanne, sangiovese, tempranillo, and zinfandel are sourced by a wide variety of wineries, including top boutiques such as Betz, Rulo, Willis Hall, and Syncline.

The estate wines are bottled (about 4000 cases annually) under the Alder Ridge (Bordeaux varietals) and Zefina labels, part of Corus Estates and Vineyards. A red blend on a second label, Six Prong, was released in 2005 from barrels that did not make it into the premier brands. The quality of the fruit from the well-sited, well-managed Alder Ridge vineyard shows through clearly; and as the vines age, the wines seem certain to gain density and power. Charlie Hoppes is the consulting winemaker.

Notable: The premier release of Alder Ridge cabernet sauvignon was a very fine effort, full-flavored with plenty of cassis and plum, great balance across the entire palate, and a Bordeaux-like elegance. The Zefina brand focuses on the more unusual varietals. Its Serience red is a blend of grenache, syrah, counoise, and mourvèdre; Serience white is a blend of viognier and roussanne. There is also a light, pretty zinfandel and a sangiovese.

ALEXANDRIA NICOLE CELLARS

Founded 2001
2880 Lee Road, Suite C
Prosser, WA 99350

509/786-3497
www.alexandrianicolecellars.com
E-mail: info@alexandrianicolecellars.com

Alexandria Nicole is the winery partner of the expansive Destiny Ridge vineyard (232 acres, 17 varietals). Located between the Champoux and Canoe Ridge vineyards in the Horse Heaven Hills, 90 percent of its grapes are sold to other wineries.

Much like its neighbor Alder Ridge, Destiny Ridge has planted a wide variety of unusual grapes. Upcoming Alexandria Nicole releases may include such rare varietals as malbec, petit verdot, grenache, and tempranillo. But in the early going, the more reliable wines have been Alexandria Nicole's whites. Among the reds, the syrah is the most interesting; the malbec and grenache show good potential.

Notable: The winery does a particularly good job with its viognier, which showcases vivid acids and lemon drop fruit flavors. It's a clean, juicy style, with lip-smacking tartness and excellent focus in the midpalate. The "Shepard's Mark" white is a roussanne-viognier-marsanne blend powered with flavors of pears and pineapple, light spice, light floral, and citrus.

AMAVI CELLARS

Founded 2001
635 N. 13th Avenue
Walla Walla, WA 99362
509/525-3541
www.amavicellars.com
E-mail: info@amavicellars.com

Amavi (AH-muh-vee) Cellars is one of a crowded field of Walla Walla newcomers. But for lovers of Washington syrah, Amavi moves right to the top ranks. A sister winery to Pepper Bridge, it shares a winemaker (the talented, Swiss-born Jean-Francois Pellet) and much of the same fruit. The early releases of syrahs have been thrilling wines, firm and supple and sporting a core of plush, dark fruit. These are pure syrahs sourced from the Pepper Bridge, Seven Hills, and Les Collines vineyards.

Amavi's general manager is Eric McKibben, son of Pepper Bridge founder Norm McKibben. Though McKibben père acknowledges that some percentage of declassified Pepper Bridge goes into the Amavi wines, he insists that this is not a second label for Pepper Bridge, nor does it taste second rate. These are excellent wines all on their own, but from younger vines and given more American oak and less time in new oak overall.

Amavi does a superb job with sémillon, a grape that seems to have its best expression in Walla Walla (think L'Ecole N° 41). Flavors are crystal clear, leesy, and long-lasting, blending pear and pineapple with citrus zest; there is a lively, refreshing acidity, and the neutral barrels soften rather than flavor the wine.

Notable: The syrahs are brilliant, infused with smoke and char, with extra nuances of smoked meats, licorice, and mineral. The winery also makes a soft, seductive cabernet sauvignon, with fruit flavors of plum and pie cherry and a lick of coffee in the finish.

ANIMALE

Founded 2001
PO Box 70491
Seattle, WA 98127
206/782-8047
www.animalewine.com
E-mail: winery@animalewine.com

Animale, which released its first commercial wines in 2003, is what the French call a garagiste operation. Winemaker Matt Gubitosa, a geologist by trade, has converted the basement of his Seattle home into a snazzy winery, laboratory, and barrel room. Which makes him more of a *basementiste*, I suppose.

Animale operates at the fringes of what could be considered commercial. Its entire 2003-vintage output was 132 cases, up to 210 in 2005. Small brings with it many challenges; no matter how careful a winemaker may be (Gubitosa maintains an immaculate cellar), producing wine in tiny batches makes it easier for bacteriological and oxidative problems to appear, which makes these artful, elegant wines all the more impressive.

Gubitosa is content to move at his own pace, and he is committed to doing wines his way, which includes no new oak, no fining or filtering and focuses on cool-climate flavors, producing varietal wines that are expressive in both nose and mouth but deceptively light and subtle. Don't look for the ripe, jammy flavors of sweet berry preserves or the toast, coffee, butterscotch, and vanilla flavors of expensive new oak. Instead, you may find what those bigger flavors often disguise: the true varietal character unique to Washington-grown grapes.

Notable: Recent releases included an excellent merlot and a stylish, cool-climate cabernet sauvignon. The 2005 syrah is a star, stylish and ripe but not over the top.

BAER

Founded 2000
9118 222nd Street SE
Woodinville, WA 98072
425/483-7060
www. baerwinery.com
E-mail: info@baerwinery.com

In Memorium: Lance Baer died unexpectedly as this book was going to press in May, 2007. Lance Baer began making wine as an assistant to Chris Upchurch at DeLille. When he started working on his own project, he determined not to use the same vineyards or barrels as his mentor, intended as a gesture of sincere respect. As a result, Baer's vineyard sources have changed with each vintage: Alder Ridge in 2000 and 2001; Stillwater Creek and Elerding in 2002; Stillwater, Boushey, and Ciel du Cheval in 2003; and all Stillwater since 2004. But despite the many different vineyard sources, Baer has maintained consistency by focusing on just two wines, both blended Bordeaux reds. A tiny bit of chardonnay is also produced (at the request of the winemaker's mother, who, he explains, is not a red wine drinker).

The first wine, Ursa, was made in 2000, when Lance Baer was still working out of a tiny apartment and some rented space in another winery. With the winery now relocated to 6.5 acres in northern Woodinville, moderate but consistent growth has brought total production up from 200 to roughly 1200 cases annually. For the time being, this is where Lance Baer intends to remain ("It's all the barrels we can fit," he cheerfully explains).

Notable: Ursa is a delicious blend of merlot, cabernet franc, cabernet sauvignon, and a dash of malbec. Its pricier companion wine, Arctos, debuted in 2002.

BALBOA

Founded 2004
4169 Pepper Bridge Road
Walla Walla, WA 99362
509/529-0461
www.balboawinery.com
E-mail: info@balboawinery.com

Balboa operates out of the Beresan winery, and Thomas Glase makes wines for both. His Balboa wines are value-priced, fresh, and interesting. The labels (by Amy Glase) have a childlike charm, and the wines are finished with a sensible screw cap. They are that rarity in toney Walla Walla: well-made wines for everyday consumption.

Glase's winemaking skills are topflight, and, given his connection to vineyard manager Tom Waliser, he should have no problem obtaining good fruit. Among the recent releases were excellent, fruit-driven versions of merlot, syrah, and cabernet sauvignon, a clear, tangy red blend called The Cat's Meow, and a more complex, pricier Bordeaux red blend named Mith.

We need more wineries like Balboa in Washington, with very clean, professional winemaking, pure varietal expressions, moderate but ripe alcohol and tannin, and affordable prices.

BARONS V

Founded 2001
PO Box 167
Woodinville, WA 98072
425/398-7147

A true underground mystery wine, Barons V is the brainchild of Gary McLean. McLean owns Interstate Distributor Co., a transportation service provider headquartered in Tacoma, Washington. McLean is a wine lover and philanthropist who contributes generously to a range of wine-related charities. His idea was to duplicate the style of Silver Oak with Washington grapes. He approached Matt Loso (of Matthews Estate) with the concept and brought in four wine-loving partners (all from the timber industry) as coinvestors.

Loso makes about 1400 cases of Barons V Cabernet Sauvignon annually. Ninety percent is sold through a mailing list and by word of mouth. Grapes come from Klipsun, Chandler Reach, Hedges, and Conner-Lee. Beginning with the 2005 vintage, a couple of barrels of syrah are being made using American oak; the plan is to do something, says McLean, "in the Grange style."

Notable: Barons V's first releases of cabernet sauvignon were imposing, muscular, tannic wines. Strong new-oak scents of spice and cinnamon and smoke accent the steakhouse-style cabernet, loaded with cassis and cherry fruit.

BARRISTER

Founded 2001
1213 W. Railroad Avenue
Spokane, WA 99201
509/465-3591
www.barristerwinery.com
E-mail: info@barristerwinery.com

Greg Lipsker and Michael White are Spokane-area attorneys who have quickly turned Barrister into a 2500-case red wine specialist. A new winery building (a three-story brick warehouse in Spokane's rapidly improving Davenport Arts District) was purchased in 2004; a tasting room has been renovated on the main floor and the barrel room fitted out in the basement. Cabernet franc was Barrister's first big success, but recent releases of syrah, cabernet sauvignon, and merlot have been every bit as good.

Credit terrific fruit sources, such as Morrison Lane, Pepper Bridge, and Bacchus. The style is tarry, smoky, dark, and dense. Despite their imposing power, these wines retain supple fruits and superb concentration.

Notable: Where to begin? Barrister syrah, cofermented with viognier, explodes from the glass with whiff after whiff of mineral, bacon fat, wild berry, and citrus rind. Barrister cabernet sauvignon offers black cherry, ripe berry, and espresso flavors wrapped together and spiced up with sniffs of fresh-cut tobacco. The merlot is thick, chewy, fleshy, and chocolatey, with concentrated boysenberry, blueberry, and cherry fruit.

BASEL CELLARS

Founded 2001
2901 Old Milton Highway
Walla Walla, WA 99362
509/522-0200
www.baselcellars.com
E-mail: info@baselcellars.com

Basel Cellars is headquartered in an expansive (13,000-square-foot) mansion set in rolling hills near the Washington–Oregon border south of Walla Walla. The winery, modeled rather loosely after Chateau Mouton Rothschild, makes 4000 cases annually, primarily red wines. The lineup includes everything from basic red wine to vineyard-designated cabernets and syrahs and a Bordeaux blend called Merriment.

Past winemaker Trey Busch turned out some real successes, when he got the right fruit (not too young, not too lean) and lightened up on the barrel regimen. Some excellent sources (Lewis, Seven Hills, and Spofford Station) go into the dense, black cabernets, powerfully scented with black cherry, loganberry, and cedar. The estate vineyard (Pheasant Run) has yet to show the same power.

Basel has the potential to become one of the better red wine producers in the state, if consistency (particularly among the syrahs) can improve so that the quality comes up to the level of the ambitious pricing.

Notable: The Columbia Valley cabernet is an excellent wine, usually with some syrah in the blend (the single-vineyard cabs are 100 percent varietal). At $60 a bottle, the Lewis vineyard designates are expensive (just about everything at Basel is expensive), but what great fruit.

BERESAN

Founded 2001
4169 Pepper Bridge Road
Walla Walla, WA 99362
509/522-2395
www.beresanwines.com
E-mail: info@beresanwines.com

Beresan (the name refers to a region in Ukraine) is owned by Tom Waliser, a Walla Walla native, apple grower, and vineyard manager. For the past decade or more, Waliser has managed Pepper Bridge and Seven Hills, the two biggest vineyards in the valley, and consulted for several other important growers.

In 1997–98 he planted his own Waliser and Yellow Jacket vineyards, 18 acres in all, on stony-dry riverbed. The first small crop was harvested in 2001, and, along with grapes purchased from Pepper Bridge and Seven Hills, it was made into a few hundred cases of Beresan cabernet sauvignon and Beresan Stone River red.

It's a trite but true statement in the wine biz that great wines are made in the vineyard, not the winery. It follows, therefore, that a winery based on a vineyard, with a grower-owner who has a track record of excellence in vineyard management, is likely to have a significant advantage, other things being equal, over its peers. It helps that Waliser is teamed up with a winemaker, Thomas Glase, who knows how to handle great fruit. Through its first few vintages Beresan has made some thrilling wines. In 2004, when the estate vineyards were decimated by a winter freeze, the meticulous attention to both vine tending and winemaking paid off with a lineup of releases that made the very best of a bad situation.

The prices are modest, and this is a winery sure to be discovered; the advice from here is get on the mailing list now. Production has leveled off at around 1500 cases, most of it dedicated to merlot, cabernet sauvignon, syrah, and the Stone River red. Very limited amounts of malbec, sémillon, and a late-harvest syrah are offered through the tasting room, one of the prettiest in the valley.

Notable: Beresan's Stone River red is a sophisticated blend of cabernet sauvignon, syrah, merlot, and cab franc. As with the wines of Cayuse, the secret sauce here is the river rock on which the vines struggle to produce fruit; these vineyards have genuine terroir. Densely layered, framed in vivid acids, and beautifully expressing its signature minerality, this is a deep, dark, mouth-filling wine powered by ripe black cherry and blackberry fruit. As long as it stays on course, Beresan will quickly join the top rank of Washington boutique wineries.

BERGEVIN LANE

Founded 2001
1215 W. Poplar Street
Walla Walla, WA 99362
509/526-4300
www.bergevinlane.com
E-mail: info@bergevinlane.com

Annette Bergevin and Amber Lane left San Francisco Bay Area careers in telecommunications to return to Bergevin's home town of Walla Walla. French-born and -educated winemaker Virginie Bourgue joined them early in 2003 and helped to design the new winery from scratch, expanding the all-red lineup with viognier and sémillon. Though Bourgue left in 2006 to begin her own winery, her legacy at Bergevin Lane will be the excellent jump-start she has given the first few vintages.

In the beginning, purchased grapes were used exclusively, but now a small vineyard (7.5 acres) planted to one-third syrah, two-thirds cabernet sauvignon is contributing grapes as well.

The affordable Calico Red, a "kitchen sink" blend of cabernet, merlot, syrah, zin, and cab franc, is fun and flavorful, nothing serious but good stuff. Bergevin's viognier is thick and peachy, barrel-fermented, and oak-aged. The syrah is fruit-powered, clean, and streaked with anise and pepper.

Notable: "Intuition," a reserve red Bordeaux blend, opens with a textured, spicy, exotic nose that mixes its red and black fruits with pepper, ground coffee, cinnamon, and saffron. The spice box flavors blossom into a lovely, supple wine nuanced with mineral, leaf, and leather. The extremely limited "Jaden's Reserve" syrah is the best yet from Bergevin Lane, a compelling blend of citrus, spice, pineapple, and lime over bright, sappy raspberry and cherry fruit.

BOUDREAUX CELLARS

Founded 2002
4551 Icicle Creek Road
Leavenworth, WA 98826
509/548-5858
www.boudreauxcellars.com
E-mail: rob@boudreauxcellars.com

"Rob Newsom," reads the winemaker bio for Boudreaux Cellars, "has survived a paragliding crash, a flaming helicopter evacuation, and having his tent avalanche-launched off a 4000-foot alpine wall. He's battled hypothermia, oxygen deprivation, and 85-mph winds during his 20+ years as a world-class alpinist. Nowadays he makes wine for a living." Being "avalanche-launched" is a pretty good description of Newsom's wines, which are powerfully built. A fishing friendship with Leonetti's Gary Figgins led to a midlife career change (Newsom was a mountain-climbing guide and outdoor equipment guru before turning to wine) and also to some rarified grape sources and perhaps a tip or two about making wine, Leonetti-style. Boudreaux Cellars has made just a smattering of vintages, but among the small-lot releases of sémillon, chardonnay, sangiovese, syrah, merlot, and cabernet sauvignon have been some meaty masterpieces.

Great fruit sources, as always, are the foundation, from vineyards such as Champoux, Klipsun, Sagemoor, Seven Hills, and Pepper Bridge. Newsom's chardonnays and sémillons are fat, dark, and rich, drink-now-type wines, but his reds are better structured and more successful overall. Boudreaux is headquartered in a compound that includes Newsom's log cabin home on Eightmile Creek in the heart of beautiful Icicle Canyon. The spectacular location, deep in the Cascade Mountains outside the town of Leavenworth, is well off the grid. Heat has been a problem in the barrel room in the summer, but a new winery was built in time for the 2005 crush, so look for more consistency in future vintages.

Notable: Boudreaux vineyard-designate reds, especially the syrahs and cabernet sauvignon, are big, full-throttle wines loaded with fruit and smooth, soft tannins. This 1500-case winery has already engendered a lot of buzz around the state.

BRIAN CARTER CELLARS

Founded 2006
3712 140th Ave. NE
Bellevue, WA 98005
425/895-9284
www.briancartercellars.com
E-mail: info@briancartercellars.com

A brand-new venture from one of this state's veteran winemakers, Brian Carter Cellars, is scheduled to be one of four wineries opening in the upscale Woodinville Wine Village in 2007. Carter (whose current winemaking duties include Apex and Apex II) has made wines for a couple of dozen Washington wineries going back as far as the late 1970s. Though he began making a few cases of his own wine almost a decade ago, it wasn't until 2006 that Carter arranged with his Apex partner, Harry Alhadeff, to devote at least half of his time to establishing the Brian Carter Cellars label.

Carter's goal is to make about 7000 cases of six different wines, all blends, not varietals. "That's where the fun is and that's what I want to do," he says, adding, "I think blends are a continuing trend and an area that Washington state will excel in over the next decade. Only recently has Washington had the number of sites and maturity of good sites for different varieties such as petit verdot and sangiovese."

Notable: Though his winery was officially begun in 2006, Carter was able to pull wines together from earlier vintages to jump-start it. Among his first releases were four red blends (two modeled on Bordeaux, one southern Rhône, one super-Tuscan), and a white wine called Oriana (Italian for "golden lady"), a roussanne-riesling-viognier blend. Stylishly clever, it nicely captures the best of all three grapes: citrusy viognier, floral riesling, and rich, ripe, peachy roussanne.

BUNNELL FAMILY CELLAR

Founded 2004
87203 West 134 PR NW
Prosser, WA 99350

509/973-4187
www.riveraerie.com
E-mail: bunnellwine@earthlink.net

Ron Bunnell is a 1982 UC Davis graduate whose winemaking career began with stints at Beringer, Chateau Souverain, and Kendall-Jackson. He and his family moved to Washington in 1999, when he was hired to oversee red winemaking for Chateau Ste. Michelle. In 2005 Bunnell left to start his own family winery, based in Prosser and dedicated to producing syrah and other Rhône varietals.

The winery makes two distinctly different lines of wines, which Bunnell has named *vins de l'endroit* ("wines of a place") and *vins de l'esprit* ("wines of the creative spirit"). The former are vineyard- or appellation-designated wines meant to capture the essence of a particular site. *Vins de l'esprit* are blended wines; the nonvintage "Vif" is the first of these.

Stunningly packaged in massive, deeply punted bottles, the Bunnell syrahs include brilliant examples from three distinct appellations. The Boushey-McPherson vineyard–Yakima Valley bottling jumps out for its elegance and precision, perfectly showcasing tart, cool-climate fruit flavors. The Horse Heaven Hills bottling, a pleasing mix of citrus, berry, and plum, slides through the palate with the grace of a racehorse, its smooth, ripe tannins leaving a hint of black olive and fresh herb in the finish. And finally, the Clifton Hill vineyard–Wahluke Slope bottling is the most forward and dense of all, with rich scents of mixed berries, spice, fresh herbs, and toast.

Vif is a bright, fruity country red; Bunnell also makes a pair of excellent white wines. Future releases may include such unusual varietals as Barbera, sangiovese, malbec, and petit verdot. Taken all together, this is one of the most impressive debuts for any winery in recent years.

CAVE B

Founded 2002
348 Silica Road
Quincy, WA 98848
509/785-3500
www.caveb.com
E-mail: info@caveb.com

The Gorge at George, as it is locally known, has established itself as one of the best outdoor concert venues in the world. Here, near the tiny farming town of George, Washington, the Columbia River cuts a deep channel through basalt rock, and the rugged beauty of the place, especially at sunset, is a bit like the Grand Canyon itself, without all the color.

Few people realize that the original Gorge amphitheater was just a small, grassy knoll attached to the now-defunct Champs de Brionne winery. Vince and Carol Bryan purchased

500 acres of land in 1980 and developed that original winery and vineyards, some of which are still bearing. They sold the amphitheater to fund a medical research project, which proved quite lucrative. When that too was sold, in 2002, the Bryans returned to their land and began building a new winery, Cave B. The talented Rusty Figgins, formerly with Glen Fiona and Northstar, was named winemaker in 2004.

The pre-Figgins vintages of Cave B wines suffered from inconsistent winemaking and rough tannins, but Figgins knows what he's doing and will set a course of steady improvement. This is a well-funded enterprise that has access to some unusual older-vine fruit from the original plantings, including some of the state's oldest chenin blanc.

Notable: The Cave B winery anchors a world-class destination resort that includes an inn, 15 individual cottages perched above the basalt cliffs, and a fine restaurant. In the planning stages are a golf course, an outdoor theater, and gardens. The Cuvée du Soleil Red is a nicely nuanced Bordeaux blend; the Estate Blanc de Blanc is one of the better Washington sparklers.

CHELAN ESTATE VINEYARDS & WINERY

Founded 2002
PO Box 2687
Chelan, WA 98816
509/670-6795
www.chelanestatewinery.com
E-mail: info@chelanestatewinery.com

Bob Broderick, who oversees the wine purchasing for a chain of Seattle-area supermarkets, planted the first eight acres of his estate vineyard on the shores of Lake Chelan in the spring of 2000. Three clones of pinot noir and some merlot were first to go into the ground; later he added a bit of viognier, chardonnay, and cab franc. The pinot and chardonnay are off to a good start (the cab franc has already been pulled), not entirely surprising because the area, though new viticultural territory for Washington, is strikingly reminiscent of British Columbia's Lake Okanagan wine region. Additional grapes are purchased and go into an excellent merlot. Broderick is also a founding member of the Lake Chelan Growers Association, and the group is pushing hard to get an application into the TTB for official AVA certification.

Notable: Pinot noir has never done especially well in Washington, though occasionally a light, pleasant bottle or two has turned up. But the Chelan area is unique and may be the exact right spot to grow the finicky grape here. Chelan Estate's first efforts have been promising, more elegant than most Oregon efforts, with none of the weedy, tomato flavors, yet the alcohol is a Burgundian 12.3%. Delicate, ripe, and flavorful, it actually tastes like pinot.

COUGAR CREST

Founded 2001
202 A Street
Walla Walla, WA 99362
509/529-5980
www.cougarcrestwinery.com
E-mail: info@cougarcrestwinery.com

In 1996, Deborah and David Hansen exchanged San Francisco Bay Area careers in pharmacy and veterinary medicine for life on a Walla Walla farm, where they developed 125 acres of orchard. Cuttings from Windrow (the original Seven Hills vineyard) and Cailloux vineyard went into the ground in 1998, and the Hansens now grow some 50 acres of wine grapes at their Stellar, Cougar Hills, and Golden's Legacy vineyards. Plantings include viognier, cabernet sauvignon, cabernet franc, merlot, petit verdot, malbec, and syrah.

This inevitably led them to make their own wines beginning in 2001. The winery, located at the Walla Walla airport, produces estate-grown viognier, syrah, merlot, cabernet sauvignon, and cabernet franc. The reds are given a lot of new oak, too much, in some instances, for my palate.

Notable: Cougar Crest's estate cabernet franc is one of Washington's best, supple, soft, and loaded with candied red fruits.

DOYENNE CELLARS

Founded 2004
PO Box 2233
Woodinville, WA 98072
425/489-0544
www.delillecellars.com
E-mail: info@delillecellars.com

Doyenne began as the name for DeLille Cellars' syrah, which debuted with the 1997 vintage. In 2004, in an effort to differentiate between the Bordeaux focus of DeLille and the about-to-expand Rhône

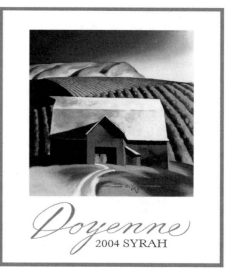

focus of Doyenne, it was officially made a separate winery. The change was inaugurated with an artist label and a massively thick bottle, heavy enough to put a hole in the Titanic.

Some recent vintages of Doyenne syrahs have been bruisers also, tight and chewy, with heavy tannins and an abundance of dark, roasted, espresso flavors. The 2004 shows the winery moving into a more elegant, more focused style, with beautifully ripened fruit that captures both the floral elegance and pure fruit power of Washington syrah.

Doyenne is rapidly expanding and has added both a varietal roussanne (creamy, and thick, with juicy flavors of citrus peel, honey-lemon, and white peach fruits), and a cabernet–syrah blend dubbed Aix. Named for the town in Provence, Aix shows some interesting hints of wild fruits and light, spicy herbs.

Notable: The newest Doyenne projects are Métier blanc and Métier rouge. The former, a viognier–chardonnay blend, is loaded with pretty white peach, pear, and grapefruit, fresh and floral. The Métier rouge (half grenache and a quarter each mourvèdre and syrah) is a Washington Chateauneuf-du-wannabe. It's a glorious effort, with a massive nose of charcuterie, wild herb, mint, and spicy plum. Concentrated and polished, it sets Doyenne on a path to join McCrea as this state's premier Rhône specialist.

DUSTED VALLEY

Founded 2003
1248 Old Milton Highway
Walla Walla, WA 99362
509/525-1337
www.dustedvalley.com
E-mail: info@dustedvalley.com

Humor is a good thing to have on your side, especially when you are a young, start-up winery with a strikingly ugly label and a lot of competition. Dusted Valley makes some fun wines and some fine wines, but I wish that wretched purple label would go away. I love the slogan, however: "As we say in the Dusted Valley, open that bottle. The first two glasses are for your health, the second two for ours!"

Dusted Valley is owned by the Johnson and Braunel families. The two couples met at the University of Wisconsin, where they individually studied food science and tourism and hospitality. Their consulting winemaker is Steve Lessard (Whitman Cellars).

Notable: The Barrel Thief red and Stained Tooth syrah are the winery's most visible efforts, but it is their old-vine chardonnay (from Kestrel vineyard grapes) and Yakima Valley viognier that have made the best impression among the early releases.

FIVE STAR CELLARS

Founded 2000
840 C Street
Walla Walla, WA 99362
509/527-8400
www.fivestarcellars.com
E-mail: info@.fivestarcellars.com

Five Star is another member of Walla Walla's airport winery fraternity, and it draws its grapes from many of the same sources as its peers. Seven Hills, Pepper Bridge, and Pheasant Run fruit goes into their hearty, tannic merlots and cabernets. A Five Star sangiovese shows simple strawberry flavors. This young winery tends to be heavy-handed with the new oak. If they can rein that in so that it matches the level of fruit intensity, their wines will benefit. Right now the merlots seem best able to handle all that wood.

FORGERON CELLARS

Founded 2001
33 West Birch Street
Walla Walla, WA 99362
509/522-9463
www.forgeroncellars.com
E-mail: info@forgeroncellars.com

Forgeron winemaker Marie-Eve Gilla-Nicault, who is married to Gilles Nicault of Long Shadows, has been making wines in America since the early 1990s. Her first years in Washington state were spent at Covey Run, Hogue, and Gordon Brothers. At Gordon Brothers she became enamored of the concept of making wines that straddled the border between American and French styles, sturdy wines with a lot of character.

"Washington sunshine," she explains, "is a lot more consistent than in France. We like the French wines because they are elegant and balanced and meant to age. So we're trying to create an elegant wine that showcases the American fruit but is subtle enough and balanced enough to age."

In 2001 she helped to found Forgeron Cellars, headquartered in a turn-of-the-century blacksmithing shop in Walla Walla (*forgeron* is French for "blacksmith"). The winery's early strengths were its chardonnay and (surprisingly) a rock-solid zinfandel. Forgeron's merlots and cabernet blends seemed to suffer a bit in 2002, but in more recent vintages it's clear that Gilla is back in top form. Vinfinity, the winery reserve, is well made but has not jumped out in front of the other wines, though it is priced significantly higher.

Notable: Gilla's Chardonnays are surefire, with crisp citrus and apple, lots of vanilla and barrel spice, and layers of buttered nuts, all in a tight, stylish frame. Forgeron's 2003 merlot, syrah, and cabernet, are all excellent wines, especially the merlot-dense, smoky, inky, and concentrated with loads of cassis and black cherry fruit.

FORT WALLA WALLA CELLARS

Founded 2002
1383 Barleen Drive
Walla Walla, WA 99362

509/520-1095
www.fortwallawalla.com
E-mail: info@.fortwallawalla.com

Fort Walla Walla makes about 1500 cases of syrah, merlot, and cabernet sauvignon, much in the same vein as many of its Walla Walla peers. Jim Moyer and Cliff Kontos are the partners. Some good syrah and merlot have been made, albeit a bit too dependent on new-oak flavors for my tastes.

In 2004, when the usual grape sources were not available, the winery made a decent red blend (Treaty Red) in a rich, toasty, oaky vein. Loaded with ripe fruit and chocolatey oak, with notes of leather and a brown sugar sweetness to the finish, it's a smooth and appealing wine, but one-dimensional and difficult to separate from the pack of similar efforts.

GAMACHE VINTNERS

Founded 2002
23509 N. Dallas Road
Richland, WA 99352
509/546-8990
www. gamachevintners.com
E-mail: bob@gamachevintners.com

The Gamache vineyards, located north of Pasco in the White Bluffs area, were first planted by Bob and Roger Gamache in 1982. Since then Gamache vineyards has been a contract grower for Ste. Michelle Wine Estates, contributing its grapes to the company's prestigious Northstar merlot, Eroica riesling, and Columbia Crest reserve cabernets. Gamache introduced its own wines with the 2002 vintage. Now that the brothers have their own estate winery, we can taste their outstanding fruit all on its own.

The first few hundred cases of Gamache cabernet were made under the supervision of Charlie Hoppes, who also guides the winemaking at Fidélitas, Goose Ridge, and Cañon de Sol. The cabernet was followed by an excellent syrah, supple, with berry and plum flavors set against hints of fresh herb and finished with dark streaks of licorice, cocoa, and roasted coffee. Still more recently the winery released a "Gamache–Champoux Vineyard Select" Cabernet Sauvignon made from 25+-year-old vines (Paul Champoux is a cousin). Sleek and sappy, it serves up a full spectrum of berries as only Washington cab can.

Notable: Gamache certainly has access to great fruit, so everything it makes from its own vines is going to be worth hunting for. In addition to the wines already released, an estate-grown viognier is in the works.

GORMAN

Founded 2003
206/351-0719
www.gormanwinery.com
E-mail: chris@gormanwinery.com

Chris Gorman, who calls himself "the anti-winery," holds a day job with a Seattle wine distributor and makes his limited-edition wines in a Woodinville warehouse, where he works "pretty closely" with Mark McNeilly, the mastermind behind Mark Ryan. Gorman's wines are good—very good—and his packaging is flat-out great. It's amazing to me that big corporate wineries, which spend tens of thousands of dollars designing labels and graphics and testing out "concepts," often fail to come up with anything really good. Then along comes a guy like Gorman, who designs his own labels and prints them out himself and debuts with names and graphics and concepts that jump out at you with their clean, startling originality.

Gorman's wines are robust and charmingly rough-hewn. Though not timid wines, they are crafted from outstanding Washington fruit and deliver concentrated flavors that showcase this state's strengths. Only 450 cases are made annually.

Notable: Among the first releases are "The Evil Twin," a monster Syrah–Cabernet Sauvignon blend, dense, concentrated, and packed with berry, cassis, caramel, coffee liqueur, black tea, and butterscotch. Equally good are "The Bully" Cabernet Sauvignon and "The Pixie" Syrah, with raspberry, black cherry, and red licorice and scents of violets, rose petals, and hints of cracked pepper.

JAMES LEIGH CELLARS

Founded 2001
16 North 2nd
Walla Walla, WA 99362
509/529-1398
www.jamesleighcellars.com
E-mail: info@jamesleighcellars.com

Established in 2001, James Leigh Cellars counts as its main strength its estate vineyard, named Spofford Station. Estate-grown fruit has been the basis for exemplary bottles of merlot, cabernet sauvignon, and syrah in the first few vintages. The merlot, thick, lush, and substantial, is about as chewy a merlot as you'll ever find. Very impressive, dense, and flavorful. The cabernet, almost as good, includes some fruit from Pepper Bridge. It's polished and sophisticated winemaking, with big, brawny, smoky, and edgy flavors. Finally, the Spofford Station syrah is packed with zingy fruit, lifted with spicy acids, tart and intense through a very long and detailed finish.

A winemaker shift shortly after the current releases were made means that the future course of this young winery remains uncertain; but the fruit speaks for itself.

LATITUDE 46° N

Founded 2002
1211 Sand Pit Road
Touchet, WA 99360
509/394-0460
www.latitude46.com
E-mail: info@latitude46.com

The name refers to the 46th parallel, which separates Washington and Oregon just south of Walla Walla. The winery is located in Touchet, a dusty pit stop a few miles west of Walla Walla and just down the road from Woodward Canyon and L'Ecole N° 41. It's a partnership between winemakers Chris Dowsett and Robert Goodfriend (of Harlequin), but Dowsett is solely responsible for making the Latitude wines. He has a fine touch with both reds and whites, which combine power and detail.

His syrah, dubbed "The Power and the Glory," is a concentrated, satiny wine that blends in up to 10 percent grenache. Released quite young and showing intense, primary fruit flavors, it hints at the layers of meat, smoke, tar, and licorice to come.

From time to time a late-harvest chenin blanc or a barrel-fermented gewürztraminer may be made. One gets the impression that a real artist is at work, making wines that speak to his particular passions. "I love complexity," says Dowsett. "If you want to be able to finish an entire bottle with a meal, it had better keep saying different things to you."

Notable: That love of complexity shows particularly in Latitude's gewürztraminers. These are true classics, styled from Celilo vineyard grapes. Fragrant, lemony, tart, tropical gum flavors abound, along with candied rose petals, breadfruit, and more. Fascinating and complex wines, they deserve a place with the best gewürztraminers in the country.

LONE CANARY

Founded 2002
109 S. Scott Street, #B2
Spokane, WA 99202
509/534-9062
www.lonecanary.com
E-mail: info@lonecanary.com

A winery named Lone Canary, with a sketchy picture of a somewhat puzzled tweetie bird on the label, runs the risk of being lumped in with critter brands such as Three Ugly Mice and the Perambulating Penguin. But there's a real story here, not a made-up marketing gimmick. Originally destined to be named Wild Canary (a nickname for the Washington state bird), winery founder Mike Scott ran "a-fowl" of another alcoholic product named for a wild bird. There was no time to start over (the wines were due to be released) and no money to fight a legal battle. Voila! Lone Canary was born.

Scott's sensitive, low-key, European approach to winemaking often recalls the similar style of Columbia's David Lake. A doomed romance brought Scott to the United States in 1979, admittedly knowing "absolutely nothing" about wine. Marooned in Spokane and looking for work ("in 1980 in Spokane all you needed was to know red from white"), he began at Worden and then joined Mike Conway (Latah Creek) as assistant winemaker. Scott's years making wine at Caterina followed, the high point of that winery's wobbly arc.

Lone Canary began with an excellent sauvignon blanc and then added three blended reds. Rosso (the Tuscan blend) is the best: predominantly sangiovese and graced with leafy, herbal tobacco flavors, much like true Chianti. Rouge (the Bordeaux blend) is a good, all-purpose quaffing wine. There is also a rather generic red called, well, Red, and a varietal Barbera. (In the most recent vintage, the Rosso/Rouge/Red concept has been discarded.)

Notable: Lone Canary's sauvignon blancs are sharp, melony, oyster-friendly wines with a refreshing, steely finish.

LONG SHADOWS

Founded 2002
PO Box 33670
Seattle, WA 98133
206/396-9628
www.longshadows.com
E-mail: info@longshadows.com

Allen Shoup, whose two-decade tenure as CEO of the Ste. Michelle wine group led to such groundbreaking joint ventures as Col Solare (with Piero Antinori) and Eroica (with Ernst Loosen), decided to forego retirement and instead set about creating Long Shadows. It's a consortium of boutique wineries, each with a focus on a single varietal or blend, produced under the supervision of a world-class, globally recognized winemaker-advisor. The first vintages were made in a leased Walla Walla facility. Gilles Nicault is the winemaker on-premise who oversees the entire portfolio.

In February 2006, ground was broken on a $4.2 million Long Shadows winery a few miles west of Walla Walla. "The winery is just a cement box buried in the ground," says Shoup. "What's going to impress people is that when you go into the bowels of the winery you will see that nothing has been sacrificed in terms of cost of equipment; you will recognize that this is a spotless, no-compromise approach." His goal, he goes on to explain, is "to create seven or eight Leonettis, free-standing, 4000- or 5000-case wineries that are meeting world standards." At the moment, each of the wines in the Long Shadows portfolio has its own name, its own label, and its own jet-set winemaker, working with Gilles Nicault.

Feather is a 100 percent cabernet sauvignon made by Napa's Randy Dunn. Soft, ripe, and plummy, it shows a good mix of red and blue fruits, amplified with lots of toast, chocolate, coffee, and cinnamon highlights, definitely a Napa-meets-Washington style.

Pirouette is a Bordeaux blend made by Napa's Agustin Huneeus and Philippe Melka. Dusty, toasty, and showing lots of expensive-oak and roasted-coffee scents, it hits the palate quite soft, seamless, classy, rich, and luscious in a Napa Valley style.

Pedestal is the project's merlot, made under the supervision of Michel Rolland in a dense, supremely concentrated, silky, smoky, voluptuous style. Lovely notes of bacon and smoked meats permeate the thick, juicy fruit; this is the best of a very strong lineup.

Sequel is a syrah made by Australia's John Duval, who was head winemaker for Penfolds from 1986 to 2002, where he was responsible for an enormous lineup of shiraz, including the iconic Penfolds Grange. Satiny and smooth, with astringent tannins, it's just a bit hot as it winds through the finish.

Poet's Leap is the riesling, made under the guidance of Armin Diel of Germany's Schlossgut Diel. Round and warmly fruity, it's a lovely mix of grapefruit, stone fruits, and light tropical flavors.

In 2007, Long Shadows debuted Saggi, which emulates a super-Tuscan blend and is the project of Ambrogio and Giovanni Folonari. Roughly one-third sangiovese, one-third cabernet sauvignon, and one-third a split between syrah and some not-so-Tuscan barbera, Saggi is smooth, chocolatey, and dark, a good first step.

Finally, there is Chester|Kidder, a red blend made entirely by Gilles Nicault. "The project," Shoup acknowledges, "only works if the wines live up to the talents of the people making them. If the wines aren't there, then the whole thing is smoke and mirrors."

Though it is important to evaluate these wines individually, they may also be considered as a conceptual group. I hope that this visionary and very expensive project can achieve its rather lofty goals. One example of what Long Shadows is up against financially: Shoup had budgeted an average of $1400/ton for purchasing grapes (during his time at Ste. Michelle, he says, the average cost was $800/ton). In fact, he's been paying upwards of $2000/ton in order to get the quality he wants and still bulking out or selling off something like half his production. That is a very expensive learning curve!

Notable: The whole project is extraordinary. So far, the Pedestal and the Poet's Leap are the Long Shadows wines that best demonstrate the distinctive power of Washington fruit. But the entire group sells out quickly—clearly it's working.

MacCALLUM

Founded 1999
Carlton, OR 98848
503/345-9218
www.maccallumwines.com
E-mail: info@maccallumwines.com

Don't be surprised if MacCallum is an unfamiliar name; the tiny (700-case) winery is based in Oregon but makes exceptional wines from Washington grapes. Owners Mitzi and Jim MacCallum intend to stay quite small because, they explain, "growing any more means employees, and we are deathly afraid of that." Three-quarters of the wine is sold off the mailing list.

Their interest in wine was piqued, they say, during a visit to Chateau Meursault in 1993. They looked at each other and knew that winemaking was what they wanted to do. They moved to Oregon in 1995, where Jim jumped into winemaking classes and part-time winery work. MacCallum made its first wines in 1999.

How they wound up specializing in Washington wines from a location in Carlton, Yamhill County, remains a bit of a mystery. But the wines need no justification. The DJ red (a syrah–cabernet blend), syrah, and malbec are made in extremely limited quantities from Yakima Valley grapes. There is also a Washington viognier and an Oregon pinot noir. I was knocked out with the winery's 2002 releases, the first I had tasted, but disappointed in the follow-up 2003s, which were not in the same league. Nonetheless, the ability to make outstanding wines is clearly there; it would be very surprising if MacCallum didn't come through with a stellar lineup in their new vintages.

MORRISON LANE

Founded 2002
201 West Main
Walla Walla, WA 99361
509/526-0229
www.morrisonlane.com
E-mail: info@morrisonlane.com

Dean and Verdie Morrison planted their first four acres of syrah just outside of Walla Walla in 1994. The vineyard has grown sixfold, and the dazzling array of varietals produced makes it one of the most eclectic in the state. Half of the 23 acres are devoted to syrah; also included in the rest of the mix are viognier, cinsault, carmenère, counoise, Dolcetto, sangiovese, nebbiolo, and barbera.

Morrison Lane grapes were a hot commodity from the very first harvest. Among the wineries lining up to purchase them are such Walla Walla stars as Seven Hills, Cayuse,

K Vintners, Walla Walla Vintners, Syzygy, and Latitude 46. It wasn't long before the Morrisons decided to make wines under their own label. The winemaker is their son, Dan Morrison, who is also the cellarmaster at Canoe Ridge. Only estate grapes are used.

The modest packaging does not entirely do justice to the gorgeous fruit. The winemaking is first-rate, and the various wines all show clear varietal identities. The multitalented Morrisons are a musical family as well, Dean on stand-up bass, Verdie on piano, and Dan on guitar. Their Main Street tasting room is often the setting for some of the town's best jam sessions.

Notable: The Morrison Lane wines are solid across the board, but the syrah, carmenère, and counoise are glorious. See also the Morrison Lane vineyard designate from K Vintners.

NICHOLAS COLE CELLARS

Founded 2001
705 Berney Drive
Walla Walla, WA 99362
509/525-0608
www.nicholascolecellars.com
E-mail: info@nicholascolecellars.com

Mike Neuffer is a third-generation builder who had long nurtured a dream to be in the wine business "one day" when he retired. "The retirement part never came," he admits. But in 2001, tired of "just managing problems," he made the move to Walla Walla anyway. Nicholas Cole Cellars is his dream come true, named for, and a legacy for, his two children.

Neuffer is hands-on the whole way. He says he was hooked on making wine from the moment he first walked through a Walla Walla vineyard with his friend and fellow winemaker Jean-Francois Pellet (Pepper Bridge). "I'm popping these grapes," Neuffer recalls, "and they're not quite ripe but they're sweet and delicious, and the air smells fresh and clean, and I'm thinking I'm going to get paid for doing this!"

The Nicholas Cole vineyard is 42 planted acres (out of 160 total) and located just up the road from Leonetti Cellar. Neuffer grows cabernet sauvignon, cab franc, merlot, petit verdot, syrah, and sangiovese along with a few rows of mourvèdre and grenache. His vineyard sits at a higher altitude than most in the valley (1100–1275 feet), which helps to protect his vines from the freeze damage suffered periodically at many lower-elevation sites.

Nicholas Cole is already making around 4000 cases of wine, and Neuffer expects to top out at around 5500 when his vineyard comes into full production. Camille is the name of his Bordeaux blend, and it is a serious and substantial wine, with interesting layers of boysenberry, blueberry, and black cherry fruit. Tight, tart, racy, and stylish, it seems to improve with each new vintage. Soon to be released are three new wines: Michele (a cabernet-dominated blend), an estate Reserve, and an estate-grown syrah. All show exceptional winemaking skills at work

Notable: GraEagle is the second label, and it is good enough to pass for the first wine of many young wineries.

:NOTA BENE CELLARS

Founded 2001
9320 15th Avenue South
Seattle, WA 98108
206/459-2785
www.notabenecellars.com
E-mail: info@notabenecellars.com

:Nota Bene Cellars stands as a testament to the steep learning curve faced by many of the tiny, underfunded start-ups in the wine business. Tim Narby and his wife, Carol Bryant, had not yet released their second vintage before they found themselves doing a complete label redesign and running way past their carefully plotted growth plans. The label redesign was prompted by the comments of a would-be distributor in the Midwest, who didn't like the old triangular style. It turned out to be cheaper to do it over than to purchase a special, $100,000 labeling machine that could place them properly on :Nota Bene's stylishly tapered bottles.

The extra production was simply the product of pilot enthusiasm. "I was only supposed to be at 500 cases by 2003, the third year," Narby sheepishly admits, "and I'm at 1100. I shouldn't have done that." One suspects that once he had his own winery, he simply wanted to open up the throttle and see what this baby could do.

Nota Bene (the name is Latin for "note well") may be the only winery in the country with a corporate leopard gecko (Samantha is its name). Narby and Bryant spent almost two decades doing home winemaking before turning pro. Using his Boeing Wine Club experience and connections, Narby has been able to snag grapes from many of the top vineyards in the state.

Releases include a pair of blended reds. Miscela is merlot dominated, with cabernet sauvignon, cab franc, and petit verdot in the mix; Abbinare is a similar blend from a different mix of vineyards. There is also a fine syrah and a Ciel du Cheval vineyard red.

Notable: The Ciel du Cheval is a gem, seamlessly complete, varied, and sophisticated, with long-term aging potential. It says something about the quality of winemaker Tim Narby's efforts that he has access to this fruit, which goes to many of the state's best wineries.

PRECEPT BRANDS

Founded 2003
3534 Bagley Avenue North
Seattle, WA 98103

206/267-5252
www.preceptbrands.com
E-mail: info@preceptbrands.com

Precept Brands is a rapidly growing group of wines based on a simple marketing princi-ple: Make wine approachable. Although the portfolio includes brands from overseas, it is solidly anchored in Washington state, with names such as Waterbrook, Washington Hills, Avery Lane, Barrelstone, Pine & Post, Pavin & Riley, and Sockeye.

Founded in 2003 by former Corus Brands CEO Andrew Browne, the company has quickly become one of the five largest in the state. A new Grandview bottling facility was opened in July 2005. New brands seem to pop up every week; among the latest are Grizz, WAWA, and Wrangler, all featuring alternative closures.

Though I cannot say that I have found any Precept wines to be consistently exceptional at their price points, I have found some from time to time that are standouts. More impor-tantly, what Brown is doing is what Washington state needs more of: smart marketing of very affordable wines. "As an industry we offer few opportunities for the average consumer to drink Washington wine daily," Browne opines. "We don't have a lot of options compared with other countries when it comes to wines under $10." Of course, much of the reason that is true is that the vast oceans of cheap juice available in California, Australia, France, and so on are not to be found here. But Precept and the handful of other large companies operating in the state are finding ways to market inexpensive wines in sufficient quanti-ties to have an impact in select markets out of state.

Steven Sealock is in charge of winemaking for all Precept Brands wines, both domes-tic and international. Resident winemakers at the facilities where Precept produces its wines work under Sealock's direction. Before coming to Precept Brands, Sealock spent years at Columbia winery and later at Canandaigua overseeing the company's Northwest opera-tions. He was intimately involved with the creation of the company's hugely successful Alice White brand.

Grapes for Precept's Washington state wines are sourced from many different vineyards, primarily in the Columbia Valley. Among the most notable are Alder Ridge, Canoe Ridge, Gooseridge, Klipsun, Sagemoor, and Outlook.

Notable: Pine & Post has done an excellent job with the $5 merlot and chardonnay.

RED SKY

Founded 1999
19495 144th Avenue NE, #B220
Woodinville, WA 98072
425/481-9864
www.redskywinery.com
E-mail: redskywinery@comcast.net

Red Sky's Jim and Carol Parsons owned a wine and cheese shop before beginning their tiny winery. The first wines (about 100 cases) were made in the family garage, the next three vintages at Woodinville Wine Company.

The Parsons like to give their wines an extra year or two of bottle age before release, so the current vintages may appear to be backed up. That is intentional. "Our wines are not made for early release," says Jim Parsons. "The goal is to make wines that increase in intricacy over time." Red Sky's limited, late-release wines have mostly gone to a few Seattle-area restaurants and wine shops. Red wines are their strength, including a very nice (and very limited) syrah, a red Bordeaux blend, and a fine cabernet franc. An excellent reserve is also in the works from winemaker John Ogburn, who, it turns out, wears a chef's toque when he's not splashing around in vats of grapes.

In 2006 Red Sky's winery moved into the space formerly occupied by Mark Ryan, and a tasting room was added. Production is up to 1000 cases a year.

Notable: The standout so far is the cabernet franc. It's elegant and complex, with compact blue and red fruits, lightly accented with sweet spice.

SEIA WINE CELLARS

Founded 2003
431 25th Ave. E.
Seattle, WA 98112
206/250-9095
www.seiawines.com
E-mail: info@seiawines.com

Seia's Robert Spalding believes that single-vineyard wines best express the concept of terroir. He makes the point with his excellent syrahs, produced in minute quantities and sold to mailing list customers exclusively. Seia (SAY-yuh), he rather prosaically explains, "is the Roman goddess of things planted in the ground." Such as grapes, perhaps? Along with the syrahs, Seia has made an Elephant Mountain viognier, and a Pepper Bridge cabernet.

Notable: Seia's Clifton Hill vineyard syrah, sourced from one of the mainstay vineyards in Washington's new Wahluke Slope AVA, makes a strong impression in a crowded field. The concentrated fruit, spicy and pure, is fragrant with berries, citrus, and mint. It explodes on the tongue with tart, snappy raspberry and boysenberry fruit, clean and bracing and powerful.

SHERIDAN VINEYARD

Founded 2000
2980 Gilbert Road
Zillah, WA 98953
509/829-3205

www.sheridanvineyard.com
E-mail: info@sheridanvineyard.com

Scott Greer is a former pension planner who confesses he was "kind of a wine geek drawn to the vineyard side of things." He wanted to own a gentleman's farm and went land hunting in the Yakima Valley. Prices, he felt, were more reasonable there. He purchased 76 acres, planted to apples, peaches, and Concord grapes, in late 1996. Chris Camarda (Andrew Will), who was advising him, purchased 36 acres adjacent to Greer's land to establish his own Two Blondes vineyard.

The first four acres at Sheridan, all cabernet sauvignon, went in the ground in the spring of 1997. "I made every single mistake you can possibly make in that first four acres," says Greer. "I'm leaving it in the ground as my ode to how naïve I was." Sheridan's site sits on a hilltop at 1200 feet, with very shallow, rocky soil and a caliche underlay. The merlot has had a hard time establishing itself, but the cabernet has done quite well. A tornado hit the vineyard in 2002; the sort of thing that seems to plague new ventures, but a fine red wine, called L'Orage (the storm), commemorates the disaster.

Sheridan's first vintage was 2000, and Greer closed his pension business soon after. Camarda mentored him with both vineyard management and winemaking, and the sociable Greer says he relentlessly questioned every winemaker who would acknowledge his presence. "I searched out the wines I had a lot of respect for, tried to learn the philosophy behind the wine as much as possible," he recalls. "I learned that you can never make the wine better than the quality of the fruit coming in the front door, no matter how good you are. But you can certainly go backwards."

His winemaking he describes as very low tech: open-top fermenters, manual punchdowns, and so on. A winery and tasting room are located in Zillah, half a mile from the vineyard. All 3000 cases produced annually are estate grown, the lion's share going into his second wine, a red blend called Kamiakin. Under the Sheridan label are a cabernet franc, a cabernet sauvignon, a bit of merlot, and the superpremium L'Orage Bordeaux blend. But best of all are Greer's syrahs, from Phelps clone vines, showing a mix of strawberry and other red fruits, hints of berry, citrus, and plenty of acid.

Notable: Some very fine wineries (Andrew Will, Cadence, Stevens, and O•S) purchase from Greer, a testimony to the high quality of Sheridan fruit.

STEPHENSON CELLARS

Founded 2000
755 B Street
Walla Walla, WA 99362
509/301-9004
(no website)
E-mail: stephenson@bmi.net

Small even by Walla Walla airport standards, Stephenson produces just four wines: a merlot, a cabernet sauvignon, and a pair of syrahs. Special kudos to the syrah, made with grapes from the Yakima Valley's Willow Crest vineyard. It's a dazzling effort, displaying elegant power. Polished red fruits with overtones of peach, apricot, and candied orange are seamlessly woven into a wine that lingers sensuously in the mouth.

STEVENS

Founded 2001
18510 142nd Avenue NE
Woodinville, WA 98072
425/424-9463
www.stevenswinery.com
E-mail: info@stevenswinery.com

A protégé of Matt Loso of Matthews Cellars, Tim Stevens worked there and at Sheridan Vineyard before setting off on his own. His first vintage consisted of just 100 cases of 2001 Champoux vineyard cabernet franc. Now, with his winery newly ensconced in a tidy warehouse space, Stevens has showcased an outstanding lineup of red wines from the 2002, 2003, and 2004 vintages.

Starkly beautiful black and white labels (from the owner's original artworks) set off wines that are trim, sharp, long, and beautifully defined. The 424 red blend is a sleek and subtle tangle of mixed fruits. The "Black Tongue" syrah, peppery and expressive, is loaded with intriguing spices and tart, compact fruit.

Notable: Stevens excels with everything, but the cabernet sauvignons are best of all. The "Big Easy" cabernet offers sharp, tangy mixed fruits and loads of sweet spices, with a grand chocolate finale. The reserve shows an extra dimension, thick and tight, with tar, licorice, and rich, black fruits set against balancing acids and nicely applied new oak.

SYZYGY

Founded 2002
405 E. Boeing Avenue
Walla Walla, WA 99362
509/522-0484
www.syzygywines.com
E-mail: info@syzygywines.com

Zach Brettler and Kelsey Harmon named their winery SYZYGY (sizz-uh-jee), a tongue twister that expresses the perfect alignment among three celestial bodies, such as the sun, moon, and Earth during a total solar eclipse. SYZYGY focuses on a syrah, a cabernet, and a blended red wine, sources grapes from excellent vineyards, and delivers a lot of flavor in all three.

The syrahs are made with Walla Walla fruit (except in 2004). These are thick and sappy wines, with a streak of citrus zest running through them. The cabernets are classically styled, 100 percent varietal, from excellent vineyards such as Conner Lee, Minnick Hills, Sagemoor, and Charbonneau. Flavors run to cassis and berry, stylishly sculpted with spicy, savory oak.

Notable: SYZYGY moved into larger quarters (still out at the Walla Walla airport) late in 2005, so production will ramp up a bit from the initial 500 cases, though this will likely remain a miniboutique. The red wine blend, which includes cabernet, merlot, syrah, and (sometimes) malbec, is the best value, sappy and ripe and high-toned, with sweet cherry and plum fruit.

TILDIO

Founded 2004
70 East Wapato Lake Road
Manson, WA 98831
509/687-8463
www.tildio.com
E-mail: milum@tildio.com

Milum and Kate Perry built this cozy winery adjacent to their eight-acre vineyard about a mile east of Lake Chelan. *Tildio* is Spanish for "killdeer," a shore bird that migrates through the area each spring.

The Perrys have more winemaking experience than most young start-ups: Kate holds a UC Davis degree in enology and viticulture and worked at Robert Mondavi, Geyser Peak, Stag's Leap Wine Cellars, and MacRostie before moving to Washington in 2000. Here she was an assistant winemaker at Chateau Ste. Michelle before starting Tildio.

Tildio's first few vintages have been a mixed bag: small lots of rosé, pinot noir, zinfandel, sauvignon blanc; an Oregon sangiovese; a Red Mountain viognier, a tempranillo, a meritage. It's hard to figure out where Tildio is headed, but once the Perrys get their fruit sources sorted out and find some sort of focus for their efforts, there is every reason to believe that they will turn out some excellent bottles.

Notable: The tempranillo, one of a handful made in Washington, is one of the more interesting wines here.

TSILLAN CELLARS

Founded 2001
3875 Highway 97A
Chelan, WA 98816

509/682-9463
www.tsillancellarswines.com
E-mail: info@tsillancellarswines.com

Tsillan (pronounced, we are told, Chelan) is supposedly the historical spelling for the Native American name for the nearby lake. Unfortunate, because it simply does not scan and most consumers will find it impossible to pronounce, it confuses pretty much everyone who sees it.

The winery occupies a gorgeous perch on the south shore of Lake Chelan and is built to resemble an Italian country retreat (at this rate, eastern Washington will soon be known as Little Tuscany).

Forty acres of vineyard are planted to syrah, merlot, malbec, chardonnay, pinot gris, riesling, and gewürztraminer, and a wide variety of wines are offered. The winemaking position has been a revolving door; most recently Brian Carter has been hired as a consultant to new winemaker Peter Devison. Unsurprisingly, the constantly changing winemakers, young vines, and unpredictable grape sources have made for a hit-and-miss set of initial vintages. But there are some successes. Of particular interest are the first estate wines: riesling, chardonnay, and especially the pinot grigio.

Notable: The estate pinot grigio is a multiple gold medal winner, but the estate riesling is the best wine made. The red wines have been unremarkable at best. The winery also presents outdoor concerts in one of the state's most impressive settings.

VA PIANO VINEYARDS

Founded 2003
1793 JB George Road
Walla Walla, WA 99362
509/529-0900
www.vapianovineyards.com
E-mail: info@vapianovineyards.com

Va Piano Vineyards is located south of Walla Walla in prestigious company: Pepper Bridge, Northstar, Beresan, and Saviah are neighbors; Rulo, Isenhower, and Basel are nearby. Justin Wylie is the winemaker; cabernet and syrah are the specialties.

The 20-acre vineyard, planted to cabernet sauvignon, syrah, merlot, cab franc, and petit verdot, was established in 1999. Two-thirds of the grapes are sold to neighbors, such as Dunham and Saviah, and the rest go into the winery's own syrahs and cabernets.

Notable: Five other wineries are also squeezed into Va Piano, each independently owned. Otis Kenyon, Rollat, Gramercy Cellars, Trust, and Tertulia are the brands. Va Piano also makes a popular non-vintage syrah/merlot blend called Bruno's Blend that honors a former university professor. An important winery to watch!

Founded 2003
50 SE Skookum Inlet Road
Shelton, WA 98584
360/426-5913
www.walterdaconwines.com
E-mail: winemaker@walterdaconwines.com

Winemaker Lloyd Anderson makes three syrahs, which he calls Belle, Beaux, and Magnifique. Heavily influenced by Rhône varietal pioneer Doug McCrea, Anderson does one syrah in French oak, one in American, and one as a reserve selection from his favorite French barrels.

Syrah grows exceptionally well in Washington, and some wineries that choose the grape as their focus have done quite well with single-vineyard selections (think K Vintners) and/or different styles of oak (McCrea Cellars). But the initial releases from Walter Dacon have not set the three wines far enough apart; they all display scents and flavors of smoke, coffee, charcoal, and tar, with dark, dark fruits.

That's less of a criticism and more of a hope: that the wines will evolve in future vintages and truly show different styles. Early releases have been skillfully made and quite flavorful. Certainly these are wines that will please many palates. C'est Syrah Belle, the French-oaked syrah, melds its sweet, cedary oak to rich cherry, plums, and spice. The tannins, smooth and soft, lead into a creamy caramel, layered finish. C'est Syrah Beaux is the American-oaked syrah, with mostly similar vineyard sources and flavors.

Notable: Walter Dacon's C'est Syrah Magnifique is a barrel selection from the French oak wines, 98 percent syrah, with a splash of viognier. Blackberry, black cherry, and streaks of citrus somewhat balance the massive barrel flavors; there's also plenty of fresh acid to provide extra thrust on liftoff. An excellent viognier debuted in 2006.

WATERS

Founded 2003
416 N. Second Avenue
Walla Walla, WA 99362
509/525-1590
www.waterswinery.com
E-mail: info@waterswinery.com

Waters debuted with a splash (sorry, couldn't resist) during Walla Walla's 2006 Spring Release weekend. Winemaker Jamie Brown, who was formerly with James Leigh Cellars, is well connected locally and was able to purchase grapes from the Leonetti estate for Waters'

Loess Vineyard syrah. Waters is planning to make at least three single-vineyard syrahs, though initially there was just a single bottling, blended from Columbia Valley grapes.

The Waters cabernet sauvignon is intriguing. Scents of tea, cola, licorice, plums, vanilla, and spice suggest nuanced flavors that don't entirely translate from nose to tongue. The winery's Interlude Red, a cabernet–merlot blend, shows well-ripened fruit, pretty cherry flavors, and barrel notes of kahlua, espresso, and smoke.

Brown and his partners are developing a 20-acre vineyard with Greg Harrington (Gramercy Cellars) south of Walla Walla, near the cluster that includes Va Piano, North-star, and Pepper Bridge. A second vineyard site has also been acquired, 14 acres in the rocky terroir first explored by Cayuse. Named "Old Stones," that vineyard will be planted to syrah, cabernet sauvignon, and cabernet franc. An estate winery is due to open in time for the 2007 crush.

WILLIS HALL

Founded 2003
4715 126th Street NE
Marysville, WA 98271
360/653-1247
www.willishall.com
E-mail: info@willishall.com

Winemaker John Bell is an alum of the Boeing Wine Club and made many vintages as an amateur winemaker before launching his own venture in 2003. The names Willis and Hall were chosen to honor his father and grandmother. Production began at around 1200 cases and will stop at around 2500.

Willis Hall's first releases were polished wines that shared many similar strengths: soft, ready to drink, and unusually pretty, with supple flavors that spoke of pie cherries, straw-berries, and plums, with a pleasing, toasty finish.

Bell's plan is to produce five mainstream wines each vintage: a pair of syrahs, a pair of Bordeaux blends, and a viognier. Very small lots of sangiovese, grenache, zinfandel, pinot noir, cabernet franc, mourvèdre, petit verdot, nebbiolo, Dolcetto, tempranillo, and rous-sanne are also made and offered to the winery's mailing list members.

Notable: Bell is convinced that Washington state is the ideal growing region for many of the world's not-so-well-known varieties, such as tempranillo. "My attempt," he explains, "is to make a tempranillo as close to a Rioja as I can, right down to using a Rioja-isolate yeast for fermentation and barrels coopered from American oak that has been aged for three years in Spain."

ZERBA CELLARS

Founded 2003
85530 Highway 11
Milton Freewater, OR 97862
541/938-9463
www.zerbacellars.com
E-mail: info@zerbacellars.com

Zerba is owned by Cecil and Marilyn Zerba, Walla Walla–area farmers who planted three vineyards in 2001 and 2003. They were frozen out in 2004 and replanted, with cuttings from Seven Hills cultivated in their own greenhouses.

Zerba's vineyards are on the Oregon side of the valley, in the section called The Rocks: dry riverbed near Christophe Baron's Cailloux. The Zerbas also purchase grapes from vineyards around Prosser, including Willard, Minick, Pleasant, and Lewis. Cecil Zerba is making the wines and learning as he goes. Given the background in nursery and farming and the location of the vineyards, this winery has a lot of potential.

Notable: Syrah is their best wine to date, although the Columbia Valley merlot is a solid effort also.

PART 3

THE FUTURE

9

WHERE THE NEW WORLD
AND THE OLD WORLD MEET

Statistically Washington is second only to California in terms of domestic wine production. But let's face it. it's a mighty distant second. However, by quality measures, the state lays solid claim to its place and, by some value metrics, even outranks its better-known rival. Year-end "Top 100" lists, a popular feature in many wine magazines, regularly include a disproportionately large number of Washington wines. In 2005, for example, *Wine Spectator* placed two Washington wines in its list, and *Wine Enthusiast* had five, including two in the top ten. *Wine & Spirits'* list of the year's 100 best wines mentioned four from Washington.

Another example, this from the Washington Wine Commission: Washington wines receive a higher percentage of 90+ scores than California or Australia across all wine styles, based on an analysis of *Wine Spectator* scores during a recent 12-month publishing cycle. Some 30 percent of all Washington wines reviewed by the influential consumer publication earned scores of 90 and above, compared with figures of 25 percent for California and 24 percent for Australia. Generally, wineries consider a score of 90 to be the tipping point for sales, especially of more expensive wines.

More surprisingly, Washington's red wines outperformed those of Napa, with 39 percent scoring 90 and above, compared with Napa's 32 percent. Cabernet ratings for the two regions were relatively close, but the percentage of highly rated Washington merlots more than doubled Napa's 90+ ratings, 43 percent to 18 percent. Even syrah, a relative newcomer to Washington state, scored extremely well, with 40 percent of the Washington syrahs earning a rating of 90 or better, while California and Australia tied at 31 percent each.

These are statistical snapshots, to be sure, and no one but a wine marketer would give them too much weight. But they do reflect a growing consensus on the part of influential publications not based in the Pacific Northwest that Washington's best wines are distinctive, quality driven, and in many instances more affordably priced than their competitors. Such comparisons are standard practices for new wine regions struggling to find their place in the world. Challenging the market leaders in blind tastings or prestigious judging events or via comparison scoring is a quick way to elbow up to the main table—if your wines are up to the challenge.

But once a region has established that it belongs among the leaders, it must stand apart from the others and define itself distinctively. This is the test facing Washington wineries today. And here there are things that can be sensed, rather than measured, that suggest that in the future Washington's wines will trend farther and farther away from the influence of California and closer to the paradigm first noted at least two decades ago.

WHERE CALIFORNIA MEETS EUROPE

In the summer of 1987, I penned an article entitled "In Search of a European Style." It was published in the September/October 1987 issue of a regional magazine called *The Northwest Palate*. Reviewing it almost two decades later, I find that much of what seemed a bit far-fetched at the time rings surprisingly true. At that time the 1983 cabernets and merlots, a glorious vintage that first brought Washington reds to the world's attention, were winning impressive gold medals around the country. Hogue's 1983 Reserve Cabernet was named Best of Show in Atlanta; the winery's Reserve Merlot grabbed first place at Kapalua. The 1983 cabs from Woodward Canyon and Snoqualmie both won double golds at the San Francisco State Fair. Regional competitions launched still more gold medal red wines. In the early spring of 1987, a blind tasting had been conducted by the wine marketing division of the state Department of Agriculture for the benefit of the New York wine press. Eight Washington cabernets and three from Bordeaux (Lafite and Cos d'Estournel among them), all 1983 vintage, were tasted blind. The New York judges voted the top six places to Washington.

Elsewhere Washington reds were a tough sell. Columbia winemaker David Lake was just back from the summer's Kapalua Bay Wine Symposium, where his 1979 Millennium cabernet–merlot blend had been featured alongside Opus One, Rubicon, and Insignia. Things didn't go all that well. "I believe we're arriving," he told me at the time, "but not by any means to a wholehearted chorus of approval. There's a certain amount of surprise that we're able to make red wines at all. Because our wines are harder, not as open and forward as the California cabernets," he added, "they are misinterpreted as being clumsy."

Time has shown that the 1979 Millennium is anything but clumsy. It long outlived the two-plus decades predicted by its ambitious name. I suspect that were the Kapalua tasting to be repeated today, the Millennium would handily outshow the California wines. Tasted as recently as 2006, it seemed to me to be still in remarkably good condition, showing a brick edge but a dark, black cherry color in the center. I found it almost Barolo-like, with mingled scents of tar and leather, rose petals and tobacco. There was not a trace of exhaustion; rather, it was a mature, confident wine, tart and tannic, its fruit still nuanced with hints of cherries, raspberries, and tobacco leaf.

Referenced in that same 1987 article was a conversation with the late Peter Sichel (of Chateau d'Angludet and Chateau Palmer), who had visited Seattle for an informal tasting of Washington cabernets. "Without being derogatory to California cabernets," he told me, "none of these Washington cabernets have that excessive weight that makes it difficult for us to relate the wine to cabernet sauvignon at all. Here they have a very similar structure to a ripe year in Bordeaux. Some of the complexities I think are fantastic. They're going to develop in bottle for years."

Early in 2003, a series of negative pieces about Washington wines appeared, written by some of the country's most influential wine critics. Writing in Robert Parker's *Wine Advocate*, Pierre-Antoine Rovani, who had tasted some 478 wines during a brief visit to the state the previous summer, stated that he could recommend only 68 of them (implying that all the rest were subpar). At about the same time, Steven Tanzer's influential newsletter issued a blanket indictment of Yakima Valley wines, and *Wine Spectator* downgraded Washington's entire 1999 vintage, calling it "an odd-man-out vintage" and implying that the wines lacked richness and opulence.

To show that perhaps California-style opulence is not the ultimate goal here in Washington (Anyone for structure, elegance, and longevity? Layers of flavor rather than having it all up front?), the Washington Wine Commission initiated a pair of promotional taste-offs. These were designed to put the state's cabernets to the toughest possible test. In Manhattan first and again in Chicago a few weeks later, four Washington cabernets competed against four highly regarded wines from Napa and Bordeaux. All eight wines were from the 1999 vintage and all were tasted blind, meaning that no one knew which was which until the final votes were tallied.

More than 50 wine retailers, sommeliers, and media representatives (by any measure some of the most hard-nosed and savvy wine buyers in the business) tasted through the wines in each city and ranked them. When the votes were counted and the wines revealed, the four from Washington had finished 1-2-3-4 in New York and 1-2-3-6 in Chicago. And it was a couple of Yakima Valley wines, from the 1999 vintage no less, that stole the show.

Give the critics points for consistency. All three publications had awarded the Napa and Bordeaux wines higher scores than the Washington wines. If their scores had been used to rank the wines in the Wine Commission's event, the results would have been completely different. To cite one example, ranking the eight wines using the Tanzer scores, the four from Washington would have finished 5-6-7-8.

What does this signify? That the critics have it in for Washington? Of course not. That California and Bordeaux have more easily identifiable (and time-proven) cabernet styles? This, I believe, is closer to the truth. The national wine press is focused, understandably, on California, and they know those wines well. And they have studied the wines of

Europe, not just cabernet, but virtually all major varietals, because these are the wines that set the Old World standard and have for centuries. But Washington? Who knows what it stands for? Critics who jet in for a day or two and plow through a few hundred bottles can hardly be expected to figure it out when even those who live and work here are still struggling to do so.

Which brings me back to Peter Sichel's prescient analysis. Though Washington's red wines have, to some degree, followed the inexorable path up the ripeness road, leading to average brix and alcohol readings substantially higher than 20 years ago, they still retain, far more than most other New World reds, a European sensibility. Now as then, the merlots, cabernets, Bordeaux blends, and syrahs of Washington state show that they can match ripe, not jammy, fruit to natural acidity, fine-grained tannins, and sometimes a gravelly minerality.

Even more than reds, Washington's white wines, especially riesling, sémillon, sauvignon blanc, and occasionally viognier, have a striking mix of vibrant fruit and refreshing acidity. These wines straddle the border, if you can imagine it, between the explosive, heat-intensive fruit of California and the more herbal, earthy, tannic, and mineral wines of the Old World.

This natural affinity, clearly a product of Washington's northern latitude, desert climate, and unique growing season, for its wines to straddle the Euro/Cal border stylistically is likely to become clearer and clearer moving ahead. Much of the hit-and-miss pioneering has been done. Washington has its own experienced growers and vintners, rather than apple farmers looking for a "safety" crop and a group of winemakers educated at UC Davis. Better still, more and more Europeans are moving here to grow grapes and to make wine.

Both Ernst Loosen (Dr. Loosen) and Armin Diel (Schlossgut Diel) are focusing their New World riesling efforts on high-profile projects in Washington. Now in its second decade, the Col Solare project uniting Piero Antinori and winemaker Renzo Cotarella with Ste. Michelle Wine Estates is beginning to reach its potential, with a new Col Solare winery and vineyard installed atop Red Mountain.

There are so many French-born and -educated winemakers in the state that Washington might want to apply for *appellation d'origine contrôlée* status. Frederique Spencer, from Provence, is winemaker at Diageo's Sagelands winery. Christophe Baron, a native Champenois, has established Washington's first biodynamic vineyard and winery at Cayuse. Virginie Bourgue, from a Luberon farming family, began at Bergevin Lane and is now beginning her own project in the area. Burgundy-trained Marie-Eve Gilla is at Forgeron, while her husband, Gilles Nicault, oversees the winemaking for all the Long Shadows brands. Serge Laville is making the wines at Spring Valley Vineyard; Christophe Paubert is at Canoe Ridge; and Swiss-born Jean-Francois Pellet, making wines at both Pepper Bridge and Amavi, rounds out the current ranks of European transplants in the state.

What brings them all to Washington? Consider that, among them, they hold an impressive range of advanced degrees in viticulture and enology. They have worked around the world as well as at prestigious wineries in their native land. Bourgue's résumé includes postgraduate work in Champagne at Louis Roederer, Nicolas Feuillatte, and Bollinger; Paubert has made wines for Chateau d'Yquem and Chateau Gruaud Larose; Pellet came directly from Joseph Heitz; and Loosen, Diel, and Cotarella, who do not reside in Washington but visit the state regularly, have world-class properties in Europe.

It is clear that none of these individuals is working in Washington because it's all they can find. They are here because they sense something special about the place, the timing, and the opportunities. Their commitments are long-term and focused. If anyone is capable of catapulting the state's wineries into making more elegant, nuanced, age-worthy, textural, and balanced wines, it is people like these, who have such wines in their very genes and bloodlines.

CHRISTOPHE BARON, CAYUSE

Christophe Baron arrived in Walla Walla in the mid-1990s, immediately bringing a distinctly French perspective to bear on everything from site selection to vineyard management to winemaking. He was born into a family of Champenois whose winemaking history can be traced as far back as the sixteenth century. But his passion was Rhône wines, and Baron traveled the world looking for the right place to plant his own vines. He found it just south of Walla Walla: an abandoned apple orchard planted along a rock-strewn dry riverbed. "It definitely looks like Chateauneuf du Pape, this ancient riverbed where I've planted my grapes," he explained to me on a tour of the Cailloux vineyard some years ago. "It's a mix of silty loam with a little sand and cobblestone for first 18 to 20 inches; from there it's pure stone for 200 feet straight down."

Digging through such rock to plant his vines was backbreaking work. The vines struggled to survive. Other winemakers scratched their heads, wondering why anyone would choose such ungenerous ground in a valley laden with chocolatey soils. But Cailloux and Baron's more recent vineyard plantings have proven him right. The wines have a particular

"There," she says, "we grow a lot of things: orchards, grapes, wheat, vegetables. I went to viticulture and enology school in Avignon and then got a master's in enology in Champagne." She followed that up with postgraduate work that provided real-world experience grappling with such issues as worker safety, worker health, and environmental protection. One year was spent working at Louis Roederer; this provided the background for a thesis on quality assurance control. "During the summer," says Bourgue, "I helped in the vineyard, and during harvest I worked in the *vendangeoir*" (a press facility stationed right in the vineyards). Her postgraduate work continued at Nicolas Feuillatte, developing a program for wastewater treatment.

Valuable though it was, the task of analyzing the winery's water from the start of crush through final filtration was not a lifetime career choice. "I wanted to do production, where you are not doing all the time the same thing," she emphasizes. Résumés went flying around the world, leading to an enologist internship at Chateau Ste. Michelle and, ultimately, to the offer to become the winemaker for a new Walla Walla winery, Bergevin Lane.

The opportunity to start almost immediately at the top comes a lot more quickly in Washington than in France, and it is one of the big reasons that well-educated and well-traveled young people choose to move here. Bourgue believes that being French with a technical education got her the job offer, but the chance to design a winery from scratch—"the flow, the tanks, what kind of chiller, all those technical questions I never had to ask myself"—is what convinced her to take it. Walla Walla itself, she maintains, was no surprise. The grapes, primarily syrah and cabernet, were familiar. It was the *style* of the wines that was different. "American wines are more powerful than French wines," she explains. "It seems the American wine drinker needs that. Here, if the nose is good—fruity, like candy—people will say, 'Yeah!' They are almost buying by smelling. If it stinks, they say, 'I may not be brave enough to put that in my mouth.' In France, it is the opposite. If it stinks, they say, 'Wow—it must be good!'"

Like the other Europeans who come to Washington, she stresses the importance of time and patience. "Success will not happen overnight; it's a lot of years of very intensive work." And most of that work, she stresses, is done in the vineyard. "If I get quality fruit, it's simple to make good wine. Washington is an emerging area. The Columbia Valley AVA is 11 million acres! There are places that are totally excellent that have not been explored. In 10 years we'll have a better perspective."

What she has already noted is excellent fruit from very young vineyards, something, Bourgue claims, she has never seen in France. Exploring the nuances of those vineyards, ever hopeful of finding that most elusive quality, that "something special" that speaks of terroir, is her overriding pursuit. Still, she maintains a certain amount of Gallic skepticism. "One vineyard," she points out, "has a thick layer of ash in the soil. I find more mineral, more smoky spice in those grapes. But I wonder, is it because of the terroir, or because they are burning the wheat fields?"

JEAN-FRANCOIS PELLET, PEPPER BRIDGE

Jean-Francois ("J-F") Pellet is a third-generation winemaker from a Swiss winegrowing family. He holds degrees in viticulture and enology and has managed vineyards and made wine in Switzerland, Germany, Spain, and Napa's Joseph Heitz Cellars. He was working at Heitz when Norm McKibben, the managing partner for the group that owns Pepper Bridge vineyard, came to Pellet with an invitation to take the head job at their soon-to-be-built Pepper Bridge winery. Pellet admits that he had "no clue where Walla Walla was, no clue at all about Washington." As he drove up to his new home, he remembers thinking "I really pushed the envelope quite far this time; it's all just wheat!"

Pepper Bridge is relatively large (200 acres) and planted with an unusual mix of red grapes (cabernet sauvignon, merlot, syrah, sangiovese, and malbec). All the vines went in at different times, beginning in the early 1990s. McKibben likes to kid Pellet, who began his tenure by immediately warning his new employer that it would take at least five vintages just to begin to understand the vineyard and its potential. The five years, McKibben gleefully notes, are now up.

It is not just the winemaker who is learning; as the vineyard comes of age there are continuous, ongoing experiments with different types of irrigation and trellising, new clones, the use of sophisticated technology (such as buried soil sensors), and, most recently, organic farming. "Jean-Francois really truly believes that a winemaker that doesn't show his terroir is not doing the right job," says McKibben. "I'm not so sure the general public cares that much about it. But to him it's a big thing to show consistently that terroir. Which means you're going to get a little more variation vintage to vintage, because you're not trying to mask it."

For his part, Pellet is delighted to be where he is, wheat fields and all. Years ago, when he first graduated with a degree in viticulture and enology, he says, he felt a twinge of envy for his classmates. Many came from well-to-do winemaking families, and they could immediately begin working in those family businesses. But now things look a bit different. "I'm almost 40," says the amiable Pellet, "and all my friends who stayed in Europe have no freedom. Their fathers are still telling them how to do things. A little bit of tradition is very good, but 100 percent? It's very sad sometimes."

On the subject of his adopted home there is no sadness. "I think Walla Walla is right between Bordeaux and Napa in style," he says. "It has the finesse of Bordeaux and the mouthfeel of Napa. I cannot really explain how you can grow cabernet, merlot, syrah, and riesling in the same vineyard. But here you can."

He is emphatic when he insists that the age of the vineyard is critically important for quality; 10 years, he believes, is nothing, just a beginning. "You don't become a fine winegrower overnight," he cautions. Drawing on his experience at Heitz, he believes that the best thing that ever happened to Napa was phylloxera. "Their biggest problem was rootstock, and they had to replant. It's going to take 15 years to judge these new clones."

Already, Pellet's combination of patience and a thoughtful, long-term approach to grape-growing is making an important contribution to the evolution of wines in Walla Walla. And the best is yet to come.

GILLES NICAULT, LONG SHADOWS

Educated at the University of Avignon, Gilles Nicault honed his skills by working at wineries in the Côtes du Rhône, Provence, and Champagne before a work/study program brought him to Washington state in 1994. When he first arrived, he recalls, he had no particular expectations about Washington wines. But early on, he now says, he was "quite surprised by the quality."

Rather than returning to France when the work/study program ended, he decided to explore further. He met Woodward Canyon's Rick Small, who offered him an assistant winemaker's job. In 1999, Nicault was put in charge of all enology and production at Woodward, where he remained until 2003, when Allen Shoup invited him to become coordinating winemaker for the Long Shadows portfolio of wines.

Shoup, who served as CEO of Stimson Lane (now Chateau Ste. Michelle Wine Estates) for almost two decades, put together a self-professed "dream team" of all-star winemakers for the new venture. "The reality," he explains, "is that someday the Columbia Valley will be in the top 10 viticultural regions in the world; I'm absolutely convinced of that." Shoup's vision for Long Shadows is based on a European model: It's a collective of individual boutique wineries, each making a single wine with a particular focus. Each brand in this portfolio of wines is made by a high-profile winemaker who jets in from time to time to visit vineyards, supervise the winemaking, and oversee the blending. The day-to-day winemaking is guided by Nicault. Now, more than four years into the project, seven Long Shadows wines have been released, and a dedicated winery opened outside of Walla Walla late in 2006.

Nicault's position seems to have evolved significantly. He now makes a Long Shadows wine of his own, a blend of merlot, cabernet sauvignon, cabernet franc, and syrah with the improbable name of Chester|Kidder. And he continues to work with six different winemakers from around the world, crafting a single emblematic wine with each of them. With Germany's Armin Diel he makes the Poet's Leap riesling; with Agustin Huneeus and Philippe Melka he makes a red blend called Pirouette. Australia's John Duval is his collaborator on the Sequel syrah. Completing the current lineup are the Pedestal merlot (made with Michel Rolland), the Feather cabernet (made with Napa's Randy Dunn), and the newest release, Saggi, made with the Folonari's of Tuscany. "It's very exciting here," says Nicault. "I am doing lots of little projects. For example, I just did a botrytised riesling. In France there is no way I could make syrah, cabernet sauvignon, and riesling all together at a single winery."

Given its ambitious scope, high costs and lack of estate vineyards, the Long Shadows project seems to be a bit of a gamble. It remains to be seen if the concept of blending wines from widely scattered vineyards will ultimately make a more quintessential Washington wine than, say, a single vineyard, pure varietal from a perfect site. Nonetheless, the infusion of experienced winemaking talent from around the world is bound to create some sparks, and it's one more example of the lure of Washington state. "This project only works," Shoup acknowledges, "if the wines live up to the talents of the people making them. If the wines aren't there, then the whole thing is smoke and mirrors."

MARIE-EVE GILLA, FORGERON

Educated in Burgundy, Gilla, who is married to Long Shadows winemaker Gilles Nicault, first helped to make American wines at Oregon's Argyle in the early 1990s. From there she moved to Washington's Covey Run and then briefly to Hogue. She found her first notable success while making wines at Gordon Brothers in the late 1990s.

There we walked through the vineyards one warm June morning, admiring the sun-silvered Snake River meandering beneath us, and she told me that "what we are trying to do here is a cross between an American and a French wine. There is a lot of sunshine here; you can make sturdy wines with a lot of character. It's a lot more consistent than France. We like the French wines because they are elegant and balanced and meant to age. So we're trying to create an elegant wine that showcases the American fruit but is subtle enough and balanced enough to age."

A lovely synopsis, I thought (and still do) of the quest to bring the best of both worlds, old and new, to Washington wines. Gilla left Gordon to found Walla Walla's Forgeron Cellars in 2001. That winery, housed in a former blacksmith's quarters (hence the name) is principally dedicated to making varietal red wines, but it has shown real strength with its chardonnays also.

Though she very much appreciates the freedom to make wines without the sort of excessive regulations one has to deal with in France, Gilla believes that the lack of strong educational programs in viticulture is a real handicap for Washington vintners. "In Washington," she explains, "I truly think that not many people know what they are doing on the viticulture side. You do not have a diploma here. You can learn to make wine, but not how to make a vineyard." On the positive side, she notes that "in France, even if something is good for the winery it doesn't mean that you can do it. Here the only regulation is economics. And the flow of energy moves so much faster."

CHRISTOPHE PAUBERT, CANOE RIDGE VINEYARD

The newest addition (as of this writing) to Washington's growing coterie of French-born winemakers, Christophe Paubert, 44, was born in Sauternes, though not into a winemaking family. His grandfather, he mentions, worked for a well-known wine merchant (Coste), and Paubert followed his own enology studies (at the University of Bordeaux) with three years in the retail trade.

Next he found a job selling winery equipment; that lasted another seven years. "I am deeply a technician," he continues, "so I took a year off and decided to go back to winemaking. All my 'practice' wines were made at Chateau d'Yquem. They hired me as enologue and cellarmaster. I was there from 1995 to 1997. It was wonderful, but . . ." He pauses briefly, searching for the tactful phrase. "There are a lot of people. I felt a little 'tight.' So I went to Chile, working for Bodegas Bebidas, starting a new project there, a joint venture with some vineyard owners. When that was done they asked me to move to Navarra in Spain to manage and improve a series of projects there. After that I made two vintages, at Chateau Gruaud-Larose and at Montana in New Zealand. But I've been trying to come to the American West Coast for the past five years."

Though a few hundred miles from the actual coast, Paubert finally made it to America. Just before the 2005 crush he was named winemaker for Diageo's Canoe Ridge winery, in Walla Walla. Visa problems delayed his arrival some weeks, so grapes were already well into fermentation when he reached the winery in mid-October. But he looks on the bright side, saying "every time you move it is complex. You have to adapt. So in one way I am pleased [for the delay] because I will have a full year to learn everything I have to learn to make wonderful wines next year. So it's not so bad. But for the wines already made . . ." (here he makes a *phhht* sound with his pursed lips). "Well, what can I say, they are made."

When a Frenchman uses the word *terroir*, it seems to carry more authentic meaning. You suspect that he knows what it is and may even have a pretty good idea about how to find it. "I am a terroir winemaker," says Paubert. "I want to express the terroir. You will never express terroir if you overripen, overoak, and keep your wine two years in barrels. First you need to want to express it; then you need to know how."

That knowing how is one of the key benefits that French winemakers can bring to Washington. They look at things differently. For example, most American-born winemakers make a fetish out of chewing on the pips (seeds) to determine ripeness. But Paubert believes it is the ripeness of the skin, rather than the pulp or the seeds, that is most important. "Lots of people are focusing on the pulp," he explains. "But red wines are made with the skin. The idea is to ripen the skin and harvest at the best moment for that. If you wait to ripen the seeds, you overripen the skin. The pulp, for me, is the least important element in determining quality."

Though barely arrived in his new home, he is confident that he sees plenty of potential for making terroir-driven wines in Washington. The challenge is to find the right vineyard locations. "I'm not sure that here we have found all the best terroir," he says. "The potentiality is there, only it hasn't been discovered. I don't see anything that would prevent wines here from potentially aging the same as in Bordeaux, if you do the maceration properly."

SERGE LAVILLE, SPRING VALLEY VINEYARD

Serge Laville's first career was working as a professional aerial photographer in his native France. When you think about it, taking snapshots while doing aerial acrobatics is not all that different from winemaking. Aren't wines just snapshots of particular grapes, places, and times? And anyone who has made wine will agree that a lot of high flying is involved. "Wine was my passion for a long time," says the soft-spoken Laville. "I was living next to Guigal—I picked grapes there one summer—and drinking mostly Côte Rôtie and Bordeaux." The wine bug bit, hard. He first studied winemaking with a private teacher in a group of 15 friends. Then, in 2000, while visiting in Walla Walla, he met his future bride and took a job as the winemaker's assistant at Spring Valley Vineyard.

Spring Valley is in wheat country, some miles north of Walla Walla's other wineries, and its estate vineyards produce quite distinctive flavors. When winemaker Devin Derby was tragically killed in an auto accident late in 2004, Laville took over the winemaking. He continues in that role under the supervision of Ste. Michelle Wine Estates, the largest winery group in Washington, which acquired the Spring Valley winery and brand in the summer of 2005.

With the infusion of new capital new equipment was bought, a new press and pump for starters. Ste. Michelle's vineyard and winemaking heads, Rich Wheeler and Doug Gore, are frequent visitors, coming over to watch and consult. Happily for Laville, the 2005 vintage, his first as head winemaker, was perhaps the greatest in Washington history. With typical European patience Laville says he has no intention of making any sudden changes to the wines. "I kept everything the same. Small fermenters. Small basket press. I love the style, and I want to keep making the same wines. It's a very tannic, big wine, but with a bit more acidity because of the location of the vineyard."

As with the other émigrés, he has had to adjust to the stylistic differences in American wines. "The first time you drink Walla Walla wine," he admits, "it's a big surprise. It's huge wine. But now, when I go back to France, it seems everything there is light! What is different here is that Walla Walla is hot and very dry. You can leave the grapes hanging for a long time. So it makes different wine. My guess is that in the future it will be syrah, cabernet sauvignon, and tempranillo that do best in Walla Walla, because it's hot here. And of course, merlot and cabernet can do well almost anywhere."

Though he came to winemaking a bit later than most, he got the same early start that all Europeans enjoy. Wine there has been a part of family life for generations, whereas in America it is only recently becoming commonplace at the dinner table. "When you start to drink wine at an early age," says Laville, "that's a big difference in the way you learn to make wine. The palate is still clean, not deformed by Coca-Cola. I have a two-year-old daughter and she has already had a sip of Champagne," he says with a chuckle, adding, "How can you learn if you don't drink?"

RENZO COTARELLA, COL SOLARE

Renzo Cotarella, winemaker and enologist for Italy's famous Marchese Antinori, oversees the production of the entire Antinori portfolio, including such iconic Tuscan wines as

Tignanello, Cervaro della Sala, Guado al Tasso, and Solaia. His collaboration with Chateau Ste. Michelle, named Col Solare (Italian for "shining hill"), was first introduced with the 1995 vintage. A decade into the project, Piero Antinori and Ste. Michelle CEO Ted Baseler broke ground for a dedicated Col Solare winery and vineyard, which has been built and planted on top of Red Mountain, between Hedges and Ciel du Cheval.

Cotarella, who visits from Italy several times annually, says he sees "huge opportunities" in the climate and soils of Washington, explaining that "this permits the possibility to obtain stylistically very particular wines also endowed with a 'soul.'" He graciously states that for their part the Italians are looking to deepen their overall knowledge of wine through the exchange of the cumulative wisdom garnered from Antinori's rich winemaking history and the "very innovative technical structure" of Chateau Ste. Michelle. With this partnership firmly in place, Cotarella's stated goal is "to make a wine that represents the two different worlds: the more traditional European one (mostly elegance oriented) and the American one (especially from Washington state), which is oriented mostly to the depth of the taste and to the personality of the product." These last, he believes, are the key strengths of American wines.

To sum up, says Cotarella, "we are trying to make a wine that can well represent the integration of these two different ways, to conceive the product in order to make an elegant, deep, savory, emotional wine, a wine that would reflect the area of production as well as the personality and attitude of people that realize it. Probably a utopia, but . . . who knows! This is the main goal that we wish to accomplish in the next five to ten years."

JOHN DUVAL, SEQUEL

John Duval is Australian, not European, but he knows a thing or two about making great syrah. From 1986 to 2002 he was chief winemaker for Penfolds, responsible for an enormous lineup of shiraz, including the iconic Penfolds Grange. In 2003 he left Penfolds and founded his own label (John Duval Wines), headquartered in his Barossa Valley home. At about the same time, he received a phone call from Allen Shoup, CEO of Long Shadows Vintners, inviting him to partner in the production of a single wine designed to showcase Washington syrah.

On their first round visiting prospective vineyards, the two recalled in a recent interview, things didn't go so well. "The first one or two vineyards we visited were very young," says Duval. "John felt that to make a really good syrah he needed some older vines," added Shoup, "old enough at least so that he could get the character he wanted."

Old vines in the Barossa generally clock in at 60–80 years of age. Old syrah vines in Washington are rarely older than a decade. Still, 10- or 12-year-old vines are better than the 4- or 5-year-old vines he was shown at first. So round two went a bit better. "The exciting thing about syrah in Washington," Duval diplomatically notes, "is if the wines are as good as they are now, off such young vines, it augurs well for the future." To be sure, syrah is a grape that seems to do very well in many places. Furthermore, it has already been "claimed" as a signature grape in both the Rhône Valley, for its smoky, meaty, pungently bloody character, and in the Barossa, for its immensely pleasurable, saturated, jammy, fruit-driven power.

So where does Washington syrah fit in? "It seems to fit in neatly," Duval insists. "True, it doesn't have the bigness of Barossa Valley shiraz, but it has the finesse and savory spice character I see in France. So I see it fitting in between the French style and the other end of the spectrum, the big bold Australian style. And we [Long Shadows] have access to some vineyards that can give a bit of both."

Duval's Washington syrah, named Sequel, has its own label, dedicated solely to this single wine. "The model is French," Shoup explains, "one winery, one wine." This is the path followed by the state's most acclaimed winery, Quilceda Creek, which for 25 years has focused on making a single wine, a cabernet sauvignon, exceptionally well. Though in recent years Quilceda Creek has made limited quantities of a merlot and a red blend, the flagship wine was, is, and always will be its extraordinary cabernet, which was awarded the first (and so far the only) 100-point Robert Parker scores in Washington wine history.

Will Sequel be able to do the same for syrah? A mix of grapes from Yakima Valley, Red Mountain, and Horse Heaven vineyards, it is designed to be what Duval terms "vibrant," showing ripe blueberry and blackberry fruit, framed in 60 percent new French oak (not 100 percent, not American oak, he emphasizes), with a nice lively acidity "to keep the wine fresh and take care of cellaring." Washington is unique, Duval believes, because syrah has been produced so much longer in other parts of the world, yet even with such young vines the early results here have been impressive. "The environment is a factor," he says. "You don't have the vigor issues that I see in other parts of the world. Syrah is a naturally vigorous plant, and here in Washington it can be controlled; it doesn't seem to be such an issue." Globally the profile of syrah/shiraz has significantly lifted in the last 20 years. "For the first time ever," Duval says proudly, "the annual 'Top 100' list of the country's most influential wine magazine included more syrah than any variety in the world."

At $55, the 2003 Sequel Syrah is not an everyday wine. Satiny and smooth, it is still in the process of integrating the oak flavors and softening the tannins. Resting in barrel are the next two vintages. Ribbon cutting on the new, $4.2 million Long Shadows winery, situated in wheat country a few miles northwest of downtown Walla Walla, took place on April 12, 2007. "The winery is just a cement box buried in the ground," says Shoup. "What's going to impress people is that when you go into the bowels of the winery you will see that nothing has been sacrificed in terms of cost of equipment. You will walk into the winery, and you will recognize that this is a spotless, no-compromise approach. There will be no road signs, just basically a hidden facility for making world-class wine, with the dream, the goal being that if John gets up to 3000 cases a year we can build a small, architectural winery for him. That's my dream."

It's a great dream. And syrah may be a great choice. Time will prove if those who make it can consistently deliver the world-class goods. Duval thinks he can do it here in Washington. "In Washington I think you've got the chance for the expression of something in between, that's got the best of both worlds, a triangle rather than a continuum," he says. "I prefer to keep away from the ripe plum and prune spectrum; ripe blueberry and black-berry rather than the next stage. It keeps the wines vibrant. In my former life, as the cus-todian of Grange, I used a lot of American oak; but I'd like to be thought of as the winemaker who created IWT [another pricey Penfolds shiraz that is aged in French rather than American oak]. I'm trying to keep the fruit as a very important part of the wine; and I'm trying to frame the fruit, using 60 percent, not 100 percent, new French oak. It's all about balance, of course. A nice, lively acidity to keep the wine fresh and take care of cellaring."

DO WASHINGTON WINES AGE?

There's no sure proof that can irrefutably demonstrate that Washington is somehow per-fectly situated to make wines, particularly red wines, that can bring the best of Old and New World styles together harmoniously. But these well-traveled, well-educated winemak-ers, who come here from all corners of the world, seem to think so. Whether or not you find such flavors in the Washington wines you taste, you will probably agree that one defin-ing characteristic of well-balanced, world-class wines is their ability to age well.

There is a mystique to old wines, or, more specifically, to the idea that wines are capa-ble of aging. Homage is paid to wines from favored vineyards and regions that have a proven ability to age gracefully. Big dollars are paid for wines from the great chateaux of Bordeaux and domaines of Burgundy, largely because of this mystique. Why should it matter? Few among us bother to cellar wines for the decades required. Even fewer truly prefer the fla-vors of older wines. Old wines require a lot of effort. Their scents and flavors can be frail and fleeting. When compared with the vivid, plump, fruity exuberance of young wines, the geezer wines, quite frankly, can seem tired.

And yet, I do think that it matters when a wine proves itself age-worthy, because those things that endure, whether songs or paintings or films, are those we cherish the most. They have stood the test of time. And wine too can achieve that greatness, can pass that test. Wines that evolve, that have a life, not just a brief moment in the midday sun, are the great wines. Places that can produce such wines are elevated to the ranks of the world's best. Is Washington such a place?

My tastings of older Washington wines have repeatedly shown that many of them do last for a surprisingly long time. Some of the state's earliest vintage-dated varietal wines have evolved quite beautifully over the decades. In recent years, as a handful of top-tier Washington wineries has reached the age where they can pull out a lineup of old wines, I've sat in on many fascinating vertical tastings. Among the best: 21 vintages of Woodward Canyon's "Dedication Series" and "Old Vines" cabernets; the first 15 vintages of Quilceda Creek cabernets; a decade's worth of Chaleur Estate reds; a dozen vintages of Andrew Will

"Ciel du Cheval Vineyard" reds; 15 vintages of Columbia "Red Willow" syrahs; and vertical tastings of Cold Creek merlots and cabernets and Otis vineyard reds going back 25 years.

But on a chilly afternoon early in 2006 I pulled together, thanks to the generosity of some readers of my *Seattle Times* wine column (and the wineries themselves), a collection of old Washington wines that truly reached back to the dawn of the state's modern winemaking age. It was for me the enological equivalent of discovering King Tut's tomb. From Chateau Ste. Michelle, and its predecessor, Ste. Michelle Vineyards, were cabernets from 1978, 1977, 1976, 1975, 1974, 1973, 1970, and 1969. From A/V (Associated Vintners), the very first winery in Washington to produce vintage-dated varietal wines, were cabernets from 1980, 1979, 1976, 1970, 1969, and 1967.

The guests at my tasting included Dr. Cornelius Peck and his wife, Gloria. Dr. Peck is a founding member of the group of 10 men, most of them University of Washington professors, who bonded Associated Vintners back in 1962. Seated next to him was David Lake, the winemaker at A/V (now Columbia) since 1979. Also in attendance were Bob and Cathy Betz. Betz worked at Ste. Michelle for almost 30 years before leaving to devote attention full time to his Betz Family winery.

The tasting began with the Ste. Michelle wines, from youngest to oldest. I spent a very pleasant hour reading and studying the labels before the wines were even opened, finding them chock-full of valuable information. The youngest, the 1978, still had its original price sticker ($6.85), as did the bottle from 1970, which had sold at the Washington state liquor stores for the whopping sum of $2.15. The bottles from 1974–78 were labeled Chateau Ste. Michelle in ornate black script and featured an oval, color woodcut of the Stimson Lane mansion, which had been acquired when the winery changed hands in 1974. The back labels were highlighted by twin maps of Washington and France, showing the 46th parallel crossing from the bottom of the state into Bordeaux and the 48th parallel crossing from northern Washington into the Loire and Burgundy. The maps' caption reads, "Washington state's vineyards are midway between the latitudes of the great wine-producing areas of France."

The two oldest bottles bore completely different labels, from the days when Ste. Michelle Vineyards was part of the American Wine Growers portfolio. In 1967, both AWG and A/V released the first commercial, vintage-dated varietal wines ever made in Washington state. Today it is hard to imagine what a radical and difficult enterprise it must have been. Very few vineyards were growing French vinifera varietals, and most were experimental. In others the vines were mixed together in hodgepodge fashion, so you couldn't really be all that certain what you were harvesting.

Winemaking techniques were primitive at best, and what little was known came largely from California, with little relevance to Washington growing conditions. But growing the grapes and making the wines wasn't the least of the problems. Consumers, with rare exceptions, didn't understand or even like dry, varietal wines. Those that did looked to France or possibly California for good wines; the generally accepted wisdom was that Washington was too cold to make decent cabernet.

The new wineries attempted to pack as much educational information as they could onto the bottles. Ste. Michelle's 1969 cab read like an entry in a wine tome. The neck label noted that this was "A Premium Wine From Personally Selected Stock." On the main label, a light cream color bordered by black vines, it read, "A Distinctive Varietal Table Wine" and then "Ste. Michelle Vineyards" in black script over "American Cabernet Sauvignon" in red script. In small type it added, "Produced from Cabernet Sauvignon Grapes grown in the Yakima Valley." There was an odd crest, and in 1970 a motto was added: *Ab Uno Disce Umnes* ("from one all others are judged").

A back label, hectoring consumers like an old-time schoolteacher, stated, "This fine wine comes from the superb noble grape from which the famous clarets of Bordeaux and America's greatest varietal red wines are made. After aging in small white oak barrels and in glass, this vintage wine is still capable of achieving further greatness in the bottle. Connoisseurs will enjoy the rewards of laying this wine aside in their cellars for as long as they can wait. This superior-quality dry wine will bring out the best in fine steaks, prime ribs, and other red meats. Store unopened bottles on their sides in a cool, dark place. Serve at cool room temperature." Whew! These days consumers are lucky to get a picture of a kangaroo and a warning not to drive heavy machinery. The pioneers really had to slog.

What did these old wines have to tell us as we tasted through them? First, that despite the primitive vineyard and winemaking techniques of the day, they had, by and large, lived their three-plus decades and still had something interesting to say. Lower in alcohol and far more acidic than today's cabernets, it seems entirely possible that, like old-style Bordeaux, they were well structured for long-term aging.

Several were standouts. The 1978: Fragrant and beautiful, the color orange/brick, like a sunset. Round and supple, fully mature flavors; plum and pie cherry, hints of tobacco. The 1976: Best of the decade. A dark wine, with more color and extract than the '78. Smooth and supple in the mouth, its well-ripened fruits mix black cherries with hints of berries and plums along with spices and caramel. The 1975: Another dark, heavy wine, quite tannic, and beginning to tire. The 1974: Bordeaux-like, herbaceous, and very light, tart, and frail. The 1973: Assertive, herbal, very deeply colored, and searingly tart. The 1970: The most like Bordeaux, elegant and delicate. Rose petals, pale cherry, hints of chocolate shavings. The 1969: Hard, tannic, and angular but quite drinkable, with notes of tobacco and caraway seed spice.

Having worked our way through eight vintages of Ste. Michelle cabernet dating from 1978 back to 1969, we continued by turning our attention to the wines of Associated Vintners. The story of this unique venture is worth a book all by itself. Briefly: A group of friends, many of them professors at the University of Washington, banded together in the 1950s in order to purchase grapes and winemaking equipment so that they could make wines for their own consumption. At first they used grapes imported from California, but by the early 1960s they had turned their attention to eastern Washington. They incorporated in 1962 and a year later purchased and planted a small vineyard, Harrison Hill, in the heart of the Yakima Valley.

Dr. Cornelius Peck, one of the 10 who started the enterprise, recalls that very little was known about what would do well in Washington. So they planted nine different varieties on their five acres, in order to see which grapes, if any, might survive. The mix included gewürztraminer, riesling, sémillon, chardonnay, and cabernet sauvignon. (Happily, some of the original cabernet vines are still bearing and are now being used by DeLille Cellars to make a vineyard-designated wine.)

A few years later, author Leon Adams (*The Wines of America*) visited Seattle, tasted some of the group's wines, and called at least one wine "outstanding." "We were winemakers," Dr. Peck recalls, "and we knew we were onto something pretty darn good. In '66 we all made wine in our basements; afterwards we said, 'holy Christopher! If it's this good, we should make wine commercially.'"

And so they did. The first commercial A/V wines to be released were a 1967 riesling and a gewürztraminer; both very well received, according to press accounts at the time. The first red wine was a 1967 cabernet sauvignon. That very wine was the centerpiece of our recent tasting. Given its place in history, I would have to say it was the most exciting Washington wine I have ever experienced.

We began with the youngest bottle on the table, a 1980 Associated Vintners Cabernet Sauvignon. By this time the winery was undergoing significant changes. A new winemaker, David Lake, had taken over in the middle of crush the year before; 1980 was his first full vintage. A little doodle in the bottom corner of the bottle, an original scribble by David Lake, shows a mountaintop and a puff of smoke and in tiny type reads, "St. Helens 1980 vintage." The back label proudly states, "Washington's First Premium Winery" and briefly tells the story of the group. Its concluding words are "Their dream of distinctive Washington state varietal wines finds its reality in this bottle."

Some of our tasters felt that the bottle we opened, from the cellar of Dr. Peck, may have been slightly tainted by a poor cork. Soft and elegant, with just a hint of chalk in the tannins and a brief suggestion of mint, it was nonetheless a fine kickoff to the second half of the afternoon. We followed it with the 1979 cabernet, which Lake explained was exactly the same wine as the legendary '79 Millennium; only the label was different. My notes call it "extraordinary, dense, hard, and rich, with traces of mineral, spice, herb, and other subtle elements. Showing beautifully well, but perhaps beginning to crack up."

On to the '76, a tinny, thin wine with an odd lift to the nose. "I'm afraid it was impaled with SO_2," Lake explained, meaning that too much SO_2 (added as a preservative) had overtaken everything else the wine may have had going for it. Things improved dramatically with the 1970, 100 percent cabernet from Harrison Hill. Deep, full, rich, and evocative, it showed a good, thick midpalate, with mixed dried fruits, molasses, caramel, and light spice. Perfectly evolved, in terms of pure pleasure it was my favorite of the flight.

The 1969, also pure cab from Harrison Hill, was flawed and beginning to oxidize, but remained interesting. I picked up some volatile nail polish aromas but also found powerful flavors of cooked cherry, sweet brown sugar, and a whiff of iodine.

We eagerly pulled the cork on the 1967, bottle number 1049. I was alive but not of legal drinking age when this wine was made. It was a lovely amber color, with a plush bouquet reminiscent of a dry tawny Port, dusty and raisined, with an extremely long finish of butter and caramel. Savoring it, Dr. Peck recalled, "We were out there every weekend, like having a new baby, topping it." The vintners believed that by the time their wine would be released, in 1969, the protective laws that had prohibited California wines from being sold here would be abolished. They felt the time was right for Washington to go head to head (cork to cork?) with California. "We were willing to be competitive," says Peck. "When the California wine bill came up in the legislature, I said 'If we can't compete, we don't deserve to be in business.' I was pretty sure we'd be able to equal the Californians; in fact, I thought we'd reduce them to raising raisins!"

As an interesting finale, I pulled a 1966 Robert Mondavi cabernet from the cellar and poured everyone a glass. It was light, elegant, and well crafted, with delicate scents and flavors. Frail but still confident, it had a solid core of mature fruits, herbs, and manicured tannin. Indeed, it was quite good, but certainly no better than many of the wines we had been tasting. Clearly, right from the start, Washington rocked.

So I think it is fair to say that the jury has delivered its verdict. Washington wines do age, in the best possible way, over life spans that can be measured in decades. The best of them don't just persist, they evolve. Like light from a distant star, they illuminate the past, the old days, when wine grape growing in this state was truly a pioneering effort. Somehow some terrific wines were made. Though they sported alcohol levels two or three degrees below today's hefty numbers (12 percent rather than 15), they made up for it with balance, elegance, and, it turns out, staying power.

Will today's more substantial, sophisticated, and (let's face it) more coddled wines perform as well? I am afraid that some high-priced, high-powered, alcoholic fruit bombs will not. But I do have high hopes for the 1999 vintage, which is already showing itself to be one of the best in Washington history. These are wines I look forward to drinking in the decade of the 2020s.

Will cabernet-based Bordeaux blends ultimately prove to be the longest-lived wines from Washington? Or will that honor go to syrah or riesling or some of the ultrasweet ice wines? It is still too soon to know. But we no longer need to wonder if any of these wines will stand the test of time. For sure, they will.

10

A GLIMPSE INTO THE FUTURE

Is Washington the Blanche Dubois of wine regions? One might well look at the industry's unprecedented growth and uncertain future and conclude that its fortunes are, indeed, dependent on the kindness of strangers. Sadly, the locals have been rather lukewarm in their support. Until very recently, it was almost impossible to find a restaurant in eastern Washington wine country that featured Washington wines. Even in trendy Seattle, it's far easier to find a sommelier praising some sultry Côtes-du-Rhône than it is to find a true believer in the quality and value of Washington's products.

The most prestigious (and longest-running) awards competition for Northwest wines has made it almost a point of honor to exclude Northwest palates from the judging panel, as if to say that only the approbation of outsiders is meaningful for these wines. A handful of wine shops, mostly in the Puget Sound region, have carried the banner for the state's leading boutiques. They are the first to offer new wines from new wineries and often initiate wide-eyed young winemakers into the harsh realities of retail. They talk them up in their newsletters, feature them at free tastings, and train staff to educate customers and get them excited about these new offerings. And as long as most Washington wineries make fewer than 2000 cases annually (many make far fewer), they can limp along with that level of support.

But it doesn't cut it if Washington has grander aspirations. At the moment, anyone (this writer included) who is perceived to be rooting for the home team is impaling him- or herself on a double-edged sword. Readers, especially those who consider themselves "collectors," will discount any efforts to explain, promote, or (God forbid!) justify the winemaking experiments, marketing faux pas, and pricing anomalies of the region's tender young wineries. And the wineries themselves, many of which truly believe that wine writing is some sort of unpaid flackery (when in fact it is low-paid journalism), tend to explode in indignant bluster at the mere suggestion in print that their baby's first steps are just a bit wobbly.

So it falls on the writers from outside the region—the national wine press and newsletter writers—to pass judgment on Washington. And more and more of them are at least paying attention, though they cannot be expected to offer more than the most superficial overview. National stories are usually cobbled together from rushed tastings and quick visits, by a writer who has spent two or three days here. Little wonder that so much of the content in these stories was stale five years ago. Too many visiting journalists either overpraise or misunderstand, but they do not, perhaps cannot, dig deep enough to give the wineries meaningful feedback. So they (and we, unfortunately) fall back on scores, and scores, as we all know, are subjective and inadequate.

The good news, fortunately, is that this state was not overly praised (as was Oregon) too soon; nor has it suffered a horrendous fall (as has Oregon) in national esteem. Equally fortunately, Washington has had a gorilla with a heart of gold (Chateau Ste. Michelle Wine Estates) to lead the way in marketing its wines outside the region. They've done so by producing significant quantities of affordable wines, establishing benchmark standards for Washington varietals, conducting untold vineyard experiments, training hundreds of workers in vineyard, lab, and winery, and even providing quality grapes to boutique wineries in freeze years. In short, they have been quietly and benignly keeping the industry going and growing while building a solid business of their own.

Despite my misgivings about the quality of the criticism leveled at Washington wines, this book would not be as complete or objective as I wish it to be were it to sidestep the issues that have repeatedly been raised by those knowledgeable writers who occasionally visit and sample our wares. These criticisms may themselves be critiqued, but I would be the first to admit that there is a lot of truth to some of them. They point clearly to perceived (if not always entirely real) shortcomings that need to be addressed. Here are the most important criticisms.

- Washington's finest wines, in the words of one critic, are "interesting anomalies" rather than indicators of an emerging, world-class wine region. Sure, there is a handful of world-class wines coming from the state, but the vast majority are mediocre.

- Washington makes almost anything you can name, but it lacks a definitive "signature" grape of the stature of Oregon pinot noir, California cabernet, or Australian shiraz.

- Outside of riesling, Washington doesn't do anything interesting or distinctive with white wine grapes.

- Washington's boutique wineries, with few exceptions, do not own their own vineyards and must truck the grapes hundreds of miles (and over the Cascade Mountains) to make the wines. Nowhere else in the world are high-quality wines produced in this way.

- Far too many Washington reds are overextracted, underripe, and too expensive.
- Washington's vaunted syrahs all taste alike and mostly of new oak.
- Washington's cabernets, especially those from its cool-climate Yakima Valley, tend to be green, vegetal, dilute, and harshly tannic.
- Washington's merlots are pretty good, but merlot is not really an important grape.
- The rapid growth in the sheer number of Washington wineries looks impressive, but in truth this has spawned a shocking number of flawed, mediocre wines from untested and untrained producers.
- Too many boutique wineries seem to believe that a heavy bottle and a long cork somehow justify a high price tag or, worse yet, that the price consumers are willing to pay for their wine is somehow directly related to their cost of production.

Ouch! Some of these criticisms, valid though they may be, can be attributed to Washington's growing pains, some to the naïveté of its winery owners, and some to plain arrogance. How do they impact the credibility and viability of the region in the eyes of the world? What should Washington's response be? Where is this state's wine industry heading in the next decade?

I invited 10 visionary leaders, all with extensive experience in some aspect of the Washington wine industry, to comment. Rather than asking them to organize their thoughts on the fly, I submitted to each of them the following questions, soliciting a written response. I expected this would result in more thoughtful comments. These are the questions I asked.

- How well do Washington wines (yours and/or others) compete in the global marketplace?
- How can they become more competitive?
- Is Washington viewed (by those outside the state) as a California wannabe? If so, can that be changed? How?
- What in your view are Washington's unique strengths as a wine region?
- What are Washington's most glaring weaknesses?
- From your specific business perspective, what are the main challenges to be faced during the next decade?
- Please respond to the criticism that Washington wines are too expensive for the quality they offer.
- Please respond to the criticism that too many varietal Washington wines all taste alike.

Here are their thought-provoking replies.

MYLES ANDERSON

> Director, Institute for Enology and Viticulture
> Winemaker and partner, Walla Walla Vintners

Myles Anderson and Gordon Venneri began their commercial winemaking in 1995, the eighth winery in Walla Walla. Over the years they have won many critical accolades for their wines while assisting other wineries (Cadence, Spring Valley Vineyards, K Vintners, College Cellars) with custom crushing and winemaking. In 2001 and 2002, they donated the use of their winery to the Institute for Enology and Viticulture so that students would have a place to learn to make wine while the college's winery was under construction. Myles currently serves as the director of the Institute. He brings a unique point of view to this discussion, as both an educator and a widely admired winemaker.

"In my opinion there are many Washington wines that can compete well in the global marketplace for both price and quality. The major issue for many wineries is that their production is too limited to supply wines in the global arena. Small producers, such as my own Walla Walla Vintners, cannot make money selling wine at distributors' prices and shipping them to Ireland or Japan, for example, although there is interest in our wines there.

"We can become more competitive by learning to market our wines both here in Washington and globally. Currently we do not do a very good job of marketing wines, perhaps because most of the best winemakers in Washington have come from careers that did not involve marketing. On the whole, winemakers do not think much about global marketing. Most of the newcomers do not want to learn about selling; their passion is in the cellar, not the market place.

"Clearly we need to do better. There are many folks outside of the state that I have run into who do not even know we make wine in Washington. Even UC Davis and the Culinary Institute in St. Helena don't offer Washington wines for tasting to their students.

"Perhaps some of us are viewed as California wannabes. The wannabes I know are wealthy individuals who own or are starting wineries as private 'trophy' wineries for their own glorification. They know little about winemaking and wine farming. On the other hand, the Walla Walla winemakers who have been making wines for 10 years or more would be making wine even if California did not exist! I include myself in that group.

"For me, Washington's unique strength as a wine region is that we are young, and yet we make world-class wines that honor the place where the wines have been farmed. The best wines in Washington are not too expensive; in fact, in my opinion they are undervalued. Another strength is that, being so young, we are open to new ways of crafting wines that reflect the region. We are avoiding making wines like the Old World and to please Mr. Parker. In fact, many of us think that we are the current leaders in winemaking and farming wine grapes in the world.

"Another strength is that our winemakers still have a collaborative spirit and are willing to share knowledge with each other while competing creatively. Most of the best winemakers know each other and spend time together.

"Finally, we are building future strength with the Walla Walla Institute for Enology and Viticulture and the WSU research center in Prosser. Walla Walla has 105 students enrolled this year [2005–06], including 65 full-time, degree-seeking students. Most of those who graduate will stay in Washington and will become primary influencers in the future.

"On the other hand, our most glaring weakness is that too many new wineries are being started by untrained owner-winemakers. Some of the wines I have tasted do not reach the world-class level of quality that I expect from Washington wines. They are hobby businesses, home winemakers, and their wines all taste very much the same.

"I have encountered many wines that taste alike. Most of them are made by new, untrained, self-taught folks who are products of very brief home winemaking experience. They may think that they are making good wine because they do not ask for independent feedback from experts in the field. Similarly, we have too many backyard vineyards that are being managed by hobby growers, nice people who do not know what they are doing. Their vines are in decline because of diseases and mismanagement.

"From a business perspective, our main challenge is to avoid making mediocre wines that are overpriced while being peddled as good wines worth the cost. About 20 percent of the new wineries are undercapitalized and on the edge of going under. I fear that this will continue until there is an economic downturn in the wine industry. There are folks getting into the business who should not be in it! They do not have marketing or business plans or money that can sustain the company.

"A different challenge is handling the success that many of the best wineries are beginning to experience. By that I mean the economic impact that success can have on winemaking communities such as Yakima, Prosser, Grandview, Walla Walla, etc. These communities are not ready to handle the growth, particularly tourism, and provide visitors with the best in hospitality services and infrastructure.

"Finally, we must avoid making wines for Mr. Parker, as so many have in Bordeaux and California. We must learn to be our own best judges of what are world-class wines, crafted for us, by us."

THEODOR "TED" BASELER

President and CEO, Chateau Ste. Michelle Wine Estates

Ted Baseler began his career at J. Walter Thompson in Chicago and joined Stimson Lane, the predecessor to Ste. Michelle Wine Estates, in 1984. In 2000 he succeeded Allen Shoup as CEO, and under Baseler's leadership the company has become one of the top 10 U.S. wine companies (according to *Wine Business Monthly*). Its annual sales of 4 million cases represent two-thirds of Washington's total production. Since Baseler took over the top job, the company has had more wines on the *Wine Spectator*'s "Top 100 Wines" than any other company in the world. Ste. Michelle Wine Estates owns or controls some 6000 acres of Washington vineyard and has placed itself at the leading edge of ecologically friendly grape-growing practices. More than any other single individual, Ted Baseler controls the future destiny of the Washington wine industry.

———————

"How well do Washington wines compete in the global marketplace? Washington wines provide outstanding quality for the money, at the top end and everyday wines. If you look at ratings per dollar or general acclaim, no region consistently is as competitive. Not the cheapest but the best value. The growth rate is up 16 percent versus California, up 3 percent versus imports, and up 10 percent overall in the last 52 weeks, according to Nielsen.

"Washington wines have two barriers to becoming more competitive. First, a lack of awareness with the general consumer population that wines are made in Washington state. Second, few tourists have been to the vineyards. We need to ramp up the understanding and positive environment for vineyards, thus the Wine Commission plan.

"It is essential that we expand winery tourism and help lay the foundation with expanded amenities in eastern Washington. This is a relationship business, and that requires the best ambassadors of the industry to travel the globe, exposing wine lovers to the wines of this state, sampling and telling the stories of artisan efforts going on in Washington. We need to encourage opinion leaders to visit the vineyards of Washington. I also like the simple theme the Commission has, dispelling the number one misunderstanding: "The Perfect Climate for Wine."

"Is Washington seen as a wannabe? I hope so! Really, people who know quality wine now see Washington on the world stage, especially for the cult labels. Perhaps as a full-force, multisegment region we need to change perceptions.

"Unique strengths, as others have also noted, include the diversity of growing regions in the state, youthful energy, and flavor profile of the wines. Weaknesses would be the name of the state and the confusion about where it is located, especially with international customers. Also, its short history relative to other regions, and, again, the lack of tourist amenities.

"Our challenge is to find a way to accelerate success for vintners who produce wines of outstanding quality and value. Other challenges will include the significant growth of low-cost imports, placing the spotlight on Washington to increase interest and esteem for the region. We need to keep the industry as united as possible so we don't lose the harmony that is one of our big competitive advantages versus some of the more established wine regions.

"Promoting with a united front is much more effective. Wineries engaging in infighting and filing lawsuits don't have the time or interest to work in collaboration to promote the region. It is refreshing, according to many outsiders, to have a region with vintners who get along.

"As for the perception that Washington wines are too expensive, nothing could be further from the truth. Sure, you can point to some labels that are overpriced, but in general most wines that are produced in this state represent outstanding value. Columbia Crest, Washington's largest brand, represents about 15 to 20 percent of the wine made here and has been called the best value brand in the world. It has produced more bottles of 90+ rated wines than any other winery.

"As time goes by, I think the 500+ Washington winemakers will develop more individual styles that reflect the character of the individual vineyard sites. The beauty of having so many winemakers is there will be many more experiments in areas such as yeasts, harvest dates, fermentation times, etc. We have a long list of ongoing research projects, including nursery clones, water experimentation, and much more."

BOB BETZ, MW

Winemaker and owner, Betz Family Winery

Bob Betz, MW, spent 28 years with Ste. Michelle Wine Estates (then called Stimson Lane), much of it as vice president of winemaking research. His final projects were Eroica and Col Solare, the company's joint ventures with Germany's Ernst Loosen and Italy's Piero Antinori. One of 270 Masters of Wine worldwide, he was awarded two additional distinctions by the Institute: the Villa Maria Award, for the highest scores on the viticultural exam, and the Robert Mondavi Award, for the highest overall scores in all theory exams. Betz and his wife, Cathy, founded Betz Family Winery in 1997 "to make small quantities of characterful red wine." He brings an informed global perspective and supremely well-trained palate to this discussion.

"Washington wines fall into quality categories, like any major winegrowing region: collectibles, midrange, and commodities. And in each tier we compete strongly qualitatively, but not so well in the esteem–price competition. When Washington wines are tasted blind against similar-tier wines from Old and New World producers we excel, but we don't carry the price tags of these other wines. I often run comparisons of the scores from the top national critics and prices of our wines against the top performers of other regions. Other wines with scores similar to our Washington wines are always notably more expensive, sometimes two or three times pricier.

"Becoming more competitive is a function of quality and time. In time the world will recognize the fundamental ability of the Columbia Valley's physical conditions to grow world-class wines. And the path to that realization is for Washington growers and producers to continuously strive for higher-quality wines. There is no substitute for quality in the bottle, and we collectively and individually must raise the bar every vintage.

"Washington is carving its own path for many wine lovers. In the beginning we excelled (and still do) with riesling, and California doesn't, and over the past two decades we have added chardonnay, cabernet sauvignon, syrah, and merlot to that list of high achievers. Each has its own sensory profile, and they are different from California. Washington's sensory character is distinctive enough that it is perceived as a different growing region, with its own identity. For me, after 30+ vintages in Washington (and still enjoying heaps of wine from around the globe), two things emerge with our wines: fruit purity/intensity and structural integrity. Regardless of variety, the top Washington wines mingle the best of the Old and New Worlds, with a definitive fruit identity and a composition that is more restrained and chiseled.

"The hero of the story is the Columbia Valley and its combination of physical factors. The convergence of climate, soil, geography, and topography is unique and creates growing conditions that lead to high-quality fruit. Winemakers are presented with intense, fully ripened, and balanced fruit. It's up to us not to mess it up. Which leads to Washington's second strength: a group of dedicated individuals, in the vineyard and the cellar, who are driven and uncompromising. They want to make good on their commitment to make this a world-class region.

"Washington's most glaring weakness is myopia: an unrealistic view of the wine world. There are many growers and winemakers who haven't explored the range of the world's vineyards and cellars. As a group we need to be very aware of the excellence of other areas, both historically and their current trends. We don't have to kneel at their altar, but learn from and improve upon what they're doing. We can't blindly state that we make world-class wines without actually knowing what constitutes world class.

"Also, there's a lack of understanding of the vinification fundamentals by some winemakers: wine chemistry, microbial and oxidative spoilage, quality assurance, etc. World-class wines don't just deliver artistry but deliver technical quality; they are capable of maturing gracefully, without spoilage, in the bottle.

"The main challenges we face?

1. *Explosive competition* from all corners of the winemaking world. Walk into the display halls at the granddaddy of all wine shows, VinExpo in Bordeaux, and you understand that the competition is on the rise. Appellations that we've never heard of produce 10 times the wine that the Columbia Valley does. And they, too, are trying to make better wine every vintage.

2. *Quality improvement.* Quality winemaking is the only major long-term competitive advantage. We must be willing to commit the resources to discover and implement those vineyard practices and cellar protocols that allow us to raise the bar every vintage. Spend the money collectively to conduct the vineyard research to grow better grapes, and expend the blood/sweat/tears individually to make better wine in the cellar.

3. *Consumer perception.* Creating awareness and enhancing Washington's image on a broad basis is fundamental to our success. Cooperative education, tasting,

promotion, and media programs nationally and abroad will continue to build the state's image and reputation.

"Are Washington wines too expensive for the quality they offer? At the high end this is really not the case. It's the disconnect in the minds of people who don't understand that Washington wines have moved from adolescence to maturity, [thereby] keeping us in the 'also ran' position versus other world competitors. To them we are not yet 'worthy' to charge these prices, although the critical acclaim justifies them.

"Here in our own state a lot of people who perceive Washington wines as expensive are well-meaning loyalists. That is, they probably don't spend a lot of money on wines from outside the area and find, in their hometown spirit of wanting to support local wineries, that Washington wines can be pricier than what they are used to."

ANDREW BROWNE

CEO, Precept Brands and Precept International

Andrew Browne brings an extensive wine sales background to his work in the Washington wine industry, including work with Southern Wine and Spirits, Chateau St. Jean, Associated Vintners, Corus Brands, and Constellation and, most recently, as CEO and owner of Precept Brands. Precept owns, develops, and/or markets a growing portfolio of wines from Washington state, Australia, New Zealand, and the European Union. In its first five years, sales have gone from zero to more than 300,000 cases, half of them Washington wines, making Precept the fourth-largest wine company in the state. Browne developed the wildly successful Alice White brand, among many others; he adds a valuable sales and marketing perspective to this discussion.

"I believe that Washington wine is very competitive from a qualitative standpoint. We have been consistent in promoting and delivering quality across vintages, varieties, appellations, price points, and brands. As the region has grown in production, we have been very careful to maintain and build upon the quality of our wine.

"From a quantitative standpoint, we have been able to sell the majority of Washington wine right here in our region and throughout the United States. We have not been forced into the competitive global marketplace on a large scale. The majority of wineries in the state are still focused on high quality, high price, and low production. While this is a tremendous asset to our regional image, we will need to have more major players enter into the value (under $12) category before we can be truly competitive on a global scale.

"We need to expand our shelf or wine list presence in all channels by offering more wines at an everyday price point. These wines need to be competitively priced and have accessible packaging, outstanding quality, and an appealing taste profile that speaks to the everyday consumer. At Precept, we are positioning ourselves to help expand the value category by producing a wide variety of high-quality Washington wines under $12. Brands such as Washington Hills, Avery Lane, Pine and Post, Sockeye, Barrelstone, Pavin and Riley, and others in our portfolio will give us the ability to compete in a global market now and in the future.

"In order to take Washington wine to the next level globally, we must educate the trade and create trial and demand as well as long-term brand loyalty with the consumer. To do that, Washington needs to define itself as a wine region. However we accomplish this, it needs to lead to consumer acceptance. Recent consumer research conducted by Constellation Brands shows that 23 percent of the mass consumer base is completely overwhelmed by making wine purchase decisions. With so many choices, we need to create a consistent message and repeat it until it becomes a household topic throughout the United States and then the world. Simplicity is *vital*.

"How can we do that? First, establish varietal focus. Choose one or two varieties that will define not only what Washington does best but also what we will become known for as we grow. Then we need to get the industry on the same page to support that message. When you look at New World success stories, you see, for example, that Australia defined themselves as outstanding producers of shiraz. They were able not only to build regional awareness and appeal, but also to help build a varietal category.

"There are many other examples throughout the world: New Zealand/sauvignon blanc; Oregon/pinot noir; Napa/cabernet sauvignon, Italy/pinot grigio; and so on. These 'gatekeeper' varieties introduce consumers and trade to the new region's wine; then they can more successfully market other varieties. We are blessed to be able to produce most of the world's finest varieties very well in Washington. Now it is time to choose one or two that have mass appeal and global acceptance to define what we become known for.

"How is Washington viewed by those outside the state? From our vantage point (many conversations with distributors and buyers), Washington has a unique selling proposition. We believe it, our distributors believe it, and the rest of the trade seems to believe it. We preach quality, consistency, and value. I think that we have differentiated ourselves from California, but the fact of the matter is that they are the powerhouse region in the United States, and it is natural to draw comparisons to a market leader.

"As a wine community we need to ensure that restaurants put our appellations on their menus, ensure that retail promotions boast our Washington appellations, and attempt to garner more articles and acclaim about our region with key trade and consumer publications.

"And I think that we would all agree that we would love to see more support here in our hometown. Washington wines still do not dominate a large percentage of retail and restaurant accounts. We have done a lot to focus and grow support through recent Washington Wine Commission programs and the efforts from our state's larger wineries, but we still have a long way to go. We need to tell locals and tourists alike that our wines are globally competitive and distinctly different from other regions in the world. It is very important that we make a strong push at home to garner more brand identity and market share with our local customers like other emerging wine regions, such as Northern California, upstate New York, New Zealand, Australia, etc.

"Beyond Washington state, a large percentage of consumers are not even aware that we produce wine! We are past the incubation stage as a wine region; now is the true growth phase. Ambassadors such as growers, winemakers, winery staff, and Washington-based business executives must choose to highlight Washington wines when they are traveling around the country and overseas. Time after time, consumer feedback tells us that our wine overdelivers for the price—when we get the trial that we are looking for.

"During the next decade I hope to see more great people and companies committing their careers and businesses to Washington state wine, communicating openly, and sharing ideas to keep the fraternity alive. We need continued quality viticulture, and the technical side of winemaking must be maintained and adhered to for quality purposes. I want the wine trade to understand that Washington is a *value* producer as well as a high-end producer and large retailers and restaurant groups to embrace Washington state and give it the space it deserves.

"I do think that Washington state is one of the greatest value regions in the world. A very high percentage of the wines we produce sell for less than $12 a bottle [for more on this see Chapter 3]. For me, the wine that we put in the bottle can and does compete with any wine region in the world and any producer in the world at the same price points, from the value wines up through the superpremium. The chances of 'missing' with a Washington wine are far less than other wine regions. Washington does not have a region like California's Central Valley. Washington state viticulture has developed immensely over the past 10 years, and with that a great deal of flavor layering has made its way down to wines well below $10 retail. A $10 wine is not going to taste like a $50 bottle of wine, but some of the distinct characteristics that are innate in Washington fruit will shine through. That backbone of structure and fruit is a fantastic base to start with."

STEVE BURNS

Consultant and founder, O'Donnell Lane LLC

Steve Burns was the executive director of the Washington Wine Commission from 1996 until 2004, when he left to create O'Donnell Lane LLC, a marketing, public relations, and strategic planning firm based in Sonoma County, California. Under his direction the image and global presence of Washington wine experienced unprecedented growth. Programs such as Taste Washington, which traveled with dozens of wineries to London, Tokyo, and major cities across the country, gave consumers, press, and trade the opportunity to taste across the full spectrum of Washington wines and grapes. During his tenure the number of Washington wineries almost quadrupled, from 80 to 350. He brings an insider's knowledge and a California perspective to this discussion.

"Japan is arguably the most quality-conscious consumer product market in the world. I am confident that if you polled a cross section of wine drinkers in Tokyo you would find that their opinion of Washington wines is much more favorable than their opinions of wine from the rest of the New World (with the possible exception of New Zealand, which is probably equal to Washington state).

"Washington vintners, both large and small, realized early on in their development of the Japanese market that Japanese consumers valued product education and exceptional product quality over value pricing and widespread availability, so they brought only their best wines to the Japanese market and introduced them in limited quantities. This effort firmly established Washington state as a producer of ultrapremium wines that should be purchased on an aspirational basis for special occasions. Of course there are now Washington wines in Japan retailing at the $10 price point. But the quality image was clearly established *before* value-priced wines were introduced to the mass market.

"Washington wine sales and marketing progress are only limited by the number of hours in the day. In an ideal scenario, an event like Taste Washington would take place in all of the major wine markets in the world on an annual or biannual basis. This effort would be followed up by an appealing, pervasive advertising campaign and an aggressive on-premise and off-premise promotional effort. In such a perfect world every influential wine writer would be invited to tour Washington wine country on a regular basis.

"Washington wines create 'ambassadors' wherever they go and whenever consumers taste the quality in the bottle and meet the winemakers. So getting the wine out there more is the best way to become even more competitive. Selling the *brand* that is Washington wine is really no different than selling a brand like Columbia Crest or Woodward Canyon—it's hand-sold, one bottle at a time!

"No one says that Napa or Sonoma wines are too expensive for the quality, and yet Washington wines are priced well below those wines and consistently outscore those wines in most competitions. Maybe the fact that there aren't any Washington 'Two Buck Chucks' helps to underscore the misperception about Washington wines being overpriced. But in reality Washington wines function in a much tighter price range than most of their New World competition.

"I believe that retailers and restaurateurs in places like San Francisco and Boston view Washington wines as a fresh alternative to California wines, something new to add to their shelves and their wine lists. They often comment on the brightness of the wines and the crispness of the flavors and how complementary Washington wines are to most cuisines. Even when Washington wines mirror varietals from Australia or California, wine aficionados often comment that Washington wines have a style that borrows the best from the Old World and the New World, wines that create a style uniquely Washington state.

"Washington vineyards are capable of producing a large range of varietals on a high-quality and consistent basis. Is that a perceived weakness? Some consumers will continue to search for the 'what Washington state does best' varietal; and yet Washington is capable of making cabernet sauvignon, merlot, syrah, riesling, and more with the best in the world. Washington vintners as well as Washington wine drinkers will need to work the inclination of the marketplace to try to pigeonhole the industry. No one puts that kind of expectation on the state of California; and in my view they shouldn't do it for Washington either.

"The challenges coming up will remain the same as they are today: first and foremost, increasing awareness and knowledge about Washington wine among the wine trade, media, and consumers around the United States. With this country slated to become the largest wine-consuming market in the world in 2008–09, it's inevitable that all of Washington's competitors will be increasing their promotional budgets for the American market. Washington has to keep up with that challenge, or some of the market share gains that Washington wines made over the last decade will be erased."

TOM HEDGES

Founder, Hedges Cellars and Hedges Family Estate

Tom Hedges began his wine industry career marketing American wines in Taiwan in the 1980s. Hedges Cellars was founded shortly thereafter, initially as a "virtual" winery whose cabernet–merlot blend was sold in Sweden for two years before a "real" Washington winery existed. In 1990 Red Mountain was chosen as the site for the winery's French-style chateau and estate vineyards, which were completed a decade later. Hedges led the way in applying for Red Mountain's official AVA certification in 2001. Together Hedges Cellars and its sister winery, Hedges Family Estate, comprise the largest family-owned winery operation in Washington.

"How can Washington wines become more competitive? I believe that this is purely a question of perception. Ten years ago, at a board meeting of the Washington Wine Institute [the lobbying arm for the Washington Wine Commission], I proposed that Washington state market itself as a producer of high-quality merlot. The initial response from the other members was 'no.' After a couple of hours of discussion, however, we pretty much agreed it was a good idea. Sell whatever you produce, but concentrate your marketing on one wine, à la Oregon pinot noir, New Zealand sauvignon blanc, even Australian shiraz or Argentine malbec.

"It's clear that our quality is there; but our *message* is not. You can count all the wine regions in the world that are known for more than one wine on one hand. Merlot would have been a good choice and could still work, though cheap merlot from other regions hasn't helped its image. Syrah could be okay, but frankly it is already 'taken.' Merlot really hadn't been claimed 10 years ago.

"When you produce only two out of every 1000 bottles of wine made in the world, for your message to stick it must be real simple. The best-ever branded region, in my view, is Champagne. The name alone is so strong that the CIVC [*Comité Interprofessionnel du Vin de Champagne*, a growers' public relations group] sued Yves Saint Laurent for using the word *Champagne* on a perfume. And they won! I find that incredible; but think about it: What other wine word has more power than Champagne?

"So as an industry, let's pick something, or it will be picked for us, either pretty soon by the marketplace or more long term by terroir. Speeding up that process by simplifying our marketing would make everyone richer quicker. And I didn't say this, but we don't really need a white wine. The white can come later, after we're famous for the Bordeaux blends (my pick, but then I'm biased).

"Secondly, we should quit making the Parker wines, which are proliferating. If we as an industry feel strongly enough about the subject, not sending the wines is the next step. I tell all of my friends that 'Parkerized' wines are not good wines and will help ruin the wine industry as we know it.

"Washington is *not* viewed as a California wannabe by those in the trade with an ounce of knowledge. In fact, it's not viewed at all by those who are any less than fairly serious wine consumers. It just often is *confused* with California as one of their own, especially since 90 percent of the wine produced in this state doesn't even use Washington state for an AVA! I would propose using Washington state in conjunction with the smaller AVAs (Walla Walla Valley, Yakima Valley, etc.) to send a clearer message.

"To work long term, AVAs must be real. Broad AVAs, such as Coastal or Columbia Valley, don't add value. They don't point to a wine style. Red Mountain works as an AVA because it was written to reflect a wine type (red) and style (big, tannic, etc.). And it is a small region; you can see it all at once.

"Walla Walla works well for different reasons. The name sounds great, classier than the surrounding wine destinations. And it has the highest concentration of great wineries in the state. For now, the wineries get confused with the wines and terroir, the high-end public who buys them thinking they are one and the same. But once a majority of the wine that is made in Walla Walla has a Walla Walla AVA [currently most carry Columbia Valley AVAs], then they will be authentic and have a more powerful, long-term AVA draw.

"The most glaring weaknesses that I see in this state are the lack of focus I mentioned earlier and, secondly, the fact that eastern Washington has only minimal charm and is spread out and a bit hard to get to, especially in winter. This is limiting new investment in complementary infrastructure (for example, great food and great lodging), and discouraging 'big names' from establishing a presence here.

"So what are the challenges we face in the next decade? First, keeping the different AVA winery groups together. In the beginning, it was pretty much concentrated in the Yakima Valley. Grape and wine prices were fairly homogenous. Now we have Walla Walla, Horse Heaven Hills, Columbia Gorge, Wahluke Slope, and the rest. Red Mountain has a superiority complex, but only for grapes. Zillah [a little town in the Yakima Valley] . . . who cares? The 'haves' do not want to be associated with the 'have-nots.' The have-nots may try desperately to make great wines, but those with inferior terroir and infrastructure will be left behind. This presents a real challenge for the Wine Commission, because unity and friendship have historically been some of our real strengths.

"The second great challenge we face is consolidation at the wholesale tier, which will by nature tend to eliminate the smaller, independent, family-owned wineries in favor of the brands. In this environment Washington's two big groups [Ste. Michelle Wine Estates, Constellation] will do well, but the smaller guys could suffer.

"Are Washington wines too expensive? Bull crap! Washington has more 'best buys' per capita than just about anywhere. Supply and demand rule. Match us variety per variety with Napa, etc., and we'll see who's expensive. As for the criticism that Washington wines all taste alike—versus what, where? This is somewhat a function of high alcohol 'Parkerization,' which, as you know, kills a sense of place and variety. Hey, Volvos are starting to look like BMWs, and don't all big cities kind of look alike these days? It's called globalization. It's mostly a good thing, but it tends to eliminate uniqueness, which for wine (and cars) is not a good thing. That and consolidation at the production level, along with the Parkers and Rollands of the world, can produce taste-alike wines."

DAVID LAKE, MW

Retired winemaker, Columbia Winery

David Lake was awarded his MW in 1975 in the UK and then studied viticulture and enology at UC Davis. In Oregon in the late 1970s he worked with Eyrie's David Lett and did brief stints at Amity and Bethel Heights before joining Columbia Winery (then called Associated Vintners) in 1979. He was the first winemaker in Washington to release vineyard-designated wines, the first to produce syrah, cabernet franc, and pinot gris, the first to blend merlot with cabernet franc. Now retired, he was for many years a featured speaker and panelist at wine forums and the Chief Judge at the San Diego National Wine Competition.

"How well do Washington wines compete in the global marketplace? Not as well as one might expect. We have no really low-priced wines like those from California, Australia, Chile, and Argentina, because of our climate and production costs. Foreign consumers might reasonably expect wines from a generally unknown region of the United States to be offered at lower prices.

"Furthermore, Washington wines are typically different from the New World wines from Mediterranean regions, not what many people in foreign markets anticipate. This can confuse them. I do find that saying Pacific Northwest wines are as distinct from California as New Zealand wine is different from Australian resonates with most customers abroad.

"To become more competitive, Washington must carve out a recognizably different identity. Educate! The New Zealand comparison is useful in the UK and elsewhere. People accept that New Zealand wines should command higher prices than most Australian. Washington must emphasize the quality edge—we make no basic plonk, jug wine, *vin ordinaire* in Washington. Stress the drinkability and food compatibility of Washington wine.

Stress the continental nature of our climate (versus Mediterranean). Be proud of our individuality.

"There is a growing disenchantment with high-alcohol, superripe, overwrought reds from California that show an almost Port-like intensity and weight. Extreme late harvesting blurs varietal character. Such wines also tend to lose their regional identity. This disenchantment is still a minority view and is only just starting to influence point scores, but the fact that these wines are tiring to drink and better consumed in the absence of food is starting to be appreciated by opinion makers here as well as in Europe.

"Washington enjoys a unique situation and growing climate: a continental, rain-shadow climate at the same latitudes as southern Burgundy and northern Rhône. Despite occasionally severe winters, our dry growing climate is ideal for cultivating quality fruit. Irrigation gives us great ability to balance the canopy with cropping level. We pick on flavor and ripeness, not because of weather concerns.

"Because south central Washington spans the degree-day, heat-summation zones from Region 1 to Region 3, we enjoy remarkable versatility and are recognized for a spectrum of excellent wines, from riesling to syrah. The unity of our industry is also rare among wine regions. Growers and wineries put the reputation and quality of our wines ahead of narrower rivalries and interests.

"On the downside, our very uniqueness makes us somewhat difficult to understand and categorize. There is ignorance of Washington (the state, as opposed to the nation's capital) and the image of it being the land of rain and evergreen forests. This confusion is exacerbated by the absence of a leading varietal identity (such as Oregon with pinot noir). Stylistic variability can also confuse outsiders, although given our differing meso-climates this is only to be expected. When we aim too low on quality, our wines can be lean, unbalanced, and bad value. We can only hope to succeed if we seek to make wine at least at the premium level.

"The other challenges we face?

1. Finding ways to continue to improve quality so as to maintain competitiveness.
2. Remaining sensitive to the market while maintaining our Washington identity.
3. Balancing the grape supply with sales (currently we have an oversupply of merlot and chardonnay, not enough riesling, etc.).
4. Improving the profitability of some wines, which are underpriced, given the quality in the bottle.
5. Educating sales personnel, wholesalers, retailers, and customers on our wine styles and strengths.
6. Adjusting our winemaking and viticulture to global warming.

"Are Washington wines too much alike? Currently, winemaking decisions can often obscure vineyard and regional character. It's true of California too! It's a lot safer to be one of the herd than to be doing something different and risk a really bad review. Chardonnay seems to be particularly prone to this. Harvesting very late also tends to reduce individuality, and this has become increasingly common. (I was sad to hear a Napa winemaker say recently that he aims to pick so late that his merlot and cabernet sauvignon often cannot be distinguished from each other, and he was content with this!) But this sameness will prove to be a passing, youthful phase. I think that the new, emerging Washington appellations will start to differentiate themselves in character, and new areas will continue to emerge as the Washington wine industry matures."

DAN MCCARTHY

Partner, McCarthy & Schiering Wine Merchants

Dan McCarthy has spent his entire professional life in the wine trade, first in wholesale as a salesman and manager and since 1980 as a partner in McCarthy & Schiering Wine Merchants, Inc. In 1991, he wrote *Pick the Right Wine* (Doubleday), a book of food and wine pairings. In 1996 he coauthored *Northwest Wines*, a pocket guide to the wines of Washington, Oregon, and Idaho (Sasquatch Books). Currently, he writes a monthly wine column for *Seattle Metropolitan Magazine* and contributes the Northwest sections to *Oz Clarke's Fine Wine Guide*, *Oz Clarke's New Encyclopedia of Wine*, and *Oz Clarke's Wine Guide*. McCarthy & Schiering Wine Merchants have been instrumental in introducing and supporting dozens of top Washington boutiques over the past two decades. Dan McCarthy is widely acknowledged as one of the very best palates in the state.

"The world of wine is a vast arena; in the global perspective Washington is virtually unknown. Save for hostess gifts carried to Europe, the Far East, and South America, only informed winemakers and wine professionals know that wines are made in our state. Washington wines are just now being noticed in many eastern seaboard cities. It is not only for their relative value. They are becoming trendy and recognized as high in quality. But just as quickly as they are noticed, the supply disappears. The problem is that most of our wineries are tiny. They don't have the production, marketing budget, or knowledge to actively establish national distribution, let alone an international reputation.

"That said, I am not sure that being more competitive is all that important. Trying to sell turducken in French bistros may not be the most successful business plan. Trying to sell highly allocated Washington wines around the globe only rewards the ego, not the bank account. Washington wines are an American gourmet specialty item at our current level of output. I don't expect that I'll be sipping Quilceda Creek cabernet sauvignon on airlines soon, even in first class.

"A California wannabe is something I trust that none of our wineries want to be. We have different flavors to offer consumers. Being a Rhône wannabe or a Bordeaux wannabe, now that is a question worth exploring. I think very few Washington winemakers would say they want to emulate southern Italian wine styles. Leave the zinfandels in California and the primitivo in Puglia.

"Washington's unique strengths as a wine region?

1. The flood plains of the Yakima valley and, to a lesser degree, the exposure (wind, warm moisture from the Columbia River, and the heat) of the Walla Walla Valley. These factors accent flavors in our wines.

2. Washington has many sites where the wines show terroir: Red Mountain, Celilo vineyard, Cold Creek vineyard, to name three. We are just now beginning to discover the best sites in the state. Many new vineyards will bear fruit of high quality, and a few will deliver grapes with genuinely noble characteristics.

"Washington's most glaring weakness? Education. We need to have more programs to educate potential winemakers into professional winemakers. Right now anyone can get a winery license. I am not sure that is a helpful fact for the future of this state. Taking a minimum of winemaking courses before being able to apply for a license is something I would like to see legislated. Our state's financial future has a vested interest in the results of such a law.

"Ferreting out the new talent from the 500+ Washington wineries will keep my palate at work for decades. Only 25 percent of these wineries are making wines worth selling. And only 10 percent of those are special enough to promote. But are Washington wines too expensive for the quality they offer? Balderdash! When you can clean house against Bordeaux classified growths and Napa Valley classics in blind tastings, don't talk to me about price. Many of our best are precious, priceless. The world is filled with wineries that have a monetary agenda. Many of our wineries seek to make only the best. After all, living and working in a desert [eastern Washington] isn't very prestigious.

"I taste wines every day in large numbers. I can say with certainty that our wines have more character than the myriad Italian sangioveses and pinot grigios, California merlots and chardonnays, Spanish cavas, German rieslings called Piesporter, and Australian syrups called shiraz that I am confronted with each week. Generic flavors are the biggest problem all over the world. Washington wines can only be made in our curiously wild, wonderfully different, and uniquely fruitful growing environment. Call us what you will, but don't suggest that our wines are generic."

ROBIN POLLARD

Executive director, Washington Wine Commission

Robin Pollard was named executive director of both the Washington Wine Commission and Washington Wine Institute (its lobbying arm) in June 2005. Prior to that she worked in the Office of the Governor of the State of Washington. During her tenure there, she managed the high-profile Boeing 787 Project and served as director of the Economic Development Division at the Department of Community, Trade, and Economic Development. Pollard's work background also includes time as director of the Washington State Tourism Office and staff positions with the Washington State Office of Financial Management, AgriShip International, and the Missouri Department of Agriculture. She is making the development of Washington wine tourism a priority for the Commission and supervising the state's first national wine-marketing campaign.

"While the Washington wine industry is still relatively young compared to other wine regions, Washington wines are now found in more than 40 countries and continue to attract international interest. The Washington Wine Commission manages export programs in three primary markets: Japan, the UK, and Canada. We are rapidly gaining ground in these countries, with a 47 percent growth in export sales in 2004, building on a gain of 28 percent the year before.

"To continue to expand our international market share, we must raise awareness of Washington state as a world-class wine region. As the number of new wineries continues to rapidly increase, the Commission is encouraging more wineries to participate in our national and international programs in an effort to expand their markets. Last year, we embarked on an ambitious new branding campaign to create a distinct image for the Washington wine industry, differentiating our wine-growing region from our global competitors. We are confident that over time, our branded Washington wine industry message ('Washington State—The Perfect Climate for Wine') will resonate with both trade and consumer audiences and increase Washington wine sales locally, nationally, and internationally.

"I don't believe that there is a general perception outside of Washington that we are simply a California wannabe. Anyone familiar with Washington understands we are distinct from California in terms of wine grape–growing conditions, wine quality, and the unity of our industry. To California's credit, it has become synonymous with 'wine country,' enjoying the same widespread awareness as the preeminent wine regions of Italy or France. To that end, our challenge is achieving the same level of awareness, so when the average consumer thinks of Washington, he or she thinks 'premier wine region.'

"We are taking an entirely different approach with our marketing efforts. Instead of solely promoting specific AVAs, Washington's wine industry has embraced a statewide brand (again, Washington State—The Perfect Climate for Wine). We feel strongly that a statewide branding platform is the best way to enhance overall consumer awareness so that individual wineries and wine grape growers located in nearly every corner of the state can achieve long-term business success.

"It's not just a slogan. We really do believe that Washington state is the perfect climate for wine. Washington's unique growing conditions, with long, warm summer days and cool nights, create world-class wine grapes with the perfect balance between fruit and acid. Washington wines pair exceedingly well with food, providing both the structure of the Old World and fruit of the New World wines. Our climate, topography, and soil are unlike any other wine region in the world. The unity and camaraderie shared by the wine producers and growers in our state also sets us apart from many other wine regions.

"Are there weaknesses? Sure; with more than 500 wineries, Washington's wine industry has more than doubled in the past decade. Such unprecedented growth brings with it the challenge of maintaining quality and consistency. It is more critical than ever that we continue to invest in Washington wine industry–specific research and education. The Washington Wine Education Foundation and Washington Wine Quality Alliance are two initiatives that illustrate the industry's recognition that continued emphasis on quality is vital to our long-term success.

"The premier Washington wineries are extremely careful about which grapes they use. Their winemakers know where every premier grape is grown in the state; they spend time in the vineyards tasting the fruit throughout the growing season, to ensure the end product is exactly what they want. This is the standard we must maintain throughout the industry.

"Without sufficient funding for research and Washington-specific education in viticulture and enology, quality control could be a challenge moving forward. We must continue to raise awareness of Washington state quality to solidify our position as a global wine industry player. As our industry continues to mature, wineries will need to develop a more global view and market their products beyond our borders.

"I would argue that the best Washington wines offer tremendous value. We are producing world-class wines, particularly cabernets, that continue in blind tastings to beat out wines from other regions, often wines that sell for twice as much as ours. Washington state can produce superior wines at all price points, but particularly in the $12-and-under category, which comprises more than 85 percent of Washington's total wine sales.

"The criticism of 'sameness' could be leveled at any wine industry in the world. However, Washington has tremendous variety in its soils, which affects the degrees of irrigation, which in turn impacts grape flavors. We have significant elevation differences, slope aspect, and the ability to irrigate when we need to. We have nine federally recognized AVAs, which underscores the diverse growing regions within the state. As a relatively young industry, the nuances and uniqueness we seek in our wines will continue to mature as our vines get older and the roots grow deeper."

ALLEN SHOUP

Founder, chairman, and CEO, Long Shadows Vintners

Allen Shoup began his wine career in Modesto, California, where he reported to Ernest Gallo. In 1979, he joined Chateau Ste. Michelle, where, as CEO, he developed a portfolio of Washington and California wineries under the Stimson Lane Wineries and Estates umbrella. He initiated joint ventures that brought Tuscany's Piero Antinori and Germany's Dr. Ernst Loosen to Washington. Shoup is also a founder of the Washington Wine Institute and the Northwest Wine Auction. He helped to create the Washington Wine Commission and was instrumental in organizing the American Vintners Association. His newest project, Long Shadows Vintners, is a consortium of wineries, each individually owned and managed, with a marquee winemaker overseeing production. A dedicated winery just outside of Walla Walla, opened in the spring of 2007.

"While a few Washington wines have had moments of success in global markets, most notably in London, it must be conceded that at the moment we are not on the radar screens of any of the important international markets.

"I don't see a short-term correction for this situation (although I do hope that my project, with its international portfolio of winemakers, might do slightly better than most). Washington viticulture doesn't have the critical mass of awareness, the arsenal of marketing tools (or the financial capability to create them), or sufficient volumes of low-priced wines to support a marketing drive. Nor do we have sufficient volumes of high-demand fine wines to aggressively penetrate these markets.

"More significant is the fact that we still have not effectively developed the domestic market. While the West Coast is relatively well informed about Washington wines, we are still somewhat a novelty in the East and Midwest, and for most unsophisticated consumers we are virtually unknown. Therefore, the marketing dollars needed to build awareness and market share are far better spent in the still-undeveloped domestic markets than in global markets where consumption is declining. The long-term growth markets in Asia and the Pacific should logically be developed by those more desperate wine regions that are losing share in their home markets; once done we should ride on their coattails.

"I think we could be logically viewed as a 'California wannabe,' but after all they paved all the roads we are now traveling. We should not reinvent the wheel in this effort. Having said that, long-term we must lay down our own trail, our own unique reason for being. We do that by promoting the uniqueness of our viticultural region while at the same time continuing to improve both our viticulture and winemaking.

"We are a very different growing region. The uncontrolled variables of the other great regions—spring frost, cloud cover, rain and mold-causing humidity, rain at harvest, disease, lack of moisture when needed (in areas that don't allow or won't support irrigation)—are all virtually nonfactors here in Washington. That's not to say we are totally immune to these problems, but for now they seem to be rare. Of course, winter damage is a problem, but it seldom affects quality, and with better site selection and viticultural practices this problem has been minimized for most growers.

"We have other advantages that are shared with some regions but not most. Being free of phylloxera, we can plant on natural rootstock, and our vines go dormant in the winter, both of which allow for greater expression of fruit (just as with lilacs and roses grow in northern climates, they have more fragrance than in southern). We have ideal, low-vigor soils and unique temperature conditions: high sunlight (extra hours due to northern latitude) yet moderate heat units (due to cool nights).

"Our weaknesses are mostly attributable to our youth. We have too few well-trained, broadly experienced wine professionals in the state, not just in viticulture and enology but also in marketing, PR, packaging, etc., literally all the attendant business issues. And many of our wineries reflect these deficiencies. Our industry also lacks a focal point. We are geographically, viticulturally, and structurally scattered, with wineries in metro areas hundreds of miles from vineyards. Even most of the wineries near vineyards are in less than ideal locations or facilities.

"And finally, with the possible exception of Walla Walla, we do not have the type of natural beauty consumers normally associate with fine vineyard regions. All of this will change over time (much can and will be done to beautify the areas around the Tri-Cities, etc.), but for now we have try to find ways to overcompensate for these problems. The most obvious way is, for those who can, to make world-class wines.

"We must remember that youth is both a strength and a weakness. We get strength from the fact that we know we are still learning how to optimize these natural advantages. We do not fight change and new ideas; in fact we embrace them. This is particularly true for the grape growers. Said differently, I believe we have only climbed to about 10 percent of our eventual knowledge and understanding of the Columbia Valley viticultural region. We have just started doing the clonal research, experimenting with water management techniques and trellising, and matching site selections to specific varietals. We have yet to attract a critical mass of well-trained enologists and experienced wine grape growers who can take advantage of what mother nature has bestowed upon us.

"But this is as much good news as bad news, for we are already making wines that compete with some of the finest wines in the world, not a lot yet, but still more than one would expect given our youth. To come this far so soon with only 10 percent of the knowledge available begs the question 'How high is up?' Washington's future, with the proper commitment to excellence, could be very bright indeed.

"For the last two decades we have been the overachieving child of the wine industry, and we have received a disproportionate amount of acclaim as a result. We have deserved much of this acclaim, but as we grow we will be held to a higher standard. Wine is the world's most competitive consumer product, and even major wine-producing regions in the Old World are seeing their centuries-old wineries struggling to survive. Meanwhile, as the world gets smaller, new rivals are surfacing: eastern Europe, Asia (particularly China), South Africa, South America, Canada, and with new technologies still more that we haven't yet considered. It will get harder for us to compete unless we shore up our weaknesses and coalesce as an industry with a fervor for quality.

"I think that Washington wines are priced at the same value disparity as wines from most other regions. Our finest wines are often cheaper than their counterparts in better-established wine regions, and our best-value wines will compete well anywhere. We cannot grow grapes at a cost that allows for the production of economy-priced wines, because the yields necessary for this pricing would destroy the vines in a harsh winter. On the other hand, we have too many premium-priced wines that are riding on the fame of others and are clearly overpriced. But marketing forces will cause that problem to self-correct.

"It is true that many if not most of the varietal wines of Washington are not individually distinct. This is not surprising as 80 percent of the wine is made in the vineyards, and too few winemakers spend much time there. I would prefer to concentrate attention on the 10 percent of the growers and winemakers who *are* deeply involved in vineyard management and who are making outstanding wines that are being recognized by wine critics throughout the world. It is not coincidental that this ratio is about the same for every wine region of the world.

"Ninety percent of the wines of Bordeaux, California, Australia, or Italy are mediocre at best; it is why the exceptions get the recognition and high prices that they do. As easy as it is to make great wine, few seem able to put it all together; it's no different than art, cuisine, architecture, fashion design, literature, or any other creative or qualitative human endeavor. In all these competitive arenas of talent, thought, effort, and commitment, there is no margin for error if you are aiming to reach the top."

CONCLUSION

No matter how loud and long the hometown writer cheers for the home team, there will never be a sense outside the state that Washington wines have arrived until the world's most prestigious critics join the chorus.

That moment may have arrived. The tipping point, I believe, was Pierre Rovani's off-the-cuff talk (he had left his notes in his hotel) given in April 2006 at Taste Washington in Seattle. For almost a decade, Rovani covered Washington wines for Robert Parker's influential *Wine Advocate* newsletter. He is a well-traveled, well-fed, jovial, but opinionated man who had been rather severely critical of Washington in the past.

Rovani is blessed with a very sharp mind and a palate to match. Though I have heard him speak on several occasions, I had never heard, or imagined I would ever hear, the sort of unvarnished praise he heaped on the vintners of Washington state in his remarks on this particular occasion. Rovani began by recalling his first visit to Washington a decade ago, traveling with Parker and tasting wines for two days while holed up in a hotel room. Though a few good wines stood out, said Rovani, on the whole it was "depressing, hard work." At that time and in subsequent vintages, Rovani criticized Washington for not living up to its potential, for making too many flawed bottles. He seemed puzzled, distracted even, by the fact that there were wineries in the western half of the state located hundreds of miles from the vineyards.

But on this occasion, speaking of the glowing reviews about to appear in the next issue of the newsletter, he had only the highest praise. "I can tell you," he gleefully told an audience liberally sprinkled with growers, winemakers, distributors, and Wine Commission staff, "that two of the highest scores in the issue go to Washington wines [these were the

100-point scores given to Quilceda Creek]. Across the board, expensive to value, Washington leads the pack. I think Washington's growers are at the peak of their profession. The vineyards are making incredible fruit. The future is unbelievably bright. We're not talking potential. You've achieved it."

Rovani went on to speak eloquently about the quality of Washington cabernet, calling it "the best in the world." He had high praise also for the state's merlot, riesling, sémillon, chardonnay, and syrah, though he believes there is room for further improvement. "If winemakers approached syrah as a totally different variety," he admonished, "rather than making it like cabernet, the quality would go through the roof."

He finished with a flourish, enumerating numerous advantages that Washington enjoys: a perfect climate (wonder where he got that phrase?), great land ("cheap!"), and control of water via irrigation. "You can play God," he said. "None of your competition has this advantage. The Bordelaise are on their knees in a chapel praying for rain, you guys just turn on the spigot. My money is on you. Basically, Washington, you've arrived," he concluded, predicting "an enormous influx of money, tourists, and wine writers from around the world."

I'm not sure we need roving packs of wine writers stomping through our vineyards, but the rest of it is well deserved and hard-earned. It's about time the rest of the world took notice. Washington has arrived. And the best is certainly yet to come.

INDEX

"perfect climate" advertising campaign, 29, 287
Pollard as director of, 286–288
on scores received by Washington wines, 249, 251
Shoup in creation of, 289
tourism as focus of, 25
wine promotion activities of, 21, 23–24, 286–288
World Vinifera Conferences, 21, 22
Washington Wine Education Foundation, 288
Washington Wine Institute, 21, 286, 288–289
Washington Wine Quality Alliance, 29, 288
Washington Wine Writers' Association, 20
Water supply
from annual average precipitation, 31
from irrigation, 31–33
regional variations in, 14
Waterbrook, 43, 80, 169
profile and score, 184–185
red wine grapes, 72
white wine grapes, 59, 62
Waters winery, 243–244
Weather of Washington State, 29–33. *See also* Climate of Washington State
Wheeler, Rich, 261
Whidbey Island Vineyards and Winery
profile and score, 212
white wine grapes, 53, 54, 55, 61
Whisky Creek vineyard, 106
White, Michael, 219
White Heron Cellars, 37, 58
White wine grapes, 50–62
Wild Canary, 232
Willamette Valley, 17, 30, 40
Williams, Ann, 200
Williams, John, 2, 17, 43–44, 92, 100, 200
Williams, Scott, 45, 200
Willis Hall, 244
red wine grapes, 67, 68, 69, 70, 75
Willow Crest, 38, 39
profile and score, 211–212
red wine grapes, 72
white wine grapes, 55
Wind River, 78
Windrow, 176
Wine Advocate (Parker), 140, 251, 291

Wine and Spirits, 20, 249
Wine and the Good Life (Pellegrini), 16
Wine Business Monthly, 24, 273
Wine Country, 21
Wine Enthusiast, 249
Wine Project, 14, 15
Wine Spectator, 21, 22, 249, 251, 274
Wineglass Cellars, 85
profile and score, 213
red wine grapes, 77
sources of grapes, 109
Winery Trails of the Pacific Northwest (Stockley), 3
Wines of America (Adams), 14, 52, 67–68, 267
Wolfe, Wade, 39, 90, 210, 211
Wollmuth, Duane, 208
Wolverton, Joan, 17
Wolverton, Lincoln, 17
Woodinville Wine Company, 238
Woodinville Wine Village, 223
Woodward Canyon, 91
awards received, 20, 250
in Champoux vineyard partnership, 90, 91, 143
profile and score, 142–144
red wine grapes, 23, 62, 64, 65, 66, 67, 72, 77
sources of grapes, 40, 43, 45, 90, 91, 106, 143, 175
tastings of older wines, 264
white wine grapes, 51, 57, 60
Worden, 20
World Vinifera Conferences, 21, 22
Wyckoff Farms, 47
Wylie, Justin, 242

Yakima Valley, 16, 17, 19
in AVA system, 20, 23, 34, 37–39
climate and viticultural practices in, 38
Yeaman, Becky, 210

Zebra Cellars, 245
Zefina, 215
red wine grapes, 79
white wine grapes, 58, 62
Zerba, Cecil, 245
Zerba, Marilyn, 245
Zinfandel grapes, 78–79